I Have Been

I Have Seen

I Have Been Blessed.

I Have Been
I Have Seen
I Have Been Blessed.

BOB COYLE

I HAVE BEEN I HAVE SEEN I HAVE BEEN BLESSED.

Copyright © 2020 Bob Coyle.

All rights reserved. No part of this book may be used or reproduced by any means, graphic, electronic, or mechanical, including photocopying, recording, taping or by any information storage retrieval system without the written permission of the author except in the case of brief quotations embodied in critical articles and reviews.

iUniverse books may be ordered through booksellers or by contacting:

iUniverse
1663 Liberty Drive
Bloomington, IN 47403
www.iuniverse.com
844-349-9409

Because of the dynamic nature of the Internet, any web addresses or links contained in this book may have changed since publication and may no longer be valid. The views expressed in this work are solely those of the author and do not necessarily reflect the views of the publisher, and the publisher hereby disclaims any responsibility for them.

Any people depicted in stock imagery provided by Getty Images are models, and such images are being used for illustrative purposes only. Certain stock imagery © Getty Images.

ISBN: 978-1-6632-1300-6 (sc)
ISBN: 978-1-6632-1301-3 (hc)
ISBN: 978-1-6632-1299-3 (e)

Print information available on the last page.

iUniverse rev. date: 02/25/2021

Family and Friends, Church, Travel, Sport
Each One Receives, A More Than Favourable Report
Lest Anyone Critique, I Can Proudly Retort
The Road That Was Mine, One Just Cannot Outshine.

CONTENTS

Acknowledgements ix

Part 1: Edinburgh 1
Part 2: Vancouver 35
Part 3: Calgary 53
Part 4: Ancaster 59
Part 5: Vancouver 73
Part 6: Unionville 85
Part 7: Aurora 101
Part 8: Ballantrae 171
Part 9: Ballantrae 213
Part 10: Ballantrae 263

ACKNOWLEDGEMENTS

Eleanor and I met in 1962. Without her memory and support, this challenging undertaking, would not have been possible. She has also reminded me on numerous occasions, as I penned this life story that, "This is mainly about you Bob. Don't expect everyone to be quite as enthusiastic".

Writing, corrections, and typing have taken place over 21 months, mostly in Ballantrae, but in more distant places such as Sarasota, Florida, and Antigua.

We have all heard the expression, "Seize the moment". For many, this can come suddenly, and if not acted upon, can depart just as quickly. My moment, was the major decision to leave my birthplace of Edinburgh, Scotland in 1961, at the age of 20, to emigrate to Canada, after a series of events were woven into my life. Richard Gwyn, who was one of Canada's most influential political journalists in his day, wrote in 1997, "The Canadian values of tolerance, civility and decency are precious, and are becoming more rare, the world over".

I have been blessed to be a Canadian citizen, for the majority of my life.

EDINBURGH

1940 - 1961

Robert Rodger Coyle Born July 19, 1940

I Have Been. I Have Seen. I Have Been Blessed.

The seeds of memories past, if nurtured with care and love, will bring fruit to those in the family tree.

My birth certificate states, that I was born July 19th 1940, in a nursing home at 71 Great King Street, Edinburgh, Scotland, during the Second World War. My father, Ronald William Coyle had joined the Royal British Navy, to serve in World War 11. I did not see him until I was age 4.

My parents had the basics of life, but in no way were well off. How I entered life, in a nursing home in one of the most prestigious streets in Edinburgh is beyond me, but that is what my birth certificate says. Eleanor and I have visited the location, which is still there, as part of a beautiful Georgian Row building, just north of the now famous Princes Street, the Gardens and Edinburgh Castle that tourists celebrate. A two-bedroom suite in the building is currently available at that address, for about $750,000 Canadian. I found support for this, on the internet, with individual testimonies, confirming the address was indeed a nursing home, with births during those years before and after 1940.

My sister Maureen, who passed September 15, 2016 in Vancouver, suggested that "Mum", Mary Macdonald Coyle may have had a lung infection or pleurisy at the time and somehow our GP doctor, Dr. Watt, had the influence to admit her into this special care facility, to ensure both of us survived.

Our home in Edinburgh was always 48 Pilton Park, a 2- bedroom apartment in a 2 level, 4 apartment stucco building that looked out onto a public park, where I constantly lived out my sporting appetite, for soccer, cricket and tennis. As a permanent residence for the first 21 years of my life, most of my young neighbours became friends, and my childhood years were comfortable with both boyfriends and girlfriends alike. In those early days, all kids on the street from the age of 4 and up, were just good friends, totally unsupervised, with lives highlighted by, the odd fight, sports, school, pranks, playing soccer during the day and of course playing soccer at night. Scotland is fairly far north, and in the summertime during school break, you would have daylight hours until at least 10:30 at night.

My memory of the war years is limited and I do not want to make things up, but I do recall a Mickey Mouse gas mask that all U.K. children under a certain age were given, in the event of a gas attack. My sister who was 4 years my senior, did not covet much of what I had, but she was envious of that mask. Edinburgh, unlike many other U.K. cities was not a target for enemy bombers, but was bombed on the odd occasion by German planes that were lost and jettisoned their payload, to escape U.K. fighters. We escaped such an incident, by perhaps 2 or 3 blocks, with significant damage to some residences, and I do recall being in a primitive bomb shelter in our garden. Fashioned out of tin and sod, it was symbolic, but not practical. We sat on benches, facing each other with our feet dangling above water.

Mother was short, but at times a bit fiery. Given the chance to move to the North of Scotland with Maureen and I, she did. But in short order returned to Edinburgh and "her way of life". She also stopped going to the bomb shelter when the warning sirens sounded, complaining that "it was just a waste of time". Hey Mum! Did you consult Mickey and I. Forget Maureen, she was just my sister!

My street friends were Peter Hempseed and Charlie Porteous. Peter was favoured, mainly because his father worked at Duncan's chocolate factory and Peter was well supplied with "broken" chocolate pieces. Could I pick the right friends? Probably this explains my heart disease later in life. September 1944 was my initial daytime departure from the family, as Scotland's educational rules required entry to Grade 1 at the age of 4. Our residence was south of Granton Primary, by a 10- minute walk. South was considered the posh area, as the north side had a reputation as being "poor". It really was poor, and a tad dangerous. If you ventured in there, it was smart to be accompanied by a "north resident". I had such a friend by the name of Charlie Rennie. He was my first close friend.

I was too young to understand poverty, but I do recall that we would get a half day holiday every so often, to account for the fact that many of my school mates from the "north" did not have proper footwear, to stand up to the many rainy days of Edinburgh's fall and winter seasons.

How times have changed! My mother walked me to the school yard gates that first school day. Probably kissed me on the cheek or patted me on the head, and then definitively said, "I'm not doing this again, you know". And she didn't! She was the "master" of the short sentence!

Time plays no favorites with family and friends. The older you get, the more you are likely to lose those who are close to you, and were instrumental in developing your character and joy of life. This happened at a very early age to me. Charlie Rennie and Dougal Herd, both at age 10 or so, teamed up to ask my mother's permission to have me join them, to catch tadpoles at a local quarry. An emphatic "no" was the reply. "Too dangerous". I was furious and somewhat embarrassed by this unwarranted maternal protection in front of my friends.

Charlie fell in the water, probably could not swim, became entangled in the weeds and drowned. Dougal did not stay, panicked and ran all the way home to his parents. I had lost my first friend in life.

Quite honestly, I found primary school a breeze. I liked school and the marks I received reflected this. I was to get a shock and, a well-deserved kick in the rear, when I entered High School.

I was a cocky kid, and it took the odd incident to bring me back down to earth. I recall begging my mother to agree, that we could board a South African student for a week, as part of an exchange program. He stayed with us for a week, and the day before he left, I asked mum for money to let me take him through Edinburgh Castle and other tourist sites. She said no, and when I pushed her to agree, she said, "We don't have any". It was said in front of him and I was mortified. I had learned a valuable, lesson. You do not get everything in life that you want, or ask for.

My father "Ronnie" spent a fair amount of the war in a gun turret, aboard the Royal Navy cruiser "Cleopatra", in the Mediterranean. He was not forthcoming about events, but when pressed, he did tell me that he was severely injured in North Africa after a truck accident, while ferrying supplies to the British troops fighting on shore. He was taken by hospital ship to Durban, South Africa, which had the primary long-term care facility for allied servicemen and women wounded during the North African campaign, which lasted from June 1940 to May 1943.

I was not my father's boy. We did not know each other. But I do recall being carried on his shoulders to a fire-works display to celebrate "V" for Victory Day, and the end of the war. For many the war was not over; the memories, the being apart from wives and sweethearts, the lingering effects of physical injuries, and the lack of relationships with children they had never seen before, still existed, and were not to be easily overcome.

My father's return from the war was a shock to me and to him. When I toddled in to my parents' bedroom about 2:00 in the morning, I was told by him, in no uncertain terms, to get back to my bed. Mum explained to him, that even in the safety of the home, war conditions made children uncertain and fearful. Never the less, I never made a return visit to "my mummy's bed".

The late 40's and 50's saw the U.K. ravaged with health problems. Tuberculosis was a major problem and there was country wide inoculation against that disease. Dad did not escape being a victim, and in the 50's was dispatched to a Sanitarium, the then expression for an isolation medical hospital. I, being under the approved age of I believe 16, was not permitted to visit him for many, many years. There went another 5 to 6 years or so, of being separated from my father. Dad died on June 09, 1960, at the age of 50. I was 19 on his death, and therefore we were apart for a minimum of 50% of my then young life.

A few years after being cleared T.B. free, he complained of stomach pains. The initial diagnosis was a broken rib. The reality was stomach cancer. He was not a complainer and probably, no definitely, had suffered in silence for a long time. His time in hospital was short…6 weeks. I visited him often, and the memory of his skeletal appearance in those last days, will remain with me forever. We have to be thankful today for modern medicine, and the more dignified manner in which patients are now treated in their last days. I can volunteer in a heart problem environment, but not cancer. The memory still haunts me!

My sister, Maureen, who had emigrated to Vancouver in 1957, had returned for a vacation in 1959 and I recall having a drink with her in an Edinburgh bar, discussing the then obvious tension between Mum and Dad, and what action might have to be taken. Because of his pride and history of illness, Dad did not reveal, even to Mum, the discomfort he was then suffering from, as a result of the onslaught of stomach cancer, and the effects upon his personality, and their relationship.

Father/son relationship was, as mentioned above, minimal. I do recall playing soccer for a club team in Edinburgh and our game was at Pilton Park, right in front of where we lived. Mum must have mentioned this, because Dad "escaped" from the T.B. Sanitarium on the Saturday in question, to watch the game. I was not aware of this, but before he returned to the T.B. facility, he spoke these words, "you are quite good". Corny although this might sound, these words, became a treasure to me in developing my future soccer ability and the fatherless days that lay ahead.

Sister/brother relationship was also minimal in Scotland. At 4 years my senior, my sister Maureen had little to do with me. I always viewed this as normal behavior, and it was. With a 4- year differential and being a female, she considered herself much more mature, and she was. Several incidents of "brotherly love" do however stand out. I would continually annoy her, by quietly standing outside the bathroom, in anticipation of her shriek at being surprised by me as she opened the door. I did this time and time again." Mum! He's doing it again", was the outcry. She and her female friends would corner me when short of money, and turn me upside down to shake loose, any change in my pocket. We are talking pennies, not pounds.

I had my tonsils removed at age 4, and Maureen and I were treated on recovery, to a visit to the cinema, to see "The Wizard of Oz". As soon as The Wicked Witch appeared, I started to cry. I was apparently scared out of my mind. We had to leave the theatre. Maureen did not forgive me ever, for ruining her first trip to the movies. I was only 4 and just recovering from surgery. What a wimp!

Her boyfriends were to be disappointed, as she was determined along with 3 of her friends to leave Scotland for Australia or Canada. The fellow I wanted her to marry was Tony. I think I liked him more than Maureen. I would save and cut out "Tony the Tiger" faces, from all the Kellogg's cereal boxes and scotch tape them to the wall area at the bottom of the stairs, where they sat at the end of their date. Tony had a motorcycle, goggles and an infectious laugh. He was my hero.

Maureen's health as a teenager was not good and certainly not appreciated by me. When I brought friends to the house I would say, "This is Mum's bedroom, this is my bedroom and this is the sick room." She had various childhood illnesses and contracted scarlet fever, thereby missing a major part of a school year. She was probably home schooled by Mum, and amazingly graduated her high school commerce class at the age of 15 years 3 months, and was employed right away, as a shorthand typist, by an Edinburgh chartered accounting firm. Quite a feat! She was bright.

As a precursor of their leaving, Maureen and her 3 friends (Winifred, Ruth and Frances) would go on cycling trips. One such trip took them to the North of Scotland, I really did not care if they took off on such trips, except that Maureen was using my bicycle. A Dayton Roadmaster, that I had acquired from one of my cousins, at great expense, I might add. To practice before going to Germany at age 17, they cycled to Queensferry, a small coastal community on the Firth of Forth, where Robert Louis Stevenson penned the famous novel "Kidnapped". Eleanor and I have been in the room at the Queensferry Inn where he did the majority of his writing. It was first published in 1886 and is set around the years following the Jacobite rising of 1745, and the famous Battle of Culloden, where the Scots were defeated by the English, in the last pitched battle fought on British soil.

The road to the Queensferry Inn, drops down, as a steep hill. Maureen had an accident, fell from her bike and was stunned. The rest of the story for a younger brother is hilarious. The locals carried her into the closest shop, which happened to be the local butcher's, and deposited her on the white granite counter. Imagine her reaction when she came to, to see a fellow with a bloodstained apron and a butcher's hatchet hanging on the wall. Use your imagination!

As a teenager I delivered morning and evening newspapers locally and part of my route led me past a small private tennis club, where Maureen was a member. I could hear her voice on my after- school route. Jealous...... probably. No, definitely. This would stand her in good stead as she joined Jericho Tennis Club in Vancouver B.C. and had years and years of happy memories. She was also a very good doubles player in a very competitive club environment. I played a lot also, but not at her level. She always referred to me as a blocker, when we played in Sarasota. We did not play often together.

When Dad died, we persuaded Maureen to stay abroad in Vancouver, and not come home for the funeral, especially as she had been with us in the prior 12 months. I have the wire we sent to her advising of Dad's passing, which she had kept all these years. Mum would not attend the funeral as she was devastated at his passing. She was then age 47 and they had been married for 24 years. At the time, I did not think of her as young, but at 47, she had a lot of life ahead of her.

I represented the family, and I am sure I was coached, and protected by other senior family members. I cannot explain, but I have virtually no recollection of events, after being told by Mum that she was not attending the funeral. I had always thought of her as being stronger than that.

These family memories, although short, heighten for me, the importance of family and the effects and obligations that parents have for and to their children, through thick and thin. As will be established later, Eleanor did most of the parenting in our family relationship, and I chipped in with the providing. Parents do not have to be perfect, but they have to be there for their children. I consider this to be an obligation. War, or being apart, does not always permit that formula to work, and we perhaps will never understand the effects of parents being separated for such long periods, and the stress of being reacquainted again.

Mum and Dad were married in 1935. He was Protestant. She was brought up in the Catholic faith. Mum's family was larger or stronger, and they would only approve the marriage in these days, provided the children were raised as Catholics. Mum and Dad were married. Maureen and I were raised Protestant. Mum did not like to be dictated to.

As a "form of punishment", we were still invited to Mum's family's social events, but the four of us most often, sat at a separate table, while the rest of the family and the local priest sat at the long dining room table. I was too young to understand the significance of this arrangement.

Aunt Sarah, (Mum's sister) was the hostess. A plump but really happy woman. The meal was usually soup followed by a sandwich, with a request that the same soup plate be used to accommodate the sandwich that followed. Maureen was pretty fussy and asked, probably about the age of 10, that she have an extra, clean plate for the sandwich. Aunt Sarah obliged, but countered with glee, by depositing her one glass eye on the plate, beside the food. I can still hear Maureen scream. Weird, but the message was, don't ask for an extra clean plate again.

Uncle Tom who was married to Auntie Jean, secured a position with the Gas company. In these days you had a natural gas meter in your house, which you fed coins into, to provide the supply of gas required for heating and cooking. Tom's job was to empty the meter, and turn the money over to the gas company. It was rumoured within the family, and perhaps unfairly, that he maybe did not comply with all the rules, and his time with the company was cut short.

Uncle James (mum's brother) worked for the Edinburgh transit (bus company). I would see him from time to time as a conductor (ticket collector) on the famous double decker buses. He loved dogs and had 2 German Shepherds, which contrary to transit policy, would sometimes accompany him on his shift. They would lie hidden under the stairs, that led to the upper deck. Any problem with a passenger, would be solved by a quick whistle, and the emergence of at least one snarling brute.

Uncle Johnny (mum's family, and another brother), was a house painter, who probably did favours for family members, but had a weakness of over imbibing from time to time. When he realized that climbing scaffolding or ladders was beyond him, he would quietly settle in a corner and go to sleep. To make him more comfortable, family members would take off his long sleeve shirt or T shirt, and then another one, and then another one, and so on. His idea of changing his soiled shirts, was to put another one on top, and another one, and so on.

Mum's family were loveable, but different. A joy of the 3 sisters at every event was to sing "Sisters, sisters, never were there such devoted sisters". And although they were different, they truly liked each other, and our get togethers were happy times. A negative memory was of my father, when he was around, always coming home from these family get togethers happy, but totally inebriated. He did not drink much, but the wartime injury affected his tolerance. I still become annoyed at the possible effect alcohol has on the personality of anyone. Sorry, but true!

I have little or no knowledge of my father's family. He was not a communicator. We have a precious photograph of his mother Euphemia, holding Maureen, taken in 1937 or 1938. She owned a confectionary store (a sweetie shop) in Edinburgh and may have been the source of funds, after her death in 1938, that supported the cost of the fancy nursing home, where I was born. Gramma Coyle, whose given name was Euphemia, was reported to enjoy smoking a pipe. She was married to Francis, a postal worker, who died, in 1913, from heart disease. Oops! My Dad, his son, was only born in 1910! Euphemia was obviously a strong willed and capable woman.

I received my first pair of soccer boots at Christmas when I was age 4, and spent most of my young social life kicking a soccer ball, with my local friends who felt the same way. Even in winter, we played until it was just too dark to see. We played in the rain, and in sleet, and in wind. The muddier the ground, the happier we were. We all wore short pants. Either long pants were not in, or we could not afford them. The tops of our legs were chaffed with the wind, rain and cold and I can remember many a night sitting with my legs in the kitchen sink, and grimacing, as my mother washed the top of my muddy, frost bitten legs and Maureen taunting me, with comments like "stop whining, don't be a sissy".

I was a soccer fanatic. I played for my primary school Granton, and was team captain at age 10. Although, I notice that in next years' team photo, I was not captain! Hmm. Their mistake! I also enjoyed being a boy scout. Similar groups of young boys today have terrible stories to tell. I may have been naïve, but I have no recollection or insight of any improper behavior, while a member of the Granton, Boy Scouts group. I only made it to the position of 2nd in our patrol which was named the Cobra Patrol. The leader or 1st, was permitted to take patrol members overnight in the Pentland Hills, bordering the famous Edinburgh castle. He, begged off, on one such occasion. Two of our patrol still wanted to go, and as I was the second, it fell to me to meet their request.

I, at the age of 15, was therefore assigned the task of taking 2 younger members overnight as described, to earn additional boy scout badges. A big mistake, was in the works! I had done this before and knew the ropes, but had not led. We hiked for the day, made our campfire, set up the tent, had our supper or dinner or "high tea" as we Scots then called it, and prepared to bed down for the night. It was not Canada cold, but it was cold and damp, as Edinburgh can be for most of the year. Time for the "Coyle keep warm plan".

The plan was simple and effective. Take the stones that had been used for the campfire, and place them in your sleeping bag at the "appropriate time". I was anxious to get these young bucks bedded down, for the night, and botched the "appropriate time". The net result was that the hot stones burned holes in their sleeping bags. They were not pleased. I was mortified. Maybe the Scout group helped indemnify the families, or my family paid. I have conveniently forgotten that part of the story.

The scout group as a whole, would head out each summer, for a week of camping outside of Edinburgh. Digging latrines and preparing moats around one's tent to keep ground water out, was not my idea of having fun, and I think I only participated once, probably before the sleeping bag incident. Our leaders, were about as smart as I was, at camping. We arrived late at the campsite, unloaded the truck, pitched tents, dug holes and moats around the tents, and prepared a fire for cooking. Based upon our numbers, a single fire would have meant some of us eating, about three in the morning. With darkness settling in, our intrepid leaders, ordered some of us to collect firewood "tout de suite", to start more fires. Unfortunately, in the darkness and rush to get the job done, one of our groups disturbed a ground nest of angry wasps, who proceeded to chase us all over the campsite, before we could escape to the safety of our tents. Most of us went to bed hungry, scared to venture outside. That was my last scout camp.

Boy scouts greeted each other, in what I can now say, was rather a strange way. Our patrol was the Cobra Patrol, and to identify ourselves to each other, we would say "Deb, Deb, Deb, we'll do our best… Dob, Dob, Dob, Woof! I leaked this information out to my barber in Edinburgh one day, and he delighted in having me recite this every time with full actions, to all in his shop, before he would cut my hair. I didn't even get a discount on the cost of my haircut!

Life as a youngster is full of experiences. If harnessed properly, they serve to prepare you for the ups and downs, of what lies ahead. Scouting taught me many basic things, but most of all, it taught me that teamwork can be effective, and that managing others, is a skill that must be worked at, and applied to different people, in a customized manner, and not as "a one size fits all" package. I did adopt this approach later in life, while managing a sales group, each with individual skills and egos.

I was bullied at primary school. Bullies tend to be stronger as a group. I managed to talk them into some kind of separation, had my fisticuffs with probably the weakest one, and it stopped. My only medical problems in these early years were toothaches, and an Achilles' heel problem. During the war years, almost all food was rationed, and there were very few sweets. Following the end of the war in 1945, we made up for this and no doubt overdid the "sweet thing". Dentistry and flossing were almost ignored, and I suffered accordingly. I do not have strong teeth, but I have deep roots. Having a tooth pulled was an event for me, and accompanied by swelling and bruising.

I also had a heel problem. This was serious. No soccer for several months! The doctor prescribed some black paste to put on my right heel every night and to cover it with a warm sock. At the time, and even now, it seemed as though I was dealing with a witch doctor. But you know it worked, and the heel became pain free. I encountered this problem again in Canada in the 1970's, and it was solved by casting my feet for shoe inserts, as the arches on both feet were pronounced as "leaving room enough to drive a double decker bus under". Inserts were expensive. I suspect the magic black paste would have done the job at much lower cost.

My mother, on the basis of my primary school teacher's comments, suggested I apply for a high school scholarship at Fettes college in Edinburgh. Fettes, was what I would call "a pretty posh and high-falutin academic college", which I did not feel my status warranted. I attended the testing day, and at least 200 students were asked to write an essay on subjects chosen by the college. I wrote about a German fighter pilot in the last days of the war, when all was lost and it was just a matter of time, before he was shot down or killed. Why I chose that subject, I do not know, but who so ever read it, was obviously not impressed, because I never heard back from the college. I was not upset.

I was enrolled at Trinity Academy High School as a then, 12 year- old, cocky, high school academic and sports loving kid. I was in for a shock, as the competition among the 30 or so male and female classmates was fierce. When I graduated 5 years later at the age of 16, I had fought my way up to 15th in the class This position, fairly represented my academic ability as average, but sports and soccer in particular, had taught me not to be satisfied with anything, but winning.

Being fairly short in stature, I planned my days ahead by teaming up with Allan Romanes. He was all of 6 feet tall. Bullying was not a problem for me in high school. Nicknames are common among school chums and I was assigned the name of Toto, based on a "character" in our French reader. Unfortunately, Toto was the little boy's dog!

High school sports for boys at Trinity were rugby and cricket (no soccer). Can you imagine a high school in Scotland, without "the beautiful game"? I was scrum half for Trinity's second rugby team, and ended up loving that game also. I probably enhanced my soccer abilities later in life, by being able to run free and swerve as you could in rugby, until someone landed on top of you like a ton of bricks.

I was an off- spin bowler for Trinity's second team and was promoted to the first team. My first ball in my first game, was hit for 6 runs (the ball crosses the boundary line without a bounce). The second ball suffered the same fate. The third ball was hit for 4 runs (crosses the boundary line on the ground). The umpire then turned to me and said, "You are getting better son". I was not promoted to the first team again. Their loss!

My years in high school were engaging, full of fun and educational. I enjoyed school. You were required to continue your education during the summer break and although I played a lot of tennis in the public courts, in the park close to our house, we were still required to do some school work. This meant writing an essay on a range of subjects each week during the 2 months of summer break. Our teachers with their flowing black robes were talented and professional, if you paid attention. They all had their own personalities. One might add "strange personalities".

A perfect example was Molly McKay. A diminutive, grouchy English teacher, who always carried a small handbag. When she arrived in a hallway, jammed with yapping, noisy students, who appeared not to be paying any attention, she merely had to hold this handbag out, and in front of her, and as she walked, the talking stopped, and the milling throng of students parted, much like Moses' parting of the Red Sea during the Exodus. Maureen had her as a teacher as well, and was not a fan.

Miss Murdoch, was an English teacher with wonderful words and expressions at her fingertips. On catching one of her class students, John Anderson, glancing at a photo magazine, with an "a la penthouse style", she almost had an apocalyptic fit searching for the right words to admonish him. She finally said, "Anderson, Anderson, your nothing, but a garden slug!" Wow! What a putdown! The rest of our class was fairly obedient, after that incident.

Our French teacher taught in a wooden trailer, which was added to the school grounds as a portable temporary measure, to handle the enrollment growth, pending the completion of a new building. Very common in all schools today. We removed nails from some of the wooden floor boards, and when she turned her back to write on the chalk board, one or two students would disappear "a la" the prisoner of war, "Stalag 17 movie", by removing the floor boards, and dropping to the ground below. If she did notice that about one third of the class was missing, at the end of the 40-minute period, she did not mention this, or did not care.

Our geography teacher, Mr. Smiths' favourite words were "Someone is talking in here". Meanwhile elastic bands and paper planes, were flying all over the room, and everyone was talking. It was absolute chaos!

Our history teacher was Scott Allan, a man who had a pronounced influence on me. History was the subject that I majored in, at high school. I was fascinated by it, as a subject, perhaps to the detriment of other subjects. I also admired him and perhaps in some way, considered him as the father figure, that I had not had the opportunity to bond with. David Duff, a fellow student and I, felt comfortable with him, and I must stress, in a healthy way. We revisited him as a pair every so often, up to 2 years beyond our graduation, and in no way did he show anything other than friendship for us. I suspect that he was a tad lonely, and that we filled a void in his life, as the children he never had.

He was extremely talented, and always had the time and the inclination to direct and produce a concert at the end of each year, centered around abbreviated Gilbert & Sullivan operettas, such as H.M.S. Pinafore & The Pirates of Penzance. They were part of our graduation closing school concert, at The Usher Hall in Edinburgh. They were truly spectacular and bordering on professional, as Mr. Allan did not tolerate anything, but the best in effort and performance. I watched Maureen participate, before I attended Trinity, and was spell bound by the sight of the choir coming into the raised auditorium, overlooking the stage, as they weaved their way back and forth down the rows, all in white shirts, ties, and navy pants or skirts, accompanied by triumphant music. There seemed to be about 300 participants (students) and they marched into the auditorium to the music, and in a precision that any regimental sergeant major would have been proud of, coming to a simultaneous halt with the music, in a standing position in front of their specific seat. It was like a master puppeteer handling 300 puppets on strings at the same time. I suspect, that Scott Allan had his outside theatre contacts. He was talented.

I was fortunate to be part of a school group of maybe 12 or so teenagers, that played the part of urchins in Bizet's, Carmen, that was presented by, a part of the Covent Garden Opera Company, in co-operation with the Edinburgh Grand Opera Company. The internet shows Carmen being presented in 1955 at the Usher Hall in Edinburgh. This looks like solid confirmation to me. We appeared in Act 1 as urchins, imitating the changing of the guard and singing "When the soldiers march on guard, we march with them, one by one…". We were made up to look like street urchins, with wooden swords and were probably only on stage for about 7 minutes, singing and pretending to sword fight with each other, but what a thrill! The then law, required that kids of our age had to be off stage by 8:00 p.m., and Carmen Act1 accommodates that. Our make-up was applied by one of the young chorus ladies, who to us boys, at the age of 15 years, appeared as a goddess. We were speechless, in awe, and immediately fell in love, as she applied the make-up.

A 1950's Scotland was cool, wet and bleak in the fall and winter, and you required many calories to feel warm and comfortable, while outside during the day. I cycled the 15 kilometers to and from high school 4 times a day. Lunch in Scotland, included dessert and was highly calorific. Gall bladder operations are still commonplace, in the whole of the U.K., even today.

Relationships are precious at any time, but so important during school years. Names like David Duff, Alan Proctor, Alan Romanes, George Bennett, Dorothy, Morag Beveridge and Margaret Webster, stand out in my memory. As a young man, I also had many girlfriends. How long the relationships lasted, I do not recall, but in my opinion, that was a healthy way to enter manhood, and was also very enjoyable. No commitments!

Margaret Webster and I, were very close. She, was 2 grades behind me when I graduated, which meant we were at the same maturity level. I was smitten, but Margaret, even at her young age, realized that we were not "cut from the same jib". She was arty and I was academic, and we were not destined to be with each other. Tell that to her mother. She really liked me.

We maintained a close relationship, even after I emigrated to Vancouver. We wrote to each other often in the first year, and then it happened. She married a fellow art student. I met Eleanor and that was that. But that is what life is all about. Meeting and cherishing others, who have a positive impact on your life, and shape you hopefully, into a loving, caring person.

Outside of school, I dated a young lady by the name of Veronica, who later married my close friend George Bennett. I recall George approaching me on a double decker bus, coming home from the Palais Dance Hall in

Edinburgh, and asking me, if it was alright if he took Veronica home. Eleanor and I met up with both of them in Glasgow, Scotland, in the 1990's. I introduced El to Veronica, who denied ever having dated me. I replied "Not so, I was introduced to your grandmother". My memory says that, it was a Scottish tradition at that time, to have your date introduced to your grandmother for pseudo approval, and that happened Veronica!

George and I were very close in Edinburgh. We both loved soccer and George was "a tough as nails half back", playing for an East of Scotland semi- professional soccer team. We keep in touch and I call him at Christmas each year. I however find my Scottish friends who stayed, to be much more insular, than those who emigrated! George now, unfortunately has a form of dementia.

At the time his older brother Alex, who was the spitting image of the Man from Glad, shocking white hair and all, was dating my sister Maureen, who spurned him. He later married Dorothy, who Maureen thought was a bit of a witchy poo. Dorothy felt the same way about Maureen. C'est la vie! George Bennett CBE FRSE was an engineer and Corporate V.P. of Motorola Ltd. in Scotland.

When El and I went to Scotland in 1990 on a Standard Life reward trip, we were entertained by George and Veronica at a level, which stunned us at the time. Picked up at our Glasgow hotel by a corporate limousine, driven by a female chauffer, complete with chauffer's hat. Registered at a small private hotel. Given a personalized tour of the Motorola plant (2,000 employees), complete with safety uniforms and masks. Every employee called Corporate V.P. George Bennett, "George". We were driven to Edinburgh (about 75 km), and entertained in the evening, at a cozy Edinburgh restaurant, "The Witchery", located in the old town, just off the Royal Mile. They were so kind to us. But that was George. Alex and Dorothy were present at dinner, and the only negative was that Alex seemed to want to play big brother. Maureen and I never had that annoying sibling rivalry.

Mum and, Dad when available, would take Maureen and I to Kinghorn for a 2- week summer vacation, during what the Brits called "The Trades", the first 2 weeks of July. Kinghorn was a delightful small coastal town on the Firth of Forth, less than 2 miles across the water from where we lived. However, to get there; the cab to the railway station, the train trip and the cab to the boarding house, took at least 5 hours. My memories of family time, especially on the beach were wonderful. An exception was, when I persuaded Mum, to let my friend Peter Hempseed, join us for a week. Peter unfortunately had a bad habit of smacking his lips with every bite of his food. He was not invited back. I can still see Mum's reaction of shock and astonishment, at the first smack!

We broke the Kinghorn chain of summer visits, and went to the Isle of Arran one year, on the West Coast. I so wanted to take a rowboat out on my own. The boat rental employee accepted my money for a 30 -minute rental. "Have you done this before son?", he barked. "Of course, I have" I replied, with a slight edge of indignation. "Well son", he said "of course then, you will know that you are facing the wrong way".

The last summer vacation I took with Mum and Dad was the summer of probably 1958, at a seaside resort called Lytham St Annes, just south of Blackpool, England. A vivid memory of the small boarding house we stayed in, was the serving of Yorkshire Pudding at every meal, including breakfast. I quite like it, but not for every meal! Maureen was now in Canada. Mum was probably trying to keep what little family we had left, together. And Dad was finally out of hospital.

I must have enjoyed the area, because I went back a year later with 2 male friends, Gordon and Steve. I have photos of them, but do not recall really who they are, and how we met. I celebrated my first legal alcoholic drink, a beer, on the Blackpool pier. England's laws were more laxed than Scotland in those days. You had to be 21 in Scotland to enter a pub which closed at 9:00 p.m.

After the visit to the pier we fancied dancing, at a marvelous Blackpool dance hall, complete with a revolving stage. This allowed a band to play for about 40 minutes, and then the stage revolved to reveal another band playing the same music piece, You, did not miss a beat. One of the bands, was Johnny Dankworth's Orchestra, which became world famous. His wife, Cleo Lane, was the lead singer and a very, very good singer. They were both recognized later in life by the Queen. He with a Knighthood, and she with a Dame appointment.

Most of the attendees in the Blackpool dance hall were single. Males on one side of the hall, females on the other. I had decided to ask this very attractive young blond girl to dance. I undertook the long walk and politely said "May I have the pleasure of this dance". She looked me up and down, for the longest time, and said "f.....off". I took that as a no, and retreated to the male ranks, much faster than I had taken towards the "ladies" section.

I enjoyed dancing and this stood me in good stead later, because El loved dancing also, and she was very, very good. This common element was more than helpful during a flourishing romance.

As a 17 plus year old, I went to the Palais dance hall in Edinburgh every Saturday night, and had much better success than Blackpool. If, however, one did not go home with a date at the end of the night, the remaining single lads journeyed home by tram, and always ended up buying fish and chips or black pudding (sausage) and chips, before walking home the remaining miles, while discussing and exaggerating earlier events of the evening.

Every Sunday morning, a bakery truck delivered pre ordered fresh hot buns to the house, and Mum prepared poached eggs. Sounds yummy, but Saturday nights and Sunday mornings were becoming repetitive. The script did not change and itchy feet were in order! But as Maureen had gone, it was my turn to be the additional breadwinner for the family. I did not realize it then, that this was to be a must!

On graduation from High School at the age of 16 in June, 1957, my first thoughts were rest and relaxation for the summer months ahead. Mother's thoughts differed. "Will it be banking or insurance?", she offered. I replied that our neighbour, and Maureen's friend, Winifred Mackie, age 21, whom I secretly admired from afar, had just joined an insurance company, called Standard Life. Perhaps I should apply for a position there, and I did.

Little did I know, that I would spend the next 40 years as an employee of Standard Life, in 6 different cities on 2 continents, from the position of mail boy in Edinburgh, to corporate group pension sales manager in Toronto, plus an additional 9 years as a defined benefit corporate pension consultant with Standard Life. In those 49 years, I travelled thousands, upon thousands of kilometers, to a final retirement in Toronto, Canada, and I have been the beneficiary of corporate pension, dental and medical benefits for the past 23 years, after formally retiring at the age of 57, in 1997. I "double dipped" for 9 years, from 1997 to 2006, receiving my retirement pension income, while also being paid as an arm's length pension consultant, to Standard Life's Ontario based defined benefit group pension clients.

How does one make an irrational decision like that, and end up winning, not only the Stanley Cup, but the Super Bowl and the World Series, all gift wrapped together, in a single lifetime? One cannot call that luck. I really believe, that I was chosen to be blessed! I know not why.

I know you sometimes have to do "stuff", to make things happen, but in writing and reflecting on these memories, it has become more apparent to me, that I was being led, in my naivete, on a path that would be productive and meaningful, as a human being on this earth. I accepted Christ as my Saviour, in 2006. Some might say, I took my time. Others, that it was just a matter of time.

Neighbours are so important in life, and especially when you are all in the same area, and close to each other for 20 years and more. While Dad was in the TB Sanitarium, Mum became very friendly with a nearby neighbour, by the name of Jessie.

Her husband Dod, yes Dod, a shortened Scottish name for George, was an engineer, and away on offshore oil projects in the North Sea, for 6 weeks at a time. Mum and Jessie were probably similarly lonely, and Jessie spent a lot of time at our house. She was the epitome of a noisy, happy lady, and Dod, when we saw him, was of a similar nature and I recall, always carried a remarkable amount of loose change in his trouser pockets, which he jingled continuously.

El met Jessie on our last trip to Scotland. Jessie would console me as a youngster, on hearing late afternoon, that I had broken up with a current girlfriend, by reassuring me, that by the next day afternoon, I would have news for her, of a new relationship. She was mostly right! Dod and her, were such down to earth, happy people, and did a lot to make our home active, and full of laughter, in these months before and after Dad's death.

A sad commentary was that one of her grandsons, who was a member of the Household Cavalry, her majesty, Queen Elizabeth 2nd's official bodyguard regiment, was killed, among 10 others, while parading in Hyde Park in London, following a bomb explosion in July 1982, attributed to the IRA. Seven of their horses also died in the explosion.

The Gammie family were also Edinburgh friends, living only four houses away. Their daughter Rae, a beautiful girl, was in my opinion overly sheltered by her parents, and I set about to introduce her to the world. She was my date at a Standard Life annual soccer dinner (black tie and all), and I must have impressed her parents, because they allowed me to take her on a day trip to Gullane, which is about 25 km outside of Edinburgh. It is famous for its' beautiful beaches and sand dunes. We were both badly sun burned, and I left her at her front door, with her face radiating heat and colour, similar to a traffic stop light. We did not date again! I wonder why?

The Sutherlands next door, were busy people. The father had a car which never seemed to work, and most memories of him, were of his feet sticking out from underneath it. The daughter Sheila was much younger than I, and visited Maureen and I in Vancouver, much later. I asked her what type of soft drink she wanted, and she replied "Scotch, neat, no ice, no water". Oops, she had grown up!

Her brother Douglas was even younger, and I recall his mother despairing, that he would ever get out of diapers. They finally had the problem corrected. Mr. Sutherland was a generous man and when Maureen and her 3 friends proposed, that they should hold a concert on the street for charity, he re- configured his huge shed in the back garden, to create a stage. It was a great success. Tickets were sold to all the neighbours.

I was permitted to be the Master of Ceremonies and to introduce the singing and dancing acts for the four "mouseketeers". My sister, and her three friends all attended a professional dancing school, and had already done some of their acts in front of the public, in Princes Street Gardens, at the bandstand. To qualify for this, you were auditioned by the parks department, and had to have talent. They truly were talented, and their show was a great hit. Where the proceeds went, I do not know. They, or a part of "they", certainly did not end up in my pocket.

Mr. Sutherland was so busy doing things, that everything he touched was done at high speed. During one of his many "Mr. Fixit" jobs, he swallowed, what he believed to be tap water, and it turned out to be some clear cleaning fluid, that had been left in the kitchen. You would not find that product today. He survived, but he probably had long lasting physical damage.

The family called the Mackies, were our neighbours and best friends. Mr. and Mrs. Mackie, and their children Rita and Winifred, were just like extended family to us and we spent many happy hours visiting each other. They had a small black "mongrel", that Mrs. Mackie adored. He went missing for months. One day, when I was outside, he came tearing up the street on his own, spotted me and leapt up into my arms. The look on her face, when Mrs. Mackie answered the door, and saw us and in particular her dog, was beyond description.

A family by the name of Russell, lived in the semi-duplex below us and we feuded with them, over I know naught. We lived as neighbours for over 20 years, never speaking to each other, and yet with an ongoing tension, that was never explained. There was no doubt that Mr. Russell was "strange", to the point that I would sometimes see him, literally doing mathematical calculations in mid- air with his fingers. It seems ridiculous, especially as their daughter Irene, was my classmate for 5 years of high school. But Irene had also fallen under the "Hatfield/McCoy curse" and I know she never acknowledged me, or spoke to me at any time during our school years.

Mr. Mackie had a position with the NAAFI, (Navy, Army and Air Force Institute), formed by the British Government to provide food and services to the British Armed Services, during the Second World War. He was instrumental in helping our family supplement our need for food during the war. Probably illegally, but we were blessed by him. He like many other Brits, was jealous of the American Armed Servicemen, who were stationed in Britain, prior to the invasion of Europe on June 06, 1944, referred to as Operation Overlord or D-Day. This jealousy centered around, higher pay, safety of their families in the USA, and an American attitude of superiority. This was very real. There were well over 1 million American troops in the U.K., prior to the 1944 invasion.

Many a young British woman found herself pregnant, following a relationship with an American serviceman. There were even roadside signs, warning the servicemen to be careful driving, such as "Drive carefully, the woman you hit, may be carrying your child". Hard to believe, but true.

After Mr. Mackie's death, wouldn't you know it, both daughters married American servicemen and emigrated to the U.S. The eldest Rita, married a young man, who was nicknamed Shane, because of his likeness to the Alan Ladd character in the movie of the same name. Her sister, Maureen's friend Winifred, married Virgil, who I was not too keen on. He was unusually quiet and as it turned out, I think the carrier of a gene, that led to their first born being a troubled child. Winifred was a patient and loving caregiver, who mothered her boy under difficult circumstances into manhood, and beyond. She made the most of a difficult life, which never went away.

Both sisters and Virgil are dead. Shane was still alive in 2017, but we have not been in touch with each other. Winifred taught English in foreign countries for many years. I spoke with her, while visiting Maureen's other friend and neighbour Ruth Hamilton Nordhoy, on Whidbey Island in Washington State. Maureen, Ruth and Winifred, are three of the four dancers, who entertained our neighbours, so many years ago, and remained firm friends for over 60 years.

Ruth married a Norwegian engineer by the name of Reidar Nordhoy, who attended and was accredited at the engineering school at Edinburgh University. They both emigrated to Toronto, as Reidar had been offered a position to work on the development of the Avro Arrow jet fighter, that Canada was pioneering. The project was scrapped by our then Prime Minister, John Diefenbaker, following pressure from the American government.

Reidar accepted a position with Boeing Aircraft in Seattle, and became one of the many engineers employed to develop Boeing's 747 monster passenger jet aircraft. He and Ruth live on Whidbey Island in Washington State, home to a naval air station, with 7600 military men and women, housing different navy military jet aircraft and in particular the infamous spy plane, that a Chinese military jet almost collided with many years ago. They have a beautiful home, on a huge piece of property overlooking the sound. El and I have been there several times. Lovely couple.

Reidar is very much a Norwegian, and does not demonstrate much excitement. When asked by me. "What speed does a Boeing 747 passenger jet land at?". His serious response was, "I don't know. My job, was to get it off the ground". His son Ian, is now a Boeing engineer, and travels extensively to assist other airlines customizing Boeing planes that they purchase. The 747's maiden flight was over 50 years ago. I asked Reidar, if he had witnessed the flight, that many years ago. His answer. "No. I was busy working on the design of the next passenger Boeing plane to be introduced, the 767".

I began my working life, by being hired by Standard Life Assurance Company, as a clerk on July 01,1957. A career that would last 40 years as an employee and an additional 9 years as an arm's length consultant. My initial pay was 200 U.K. pounds a year. I started in Edinburgh, and retired in Toronto. My initial interview and only interview for a job, was conducted by Mr. J.B. Dow, who was then an Asst. G.M. of this large life insurance and pension organization. He became the General Manager (President in North American terms) of Standard Life. Why take up his time, to interview me? I do not know. I believe my soccer ability secured the job, over my academic ability.

My first position was in Pensions Q to Z (pension clients who had first names in that alpha range) and were serviced by our department. Within 2 months I received word that I was being transferred. The new department was Pensions H to P. I felt like I was going backwards! One of my very important jobs, was to sort the mail for all H.O departments. This was dumped "en masse" on the Boardroom Table every a.m., and we had to sort and distribute it by department.

Access to the Board Room, was very much restricted to the Directors and a few senior staff, and the only direct route was up the red carpeted central staircase, which was off limits to the general staff. Being rebellious, I would run up there on occasion, and if challenged, I would yell out "Mail sir", to which the answer would be "Use the other stairs the next time, and don't run".

3 George Street, in Edinburgh as the Company's world headquarters, was the "Holy Grail" of financial institutions in the city. It has been a well- run company since 1825, with good people. In recent years, Standard sold its Canadian life and pension business to Manulife, and has now also sold its remaining world, life and pension business, to a U.K. organization. It is now solely, a multi- national, giant investment management organization, with the name Standard Life Aberdeen. With Brexit looming on the horizon, we will see, if Edinburgh is maintained as its Head Office, or if it moves to say Dublin, Ireland to stay, within the European community.

I certainly have no regrets and with positions in Edinburgh, Vancouver twice, Calgary, Hamilton and finally Toronto, Eleanor and I and our family were treated fairly and with dignity. We gave to Standard and they gave back. Oh, and a nice pension too!

As a young man with Standard in Edinburgh, I was fortunate to meet so many fine young peers, who through work, sports and general camaraderie, made life so pleasant for me in these formative four years, before I left for Canada. Friends like Derek Short (now in Burlington), Eddie Shallcross (from Liverpool), Brian Robb, Jim Gibson (an actuary from Newcastle), and Scott Bell (an actuary from Falkirk, who became President of Standard's world- wide operations).

We met most weekday afternoons, after work, in the backroom of Milnes' Bar, a stone's throw from the office, for a pint or two before heading home. We did some silly but harmless things, a prerogative of young men. El and I visited the pub on a trip to the U.K. We arrived late, and knocked on the locked door. I apologized and explained quickly to the young lady who answered, of my history with Milnes' Bar. She said "Very interesting, but we are closed. Good night".

El and I went for supper at a restaurant nearby the next day, and the waiter said" You are from North America aren't you. I suppose you want fettuccini and Caesar salad. Well you are not getting it". Strange, but true! I think we ate elsewhere. That's not the Scotland I remembered.

All my Standard Life friends, were members of the company soccer team or the hiking club. The hiking club was a bit of a farce. We would drive in a mini- van to a town in the south of Scotland or North England, park the vehicle, and walk the last 200 meters to the YMCA, faking total exhaustion. The very reasonable YMCA accommodation, plus a strategically located pub, made the weekend very tolerable. I believe that someone snitched on us, because the Hiking Club, probably deservedly so, was dissolved in its second year of existence.

We were challenged as soccer players, to play against the Standard ladies, field hockey team, on the condition that we dressed up as females, gym slips, pigtails and all. I have a photo, of our male group dutifully dressed, and we actually look good. Blackmail could have been in order, years later, as two of the "male models", achieved lofty status in Standard Life management, including the Presidency.

Our team soccer ability was passable for two years, and then we got serious and were quite good. Scott Bell, who became our President was our left back, and I would often praise him as the team leader in goals. Unfortunately, most were for the opposition. He certainly did not, in any way try to stop or impede my move to Canada, later on.

We won the Scottish Insurance soccer league in our 3rd year and were invited to play against our London, England office. We travelled overnight on the Flying Scotsman train (400 miles in less than 7 hours), which was pretty exciting in 1959. Several of us had severe cramps the next day and lost to the London team. Defeated on the field, but we held our own at the social they threw for us that night. Good memories, if I could only remember what happened that night!

After a year or so in the Pensions office, I was transferred to Agency Dept. led by the marketing vice president, Mr. Graham Pullar, who was a dynamic individual, but a bully. Agency Dept. was the H.O. new business life insurance department that controlled over 300 new business inspectors, who "sold" or acquired individual new business applications from insurance brokers across the U.K. Inspectors were salaried representatives, with expense accounts and cars, not car allowances, paid for by Standard. My initial functions were pretty minor, and included coding all new business individual insurance applications, to allow the key punchers to input the new business data, on Standard's "super computer", of over 60 years ago.

Graham Pullar's office was huge. His assistant Arthur Stepney, whom I liked, had a much smaller office and our clerical office, managed by Steve Aitken, with Phil Peniston, Tom Pemberton and myself, was reasonable in size, for the four of us. I mention these names, because these gentlemen were so helpful in shaping my future, and gave me every opportunity to "get ahead".

The office space for the department typing pool was fairly large, and was managed by a very severe hair bun wearing lady, who only smiled, when she was dressing you down. The stenos, all female, were older than I, and used every excuse to tease me, when I walked into their room, especially when "witchy poo" was not around. Consequently, I was always in trouble with, "you know who", for being caught talking to them. I do not know how I survived.

Before leaving for Canada, I urged a steno, Margaret Jamieson, who I liked very much, but, was older than I, to consider going to North America, based upon comments she had made. Months later she tracked me down by mail from San Francisco, through Standard Life U.K. staff, to confirm that she had indeed emigrated to the United States and had been hired as an airline hostess with Trans World Airlines. Good for her! The letter invited me on arrival in Canada, to stay with "them". I wanted to, but I did not, as I felt that the "them" expression, might disappoint my amorous ways.

An interesting point is that about 10 years following my years in Agency Department, Eleanor and I entertained both Graham Pullar and Arthur Stepney, in Calgary on separate occasions, as they toured Canada in their final months before retirement. Both men and their wives were extremely courteous, and friendly towards us. However, when I was in Edinburgh, I had seen some of the reports Graham Pullar had written about some of the Canadian managers and sales reps., that he and his wife had met. They were not at all glowing, quite critical and very pointed. El and I were on our best behavior, during the time we spent with both of them.

Each U.K. inspector in the U.K. had a Company car (mostly Morris Minors). Agency was in charge of all facets of the cars from leasing to servicing. Tom Pemberton, was responsible for the work involved, and was approached by car dealers and manufacturers alike, to test their vehicles for possible additions to the fleet. I was sometimes included in the test rides and subsequent suppers, to listen to their offers, as long as I was quiet. I do not recall any changes to the Morris Minor fleet, while I was there.

The manager of our clerical staff in Agency was Steve Aitken, a real gentleman from Peebles, who was also responsible for Standard's country cottages in Peebles, that the Company rented out to staff at discount prices, on a lottery basis. I only applied once, while in Canada. No luck!

Steve was also responsible for furthering my soccer career. He persuaded a scout from Peebles Rovers, an East of Scotland semi- professional soccer team, to come to a Standard Life game and watch me. The scout approached me, and at the age of 18, I signed a contract, with very little thought, but with a very big head, at the realization of what I had achieved and what might lie ahead.

I was effective on the field in my first season, but tailed off later. Dad died when I was 19, and that may have had some influence on me. The organization was very good to us. Rides to and from the games. A wonderful team meal after every game. What were we paid? Probably not very much.

Following a game for Peebles in 1969 against Ayr United, a Scottish Second Division professional soccer team, I was given permission to play a "trial" game for the pro. team. After the game in which I did not exactly shine, the team coach approached me and asked what my plans were. I stated that I was considering going to Canada. "Take my advice son, go to Canada", he said. I like to muse that, that was the end of my Scottish soccer career.

A highlight of my Scottish soccer was playing for Peebles Rovers against Hibernians of Edinburgh (Hibs, as they were called), in a Scottish cup tie at Easter Road Stadium in Edinburgh. This was big time stuff and realized, a childhood dream. We lost by 9 goals to 1. Graham, a son in law of Uncle Tom (remember him), was at that game, and in a 2015 conversation, stated that he did not remember me, but that as a team we were rubbish! I quite enjoyed talking with Graham, up to that point.

Seriously I got along with Graham very well. His life was difficult, as Kathleen, his wife and my cousin, sustained a head injury, when falling while leaving a theatre in Vancouver. She due to alcohol consumption, may have not been in full control, but the brain damage was more than severe and her life after that tragedy, was limited to a wheel chair, lack of speech and cognitive capability. Graham was a retired firefighter who gave more than most, to care for her at home. She was finally transferred to a care facility in the last few years, and Graham was free, but still somewhat shackled with a guilt complex.

After Dad's death on June 09,1960, Mum and I started to make plans to join Maureen in Canada. Even in those days, Canadian immigration rules were strict, and it took 9 more months of planning, before we finally received approval. To obtain immigration papers, we both had to pass extensive medicals, have written confirmation from employers in Canada that we had employment, when we arrived, have U.K. passports and funds to purchase passage by air or sea.

Task number one, was to ask Standard Life, for a transfer to their Canadian operations. Mr. A.J. Bromfield who was the corporate pensions manager, was also responsible for staff transfers. I requested an appointment, and arrived at the door of his mammoth office. I felt like Oliver Twist in the Charles Dickens novel, asking for more soup. "Yes, what do you want?", he said gruffly. I replied that I wanted to go to Canada and would like to join Standard there. To my surprise, he said "Excellent idea, we should have more young people transferring to the Colonies. I will make inquiries about positions in our Montreal, Canadian head office". "Thank you, sir", I mumbled," but I would like to be transferred to Vancouver"." No one gets transferred to Vancouver", he roared. I left the room somewhat traumatized.

Unknown to me, my sister Maureen, had spoken with her Vancouver boss, Byron Straight, an independent pension consulting actuary, about the possibility of Mum and I emigrating to Vancouver. Byron wrote to our Canadian President, George Westwater, who he knew, and who was also an actuary. His comments included "if the lad is half as good as his sister, you will have yourself a winner." My destiny, was being prepared. Do you doubt the path was being readied?

I was informed in October, 1960 that my transfer to Standard's Vancouver office, was approved, subject to medical and immigration approval. I passed my medical. Mum did not. The examination revealed a lump on her thyroid gland and at age 47, she was required to have surgery and a diagnosis as to whether the tumor was malignant, or not. This all took time and we were now into 1961, and Standard was questioning, if I was serious or not, about emigrating.

The wonderful news was that the tumor was benign, and Standard being the great company they were and are, celebrated the good news, by offering to pay both our one-way air fares, on the condition that I remained with them for at least 3 years. Nothing in writing, just a verbal agreement. They got 36 years from me as an employee, not 36 months!

The next few months, were spent saying our goodbyes and gifting our household goods, including my collection of movie star photos (don't ask why), my stamp collection and my, previously my Dad's, collection of Edgar Rice Burroughs' books (Tarzan and Mars adventures). I like to keep memorabilia for a while before dispensing of it, if ever, and I have always regretted giving these treasures away, for others to enjoy. Dad, was also a romantic, and was really fascinated about space. I recall listening with him to a radio series in 1959, the year before he died, called "Dan Dare, pilot of the future", which seemed to intrigue him. He stated quite clearly to me, years before it happened, "that man, would be on the moon before long." The U.S. manned Apollo11 module landed on the moon's surface July 20,1969, fulfilling his premonition.

I was still young, and my friends and I, although sorry to say goodbye to each other, were realistic. Our lives lay ahead of us, and so as so many stoic Scots, who have the habit of leaving Scotland in droves, we accepted the facts and moved on. The odd young lady, (Jaqueline, Margaret, Christine, Dorothy, Morag and so on), maybe shed a tear or two, and then no doubt also moved on!

My soccer friends farewell night in Edinburgh, started in Milnes Bar, and proceeded to move East along Rose Street, a laneway and part of what is called New Town. Construction of this area started 200 years ago, to handle the growth of Edinburgh. It also helped solve the unsanitary and cramped conditions existing in the Old Town, which is south of beautiful Princes St. Gardens, formerly the site of Nor Loch, before it was drained. There are now a number of bars on Rose Street and we did not wish to insult any of them, by not dropping in. The 7 of us eventually hailed a cab and piled in. Totally illegal to transport that number, but the fare we offered, persuaded the driver to take us somewhere, until someone suggested, that they were not feeling well. The cab screeched to a halt, and we were ordered out. My last strong memory of that evening was of us booing, as the driver with a limited payment, sped off. Somehow, I was escorted home, expecting to be scolded by my Mother, for my condition. She was not even home and I crawled into bed, to get ready for the big day ahead of us.

I still have the letter from American Express, confirming our travel and flight details. We flew out of Prestwick Airport (south of Glasgow) on a Douglas DC8 jet aircraft, and were welcomed by 10 feet high, walls of snow lining the runway in Gander, Newfoundland. The next leg was to Winnipeg, to repair some minor engine problem. Mum expressed astonishment there, at the size of Canadian coffee/tea spoons, by questioning why Canadians use soup spoons to stir their hot drinks. We arrived in Vancouver on Saturday, April 01, 1961. Maureen's first words were, "You smoke, Robert!"

Maureen's senior friends, Kay and Art Liss, and Ed and Dorothy Meade, had arranged for a letter of employment for Mum at a bakery in Vancouver (but just as a front). She accepted the position anyway, and it probably helped, because if not occupied, you can feel very much alone, when you arrive in a new country. In Edinburgh, Mum had managed a confectionery shop, and also waitressed in a very "posh" restaurant called the "Wee Windaes", which has just gone out of business on the Royal Mile. Edinburgh's professional soccer teams dined there frequently, and she knew several of the stars, and obtained many an autograph for me, which I stupidly left in Scotland.

Ed Meade was with the B.C. Provincial government, in a senior role with the Fish & Game Dept. and it was not unusual to be fed cougar as a delicacy, and part of the evening meal. In B.C. cougars were not permitted on any of the islands and were hunted, if found there. Dorothy was with the Bank of Montreal. Kay Liss was a private secretary for Walter C. Koerner, who was a businessman in the forestry business and a philanthropist, who is now recognized, by an academic library in his name at the Vancouver campus of The University of B.C. When Kay was unable to continue her work for Mr. Koerner, Maureen took over, and she was his part time stenographer for many years, in addition to her sales position with Standard Life. In Maureen's words "Mr. Koerner more than assisted me, in paying off my first mortgage".

Walter Koerner was Austrian. A man of short stature, but very trim. He loved riding and Maureen said he often appeared to dictate to her in full riding gear i.e. breeches, boots and all, prior to leaving for his riding appointment. Art Liss, was an employee with B.C Hydro and a man of many means. He was the one who taught me how to drive a car, and on many of the Sundays we spent in Richmond, he would risk his life, by letting me drive, before I had my license.

VANCOUVER

1961 - 1966

Maureen had rented an apartment in Kitsilano, with a view of the outer Vancouver harbour and Stanley Park. It was stunning. I started work at Standard, the Monday after we arrived. 1281 West Georgia St. was to be my business home for the next 5 years. Canadian Pacific Airlines, were also in that building, with a reception desk at the end of the lobby, occupied by a receptionist, in full air hostess uniform. We never spoke, as I secretly glanced at her, while awaiting the elevator. She was the secret love of my life for many, many months, before CP Air moved their offices to the airport.

Ron Moir was my boss in the Group Life and Pension office. George Weld and Bill Akeroyd were my fellow staff supervisors. My work was probably meaningless in the early months, but these gentlemen did give me the grounding, the start, to work my way up in the organization, from the group pension clerical position, to a Regional Manager position in Toronto, after 20 years. I accepted all the challenges, but am grateful to all the good people, who honed my skills over this period.

Those early months in Vancouver were lonely months. I was working and had family, but I missed my many Scottish friends, and only time can heal that feeling of not belonging. My best friend in these early months was the CBCs' Knowlton (K)Nash on the (K)National (K)News.

Thanks to Ed Meade, I was contacted fairly quickly by the manager of Westminster Royals soccer team, which played in the Pacific Coast League, a forerunner of the major soccer league, that the Vancouver Whitecaps play in today. We were sponsored by Canadian Forest Products, and received $13 for a win and $10 for a draw. My first game was against Victoria on Vancouver Island. Apart from the beauty, experience and success of the memorable ferry trip, I received my first $13.

My other outlet was badminton. Maureen played, and introduced me to the sport and the Shaughnessy Social Club, in which she was a member. We played one night a week, sometimes we went swimming afterwards in Vancouver's outer harbor, from a Stanley Park beach. This would not be possible today. The sea water was pure and clean, 60 years ago.

The "badminton night", was ended with a drink, and then food and coffee. In these days, access to a pub was separated. Males only in one section, and single females or females with a male escort, in another. I experienced an embarrassing incident the first night of joining the club. We had gone for coffee after our pub visit, and when asked by the waitress, if I wanted my apple pie "a la mode", I answered "No just with ice cream!" Oops, that exposed my sheltered Scottish background.

As a group we went camping in the Okanagan, where one couple had a beautiful summer house, beside the area lake. I learned to water ski and we spent hours trying out multiple skiing tricks behind a powerful boat, towing as many as 5 of us, at one time. We were young, we were silly, we believed that we were invincible, and the good news was that, nobody died.

As a family we had moved from Kitsilano to rent a house on 18th avenue in Dunbar, on the west side of Vancouver. Mum and Maureen threw a 21st birthday house party for me, and anyone I or Mum knew or even met in the 4 months we had been in Canada, and of course Maureen's friends, were invited. It was raucous and went on to the "wee hours" of the morning. I am surprised, on reflection, that the police were not called, or that we were not evicted. Without sleep, I took off early morning, for a weekend in the Okanagan. In the car I apparently rested my head, on the lap of a close female friend of Maureen, and snored the whole way. The friend, Diana Flostrand, who I had not met before, was very gracious, but thought I was quite disgusting. Yes, I was a selfish youth, of now 21. Time to grow up and take responsibility.

Westminster Royals had qualified for the John F. Kennedy Cup tournament in Los Angeles in May, 1961, the month after I arrived in Vancouver, as a young and naïve immigrant. According to the press clippings I retained, I was part of that team, and even scored a goal in the first game, before being outscored by the Mexicans in the final. Call it, too much, too soon, but I have no real memory of that trip, and have to rely on these press clippings, to confirm that I was there. We probably lost because most of our team, although experienced and talented, were in the twilight of their careers, and the members of the Mexican team were younger, and much more athletic.

Back in Canada, the Royals were transitioning to a much younger team and the old hands were either retiring or being pushed out. I decided to leave them in 1962, and join the Vancouver Canadians, who also played in the Pacific Coast League. I was not yet a Canadian citizen; the only non- Canadian on my new team. They were young, and had all come up through the Canadians juvenile system. They also were hungry and wanted to win. Ken Howarth was the manager and I was taken by his charm and enthusiasm, and his desire to win.

There were 4 Bobs on the team; Bob A_llen, Bob B_isset, Bob C_oyle and Bob D_urante. On the field we were simply referred to as Bob A, B, etc. I played 5 seasons with them before leaving for Calgary in late 1966. They were good years soccer wise, and I probably played my best soccer as a member of that team, and was picked on at least 2 occasions to represent the B.C. Pacific Coast Soccer League Allstars, in games against touring U.K. professional teams.

Our club games were played at Callister Park, which held about 5,000 fans. It was a waterlogged park, and after days of torrential rain, a fan of ours, who always seemed to be, and was a bit tipsy, gave what I consider to be, one of the best one lines, I have ever heard, before our upcoming game. He said to our captain Neil McKechnie, "Neil. Neil, if you win the coin toss, choose to kick with the tide".

I was selected to play for the B.C. Allstars Soccer Team against Toronto F.C., which consisted of professional U.K. soccer players, who had been given permission to tour Canada in 1961, in their off season. The likes of Stanley Matthews (a soccer legend), Johnny Haynes, Tommy Younger and Danny Blanchflower were on that team. An incredible honour, but the talent prevailed and we lost convincingly. I was also a member of the B.C. Allstars Team that played against Wolverhampton Wanderers, a year later. They still are a top English premier league team, and they also defeated us handily.

Probably the most rewarding experience of my soccer career, was playing for New Westminster Royals and Vancouver Canadians, representing Canada in both years, for the John F. Kennedy soccer trophy, in the summers of both 1961 and 1963 respectively. The Kennedy Cup as it was called, remains unique even today, as it was the sole sporting award in which the late President ever allowed his name to be used. The opposing teams in both tournaments, were from Los Angeles, San Francisco and Mexico. The games were played in L.A., and were the precursor of North American international soccer, as we know it today. At the time President Kennedy was campaigning for physical fitness in the U.S., and recognized the level of fitness inherent in the game of soccer, hence the naming of the trophy.

In the 1961 Los Angeles setting, we defeated San Francisco 3 nothing in the first game, and I, apparently, scored the first goal, which according to the article written by Jeff Cross, the sports columnist of the Vancouver Province (who died just a couple of years ago at age 92), took it's time to limp slowly cross the line. As stated earlier, age prevailed and we lost to the Mexicans in the final.

In 1963, I was playing for the Vancouver Canadians in L.A., and we won the first game in the John F. Kennedy tournament over San Francisco, 2 goals to 1, in overtime. The game was played in a huge stadium, under a searing sun and cramps were the order of the day, especially in overtime. Ken Ferrier and I scored the Canadians goals. We celebrated that night in an L.A. hotel, by crashing a Mexican wedding reception. We were all young, crass and cocky. We were subsequently escorted out of the banquet room, rudely protesting that we had only been recognized, because we were taller.

The final was against Mexico and we were flabbergasted to see that their entire team looked not only athletic, but were all at least 6 feet tall. We were a beaten team from the start. They were very good, and beat us soundly. Once again what an experience, what an honour, to be a part of the only sports trophy, that President John F. Kennedy granted his name to. What a memory! I have the individual trophy, indicating that we were J. F. Kennedy cup finalists. He was to be assassinated only 4 months later.

During that trip, I was fortunate to be able to attend a baseball game in L.A. The Dodgers were playing San Francisco and Sandy Koufax was pitching for the Dodgers. Even then, he was a legend in the game. I sat beside Dick Beddoes, who was a sports journalist for the Vancouver Sun. I never warmed to him, and when I read his column the next day, my first thought was "What game were you at". His story line on our loss to the Mexicans, was not cruel, but was not heart- warming. When our family went on vacation to Parksville on Vancouver Island, over 15 years later, he was renting a cottage at the same resort. We met, acknowledged each other, and went our separate ways. He became a writer for the Globe & Mail and an Ontario TV personality and died in 1991 at the age of 65.

That soccer tournament introduces the love of my life, Eleanor Elsie Jane Storey. We had been dating for over 1 year, and while I was in L.A., Eleanor was visiting her parents in Peterborough, Ontario. We had not been apart for more than 24 hours over the past year in Vancouver, and this separation was a true test of how we felt about each other. The words in some of the letters we exchanged were sizzling, and will not be provided or copied. How did we meet? Where did we meet? You are about to find out.

The development of the individual pathways our lives would journey on and finally intersect, is more than interesting, and once again involves Standard Life. I left Scotland for Vancouver in 1961. Eleanor was just as antsy, and left Peterborough, Ontario for Toronto, in 1962. Separate paths, but destined to cross. As a bridesmaid at a girlfriend's wedding in Ontario, she was drawn to considering a move to Vancouver, after her girlfriend moved there, and commented on the physical beauty of Vancouver's setting on the West coast.

On arriving in Vancouver, in the summer of 1962, Eleanor was referred by an apartment supervisor to two girls, who had just arrived from Ottawa, and were looking for an additional roommate to share the cost, as their 3rd roommate had decided to return to Ottawa. Eleanor was welcomed by Hilda Ramsay and Barbara. Hilda was sweet. Barbara not so much. Now here is the rest of the story.

We had just lost our junior steno at our Vancouver Standard Life office, and subsequently hired a new girl by the name of, you guessed it, Hilda Ramsay, whom I had never met. As a newcomer to Vancouver, she professed to being a bit lonely, and I offered to take and introduce her to the Shaughnessy Badminton group. There was nothing romantic about it. Just a goodwill gesture.

A "friend" of mine, Bill Gates who had a car, drove me the next weekday night, to pick-up Hilda at her apartment and introduce her to the badminton club. I went to the apartment door and knocked. A "blond' answered the door. I stuttered "I have come to pick-up Hilda for badminton". "She has not returned home yet. Would you like to come in and wait?", she offered. Boy, would I like to come in, I thought. I was smitten and decided then and there, that this no name blond is in, and Hilda is definitely out! I mumbled "No thanks", and took off.

The message to Bill was that this unknown blond I had just met, was coming to badminton, whether she liked it or not, but if he felt the same way after meeting her, then he could date her first. Why I said that, I do not know. Unfortunately, his idea of the difference between dating and possession, was different from my Scottish cultural version. He, after a week or so of dating Eleanor (the blond), left to play in a badminton tournament, out of town. I seized the opportunity to ask her out to dinner and dancing, in a hotel setting. She accepted and we hit it off. Not a home run, but a triple.

The next weekend, I took Eleanor to a badminton party. Bill was more than upset, got drunk and wanted to fight. He had a beer bottle in his hand and while waving it around, he accidently, I think, broke it at the neck. We stared at it, for what seemed a lifetime. He was certainly drunk and angry enough to cause me bodily harm, but after a while my words were enough, to counter his fists. I certainly had miscalculated his "North American" view as to what constituted dating, and realized how I had hurt him. We probably agreed that Eleanor would make the ultimate decision. Poor El, she had to counter her emotions and embarrassment, and was not feeling well, when we left the "party".

If it did anything, it strengthened our desire to be together, but of course we had to counter our differences in backgrounds and cultures. My Scottish humour, did not go over particularly well on the phone, and my teasing was usually received with, the silent treatment. We were in love, and this conquered the odd spat and disagreement.

We had no car, and walked many miles in the rain, under an umbrella. El. says that I sang to her quite often, and though I do not remember, I will not disagree. She lived in an apartment downtown Vancouver, and I lived on 11th Avenue, the other side of False Creek. I walked several miles over Burrard Bridge, many a night, after midnight. If there were buses, I never took one. I was more than fit from soccer, and being Scottish, preferred to walk. It was cheaper.

Her mother wanted her home in Peterborough for Christmas 1962. She countered that the only way she would come home was, if I was with her. Told you, this relationship was strong. The first words spoken by her father were "Are you a mick?" I countered," No, but why would it matter?" Oops in those days and in many towns in Canada, religious differences really did matter. Shades of my family differences again! I recall that the 7 days or so, we spent in Peterborough, the temperature never got above minus 30 degrees Celsius. It was cold, but we were in love and got around to meet Els' friends and various family members. Elsie, her mother, viewed me with obvious suspicion in these early days. Her father invited me to the Legion, for the approval test set up by he and his drinking buddies. I passed!

1963 was to be the historic year. We enjoyed our courting and were now recognized as an item. We played badminton, and attended various house, badminton and soccer get togethers weekly. El was working as a steno in Gastown. I was clerking at Standard. We did not have any money. I was approached midway through the year by Doug McArthur, then Standard's Vancouver Life Manager, who became a wonderful senior friend and confidant, about purchasing a car, which his 14 year- old daughter, had won in a radio quiz program. His asking price was $1200. I indicated that I did not have the money, to which he replied "Don't worry I will arrange the loan", which he did, that afternoon with a branch of the Bank of Montreal, that was in our building. No collateral required by me. Doug was a man of action, and was making sure that his daughter, was not having any thoughts about keeping the car!

The car in question was a Renault Gordini. A beep, beep, type of vehicle., similar in looks and size to a Volkswagen beetle. I drove to Eleanor's with pride. She was not overly impressed, and really neither was I, but it was my first car and it did the job for us, for almost 10 years. Being a French manufactured car, we gave it a French name, Chou, Chou, which means Little Cabbage.

I have no recollection of obtaining my driver's license, but I do recall having an accident, while learning to drive Bill Akeroyd's car from the office. It was a massive Plymouth with the large wings in the rear. On turning left from Granville St. south, onto 11th Avenue, I oversteered and hit an oncoming car, just a block away from where I lived. I prayed neighbours, and family would not come by and see me. The police arrived and really were extremely courteous and helpful to me, considering I had caused the collision. How Bill managed the claim, I never asked.

I proposed to El in a lookout parking spot in Stanley Park, and indicated that I had scouted rings in a jewelry store on Robson St., and preferred that we shop together, which we did. I hastened the wedding, with an indiscretion, but a very nice one. On finding out that Eleanor was pregnant, we managed to make arrangements for a mid- November, 1963 wedding.

We did not escape the aura of embarrassment that accompanied being with child before marriage, but we were deeply in love, and all family members and friends were understanding, and although not approving, were very supportive. After 55 plus years, I think we can relax.

In the months leading up to the wedding we had met Bill and Sylvia Nicol, Bill and Leone Watson, David Smith and Barry Sanderson. Sylvia is still a close friend of Eleanor's, Bill Watson (deceased) gave Eleanor away, as Els' father was unable to be present, Maureen was Els' bridesmaid, and David Smith was our best man. David and his wife Jana have been friends, for all these years, and now live in Tempe, Arizona. I do not know where Barry is. He was last heard of, coaching tennis in the U.S.

The Watsons were like mother and father figures, to El and I. They lived next to the Coyle family in the Dunbar area of Vancouver, and El and I watched several Grey Cup games with them. Bill and Leone were so prim and proper and businesslike during the day, but had a bit of a drinking problem at night. We tried to keep our relationship with them to daylight hours. David Smith had dated Maureen and he and I had skied together and were friends. In choosing the best man, it was a coin toss between David and Barry Sanderson. Barry was a sales rep. for Cunard Ship Lines and a confirmed bachelor.

El and I had little money, and David Smith helped us out for the wedding. He was repaid, because, since then El and Maureen stayed with the Smiths in Mexico City and we stayed with them in Tempe, and I was his best man when he and Jana were married in Victoria. David would have let me know, if I had not come through. David was a talented engineer and held major positions with companies in Vancouver and Mexico City. His later consulting roles included, the design of jails in California, during Reagan's administration, and cement plants for Cemex, the multinational building materials company, based in Mexico. His last major design project was a cement factory, located near the San Andreas fault in California, which he thought was a bit silly.

Our wedding was scheduled for 7:30 on Friday, the 15th of November, 1963 at a United Church presided over by the Reverend Gardiner, an extremely handsome photogenic, white haired man. We had met with him much earlier, to discuss the importance of marriage vows. When my mother married Ralph two years later, he was also the presiding minister, and remarked to El and I, "Are you two, still together?" An attempt at humour I think, which seemed out of character, and was not really appreciated.

As the best man for our wedding, David Smith arrived at Mum's 11th Avenue apartment, after driving several hours from his engineering duties in the interior of B.C. My mother said "David, you must be tired and hungry. Come with me. Bob, wash the car". There I was, 2 hours before my wedding, washing B.C.'s interior mud, of the wedding car. Wedding or not, I was not about to cross my mother!

The wedding vows were exchanged. The ceremony went well, complete with official wedding photographs, taken at a studio. In those days, the setting for wedding photos was more than formal, and lacked the spontaneity that we see today. As mentioned, the Reverend Gardiner was quite photogenic, and every female attending the wedding, wanted to be in front of the lens with him, for casual photos taken in the church, after the service. I managed to be included in 1 or 2. Our reception was held at the Cave Supper Club in downtown Vancouver. El and I had been frequent attenders of the Club, and had personally met the likes of Pat Boone and Louis Armstrong backstage. These and other stars, used the Club as a precursor for their Las Vegas tours, to iron out the kinks. The entertainer, the night of our reception, was the blues singer, Eartha Kit, who was a star performer in those days.

Our numbers were minimal, about 18, including the Mums, Maureen, and the other wedding guests. Eartha Kit was so gracious, coming on stage to say, that as soon as the Coyle wedding party had completed their toasts, she would start her show. Our table was by the stage. The food was as usual very good, and the show so entertaining, that after our guests had gone home, El and I stayed to watch the second show. Maybe my Scottish heritage was already rubbing off, on my Canadian wife.

To be truthful, our honeymoon night was not in a romantic setting, but in a Burnaby motel. El was not feeling well, and was exhausted. We left Saturday morning for Harrison Hot Springs, a resort in B.C., which features natural hot springs. On arrival, we took advantage of the springs, had a memorable dinner, went to bed and slept around the clock. Weddings can be exhausting!

The resort is a number of driving hours from Vancouver. The dining room was splendid, and while we were awaiting service, the in-house orchestra leader announced that they would now play The Anniversary Waltz, for a couple that had been married for "25 (pause) hours". There, sitting a few tables away, were Standard Life's, Doug and Joan McArthur. It can be a small world!

As required, we were first on the dance floor to show that we could waltz. Thanked the McArthurs, and their guests, sat down and tucked in to a quality dinner. We both had ordered steak as our entrée, and not long after the main course had arrived, and we had started to eat, the waiter came over and asked if there was something wrong with my meat. Was it too tough, or was it not cooked, to my satisfaction? "Not so", Eleanor chipped in," He always carves his meat that way". We had gone from a 24-hour married couple, to a 24-year married couple, in a blink of an eye.

A reality check came with the serving of coffee at the end of the meal. Neither of us knew or remembered, what cream and sugar either used, if any. Why indeed! It had only been 24 hours.

It was November and our stay there, was dominated by cold wet miserable weather. We took a drive one day, through a Doukhobor encampment consisting of tin and plastic temporary structures. These people had originated in Russia, and were a self-proclaimed pacifist, religious group, who had been persuaded to leave Russia, for Canada, but who now would not even adhere to basic Canadian laws of the land. Their commune had been raided by the authorities, and their temporary camp outside the resort was a symbolic protest against the B.C. provincial government. We were probably wrong to do this type of ogling, but this group turned out to be quite hostile, and some members were ultimately responsible, for bombings of schools, railway lines and power generators in the province, before multiple jailing of members occurred. Their number of members today, has dropped dramatically to about 2,000 and the problems they caused 60 years ago, no longer exist.

Back to Vancouver and reality, and a sad reality it was. Our wedding day was Friday the 15th and President John F, Kennedy was assassinated on the following Friday, the 22nd. Most people of that era know where they were, when that disaster occurred; in Dallas, Texas, at 12:30 Central Standard Time. I was in the office, when the tragic news was released.

The following Friday, the 29th, Trans Canada Air Lines supper time Flight 831, bound for Toronto from Montreal Dorval Airport, with a crew of 7 and 111 passengers, crashed about 20 miles north of the airport. It dived nose first into the ground at an estimated 800 plus km/h. Why? How? The cause was speculated as technical, but not proven, unlike the suspected technical issues involving Boeing's 737 Max 2018/19 problems. I mention this tragedy because, although I did not visit our Montreal Head Office frequently, it was not unusual for me, when in Montreal, to take a similar Friday supper time Air Canada (TCAs' successor) flight as this. I had been blessed again.

At the time of our marriage, Eleanor was renting an apartment on 1st avenue, in the Kitsilano district of Vancouver. I moved in with my worldly possessions; a suitcase with some clothing, a record player and two '78 records (Bill Haley & His Comets, "Rock Around the Clock", and Dave Brubeck's, "Take Five"). "Is this all you have" she exclaimed. "Yup", was the answer. Two other young ladies also rented rooms there, and the 4 of us shared one bathroom. I think I got up at 5:00 a.m., to get any time on my own.

We stayed there until spring 1964, and then rented a larger and much nicer apartment, still in Kitsilano, but on 4th avenue, in anticipation of the birth of our first child. It was new and we were among the first occupants. The next couple who rented above us, were German, who turned their stereo up every night, to an ear shattering level. I had to confront them, and although not happy, they complied. I think the thought of a crying baby convinced them. We had a weapon in the wings!

Babies can cause friction. Babies, can make friends. We were blessed through the pre- natal class that El and I attended, to meet a couple who have been lifelong genuine friends. Life should be about bonding with people through time, but geography and circumstances, often put a roadblock in the way. Nick and Diane Scharfe have been our friends, from that time in 1964 to the present, and we were flattered and so pleased that they attended our 50th wedding anniversary in Toronto. They have always lived in Vancouver and as you will read, we have bounced around many parts of Canada, but the relationship and friendship with them has matured and prospered through these many years.

The males did not attend every class, and usually met in a pub, to discuss "the difficulties of having a baby, but that we could do it". In between "sips" of beer, we would practice our, "assisted panting procedure", which in those days was really never exercised, as males were rarely present at the birth.

July 1st,1964 was a momentous day, the birth of our first born, Susan Jane, weighing in at 7lb 2oz. In these days, fathers of newborns, were allowed 1 day of paid leave. July 1 was Canada Day, so I lost out on that one. Way to go Susan! The other quirk of these times was that fathers to be, were not exactly welcomed at the birthing stage. I was told by the nursing staff at St. Pauls' Hospital to go home, as the child would not be delivered until long after suppertime. I went to 2nd beach in Stanley Park, in the afternoon, enjoyed the warmth of a beautiful day and arrived back at the hospital, to find that El had delivered Susan at 4:00 p.m. Double oops! But good news, Mum and baby were doing well.

We were not financially well off in these days, by any means, but decided that once a home mum, always a home mum, and that El would not go back to work. We managed somehow to make that stick. This is not the way of todays' world, but despite the hardships, I firmly believe that the full-time mother, availability, attention and bonding, enhances the family relationship in the future and for all time.

As a son, I thought I knew my mother. As a grandmother, however, it came as a bit of a shock, when she saw Susan, commented on how beautiful she was, and then proceeded to say "I don't babysit you know". I never figured that one out! She was the master of the one liner, but that did not seem to fit.

Susan was a happy baby, and El and I were comfortable in the rented apartment, but became equally driven, when El found out that I could qualify for a Standard Life 100 percent mortgage, equal to 3 times my salary, which then amounted to $5,000 per annum. El found a beautiful bungalow, at an asking price of $16,500. Standard said no to us despite our appeals. El was not happy, but we continued looking in the Dunbar area and found a home at 3777 18th Avenue West for $14,500. We have since seen this property, which has added a "lane home", where the garage was at the rear of the property, and both residences combined, have an estimated current value of $1 million. But that's what real estate demand, and 55 years of inflation, do for you.

Our offer was cemented by a good faith cheque dated December 1964 for $100, payable in trust to our realtor "Joe", with a firm demand that he not, cash the cheque, as we did not have enough money in the bank, to cover it. He initially thought, and later actually expressed an opinion that we were crazy, and that the deal would not go through, but bless him, he did not cash the cheque, returned it, and I still have it in my possession. We also have been blessed by parlaying a $14,500 mortgage debt into a $1 million wholly owned real estate asset ourselves, in just over 50 years.

It is hard to believe that in the late summer of 1964, the Beatles made their maiden trip to Canada and appeared at the Pacific National Exhibition grounds, August 22. I was there that day due to soccer, and I noted young girls walking through the grounds, virtually screaming and talking excitedly at the same time. I asked why they were so excited, and they bubbled out their delight, at going to see the Beatles perform. The Beatles? Who and what are the Beatles? At the time, I didn't know what they were talking about. Was I the only uninformed one on the planet?

The winter following the house purchase, was for Vancouver unusually cold and snowy. Then everything woke up. We had noticed the odd ant interrupt our social life in the house, but as the warmth of spring brought back life, we found ourselves inundated with an army of Carpenter ants. Yes, the large ones. A desperate call was made and the advert free van arrived with men in suits. Were the neighbours fooled? We did not care. Holes were drilled into the stucco walls, around the house, and we were asked to vacate the premises for 48 hours to allow the poison to do its' job. We returned relieved, only to find that there were other nests in the house walls that they had missed. They followed up and we were finally rid of the critters. House inspections were common in these days and someone missed the signs or due to the wintry cold conditions, they were just not visible.

There were at least 2 major incidents in that house, in the short time we were there. The first involved Susan. We had a habit of sterilizing her plastic bottles and caps every night in a pan of gentle boiling water. We forgot to turn off the burner, and once the water had disappeared the contents melted, causing smoke to fill the kitchen, and the bedroom where Susan was sleeping. We eventually smelled the smoke and found Susan still sleeping happily and sucking actively on her soother, as she was prone to do. All was well, but her whole face was as black, as an often, used flu, in a chimney. Sorry Susan! We promised to be more careful.

The second was, experiencing a 6 plus reading on the Richter earthquake scale. We were sitting in the kitchen, when there was a loud rumble, which resembled a truck driving through the house, followed by absolute silence, and then the experience of floating in midair, as the kitchen floor appeared to disappear under our feet, and furniture and dishes alike, shook and rattled violently. The incident was short, but left you with a feeling of total helplessness, and uncertainty. Vancouver sits close to the Western fault line and one of these days. Well, you never know!

We had a family visitor at the house in the shape of John MacDonald, my cousin from Edinburgh, who had decided to follow my footsteps and emigrate to Canada. El and I were slightly concerned that he might want to board with us for a while, and although deemed selfish, we were on the edge money wise and not the "rich" Canadians that some of our relatives thought we were. We wanted to help, but wasted no time in strongly encouraging him to get out and look for employment. He had skills and found a job fairly quickly, although his employers' location was a long way from where we lived.

He stayed for a few more months, but due to travel time, found a place closer to his work place, once he had built up some savings. While with us, he took Susan to the Pacific National Exhibition, when she turned two. We trusted him and he truly loved children, but we became concerned when he had not returned by the supper hour. We checked down the long street that we lived on, and about 7:30, they could be seen walking towards us from the bus stop. Susan's face was covered in what seemed, at a distance, as chocolate ice cream, and her dress looked like she had not changed it in six months, but the smile on her face was something to behold. Boy, was she happy! That was John and he has not changed. We are not close, but one has to respect anyone who can put a large as life smile, on a two- year old's face, and fill her with genuine happiness.

We had lived in the west end of Vancouver for less than 2 years, when I was offered a position, as manager of our Calgary pension office. The only person who would report to me, was a shared steno. Not much to manage, but I looked at it as a foothold on the first rung of the Canadian corporate ladder. El was supportive, and we began the real estate buy/sell scenario. We sold the Vancouver property within two years of acquiring it, for $18,000, probably due to Els' decorative abilities, and on a short company paid trip to Calgary, purchased a split- level home at 27 Gladys Ridge Rd. in Calgary for $19,500.

Ron Moir was still my boss. Ron and his wife Pam were truly nice people. Pam was in the WAAFs' during the 2nd World War and had the huge responsibility in a secure war room, as one of the staff, to plot the course and the destination of German bombers for interception, using the radar technology that Britain had secretly invented, without German knowledge. She was generous with her time and loved to entertain, producing mountains of food in record time.

Ron was sparing with his time, unless you responded quickly, and produced positive results. He and I seemed to hit it off. He was an advocate for spending on a limited basis. Our wedding gift from him was a kettle. Practical and useful, until it developed an early leak. The repair technician on examination said to me "Nobody, made this", "What do you mean, nobody made this", I said. He countered that any kettle he had ever seen had a logo or stamp on it. One of Ron's favourite corporate clients in Vancouver, was Canadian Stevedoring. I would surmise that he acquired the odd product from the arriving merchant vessels, through this source. Ron was dealing in "knock offs", before anyone knew the terminology.

His frugalness, almost proved our undoing. He had decided, that after shipping our furniture to Calgary, courtesy Standard, that he could limit company cost, by having us drive there. We had already stayed in a motel on the North Shore of Vancouver for a month, after the house sale, to keep our costs down. El was stuck there with Susan, without a car, and in the early stages of pregnancy, with our second child. She was not a happy camper, and when the news came to travel to Calgary, even by car, we quickly chose the "get out of town option", that was offered to us. Not a bright decision! We set out on New Year's Day 1967, in our beloved "Chou, Chou ". Any nasty weather covering B.C. and Alberta, had been delayed and stored in readiness for our travels.

To say, we had multi problems was an understatement. Susan contracted tonsillitis. El had morning sickness. We skidded off the road, on a hill before the Rogers Pass, and I had to get out of the car, run up the road and stop the oncoming traffic, to get assistance in pushing our car out of the snowbank. We had to buy chains to travel the Rogers Pass, which was then closed for at least 24 hours, due to avalanches.

We stayed in Revelstoke until the Pass was opened, and used our time to try and repair the locked door handles, which had frozen overnight. We ended up, breaking the locks and roping the doors together. When we arrived in the valley beyond the pass, there was no snow, and the chains tore large chunks of rubber out of the tires. This French manufactured car, was not up to the rigors of a Canadian winter, and neither were we! I did however, assist another traveler to change his flat tire, by the side of the road. Man was I stupid!

I should add that Eleanor and I, did not get divorced after this trip, but based upon what she and Susan went through, I think a good lawyer, could have presented sufficient evidence to the court to obtain a positive judgement, on her behalf. I salute both of them for accepting the difficulties encountered, without any meaningful complaints. The travel part was still exciting for us, and once again we were being escorted on a journey, without realizing why or where we were going.

3

CALGARY

1967 - 1971

We made Calgary, without further incident. The first thing on arrival, was to tuck Susan inside my coat, and rush into a department store to buy her a snowsuit. When questioned by Doug McArthur, about whether or not the Coyles had left for Calgary, Ron innocently answered that we had left by car on January 1st. "What" Doug exclaimed apparently, "You sent a pregnant woman, with a small sick child, in a small car, through the Rogers Pass at this time of year!" No such thing as cellphones then. I believe Ron made several calls to his Calgary contacts to try and locate us, and confirm that we had made it. Nobody called. No apology was ever forthcoming. That unfortunately was Ron.

We were still in Canada, but it was so cold. The first morning after our arrival, I looked out the window of our motel room at the snow, and the line of cars, with their exhaust fumes suspended midair in a frozen state, and thought. What have I done?

Before long the moving company called, and we left for the house. We had just arrived and the door- bell rang. It was Don and Peggy Ramsay. Don was the manager of Standard's Calgary individual sales office. This started a friendship which lasted for many years. They were so good to us, and in addition, patiently taught us to play bridge, through the long cold Calgary winters. El suspects that Ron Moir called them, to make sure we were still alive, and he was not facing triple homicide charges!

The moving truck arrived later that night, and they began with the following "good news". "We have to be in Edmonton tomorrow morning to deliver parts for a hotel finalizing its construction. We will unload your furniture, make up your beds and staff will come tomorrow to help you put the house in order." Because of the cold, the stationary truck rumbled well into the night, until they finally left. I am sure the neighbours, who we had not yet met, were really impressed. But wait there is more to come.

We received our help the next day, and organized as much as we could. Got Susan settled, sat down wearily, to receive another night time knock at the door. It was a friend of Eleanor's, from Peterborough. A former boyfriend no less, whose family owned Trentway Bus Lines, a private luxury coach bus line. Mr. Gerry Bolton not only came, but he brought the bus, whose engine of course rumbled away in the cold of the evening, for fear of not restarting. Our neighbours, I am sure, were wondering what had landed on their street, and what more could happen to shake up this formerly peaceful part of the world, as we had only been there for less than 30 hours. Oh yes, and by the way, how did Mr. Bolton get our address in that time frame? Hmmm!

Our next door neighbours, Bill and Yvette, were indeed friendly and understanding. He was an engineer, who travelled a lot. His one son aged 10, was soccer mad, and would often come to our door after supper and ask "Can Mr. Coyle come out and play with me?" He had lost a brother to a household accident, and many times I felt it difficult to refuse him, especially when his dad was away on a business trip. His father was a talented, balanced man, but to this day, I remember his obsession, which was that the U.S. marines would invade Canada at any moment, to seize control of our fresh water supply, which he insisted, the United States was about to run out off. I am still waiting.

Our neighbours across the street were Bob and Judith Young. He was out of character as someone with a chemistry background, because he was a master at leading people astray, but in a loveable sort of way. After my promise to mow the lawn, El would leave to shop, and come home to find Bob and I, sitting on the porch, beer in hand, with my task not even started. She would be pleasant to Bob, and give me heck. To me, Bob was the 20th century Peter Pan, and when we met years later in B.C., he had not changed, and as you will read below, he has become an even more "Will-o'-the wisp" character.

The Youngs eventually moved to Salt Spring Island on the west coast. He is part of a big secret, that cannot be revealed. So, do not read this page, if you cannot keep a secret. The mountain on Salt Spring is Mt. Erskine, and it is inhabited by gnomes, courtesy of Mr. Young. (Shh). He has constructed multi gnome villages all over the mountain, complete with doors and windows cut out of tree trunks, with little pathways, mail boxes etc. Many a person has tried to determine who painstakingly has built these miniature villages, and some have claimed to be the ones. But now you know the truth, and having read this far, you are bound to silence, or else!

Our second child, Michele Maureen Coyle, was born in the afternoon, of June 14, 1967. El felt that a beckoning vacation, caused the doctor to force the birth, to her great discomfort. We were excited to bring Michele home. Susan also, was caught up in the excitement of the birth, but somewhat in the wrong way. She was astonished that we were going to keep Michele. We believe her words were, "Send her back, you have got me!" Three- year old kids, are not receptive to competition.

Life in Calgary was not easy. I was not earning enough money, for us as a family unit, to get ahead. I had obtained an insurance license in B.C. and had this approved for Alberta. I approached Don Ramsay, and he undertook to obtain Head Office approval, to allow me to sell individual life insurance, while maintaining my group pension division position. They agreed. I then asked Ron Moir, my immediate boss, on his only trip to Calgary in 4 years, for a raise, or I would be forced to leave the group division. Somebody at Head Office knew something, I did not. I received a 30% increase in salary. Yes 30%!

To make up for the small income I had been receiving, I finished my group work at 5:00. Cold called university students between then and 6:00. Went home and had supper and then met with those prospective buyers, who had agreed to talk with me. We survived, but El was lonely and unhappy. In my attempts to get ahead, I had left her behind, and with 2 young children and my busy, busy, selfish life, there was not much for her to get excited about. These were tough days but we survived, and yet once again I salute her for her patience and faith in me.

Socially, I played soccer with a team called the "Callies". El played badminton. The Ramsays continued the bridge lessons. We did not socialize with the Standard field staff and at times they were not exactly friendly, especially if in any week, I sold more individual business in my part time position, than they did. We also had group clients in Edmonton and Medicine Hat and I recall fondly, (yeh, right), leaving Calgary at 6:00 in the morning and driving 3 hours, for early morning meetings in the middle of a bitterly, cold Alberta winter. The road conditions were not pleasant, with frost free weather in Alberta limited to about 90 days a year. I was dedicated, but stupid. Of course, I had the car, and El was "stranded", and probably felt very isolated.

Susan was developing, a "Miss Susan personality". I drove her to nursery school in our beloved Renault Gordini, which by now Susan had decided, was not a 5- star vehicle. If we arrived ahead of the school bus, all was fine. If not, she would slip out of the front seat and hide on the floor well of the car, imploring me not to open the car door, until all the kids were off the bus and out of sight. What 4 year- old doesn't do this? She reassured me, that it was the car and not me, that she was not particularly proud of. Phew! That was a relief! At age 5, we ensured that she was taken to school in the school bus.

We were finally heading in the correct financial direction, and were now able to finance a new car, a gold Plymouth Valiant. Not much later, this car was hit by a motorcycle running a red light. Police on nearby radar duty saw, and confirmed this fact, but for some reason backed off witnessing. El, Michele and the 2 boys on the bike were not seriously hurt, although one of the boys had tumbled off, hit and smashed our windshield, while luckily wearing a helmet.

A father of one of the boys, who was a lawyer, decided to sue us, as El was turning left in the intersection, and left turners are inclined to be blamed, for such accidents. The lawsuit delivered one night to our front door was a bit of a shock, but was a scare tactic, as the young boy had caused the accident, and did not even have the proper license to have a passenger on the bike. The discovery meeting sorted things out and the final decision was a 50/50 settlement. We ended up paying 50% of our deductible, or $50. To wrap up, the car was repaired and delivered to me at the dealership, with the assurance that all repairs had been completed. "And, the fact that the windshield is still cracked?", I said. Oops! We were on our way within the hour, as this "minor" detail was attended to.

We did not vacation much in the 4 plus years in Calgary, but we did visit Vancouver twice. and stopped in the Okanagan for a few days each time, once with the Nicols. El still maintains close contact with Sylvia, who has remarried, and who we both like very much. Bill and I both had played for the Canadians soccer team, and the B.C Allstars team in Vancouver. Bill was a very nice man, but quiet, and El and I probably were closer to Sylvia, and have maintained that reasonably close relationship through today.

Mum and my stepfather Ralph, both visited us in Calgary one Christmas. It was bitterly cold and the Hong Kong flu was raging through B.C. and Alberta. We were all stricken, and try as we might, we could never register enough of the family at one time, to celebrate with a Christmas dinner. Mum, the master of the one liner, turned, as she headed out on the tarmac to board her plane, (no telescopic passenger runways in these days) and said, "I'm not coming back, you know".

Alberta is quite beautiful and when you are close to the Rocky Mountains, the visual scene can seem unreal, as if Hollywood had built and placed a painted prop in front of you. Calgary however, was a test for both El and I. We did not warm to the long winters and the cold. A tight budget and two young children did not provide us with the opportunity to take advantage of what Alberta could offer, such as skiing etc. Stampede Week and its' outlets, bridge, badminton, soccer and membership in the 400 Club, offered us some social relief, but something was missing, and I think we both were hoping for a change of venue, having experienced living in areas where the four seasons were somewhat more identifiable.

4

ANCASTER

1971 - 1978

In 1971, I was approached, about transferring from Calgary to our Hamilton, Ontario pension sales office, with more responsibility and a larger salary. As indicated earlier, a possible further move was on our collective minds, and we both accepted the next step on our journey, without question. Standard offered to buy our Calgary residence for $29,000, and we were off to Hamilton to house hunt, and meet my new boss. Maureen "volunteered" to come from Vancouver and babysit our now 7 and 4 -year old girls. They were going to be a handful.

Being single, it took a while for Maureen to dress the girls to go outside in the cold, and of course, she did not consider the effect that the weather would have on their bladders. They no sooner got outside than, they wanted to go to the bathroom, and the dressing process started all over again. Susan exerted her independence and one day, Maureen had to send her to school in a dress and rubber boots, even though the temperature was a wee bit chilly. She was grateful, when we returned. In Hamilton I went to the office, and El teamed up with a realtor named Joanne, who was a real sweetie. Our agreement was, that El would spot houses for sale in reasonable areas, in a price range of about $35,000 to $40,000 and I would then be involved and we would make the final decision. Multi homes were available on Hamilton Mountain, and in Burlington, Dundas and Ancaster. Multiple choices made it very difficult to come to a decision.

We chose a 2 story older home on Jerseyville Rd. in the heart of old Ancaster. I liked it, El loved it.! She was smitten. Our buying price was $39,000. A Standard appraiser approved the mortgage, but felt we had overpaid. A trying time ensued, but our logic prevailed, and based on the neighbours we enjoyed for years, the schools, the services, our experiences there, and the house itself, we made the absolute, correct decision.

The Regional Manager for Southwest Ontario was Lloyd East, my new boss, a very tall man with a personality like a high school principal, studious and a very slow but deep and thorough thinker. Lloyd obviously had had problems retaining staff, because his wife Ida, who El and I grew to really like, spent a considerable amount of time explaining to me, that if I could put up with Lloyd's idiosyncrasies, I would benefit greatly from his knowledge and wisdom. She was correct about the benefits, but the trials and tribulations in acquiring these, were at times painful.

Lloyd was an unexplainable character, and there were an amazing number of incidents in the seven years I worked under him, all the while gaining the knowledge and business experience that Ida had alluded to. His continual and deep thought processing, made it difficult for him to remember simple detail. We were on our way to Brantford to meet with Harding Carpets. I arrived home one afternoon at about 1:30, and explained to El that Lloyd would be around "shortly" to pick me up. "Shortly", turned out to be about 60 minutes, as Lloyd realized half way to Brantford that Bob and the files were not with him. When he finally picked me up, he greeted me with his usual phrase "Bob so good to see you again", as if his oversight had never happened.

Lloyd was a cigarette smoker and when deep in thought, he would sometimes throw his stub into the garbage can in his office. I would notice this , but only alert him when the flames were rising above the top of the can. I refused to mother him, but I had to be 2 or 3 steps ahead of what might happen next. In essence I did not stop him from doing things, that most would consider strange, but I had to be aware at all times, to fix any problems, such as our presentation to a potential client.

The Kitchener Waterloo Record newspaper, which became a client, was a classic situation. We had arrived early, decided to have lunch and review our proposal. I watched carefully as Lloyd read the original copy intended for the Company, and then put it inside his menu on the table. Our order was taken and the menu disappeared with the server. We of course, could not locate our material, as we were about to leave the restaurant, and head for the meeting. Lloyd was beside himself. I knew where it was, commented that it might have been caught up in the menus, and we waited patiently at the front of the restaurant, as the maître d' opened every hard cover menu, finally locating it. Naughty of me, but I believed, that he also had to share my discomfort.

I made it my doctrine to either use my car, have the files required for the meeting, or have the keys to Lloyds' car, to avoid being a victim of his forgetting. On the way back from Toronto, I noticed that his gas tank was registering empty. "Lloyd, we are out of gas and it is only Oakville". "I thought we would have at least made Burlington" he said, which had nothing to do with the problem, as we still had a further 25 kilometers to get home. We pulled to the side of the QEW freeway, where Lloyd suggested that I use his old raincoat to cover the wire fence at the side of the freeway, scale the fence and leave a $5 bill, as compensation for using the contents of a lawnmower gas can, that we could see in a garage on the other side of the fence." But it will no doubt contain oil as well", I said. "No worry", he said. I complied. Nobody was around as I filled the tank with the oil/ gas mixture, scaled the fence, returned the can, and we went on our way.

Our third child, Fiona Mary Coyle was born April 24, 1971, not long after we had arrived in Ontario. A child born in each of 3 provinces. El threatened, that if a further move to another province was in the works, an operation would be in order. Ouch! Quebec was out.

We really enjoyed Ancaster. El loved the house. The neighbours on either side were great, and there were only woods across the street, where the T.H.

and B. Railway had a right of way. This large company was to become a pension client of ours, while I was in Hamilton.

We met some lovely people in the 7 years we were there. The Hunters, the Jepsons, and the Jopsons, who lived next door to each other (a postman's worst nightmare), the Burleys and the Becketts. El had met some active ladies, mainly neighbours, and was able to walk with them, cross country ski with them, and play bridge with them. Susan and Michele were settled at school. Fiona of course was still at home, and El really enjoyed her.

Tom Beckett was the owner of the Beckett gallery in Hamilton, and was the agent for the very talented Canadian artist, Robert Bateman who now lives on Salt Spring Island. Tom was a delightful person. He took us to the gallery one night, to view Bateman's recent work, that was being sold the next day, based on closed bidding. We had barely been in the gallery, when the Hamilton police burst in the door. Tom had forgotten to turn off the silent alarm.

I was in the twilight of my soccer career with Dundas United playing with a very British group with names like Davey Snowball and Brian Appleyard. I was busy with work, but had developed a firm friendship with Tom Jepson, who wanted so badly to learn to play soccer. Tom was one of Ancaster's general practitioners, and despite being a doctor, one of the most humble and down to earth persons, I have ever met. At his first soccer practice, he somehow ended up standing on the ball and rolling back and forward, like a performing seal, which is not easy to do. That mishap "sealed" the deal with our coach and he became our non- playing physio.

Tom Jepson and I became really close friends. It may be a male thing, that male bonding is not common, but in this case, we really enjoyed each other's company. Tom and I loved to run, and we were frequent participants in the Terry Fox 10k run each year. Brian Burley, a neighbour, who was a Professor of Geology at McMaster University, asked if he could join us. We realized selfishly, that if we agreed, we could use the shower facilities at McMaster after the run, and readily consented. Every such run has organized tables on the route, with water bottles. Most runners will take a sip of water, and pour the rest over their head to cool down. Brian had observed this, and quite rightly decided to copy this procedure. Unfortunately, he had picked up a bottle of Gatorade, and proceeded to pour this over his head. Accordingly, every fly and wasp in the area joined us in the run. Tom and I tried very hard, to run at least 10 meters in front of Brian.

We originally met the Jepsons, Tom and Barbara, at a school social in Ancaster, and as mentioned Tom and I became firm friends, until I left for Vancouver in 1978. Tom as a General Practitioner, was beloved by his Ancaster patients. We drank together, smoked cigars together, watched football together, fished together, ran together and so on. We had a very healthy relationship, and even organized a fitness class in Ancaster, for about 20 male neighbours.

Tom was aware that the Jepson family had heart problems. His brother Jim, who was a London, Ontario federal MP, died at a very young age, and Tom himself died in 1993, after his heart went out of rhythm while he was playing hockey. Tom was a fine human being, and although we did not continue to keep in contact with Barb, after they divorced, we still have maintained some contact with the children, Gordon, Kenneth and Catherine.

We were blessed by having Tom Jepson as our GP, and also the fact that his office was directly behind our house, and accessible by squeezing through the hedge in our backyard. Tom lived life to the full. Initially, I did not understand why, but as I look back, I suspect that he was more than aware of his family health history, and the possibility that his life would be shorter than normal. The strides, the medical field has made in the area of heart disease over the past 25 years, should be celebrated. But for him they came, too little too late.

The Hunters, John and Alma, were just delightful and being next door, very handy for forming a close friendship. They were like understanding parents to us, and we grew to become very close. They loved Fiona, and she would visit a lot. She was the child they never had. We played bridge with them every weekend. Their card playing was normal, but John had an infuriating ability of winning the last trick, resulting in he and El, putting

Alma and I, one down, time after time. It happened a lot, and invariably his last card was a black jack. His favourite and "annoying" expression, as he put us down was, "not through the iron duke!" On being transferred back to Vancouver, 7 years later, the thought of leaving them, is now seen as one of the most difficult decisions we ever had to make. We can still see them, standing at their door as we left for the airport, waving goodbye, and crying unabashedly. Believe me, John did not cry easily!

With 3 children, vacations were not easy to come by, but we did get away on occasion. One such trip was to Daytona Beach, Disneyworld and Myrtle Beach, where we joined four other families from Hamilton. A joint desire by the Dads was to go deep sea fishing. It was a windy day and the ship captain warned us that conditions were not perfect, but we insisted. Several of the families' children were with us. Not the Mums! Sea bass was the catch. Squid the bait. Rough seas were the problem.

Susan and Michele were not ill, but were quiet. Two of the younger boys, who had flaming red hair were really noticeable because of their contrasting green faces. I had taken anti- nausea pills after breakfast and felt great. I may have been the only one who really enjoyed the trip, and wanted to eat every ones' lunch on the return trip to the dock.

Our kids pushed us to go on the famous roller coaster ride in Myrtle Beach. I am not a fan and when you look at that structure, which is not exactly new, you might agree with me. As we chugged slowly up the first portion, which takes you to the top of the ride, before you plunge into the twist and turn of the abyss below, Fiona who was sitting beside me, calmly said "I have changed my mind Dad, I want to get off". She was merely echoing my thoughts, and we clung to each other in terror, for the rest of the ride, only to be greeted by her sisters screaming, "let's do that again…please". Hearing this, Fiona of course joined the chorus. Weird!

We rented a cottage one year on Lake Huron. Not Els' favourite. No break from cooking etc. We also had a wonderful trip to Ocean Park in Maine with the Blacks who were neighbours in Ancaster, before moving to Barrie. We shared one- star accommodation with them near the beach. El became very close to Sue Black. She and her husband Doug, who unfortunately died at a young age 65, from an enlarged heart, led El. to becoming a Christian. El and Sue are still very close friends.

We spent hours looking for sand dollars in the shallow water at Ocean Park, and enjoyed a really warm spell of warm weather while we were there. Susan escaped serious injury, while we were fastening some luggage on the roof of our car. The bungy cord snapped loose (my fault) and hit her just above the eyes, in the centre of her forehead. Thank the Lord, because it could have been much worse. She did not complain, but she does want to be executrix of my will. Hmmm!

Maureen had agreed in late 1971 to let us stay with her in her apartment overlooking Vancouver's inner harbor, if we brought the baby (Fiona) with us. Susan who was all of 7, did not want to miss school. Weird, but I was sure that there was another devious explanation. Tom and Barbara Jepson volunteered to look after her and they did. More to follow!

The remaining Coyle four, flew out to Vancouver on a 747, occupying bulkhead seats, which allowed us to deposit Fiona at 4 months in a baby crib, that was attached to the bulkhead. Probably not authorized today. The flight was delayed for 4 hours and with a flight time of 5 hours, we were fairly exhausted when we arrived. Michele and Fiona were really good and slept a good portion of the flight. The only problem is the rapid descent into Vancouver, after overflying the height of the Rockies. Children do not know, or can handle the pressure problem in their ears, and because the girls had been sleeping, the wailing was real!

I was a bit lethargic during our visit to Vancouver, and seemed to spend an unusual amount of time in the toilet. Maureen (Miss Fitness) barked at me on many an occasion "to get moving". We returned home and while watching a football game at the Jepson house, I started to sweat profusely, and Tom who was not then my GP, diagnosed that I had the flu and gave me an injection. I subsequently went for a follow up medical exam with Dr. McCurlie, our then GP, who diagnosed gall stones. Oops Tom! A gall bladder extraction was scheduled for early 1972. Tom Jepson had scheduled a Caribbean trip, and was really upset that he would be away.

The Jepsons of course, had returned Susan to us, and we quickly found out that she had wound them around her little finger. The first night we were home, she came sauntering down from her upstairs bedroom around 10:30, and when questioned as to why she was up, she replied that she felt hungry, and was going to have a snack! We quickly put an end to that, and ushered the 7 year- old back to bed.

Following my surgery by Dr. Billy Barnes at McMaster, I jaundiced quite badly. I recall Dr. Barnes coming into my room while smoking a pipe, and pronouncing in between puffs, that if he had to go in again, "he would use the same hole". In these days the surgery did involve a fairly large incision. I was as yellow as Chairman Mao Zedong, who was currently entertaining U.S.A. President Richard Nixon, on his historic and surprising visit to China, in early 1972.

I probably did not feel well. I certainly did not look well. After multi questions from hospital specialists, about have I ever had malaria or any other parasitical disease, the bile duct cleared, and I returned to normal colour. Before the yellow disappeared, the children had in their own quiet way, asked El if I would always look "like the way I did". A highlight for my wife, before I completely returned to normal, was when a dietician walked into the hospital room, looked at me, looked at Els' young face complete with the jaunty tam she was wearing on her head, and then boldly pronounced to her, "that your father appears to be making progress."

Returning home was not easy, not because I was not healing, but because we encountered the worst ice storm that Southwest Ontario had ever seen. The trees were coated in inches of ice and the whole land was white, icy and more picturesque, than ever a Hollywood screen set could match. El had gone for a walk with John Hunter, and just described the scene "as beautiful beyond belief". Of course, negatively almost all power lines were affected by the weight of the ice, and thousands were without power for weeks. Hydro crews from all over Ontario had to assist. The massive storm covered the whole area from Burlington to Dundas You could not touch a tree branch without it breaking, and many more branches and trees just collapsed anyway. Ancaster is a very rural and green community, and the damage was huge.

I watched as one large tree bordering the fence line with the Hunters started to lean. It finally fell, but right between the houses. Thank you, Lord! Fiona, still not 1 year old did not understand, why after my surgery, I could not pick her up. Our Renault car, almost on its' last legs was sitting in ice, halfway up the tires and one tire was flat. I really felt helpless. "Houston, we have a problem!".

The neighbours were supportive, and the Gibbards, with a wood burning fire place, invited us to the warmth of their house and the availability of hot food, because of their fireplace. I remember distinctly, having my first bowl of Campbells' chunky soup, poured from an iron pot heating on the fire. It felt like Scotland all over again, but over there it would have been home- made soup.

The Gibbards, had two girls, one of them a stay at home daughter. An attractive girl in her 20s', who only went out at night, fully made up and dressed to the hilt, and who slept or stayed in her room all day. Strange! We never saw her, except on the odd occasion, when we observed her walking past our house, to get the bus, to go somewhere. Where she went, what she did, nobody knew. As friends of her parents, we honoured them, with a code of silence. But it was so tempting, to find out what she actually did. We never did! I still want to know!

Our time in Ancaster, has to include wonderful memories of the several trips we took with some of our neighbours, to Loon Lake Hunt Club. Tom Jepson's father was a member, and when he died, the shares and membership went to Tom, and his brother Jim. Most other members were business men, in insurance and banking, from Brantford, Ontario. The Hunt Club building lay east of Huntsville, bordering Algonquin Park, in a dense wooded area and with a private lake, named Loon Lake. To us, it was a form of paradise, and we spent many weekends there, mostly in the winter, cross country skiing, ice fishing, ski doing and socializing.

Tom and I joined a group of males on one such weekend in the winter. The weather was really bad and other than us, all left early to return home. We packed up and left, but Tom and I were stopped by the RCMP, because of strong winds, snow, poor road conditions and visibility. We had no choice but to return to the hunt camp. We had food, but "disaster", nothing alcoholic to drink. Tom knew the owners of a private lodge just north of us, and also knew that the male owner was not permitted by his wife to drink on the premises, or in front of guests. He therefore had a stash of "hooch", hidden in a small cabin, in the woods. We put on our cross- country skis and set of on our snowy journey. Tom located it, and as per the rumour, there was the cache of various bottles of rye, scotch etc. We took the rye and left a note. Tom promised to call him the next day, and "quietly" reimburse him for the "loss". We had no soft drinks, and I was forced to have my first rye and water. My favourite non- wine drink today, is rye on the rocks, without the water.

To probably accommodate Lloyd East, my client territory was outside of Hamilton. It covered Kitchener/Waterloo, Guelph, Gault, Brantford, Collingwood and various communities south of Hamilton towards Niagara. I recall watching parts of the infamous Canada/Russia 1972 hockey series on a shop window television in Kitchener, in between appointments. Being on the road encouraged improper eating of fast foods. A & W's grandpa burger was my favourite. A large number of patients I meet at Southlake's CV Surgery ward, in my volunteer role, are truck, and taxi drivers and travelling sales persons, who have inherited heart disease problems, from the food eaten at "that place, where the food was so tasty". Stay tuned!

Lloyd decided that I should cover the north as well. Communities such as Sault St. Marie, Thunder Bay and Dryden. The Sault had Algoma Central Railway, and its' subsidiary Algoma Shipping with its multi freighters on the Great Lakes. El and I were invited to the christening of a new Algoma freighter in Collingwood. What an event that was. The number of guests and dignitaries was impressive. It was more of a birth, than a christening, and the pride and warmth displayed by the Algoma staff, as it readied for its' maiden voyage was heart- warming. You feel very insignificant, standing on the dock, looking up at this massive structure. We toured the vessel, but for some reason were not allowed to see the cabins they rent out to travel, fare paying tourists. The only disappointment of the day. They probably had not yet been furbished.

Thunder Bay and Dryden had huge paper mills and our clients were Great Lakes Pulp and Paper and Dryden Pulp and Paper, both with very large salaried and hourly paid staffs. In Dryden, the only reasonable accommodation for visitors was the Dryden Hotel, with very small rooms and murphy beds, that stored in the wall. Lloyd had come with me on my first trip there, for introduction purposes. At 6 feet plus plus, his feet extended well beyond the confines of the murphy bed. Our room was above the main entrance, which had swinging doors, leading to the bar, a la the set of a Hollywood western. In bed after 11:00, we would hear the doors swing open, followed by the words "and don't come back again", as the body was flung through the doors and onto the street." Yup partner, those were the days!" Remember, this was almost 50 years ago.

Dryden was in the middle of seemingly nowhere. Your plane flew low over endless forests and then dropped suddenly into a large clearing, harbouring a commercial runway completely surrounded by trees. On arrival you were exposed to a smell, which was not nice. Dryden sits on the Wabigoon River and at that time, it was all about business and not about safety. Chlorine and Sodium Hydroxide were used to bleach the pulp, that the plant produced, and in addition to the awful smell, which you never got accustomed to, the chemicals contaminated the English/Wabigoon river system, causing mercury pollution in the fish and subsequent mercury poisoning in the local First Nations people. It was not until the middle 80's, that compensation was provided for the damage done. Dissolved mercury readings are now low in the river system.

Great Lakes staff loved to entertain. Their favourite spot was a steak house on Highway 17, which does not appear to exist today. The executives were efficient and likeable and I had many enjoyable days in Thunder Bay. They were interested in learning about new ideas in the retirement field, and although they seemed basic to me, their staff appeared to warm to them.

Great Lakes once employed 4,000 people. It was acquired in 1974 by Canadian Pacific and had a name change to Great Lakes Forest Products. Standard Life had a close relationship with C.P. and our relationship as their retirement provider did not change, but was probably enhanced. Most visits went off without a hitch, but my last visit to Northwest Ontario did produce excitement.

Options to fly to Dryden, were with Air Canada, or Transair which the locals referred to as Trashair. If the weather was really bad, Air Canada would not fly for safety reasons. Transair, possibly for cash flow reasons, had no choice. I was coming back from Dryden, and wanted to visit Great Lakes in Thunder Bay. Air Canada said "no". They would overfly Thunder Bay, because of weather and ground conditions. I had no choice, but to use Transair.

We landed in Thunder Bay, and as we rumbled down the runway, I noticed that the signs bordering the runway, had gone from single digit to double and now showed, XX, YY and finally ZZ. We kept going, and going, and going, and it became bumpier and bumpier, before we finally stopped in the middle of nowhere. Luckily enough, there was a field at the end of the runway, not entirely flat and smooth, but strong enough, to support the weight of the aircraft, probably because the ground was frozen solid. Here we were, at least a quarter of a mile, beyond the paved runway, which must have been so icy, that the planes' braking system had no effect. The silence was deafening. The cabin door did not open. No one, not even the flight attendants, spoke. We could see the flashing lights of the emergency vehicles, including fire trucks, as they made their way out to us. They finally put into position, a vehicle, with stairs leading to the front exit door. The door was opened, to reveal a very large male, in a highly coloured flak jacket.

As he entered the plane, he was greeted by an eerie silence. I will never forget the words he uttered, as he looked at us, and said defensively, "Don't blame me, I wasn't flying this thing". I flew on Air Canada to Toronto, the next evening, and the Transair plane was still sitting in the middle of that flat frozen field, looking very lonely, and I'm sure awaiting a visit from National Transport Board Safety Inspectors. Thank you, Lord! It could have been much worse. Transair was purchased by Pacific Western Airlines, within a year.

As indicated, our days in Ancaster, were happy days, for all members of the family. The children enjoyed their schools, and Susan and Michele had friends, and participated in school plays, etc. Fiona was working on her skills, to get under the skin of her older sisters. Susan was enjoying her new bicycle, which she crashed early on, because of "a swarm of bees that mysteriously appeared in front of her!" She also managed to chip a part of her tooth, in another bike fall. We found the missing piece several days later, buried in her lip. Michele fell in the house, prior to going out on Halloween night. She was bleeding profusely, but Dr. Tom was available, five minutes away, across the backyard, stitched the top of her head and like the trooper she was, she went out "trick or treating".

I was not aware that Ron Moir in Vancouver, had signaled his wish to retire within a year. I was contacted by Head Office in 1978, to the effect that The Regional Manager position for Western Canada, covering B.C., and offices in Calgary and Edmonton, was to be open in 9 months and that based on Ron and Doug McArthur's recommendations, I was being offered the position. El was supportive. Another step on the ladder. The salary change was meaningful. In fact, Michele said "I hope you are getting a large raise, because this is not going to be easy". She was 11. It was not an easy decision, and looking back, probably selfish. All of us losing close friends and neighbours. Leaving Els' mother in Ontario, to now be with my mother and sister in Vancouver. A tough choice, which El never the less supported. I have to believe, that both Eleanor and I, still had that desire and confidence to travel and explore. That we both believed, that we were still on a path, that was being determined for us, and not by us.

The Ancaster house was appraised, put on the market and sold quickly for $70,000 to a lady professor from McMaster, who loved it. She unfortunately died within 3 years, but the house has remained in her family's possession.

El and I left for Vancouver to find a house. One of the residences shown, was a just completed new house in Richmond, not too far from where Maureen lived. Vancouver homes were too expensive or required too much work. We low balled an offer on the Richmond home at about $115,000. The asking price was $126,000. The builders countered at $125,000. I suggested that this was a bit of an insult, and our realtor said, that the builders, who were brothers of Japanese descent, felt exactly the same way about our offer.

My regional manager position as agreed, did not come into effect until 6 months from then, to permit Ron Moir's planned retirement. I studied our budget intensely, and asked everyone except El. to leave the room. I requested a promise from her, that we would within reason, not buy anything for 6 months, and on receiving her agreement, counter signed the new offer at $125,000. It turned out to be a very smart move, which we more than profited from.

The final move was difficult. Lots of genuine tears and sorrow. The movers packed everything and promised to be in Richmond at a set date, allowing us to fly to Calgary, and rent a car to let the children, enjoy the scenery through the Rockies, unlike our 1967 winter trip.

We must have been a sight travelling through Toronto Airport, then called Malton, with the 3 girls, lots of luggage, and our caged birds Joey the budgie, and Dougal the canary. The birds were quite agitated, and screeching loudly and incessantly, even though their cages were totally covered. The porter who was helping us said "What do you have in there. Two roosters?"

We arrived in Calgary and stayed overnight. Then we got the phone call, from Ron Moir, to the effect, that Manulife had accepted an offer from Standard Life, to purchase the Canadian operations of Standard

Wow! There I was in between positions. I had left the security of the Hamilton office, the comfortable Ancaster home and friendships built over 7 years, to return to what I considered as our second home in Vancouver, but to an office and business scenario that I had been away from for almost 12 years, and would now presumably be competing with Vancouver Manulife pension staff, for a position of authority.

In essence, who would win out, to take the combined Manufacturers/Standard Life Vancouver pension branch management prize. Based upon what I had seen of Manulife business practices and pension staff, I was fairly confident that Standard's staff would do well. I firmly believed our overall pension operations and knowledgeable staff, to be much stronger than Manulife's.

5

VANCOUVER

1978 - 1981

The move to the house on Willowfield Drive in Richmond went smoothly and we settled in. The children liked it, because it was new. Susan loved her new bedroom. We reacquainted with Maureen, and my mother and Ralph again. El. got to work, thinking about changes to the house, when the 6 months hiatus was over, and I started to assess the client base and my new staff in Vancouver. Don Liesch would work on sales, under me, and Mary Murray was our administrator, secretary and steno.

The major problem was that Manulife would not leave me alone, to do my job. They insisted on meetings, first in Toronto and then Calgary, which were intended to either make me comfortable, or sell me on Manulife, if the takeover did not go through. On receiving a third request to meet again in Calgary, I refused to go, and spent time answering calls, from Standard sales staff, asking if I knew something they did not, and how could I refuse such a request. I merely countered, that if I was not in Vancouver, our current clients, who were already nervous, might look elsewhere.

Ron Moir was easy to deal with, and I became closer to our major clients, while the on again/off again merger saga, continued. Our investment returns at this time were strong, and we managed to add several new accounts, which kept me more than busy. Senior Standard Canadian staff, were totally against the merger, and when they revealed, that Manulife would have to obtain individual approval from each Province, that Standard did business in, the takeover collapsed. Manulife got busy, and took many of Standard's individual producers. No group staff defected.

What did I learn in the 3 short years, I was in Vancouver? I was exposed to, and much improved my skills in marketing, investments and staff development. Manulife marketing skills were better than ours and I learned to adopt them. Defined contribution plans, similar to Group RRSPs', were becoming popular and we started to sell a lot of them. Standards' investment group SLPM, had great performance, and I was exposed by their staff, mainly George Kiddell and Ron Kaulbach to major investment accounts, such as C. P. Air, which was a huge opportunity. George was a character. On being asked seriously by a representative of B.C.'s forest industry at an investment meeting, if he felt the local economy was doing well, George with a straight face, indicated that he had been propositioned by a young lady, coming out of his Vancouver hotel, and that based on the asking price, he felt that, "the local economy was doing just fine".

I also felt, that I learned to more properly determine, the strengths and weaknesses of the young field staff, that I was inheriting, and who in my opinion had not been managed. Don Liesch had been overly sheltered, Martin Horsburgh our latest addition, was young, but was full of confidence. Calgary's David Stone was impressive, but was too confident and had to suffer some setbacks. Edmonton's Julien Doucet was probably not teachable. I termed them "my youthlets". I travelled a lot, and in trying to improve the marketing and administrative skills of these young men, it helped to make certain points and then leave them to ponder, what they should be doing to improve themselves.

Don Liesch had a good relationship with the Vancouver consulting firm Mercers, and was really improving, as a sales person. After I was again transferred, I supported Don's promotion to Vancouver pension manager, against a V.P.s' strong objections. Don and Martin Horsburgh let me down badly, and that will be reflected later on, in my writing. Vancouver is a long way from Montreal's head office, and they were unfortunately left alone to develop some pretty bad habits.

I had only been in Vancouver 2 years, when I was approached by our pension V.P., Tom Goldberg, as to whether or not I would wish to put my hat in the ring for the Regional Manager's position in Toronto. Standard Life's top gun pension field position in Canada. I was 40. The current manager was being retired early, but not for a further 12 months.

El and I discussed this in detail. Another move, but once again we felt that the chosen path was being determined elsewhere, and the rewards were worth the upheaval. We were sworn not to discuss this with anyone, especially the children, during those last 12 months in Vancouver and how we survived, I do not know. We also knew that the children would be mixed in their reaction.

Before we come to the actual move and its ups and downs, there were other items to note during these 3 short years. The retirement party for Ron Moir was a great success. As a family we had very pleasant vacations in Parksville on Vancouver Island. I enjoyed going out one day, as an unpaid hand on a fishing boat, which left the dock about 5:30 a.m. and returned at 10:00 in the morning. The boat had two arms with multiple baited hooks, that were lowered in the water, and as we trolled, the fish seem to magically appear on the lines. We purchased and froze some of the fish, and brought them back to Vancouver. Commercial fishing was bountiful in the early '80s.

During an Air Canada strike, I returned from a visit to a Saskatoon client, with a small airline that had sprung up to take advantage of the strike. On the first attempt to take off in the small prop plane, the pilot aborted, and stated that all 25 or so passengers, had to crowd to the front of the plane, so that he could achieve lift off. We did achieve separation from the runway and very gradually made it to a safe flying altitude. I doubt the Air Safety Commission knew about that.

A highlight of my last year there, was being invited by the H.R. director of B.C. Forest Products, a very large client to join him, on a tour of 3 of their operations on Vancouver Island, to celebrate his upcoming retirement, after multiple years with the Company. The exciting part was that we were being flown there by helicopter. We also flew over and around the world famous, Butchart Gardens, and were hosted at a Company lunch in Victoria. Why was I the invited guest? I do not know, but I know that Don, the about to be retiree and I, had had a close business relationship, short that it was. On the way back to Vancouver, the pilot spotted and circled a pod of killer whales from a safe distance, not to disturb them. Magical stuff! A week later, that same helicopter crashed on lift off, from its pad. The pilot survived. What is this about planes and me?

Michele was starting horse riding lessons and we allowed her to go to a Christian Camp in Calgary, to further her abilities, and to foster an acquaintance that she had made while living in Calgary. I don't believe that she had as good a time as we had forecast, and her absence from home brought to light how fussy she was about food, to the point that she ate very little of the "disgusting meals" there, and came back lighter, and certainly hungry.

Michele and Susan were both bullied in school, and Susan in particular had a really rough time. She was very frustrated and upset, that she was not growing, and that her development to womanhood, seemed to be on hold. El did wonderful work with the various doctors and specialists, not to just listen, but to argue with them, before taking any steps. The best step of all was patience, and the good Lord came through, with more than reasonable height for Susan, and the eventual birthing of three healthy children.

A major blow to business development, was the stunning word that George Kiddell was leaving SLPM Investments, to set up his own investment firm, and in the process was taking 7 senior investment staff with him. I managed to have Roy Naudie, the President of SLPM, come to Vancouver, to reassure our clients that we could overcome this upset, and that "his hand was still steering the investment ship". Most clients stayed, while I was still there, despite attempts by the new group to rock the boat. I have found that Canadian businesses do not react impulsively, and that if change is handled well, and does not have a major effect on the relationship, they will remain loyal to you.

The only major client that jumped, was the I.W.A. unionized forest industry employee group, that we had acquired, after I came back to Vancouver. They were controlled by the legendary Jack Munroe, the Union President for ever, who dominated discussion at all the meetings and in essence made all the major decisions, for all the committee members. Our investment relationship with them was short, and I for one understood their decision. Mr. Munroe's position was, that as the union president it was safer for him to get out, than to risk the unknown.

During Roy Naudie's visit to Vancouver, El and I joined him for dinner one night at Hy's Steakhouse. As we were leaving, Charlton Heston stepped out onto the front porch, reflecting the growth of movie development and the now common sight of actors in Vancouver. At my retirement dinner, many years later, Roy stated in his speech, that he recalled Charlton Heston pointing at me, and shouting "Isn't that Bob Coyle over there". Roy was a quiet man, who trusted people, and was burned in the process by the actions of several of his staff. Mutinies in corporations are not uncommon and you must be on your toes at all times, and not take business relationships for granted forever. Another lesson learned. Be prepared for change!

El and I were invited back east, to attend Lloyd East's retirement in Hamilton. Held at the Hamilton Club, where at that time males and females entered by separate doors, it was a splendid evening. I had worked under Lloyd for 7 years, and therefore was one of the guests, who were able to speak, and recount about him. I did not hold back, about his unusual antics. El and Ida had grown to become close friends.

A surprise guest that night was Pierre Berton, commentator, author and well-known Canadian personality. Apparently, he and Lloyd had been in the Canadian forces together as members of the intelligence section. He told the story of their regiment being on parade in Canada, awaiting an inspection by a visiting high ranked member of the force. It was summer, extremely hot and humid, and therefore wearing on those, in full uniform. According to Mr. Berton, Lloyd became a heat casualty, and slowly sank to the ground. What to do with a 6- foot 3- inch body. The regimental sergeant major according to Mr. Berton, barked out, "Drag him outside and hide him behind the Coca Cola sign. He won't be seen there".

Just before the retirement dinner trip, we had been invited to travel and stay with David and Jana Smith, in Mexico City. I was up to my ears in the client investment protection business, that you have just read about, and felt that I could not go on vacation. Maureen agreed to join El, and after the retirement evening in Hamilton, El flew from Toronto to join the Smiths, and Maureen came out of Vancouver the next day. I can only comment on what El. told me. David's tour as the lead engineer for a company building cement factories, was coming to an end, and they would soon be leaving Mexico City.

David's wife, Jana, drove them to where their bus would leave for the day's excursion, and the 2 of them went touring. On one such bus trip, a hand came snaking through from the seat behind, seeking one of their purses. They turned around and yelled at the perpetrator. He left the bus at the next stop. On another day they went to a market, where in a shop with a narrow walkway, Maureen managed to dislodge and presumably break, some home-made Mexican souvenirs. The shop girl yelled at them, and demanded compensation, in Spanish of course. They left the store, with Maureen protesting and the girl following, and still yelling. Maureen literally threw some money at her, and said that was all she had. Once on the bus, the yelling continued from outside, but as they pulled away, they could hear the wail of a police car siren. What a relief, as the police car sped on by, and disappeared.

They spent a weekend in San Miguel, which is now a favourite tourist spot, for Canadians. The bus had many locals carrying chickens. The aisle was full of empty cans rolling around, spared from those tossed out the windows. Back in the city, they went out for dinner with the Smiths, and visited a local square, where people hire mariachi bands for the evening. A very intoxicated Mexican, decided that he wanted to marry "the blond". When David interpreted the Spanish to El., she seized his arm, and told him in no uncertain terms, to advise the Senor, that "the blond" was already married to him (David), who then left, with both wives on his arms. His actual wife Jana, is also a blond.

The Smiths had a beautiful 3-level home, in a gated community, surrounded by high thick walls. Kidnapping non-Mexican children for ransom, was becoming more frequent in Mexico, and the Smiths were not upset that their tour of duty was up. They had a cute shaggy dog, that liked Mexican food and "tooting'". The dog, always had to be removed from the room, where they were eating or drinking.

The year was up. I was the successful candidate for the Toronto regional manager position. That night we had steak for dinner, and the girls almost uniformly said "Where are we going now?" Susan was ecstatic. Michele was angry and disappointed. Fiona said, "Towonto, sounds great. Where's Towonto?" The family negotiating had begun. The sound of a pool in Toronto was exciting, the sounds of a pool and a horse, carried the day. To some bribery is despicable. In this case, the kids and Eleanor deserved to be spoiled. They had endured multiple moves, loss of friends and a constant starting all over again, for probably my own selfish gain. We were moving away from my mother and sister, but once again the lure of the challenge, was just too great. My path was again being orchestrated.

Part of the transfer agreement was that Standard would appraise the Richmond B.C. house, and make us an offer to buy it, allowing us to house hunt freely in Toronto. The residential market in Vancouver had been heating up, and the offer from Standard was $250,000. It took less than 2 seconds, to get our signatures on the agreement. The house value had doubled in value, in less than 3 years.

The Richmond house had central heating, not with air, but with heated water. There were radiators throughout the house, which more than adequately heated it, in the temperate climate of Vancouver. The house did not sell for some time, and someone made a grave error, by clicking of a switch in the furnace room, which they thought was to turn lights off, but was the switch for heating the water in the pipes. An unusually cold spell followed, and the water pipes burst, flooding parts of the house. Standard eventually sold it, but took a "bath" on the price. We were instructed never to bring up the sale again in conversation.

We journeyed to Toronto to house hunt, and were referred to a lady realtor by the name of Lou Dobson. El looked in Markham, and Unionville, while

I went to work. We stayed in a very bland motel, The Parkway, on Highway 7 in Markham, where the price of the room, was determined by the colour of the concrete wall. This property has been modernized of late, and is now so much nicer. We considered living in Ancaster again, but the commute to work for me would not have been easy, and the successor to Lloyd East in Hamilton, Mike Ion, was now living there. Standard's pension office was on Eglinton Avenue just east of Yonge St. It was "grubby" and I was told that a move was under strong consideration.

We had thought that Toronto prices would be much lower than Vancouver, and we were in line to buy a mansion. Wrong! They were pretty well much in line. We finally made an offer on a house in Unionville at 11 Russell Court for, you guessed it, $250,000. The realtor had wanted much more, but we noted, that the shower upstairs had been leaking, and that there was subtle water damage in the bathroom, and in the ceiling of the dining room below. We made our offer, subject to satisfactory repairs to the water damaged areas. They may have felt guilty, about disguising, or not noticing the damage, but they agreed to our terms, and we returned to Vancouver and our now 17, 14 and 10-year-old "babies" who, with drop ins from my Mum and Maureen, had survived the week on their own.

The chosen house was not Els' favourite. She was not fond of the kitchen, but it had space, a fully furnished basement, a circular staircase from the basement to the second floor and a huge yard for the inclusion of a swimming pool. It was also fairly close to stables, if the horse purchase was to become a reality.

Back in Vancouver. Time to start saying goodbye, to family, friends and neighbours. Time to hand over business accounts to Don and Martin in Vancouver and time to visit staff in Calgary and Edmonton to tell them that they were now on their own, without supervision from a Vancouver manager. Being cocky, they took this news in stride, as if I had never helped them over the past 3 years. Maybe I didn't.

Time to prepare for the move, and the packing that goes with it. This was arranged and paid for by Standard, but as it is an inventory of your belongings, you are very much involved. The move across Canada would take more than several days, and it was time to spring the surprise to the girls. While the movers were travelling, we were going to Disneyland in Los Angeles and then to San Diego for a week or so. We would fly to Los Angeles, spend a few days in Anaheim, rent a car, drive to San Diego, spend the rest of the week there on the beach, return to L.A. and then fly from there to Toronto.

We left Vancouver Airport on August 06, 1981. How do I recall that date? Because, that was the day after President Reagan fired all the unionized aircraft controllers, for going on strike. This left an undermanned group of supervisors, to ensure the safety of the skies in the U.S. We landed at L.A.X airport in Los Angeles, and the plane continued at high speed down the runway, peeled off a very fast right turn, onto the arterial tarmac leading to the terminal, and came to rest at the gate, with a series of back and forward motions as the brakes were applied, at the last minute. You could almost hear the pilot say, "phew we made it"! Bob and planes again!

We found a reasonably priced motel in Anaheim, near Disneyland. Susan was not pleased, having to share a room with her sisters, but it was presented to her as, "you have no choice!" We all enjoyed the Disney experience for the day, and went to bed early that night, tired from all the travelling. We awoke the next morning, to the strange sounds of roars and screams. Our motel was only separated from the Anaheim Convention Centre parking lot by a mere 5-foot wall.

To our surprise and delight, the parking lot, was full of cages. The circus was in town! Barnum and Bailey and Ringling Bros., were both starting their tour of the U.S., and we were the first stop. We freely toured the lot, and witnessed up close and personal all the animals used in the circus. El caught the eye of a toothless elephant keeper, and I had to spirit her away, as she had definitely caught his attention, and had been invited for a ride, on his 4 legged "buddy". She denies this, but I was there. It happened! We went to the show the next night, and the kids really enjoyed it. It lasted 3 hours, because both circuses performed that night before they split for their road trips, and went their separate ways. Circuses, involving animals, are not in vogue today, because of claims of animal cruelty. We saw nothing resembling this, with these world- famous circuses.

The next day, El took Susan and Michele to Universal Studios, and were somewhat disappointed in what they saw. Disney has spiced this up somewhat since then, to "scare visitors". Fiona and I had another great day at Disneyworld. We also took the girls to the Knotts Berry Farm theme park, where they loved the rides. El and I refused as they were too scary. Check out the great family photograph!

We headed to San Diego in the car rental, and decided to find a place on Coronado Island, near the Pacific Ocean. There is a marvelous bridge connecting the mainland with the Island and as you leave the bridge and drive on the island it feels so much more serene, and isolated.

We tried the Hotel del Coronado, which wanted $30 per night per person. I, discovered later, that this hotel was where the U.S. presidents stayed, when visiting the area, and is referred to fondly by locals, as the Western White House. Nice try Bob! We found a nice Mexican hacienda style hotel, for a much more reasonable price. The beach was in walking distance, and as there were military bases in the area, we found the whole experience interesting. You woke to the sound of U.S servicemen doing drills on the street, at 6:00 in the morning. Marines would emerge from landing craft on the beach, and now and again a fighter aircraft would come screaming, a few hundred feet above your head on the beach, heading towards the air force landing strip.

The vacation could not have gone better. The only "negative", was that the first day we arrived on Coronado Island, there was a dense fog, and we walked the beach, with little visibility. Despite the apparent fog, the sunrays were strong, and the next day all of us were complaining, about being slightly burned and looking as red as beets.

Eating out was a treat for our 2 eldest young ladies. They had taken to sitting at a separate table, and enjoyed the satisfaction of asking the server, to send the cheque to our table. They were sensible however, and did not splurge. We returned to L.A., having pre booked a reservation, at an Airport Hotel. When the 5 of us arrived, dressed safari like, probably looking grubby and sweaty, with multiple bags of luggage, the staff behind the front desk, visibly shrunk back on their heels, and only relaxed, when I showed them our reservation confirmation. Why, I do not know, but we may have looked a bit ill- fitting for their fancy hotel. The 5 of us shared a room, slept somewhat, and left for Toronto the next a.m. to start a new life.

As the saying goes "This was to be the beginning, of the rest of our lives".

6

UNIONVILLE

1981 - 1987

The 6 years in Unionville from 1981 to 1987, brought many happenings, and changes to the lives of the Coyle family. El and I kept our promises to the children, by having a beautiful swimming pool installed in the backyard, combined with a large wood deck with steps leading to the pool deck. Both were constructed in October 1981 by Mayfair Pools, just after we arrived. The reason was to eliminate the amount of lawn that I had to mow. I virtually spent the whole weekend cutting grass. The pool was opened, and then immediately closed for winter. I would spend the next 20 years becoming fairly efficient at maintaining, closing and opening outdoor pools. Fiona was usually the first to christen each opening, by venturing in when the water was 60 degrees.

Hilda Ramsay (now Baxter), she, who was instrumental in introducing El to me, knew a couple who bought and sold horses. We were introduced to George, an old Ontario codger who knew his horses. We purchased Copper from him, a half Arab, half quarter-horse, who although at times was stubborn, was very loveable. Michele's interest finally waned, and Fiona and El stepped in. We found a reasonably priced stable not far away off Warden, which is now the site of the Unionville High School and their Theatre of the Arts. It was run by Sue and Brian West. Horses become very expensive, if they require medical attention, and as the girls gradually lacked interest, El and I found ourselves increasingly involved in cleaning Copper's hooves every night, and in grooming him. It was however good experience for us, and our love of horses and riding, led us to spend many more years riding in places such as the hill country of Texas, the Tanque Verde ranch outside of Tucson, Arizona, and ranches near Kelowna B.C.

A house is a house, but location and good neighbours help make it a home. We were blessed with good neighbours. Notable were Rolland and Mary Hoffman from Charlotte, North Carolina. Rolland as a C.G.A. was opening up a Canadian branch for his U.S. accounting firm, and their stay was limited. Their kids loved coke, even for breakfast. Rolland installed a coke machine, that required quarters to get a bottle, to control their consumption. Mary was fascinated with snow, but had to shovel it off the driveway, long before the last flake had fallen. Many a morning in the winter we woke up, to the sound of her shovel scraping the driveway clean.

We invited the Hoffmans for Christmas dinner that first year, as they had just arrived. A hit for them, was the Christmas crackers, which they had never seen before. We remained good friends for many years, visiting them in Charlotte after their return to the U.S., and being a part of their son, Paul's wedding in Philadelphia, complete with an invitation to a major league baseball game.

Christmas for us, is a very special time, and not just for the food and the fellowship. I have written a poem about the True Meaning of Christmas and included it in these memoirs, to emphasize the importance of this celebration, and the reason that we should be relating our lives to the birth of Jesus, and the story behind the celebration, as well as the celebration itself.

Tradition is important to El and I, and we tried hard to install that feeling in the family. For at least 25 years, El hosted Christmas dinner for all family and in-law family members, that could attend. She also introduced the "String Game" at Christmas to our children, and their children for many, many years. Using a different coloured ball of wool for each child,

I would weave a spiders' web in the basement with each ball, and deposit an extra Christmas gift at the end. Initially, this would come as a surprise after the tree had been cleaned of all gifts, but after a while, the expectation was there, and when we mentioned that, that was it, no more gifts, the kids would rush down to the basement, in anticipation of the sight of the wool webs and the extra gifts.

Once the pool was up and running, we attracted the neighbours and their children, which we encouraged. A true friend to El, over these many years, is Marlene Eagan, then Clements. Marlene and Brian, now divorced, lived on another street, but the shape of our property meant that their backyard just touched the corner of ours. On foot, they were 10 minutes away, but over the fence, mere seconds. They engineered, an old fashioned, stile on our fence, and climbed over.

Their first child Allison enjoyed coming over. El and I will never forget the day in 1982, Marlene visited us in a distraught state, to let us know that their second child Lauren, had been diagnosed at 6 months, with severe cerebral palsy. Such handicapped children, do not normally live a long life, but "normally" was not a word in Marlene's vocabulary. She has been an angel in disguise, and has loved, nursed, educated, tutored and put up with a very difficult situation for many years, as Lauren has gone through her different phases of life, trapped in a handicapped body, but with a mindset that at times is joyful, clever, cunning, depressed and yet so able, beyond her years.

Brian Clements, Lauren's dad, is still Marlene's friend, and has helped somewhat with Lauren, but the bulk of the credit goes to Marlene. Most, could not have done, what she has given a huge part of her life for. Her second marriage was to Paul Eagan, who is very likeable. He, for many years, held the position as the "pitching mound groomsman", for the Toronto Blue Jays. To some, this may sound strange, but every starting pitcher wants the mound to be customized to his liking, within baseball rules. Paul was recognized as one of the best. We attended their wedding, which was held in the garden of Paul's sister's house, in Rosedale.

El was introduced to Shirley Johnston through a Christian Markham coffee hour group, and we became firm friends with her and husband Larry, who actually became neighbours on Russell Court. Larry was so sadly killed in a motor vehicle accident in April, 2002, which I will address later. We have maintained contact with Shirley ever since. We downhill skied with them in Ontario, Saint-Sauveur, Quebec, and Killington, Vermont and have so many happy memories. They were also instrumental in introducing us to the Siesta Dunes condos on Siesta Key Beach in Sarasota, where a large segment of these memoirs was penned. Thanks to the Johnstons, we have vacationed there 24 different times since their initial introduction in 1989. In many ways, it has become our vacation home, and enabled us to give back to others, including family members.

My promotion to the Regional Pension Manager position for Toronto was not well received by the staff, I was about to manage. They had been accustomed to older and "more experienced" managers, who had left them alone, and in my opinion had not really managed them for some time. They were also convinced that the successor would come from within the branch. At age 41, I was viewed with suspicion and deemed too young. I believe that they also felt that "the comfortable period" was perhaps over.

Fraser McDonald, our then marketing manager, said "You can fire the lot and somehow survive, or you can manage, educate and mold them into a more efficient and successful group, but I doubt the latter choice will work". The first choice was not feasible, the second and really only option, almost brought me down. Standard Life's Group Pension division was transforming from a slow, moving Galapagos turtle, to a fast moving, new business machine, and having expended the dollars, Head Office wanted to see early and significant results. Based on the cards I had been dealt, our branch could not and would not contribute to the rally, any time soon. The following two years were trying, and not fun. Luckily somebody, somewhere, said, "give him time".

Bruce Sinclair, probably deemed as the leading Toronto branch sales representative under the previous management, was a former miner from Northern Ontario. I had met Bruce at previous pension sales meetings and liked him, without really knowing him. He had been favoured by the Toronto staff, as the next Toronto office manager. Prior to my arrival he had a huge setback, as the flagship of the accounts he advised and administered, Thomson Newspapers, chose to move their consulting contract to T.P.F.& C., a major pension consulting firm, thereby dumping Bruce as their advisor. Bruce, bless him, was the first to readily accept my appointment, but was devastated by this news.

I was asked to accompany him to a meeting, attended by some Thomson executives and board members. He had been really close, to the company over the years, including invitations to vacation with some of their staff, and was the sole Standard Life contact. As a "newbie", I was powerless to help. I witnessed the cruelty of Toronto big business, at that meeting. No names, but it was not pretty, and any negative that could be brought to bear against him, justified or not, was raised. Bruce had a stroke within 12 months, and never worked again!

Prior to his stroke, El and I were part of connecting hospital visits, beginning with a funeral. Bill Buckingham, whom I had worked alongside in Hamilton for 7 years, died suddenly. A major business requirement sadly prevented me from attending the funeral. However, El agreed to go on behalf of the family, and Bruce agreed to attend on behalf of the Toronto office, and drive El there. On the return trip, his car coming from downtown Burlington, ran over "something" on the access road to the QEW. El let out a yell, and said "that hurt". Bruce stopped the car, got out and checked under the front passenger side. He tugged down, pulled out and held up a poker sized metal bar, that truck drivers use to tighten the straps holding their loads in place. El felt her clothes covering her bottom, and came up with a handful of blood. This inch thick, metal bar, had penetrated the bottom of the car, the front passenger car seat and Els' bottom.

Neither panicked, but both agreed that a visit to "emergency" was in order. They picked North York hospital, as the most convenient for both. Several days prior to this incident, I had admitted myself to North York emergency, on my way to work, due to extreme pain in my abdomen, which was diagnosed as a kidney stone blockage. I was kept overnight and surgery was frequently suggested by the attending doctor. I refused, received painkillers and was discharged. I was back 2 days later at emergency, and was confronted by a skeptical nurse, who suspected that I was back solely for the drugs. I passed the stone in the office washroom, a few days later.

El had arrived at North York Hospital two days later and gave her name, Eleanor Coyle, and described her problem to the emergency admitting staff. El asked if she could spell her name and the nurse said "I know, and spelled out C O Y L E". We were on their radar! The attending physician gave her a tetanus shot, stitched up the wound and said "If, that piece of metal had penetrated your body one inch or so to the left, you would have been paralyzed for life, as it would have shattered your spine." The metal had only penetrated flesh. Thank you, Lord!

El recovered and I recovered. A week later an agitated next-door neighbor asked, if I would drive her husband to the hospital. Another kidney stone incident. He was a strapping 6 foot plus, stoic German, who was reduced to the status of a whimpering child in the back of the car. Never delay getting assistance when a kidney stone blockage is suspected! The pain can be unbelievable.

1981, the year of our move to Toronto, was a tough year from a financial point of view. The prime rate was over 19%, with 5- year mortgage rates over 18%, 5- year GIC'S yielding 17%, and with a negative expectation that rates would only go higher. Within months of our move, federal legislation was passed, requiring that any employer subsidy for the provision of employee benefits, would be considered as a taxable benefit. This applied to our new 5-year mortgage on the Unionville house, as Standard Life was subsidizing our mortgage rate. It usually took us 6 months to recover from a move. This change meant we could expect, from a budget point of view, to recover no sooner than 12 months, from our arrival in Ontario. Once again, I had to ask El to go easy on spending over the next number of months.

To put these unusual times into perspective. At my introductory visit to the Toronto pension office, which I was to manage shortly, an announcement was made to the staff by the incumbent manager, Bas Spurr, who was retiring. "Listen up, he said. This is Bob Coyle from Vancouver. He will be your new manager as of next Monday. Because of wage controls, your salaries effective November 15, will all increase by 12%. Any questions, talk to Mr. Coyle next week." At the time, the office had 24 sales and administrative staff. It was not an easy ride, but when I retired 16 years later, we had experienced massive growth in pension assets under management, the branch was healthy, and our total sales and administrative staff numbered 18. All was well, when I handed over the reins of management in 1997. I told you I was blessed!

I was fortunate, that I had seen the Manulife sales process, that Standard Life had made the decision to become aggressive in the group pension market, that they had invested enough money and resources into updated technology to achieve such growth, and that I was not fired in 1982 or 1983, as our Toronto office sales were nothing less than tragic. I have to thank our then V.P. Pensions Tom Golberg, for having faith and keeping the wolves (the President) at bay.

Family wise our "babies" were growing up to the extent that out 2 oldest young ladies were married in 1986 (Michele in June to Douglas Cook, and Susan in December to Michael Hamelin). Michele had threatened to leave home, and when El and I were in Vancouver on a business/vacation trip, she did. Michele gave birth to their first child, Daric (the name of a Roman coin) on July 13, 1986, (our first grandchild). Fiona at age 15, was still at home, but we sensed trouble on the horizon, and we were not to be disappointed.

We have maintained healthy and happy relationships with our 3 girls through the years, but those particular years in Unionville, although happy at times, proved to be very trying. Especially for Eleanor, who as a mum, was mentally fighting continuously, with the girls' natural desires of womanhood and independence, that were influencing them, as they became ever more mature.

I was raised in Scotland with total freedom, but on the basis that any of my decisions would be favourable for all the family, and not just myself. Contrary to Eleanor's wishes, I was perhaps too free with the children's' desires, and unlike some fathers, I did not exercise the strong and disciplined control that others might have. I gave them freedom of expression, which I still believe in, trusting that we had parented them, with the proper skills. In the short term, I was perhaps wrong, and they were allowed to trust in their own independence more than others, but in the long term our relationship today is close and strong. We love them as much today as we did then, and they love us, and that is really the most important, and long- lasting thing.

We are extremely proud and close to our "young ladies". On reflection, some of the mayhem during these Unionville years, was due mainly to the new lives we were all living. I had pushed and pulled them across Canada east and west and then east again. Always new friends and surroundings. This together with the physical and mental desires of teenage females, had to have an effect on them. I was also laboring with a new position, new untrained staff and work challenges to overcome, if the "success" path was to continue. Of course, El had to bear the brunt of the girls' problems, and be there to steady the ship, when all seemed lost, and at the same time make new friends. Some families might have blown up. We survived and are stronger for the experience.

To put the above in perspective, we have lived in Vancouver B.C. (3 locations), Calgary Alberta, Ancaster Ontario, Richmond B.C., Unionville Ontario, Aurora Ontario, and currently, Ballantrae Ontario. I was not immune from being confused at times. Some years ago, while living in the West, I was visiting Winnipeg on a business trip, and after 2 days, booked my return trip at the airport counter with Air Canada, to go home to Vancouver. I returned to the counter after 20 minutes, to ask if I could change my destination to Calgary, without cost. "I think we can arrange that", she said. "Change of plans?' "No, I am going home, and I don't live in Vancouver. I live in Calgary," I said. She gave me a funny look, as I went on my way.

Michele and Doug chose to have an informal outdoor barbeque setting, following their wedding, rather than a formal restaurant venue for their wedding reception, which was fine. A tragedy of sorts followed them within the first year of their marriage. El and I were in our Unionville driveway, and heard a helicopter flying overhead nearby; the red Medivac helicopter. Michele arrived shortly thereafter at our house with Daric for a visit, and received a call. Doug who was a car mechanic had been injured at work, in a garage accident, by being pinned between 2 cars.

He was flown from Boxgrove, to Sunnybrook Hospital, and released after demonstrating some movement in his legs. He has suffered horribly ever since, with constant pain due to nerve damage. He has not given in to the pain, and continues to do work around the house, build various structures on the property, and work with their beef cattle and horses, that most in his condition would not attempt. Could more have been done prior to his release from hospital? In my opinion, yes, but I was not present! The diagnosis was based on no visible breaks or paralysis. They should have insisted, that he be admitted for further study. He has paid an awful price to-date, and for the rest of his life. He is not a complainer, but I know that he has had to share a great deal of the consequences from the injury. Constant pain must be terrible.

Following Susan and Mike's wedding ceremony, their reception was at a restaurant in the Beaches, where Mike was employed at the time as a sous chef. It was a fun evening, with most participating in reciting a poem, or telling a story about the wedding couple. Sue and Mike honeymooned in Jamaica, which was spoiled somewhat by the non - delivery of Susan's checked bag, until well after they got home. She had to suffer limited change of clothing during her honeymoon and received no compensation. That would not "fly" today.

I had managed, through a Standard Life real estate contact, to find an apartment for Sue and Mike at Sheppard and Bayview, in central Toronto. In those days however, "key money", was in vogue. Under this arrangement you jumped the queue, by agreeing to pay the monthly rent for an agreed-on period, but in addition you paid a lump sum payment. To avoid illegality, a set of blinds would be left on the window, or a skimpy lamp would be left, for which you paid an exorbitant cost of say $250, Totally illegal and certainly this practice does not apply today, but in times when rentals are hard to come by, people become inventive and took advantage.

Susan's music playing ability should not be forgotten, as she achieved her Grade 8 music certificate early on, at the age of probably 17. She had a very efficient, but inflexible music teacher, who would not let her play anything, but classical music. The practicing was demanding and of course her friends did not relate to what she was playing, and did not encourage her. She finally drifted away. The talent is still there however, having heard her, on her key board. The good Lord willing, she will be able to return to this part of her life, that she loves!

Business success can be achieved in many ways. My goal for the Toronto office clients was to create what I perceived, as initially not being there. That is, a feeling of comfort and a sense of belonging. If achieved, I believed, they would want to belong, and become long term clients, despite the lure of the many pension consultants. As well, apart from the satisfaction clients have in the quality of their business relationship with you, the social aspects of your relationship, have to be equally addressed, to achieve that overall feeling of being content and dismissive of change.

We held a Christmas gathering for clients annually at the Boulevard Club. This major luncheon was increased, to invite 250 existing client guests, prospects and qualifying staff. The annual address I gave, was designed to be business free, and to celebrate the season, while incorporating, hopefully in a subtle manner, my relationship goals. Best time of the year to make people feel comfortable, and for them to want to be "part of your family". I think it helped. The eventual results said it did.

El was extremely supportive in organizing a Toronto management staff get together at Christmas, which offered invitations to the managers and spouses of the various Standard Life departments throughout Toronto; Pension, Individual Life, Group Life, Property, Real Estate, Brokerage. We held them initially in our party proof Unionville home, and apart from the food and drink etc., we included challenging party games, such as the guessing of hand drawn pictures with notations, to represent Christmas carols, which brought these departments heads together for the first time, and gave them a sense of not only belonging, but in some cases of meeting each other for the first time. Head Office for some strange reason, would not provide any subsidy for a global Toronto staff party, which in my opinion was a shortcoming, but I suspect was a firm recognition that Montreal was the Head Office location, and "bonding in Toronto was not to be."

We stepped in, and to a degree did it anyway, by holding the above Christmas get together. We still had our own Pension office staff Christmas party, and this was mostly held at the Boulevard Club, in a room overlooking Lake Ontario. We were favoured by the Club staff, at a very busy time of year, and especially by a young female social director, who went on to become the social director of The Four Seasons in Toronto.

My attention to our Toronto staff weaknesses was also a priority. Changes were required, even after all the coaching and intense training provided, in my first 6 months in Toronto. I gave all concerned, a reasonable, and perhaps too reasonable period of time, to look for a new position. One such employee David Gordon, who was in our sales staff, ended up as the head of the Pension Commission of Ontario. The right man for the right job, and a profitable move for him.

Re sales, my eventual plan was to have 3 sales units, with a unit manager in each, supervising 2 other sales persons. One of the units would be an all- female group. This was a "pipe" dream in those early years, as we did not have sufficiently trained sales staff, to take on such a supervisory role. Having also taken on the management and consulting position with our larger clients, I knew I would eventually require such assistance in co-managing the sales field staff.

I also required a female administrative manager, to take a major role in dealing with administrative staff matters, such as the reality of hiring and firing. I had three such ladies while in Toronto; Joyce Stephenson, Beulah Greaves and Carole Ifurung. Of the three, Carole was the one who achieved a sense of belonging among the staff, which I favoured. Consequently, although she required more supervision from myself, she as a very likeable and trustworthy lady, met the majority of the staff needs and consequently there was less grumbling, less turnover and a family atmosphere was achieved among these administrative staff members.

The acquisition of most companies' pension plans, are acquired through a "middle man"; in essence either a pension consulting house or an insurance broker. I redirected our sales thrust to brokers, as opposed to consultants. I sensed the consulting houses were playing us, due to our ability to provide exactly the same advice and administrative skills as they did, but at considerably lower fees. We were their competition. Insurance brokers in Ontario have a strong presence in corporate business, and if they trust you, in looking after "their" clients, and in providing them a steady flow of commission payments, they will not look elsewhere.

I had charted a path, which I felt should bring results. Two problems however. How long would it take to have the plan take effect, and would Head Office give me the time to see positive results, and therefore allow me to keep my job. It did not happen overnight; '82 and '83 were not good years. The stroke and disability retirement of a senior sales staff member, Bruce Sinclair, early on, added to the pressure. Someone however had faith in me at H.O., and business started to turn around. We made our branch target in 1984, although at the time, I even deemed it a soft target.

This qualified me to be part of the 1985 stars conference held in June of that year at Minaki Lodge, which is located in the wilderness on The Ontario/Manitoba border. Originally built in 1914, it is located on the Transcontinental railroad. All meals were served in a massive dining room, staffed by young people, who were presumably university students, through for their school year. Minaki is an Ojibwa word, translated to mean "Beautiful Water or Good Land". That is so true. The scenery is stunning, but the conditions for the Ojibwa people living in Minaki, not so good. I recall a dirt road main street, with very old wooden homes and the inevitable dog lying outside each, motionless.

The meeting, mainly attended by Standards' personal life insurance producers was disruptive, as a proposed change in their remuneration package was not being readily accepted. Our pension representatives were not involved, but suffered the effects of the mood of the conference.

Spouses had been invited, therefore El and I had flown to Winnipeg and been "bussed" back to Minaki, over miles and miles of straight, endless, flat roads. When the conference ended, we returned to Winnipeg, where I had two days of meetings with clients and consultants and then we flew to Vancouver for a weeks' vacation. My diary says this. I do not recall any details, beyond the conference.

We also managed to have two, four- day visits to Loon Lake, in '85 courtesy of invitations from the Jepsons. Therefore, despite my business activities and woes, I did have wonderful breaks, with friends and neighbours.

In November I attended a meeting in Washington D.C. with an investment staff member to review performance of the investment assets we held for the Canadian division of the United Food and Commercial Workers Union. The meeting was held in a building, two blocks from the White House, and there must have been 30 plus union representatives sitting at this enormous board room table. Their assets were 100% in mortgages and as interest rates were starting to fall from their '82 peak, the fund performance was outstanding. They were so pleased, that the meeting lasted less than 10 minutes, and we were sent merrily on our way, to enjoy in our wool suits, the very warm conditions in Washington that day

The direct return flight to Toronto and other flights had been cancelled, and we were loaded onto a DC 10, to fly to Baltimore, and then onto Toronto. I recall we did not pay, until we were on the plane, via the flight crew pushing around a trolley carrying the credit card machine. The loading of 200 plus passengers was done quickly, "en masse", via the very rear of the plane, which opened up to accept us, as if we were paratroopers heading off on a mission. Probably not legal!

Just before the 1985, calendar year- end, I was contacted by a gentleman, by the name of Jeff Gray, who indicated that although he had no prior insurance or pension experience, he was extremely interested in applying for the pension sales position, that I had posted in the local papers. I decided within minutes of meeting and talking with him, that I had found the talent that was going to help mold the branch into a success. It took a bit of extended persuasion and meetings in early '86 with H.O. staff, that Jeff without any experience, should be hired. Once again, they trusted my judgement, and in this case, boy was I right!

We exceeded our production credit target of $2 million in 1985 and never looked back. When I retired in 1997, our target had grown in excess of $18 million credits, but our actual production in that year exceeded $24 million credits. I think I made it!

At the end of 1986, Mary Laudadio, quite rightly confronted myself and H.O. staff, with the status of her future, as to her sales role in the branch, improved income and future opportunities. She was fighting the anti-female trend that was fashionable in these days, and still is today. I did support her, and although Mary was always suspicious, that she was treated differently from the male sales representatives, she was a fierce competitor, always performing to the best of her ability, and became as expected by me, extremely successful. I now had the 3 people, who I felt could help carry my sales plan into effect, and spearhead the branch to the sales success that was expected of us, by H.O.

I muse, that having experienced the ups and downs challenges, presented by 3 teenage daughters, in multi locations in Canada, and an interest in equestrian affairs by owning and riding a horse, which on many occasions had a mind of its own, I had developed the proper mental attitude to deal with the wishes of a highly strung, highly motivated sales staff. I understood that the benefits derived from highly successful sales employees, would be accompanied by their constant demands, for better administrative support, product line improvement, cutting edge technology, improved income and most important of all to them, recognition. If I wanted high end results, life would not be easy, but I was ready.

Jeff Gray, Mary Laudadio and Tom McCartney headed the 3 sales units, although Tom was a loner and more interested in a title as opposed to managing anyone. Tom came in at 10:00 and left at 4:00, but always delivered his new business targets and more. I was not about to, or frankly able to change his ways!

I had promised El, that at some time, we would move to a smaller house. We finally purchased a show home in Aurora, in the spring of 1987. A lasting memory of Unionville was the police having to shoot a rabid racoon on our front lawn. A catalyst in our move, was the fact that we were uncomfortable with the impressions that Unionville High School was leaving on Fiona, and that a move north was in order. Many of the Unionville students were living a life, beyond their years and we felt that the Aurora move, would allow us to have more control over Fiona. It was also more affordable, as Aurora had not yet seen the escalation in house prices present in Unionville.

AURORA

1987 - 2001

Monarch Construction, a Taylor Woodrow subsidiary, was a pension client, and in addition Standard Life had a minority ownership position in the Company. El and I had seen some model homes, built by Cairns, a sister company to Monarch. We questioned the sales office and were told that the "Turnberry" model was spoken for, and that we were number 5 on the list of applicants. El loved the plan, and the interior was furnished beautifully and with classy paintings throughout. The name Turnberry was also symbolic, as it is a golf location in the Southwest of Scotland and only 30 minutes by car from the village of Ballantrae, which was to be our next house location in Ontario. Strange but true!

I would like to believe that this was the first and only time that I had done this; in essence pulled rank and took advantage of, who you know, and not what you know. I called Monarch's President, Mr. Colin Parsons, whom I knew, and asked him, if he could help us! His answer a week later was "I have some good news and I have some bad news." For a price set by the builder, we could have the house and the paintings throughout, but not the furniture. We sold the Unionville home for $340,000 and bought 283 Murray Drive in Aurora, for $272,000. I will not forget the look on the face of the sales representative, when we asked her for the keys to our house. She was not pleased that we had jumped her queue. El was happy and I somewhat happy. The house market took a tumble after we moved in, and our new Aurora home was now priced about $20,000 less than what we paid. But it was ours!

Colin Parsons was transferred to Taylor Woodrow in the U.K. in 1992 and appointed Chairman, with authority to finalize the completion of the building of the subterranean Chunnel linking the U.K. and the European continent, via France. According to Colin, they used in excess of 10 boring machines, with the British and the French working from both ends, while achieving a tiny minor variance when both ends met. The French had names for the machines such as Fifi, Monique etc. The Brits being Brits, named their machines No 1, No 2, etc. Vive La Difference!

After we settled in the house, we checked with Mayfair Pools, if they could safely install an inground swimming pool in the backyard. Iffy they said, because of the sloping ground which was made of fill, and not natural hard packed earth, and because a retaining wall at least 8 to 10 feet high would have to be built. We had Ian Marjerrison and his friend, build a superb wood retaining wall. However, in the absence of right- angle retaining beams near the top, a weakness would occur in time, which would cause problems and more cost for us, later on. Our fault, as a cement wall would have been more effective. We had declined the cement contractor's quote, due to the exorbitant cost, which at the time we could not afford.

The pool was installed and the setting was fantastic. The pump was installed on the north side of the house, 10 feet above the level of the pool deck, which caused a slight headache in priming, after shutdown. Stairs leading from the inter locked pool deck to a thirty foot - long wood deck, made the backyard look gorgeous. This was enhanced by the view from the deck, which overlooked a flood plain and wooded area, with a golf course fairway about 100 feet away, running alongside. El was happy with the house and we, and the children/ grandchildren were to spend many happy times there over the next 14 years. The setting was perfect, with little noise, privacy, good neighbours, a western exposure, and an unobstructed view of the sunset, each night. Our second grandchild, Jamie, was born to Michele and Doug, on July 14, 1987.

The biggest joy was just being there, to see the children and grandchildren having fun. It was their home, away from home. It was a very happy time in our lives. There are multiple memories of happenings and good times in Aurora, but before these are recollected, I would like to dwell on a story of a special short vacation that Tom Jepson and I took at Loon Lake Hunt Club Oct. 1987.

El and I rarely took vacations apart, but this time, I was invited to join the male Club members in a moose hunt, which I agreed to, provided I did not have to shoot. The members were mainly business men, lawyers and insurance brokers, from Brantford. The hunt was scheduled to begin at 6:00 a.m. on the Saturday morning, and I was assigned with an Indian guide from the Six Nations Grand River band to be beaters who made noise, and drove the moose to the waiting guns. As beaters we were provided with gold and orange flak jackets. I prayed that we would be recognized as such, and that we would not become the targets.

My fellow guide was friendly and pointed out in great detail, the recognizing signs to him, as to where animals had lain down, and spent the night etc. As a rookie, I had no reason to dispute his claims. We tromped through the bush as noisily as possible, right up to where the hunters were "hidden". Nothing, nada, not even a bunny rabbit!

The guide and I were getting along, and chose to walk back to the camp, whereas the hunters chose to return to their cars. We were in the middle of the bush, and I had no idea where we were. Suddenly the guide said "Down", cocked his rifle and literally fired over my shoulder, and by my right ear. I looked and saw nothing. "Moose", he said. "Did you hit him", I asked. "Maybe I wounded him and he will keep going", he said, as we increased our pace towards the target, that I did not see. "How will you know where to find him", this city slicker asked. "Look for the birds in the sky", he stated, as if I should know that. If you are one with nature, you should know that.

After what was a long walk, he confidently said "There, look. Birds are circling". The shooting group, having heard the gunfire were catching up with us. I found out later that this group had a license to shoot a young male, which is called a calf. The pristine animal lying there was a calf, but a pretty big one. To put it bluntly, they finished him off and gutted him, for transport to the camp. Then it dawned on them. How do you transport an animal the size and weight of this, from the middle of the bush back to the camp? Dah!

They were known in the area, and somebody knew somebody, who had a medium size tractor. The local was contacted and contracted for a fee to pull the carcass back to the camp. After a fairly long delay, he arrived with the medium size tractor and chains. The calf was hooked up and the safari group walked alongside. The ground was uneven, rocky, and with what seemed, multi streams. With each hurdle, a part of the tractor would come away, until it started to resemble a riding lawn mower, with just a seat and an engine, that was straining with the "dead" weight and the terrain. The damage was extensive and visible to all, and notably the owner of the tractor, who was getting more agitated, with every struggling few yards. The shouting became louder and the arguing more serious. He unhitched the tractor, picked up the chain, and putt putted off into the bush, while uttering some unprintable words. What were we to do?

By now, it was early afternoon, and we were all getting hungry. Out of nowhere the camp chef arrives. How he found us is a mystery. This group of 12 or so however, knows how to live and had hired a chef for the weekend. We hungrily wolf down designer sandwiches, and wine in plastic cups, in the middle of the bush and discuss Plan B. Someone knows Dave, who works for the county road department, and has access to large road equipment. He is contacted and agrees to come, once again for a price, after his shift is over mid to late afternoon.

Not long after 5:00 p.m., we hear this eerie noise approaching through the forest and suddenly as the bush and greenery part, this huge bulldozer appears, as if it is auditioning for the massive bulldozer part, in the movie Avatar. Dave is at the controls. Handshakes and congratulations all round, as we plan the final leg of this saga. By now it is dark! Do you have lights on this behemoth Dave? "Dah. No!", he says. We all agree that without lights, finding the hunt camp might be a bit tricky and dangerous. It can really get dark in the bush.

Finally, hand held lights are acquired. Once again, I do not know how. Dave scoops the moose, now clay in colour, and not looking pristine, into his enormous bucket, hoists the bucket into mid-air and we set out triumphantly on our last leg to the hunt camp. The moose carcass is transferred to hook and chains at the camp, and raised on a pulley system to a structure off the ground, and out of reach from hungry bears. The carcass is then hosed down, and starts to resemble the fine, looking animal that it was. We settle in, for a sumptuous chef prepared supper. All is well. Mission accomplished. It only took, all of 13 1/2 hours. I have pledged quietly, to never do this again!

The hunt camp building consists of 2, enormous two- story log structures, joined together. The entrance leads into the main sitting room area, with a huge fireplace, poker table and two bedrooms. The through part of the building has the kitchen, washrooms, several wash sinks, a very long dining room table and multi small bedrooms on the upper floor. I have described this image of a strong and complete structure, apparently able to withstand anything thrown at it, until on occasion a group of 20 or more visiting males go to bed. The noise from the combined snoring of this lot, I was told and now can testify, is terrifying, and usually can only be tolerated once, on a very short weekend. I endured this for two nights from a group half the size of the capacity, but never again. The noise from the snoring was earth shattering, and appeared to challenge the mightiness of the massive log walls and ceiling.

Sunday was a day of rest, recounting the ups and downs of yesterdays' events. We were all leaving after supper on, Monday, October 19th, 1987. I know that date well, because of the following. Late afternoon some of us were listening to the crackling, and in and out sounds of a portable radio, while playing cards and enjoying happy hour. Reception was not good in this remote location. One of the senior members said "What did that announcer just say? The Dow is down 20 something percent." The radio continued to crackle, and he could not confirm his comment.

"Well let's have another drink", he said, and we continued with our own conversations.

That momentous day is known in financial circles as Black Monday, when stock markets around the world collapsed in a domino like fashion. The U.S. market represented by the Dow Jones index, fell 508 points, or 22.61 percent in one single day. In todays' world, the points are meaningless, but look at the percentage loss, and you will understand the cold chills that many felt at the end of that Monday. We were spared that initial shock, until we returned to "civilization".

A dinner was arranged several weeks later, to recall the events of that historic weekend, and we were all presented with cuts of moose meat, for future family meals. You have to acquire a taste for venison, but believe me you have to really acquire a taste for moose. We tried first of all, by serving so called "hamburgers" to our young ladies. They rejected the "mooseburgers" outright from just the smell in the kitchen, and I do not believe that any of the Coyle family even tried to be converted to this "delicacy". But what a memorable weekend!

Our move to Aurora and a 14- year stay, highlighted one of the most important factors of life; the relationships that you foster with your family members. We were now in a position to assist Michele and Susan and their family members by offering our basement space to them, while they finalized their new locations. Sue and Mike gave birth to Melissa on November 18, 1988 (3rd grandchild). Fiona, also came back to live with us and brought her cat. I am not an advocate of parents, and mature children, sharing space for any length of time. I have seen too many cases where the resultant stress, takes a while to go away, especially if they have pets.

Larry Johnston finished the basement beautifully with sliding glass doors, leading to the pool deck, which were attractive and functional, while entertaining. They also made entrance to the house vulnerable and we installed a fairly sophisticated alarm system, which "dumbo" here, set off on the first night of installation. I spent considerable time on the phone persuading some alarm employee in Edmonton, that I was not the intruder. The ground level basement also made it vulnerable to flooding, which only occurred once, when our neighbour's sprinkler system, refused to turn off, causing only minor damage.

Our neighbours to the south, Ron and Fran Hine, were both psychologists. The joke was, that if invited for a drink, this had to be consumed lying down on the couch. They were good neighbours, but Fran needed more careful handling, and did not have the easy- going mannerism of Ron.

Our northern neighbours were Roy and Pat McCutcheon. Roy was the President of Seneca College and from time to time, let you know that. Pat's mother stayed with them. She had owned a ladies' fashion shop in Toronto and always dressed to the hilt. She enjoyed taking us aside, to complain that someone was taking food from her side of the refrigerator. She was delightful, but probably the worst driver I have ever seen. Backing out of their drive way was an afternoon event!

The McCutcheons could take a joke, and when Princess Margaret was in town to dedicate the new King Campus of Seneca, they of course, having talked about this for months, were dressed to the hilt, as they walked from the house to the waiting chauffer driven stretch limousine. El and I had dressed down as poor waifs, complete with the oldest garden clothes, pitchfork and straw hats, to see them off. It seemed funny at the time, but was probably quite rude!

The McCutcheons left, and the house was purchased by the Jones family. Kim was extremely friendly, as a young mother of eventually 3 children. Frank, I tagged as someone, you would never get close to. He worked at a techie start up, even then, and was not a good conversationalist. He was cautious with me, but eventually opened up and wanted to join me in my daily runs. He did not call ahead, just appeared at the door in running mode, and waited while I changed. He was very competitive, and although we ran side by side for the 5k or so, he always wanted to get his nose ahead of me, as we crossed the chosen finishing line.

Frank was full of surprises. One long weekend, he asked if I would like to join him for breakfast the next day. "Where should we go?", I asked.

"Lindsay", he replied. "That's a long drive", I said. "I just got my pilot's license", he countered. We flew from Buttonville the next a.m. His first solo. It was a single engine piper cub. On the way we encountered other aircraft and parachutists. No radar. When I look back, I realize how much I trusted this man, and how much confidence he had in himself.

Frank had found his niche, and the family moved to Saskatchewan. He was able to upgrade his flying license, and was now ferrying miners back and forth to mining locations in Northern Saskatchewan. He turned up at our Aurora door one afternoon years later, following a trip to Toronto, stayed for dinner, and opened up about how settled he was. After much studying and training, he was now qualified to fly jet aircraft, and was flying Lear jets for business men. Frank was quite the accomplished gentleman.

The Jones had a German shepherd dog named Jake, who was a pussycat. Continually wanted to be petted and loved, and would cower if reprimanded. But, had a bad habit of rearing up on his hind legs to greet you. Imagine if you are walking or running past the Jones house, and this German shepherd "beast", suddenly comes along side you and rears up to lick your face. The family was not good at keeping Jake on a leash, and he wandered a lot. Suffice to say our street was devoid of walkers or runners.

Jake, aimed to please and this caused problems. Other neighbours nearby, brought home some domestic rabbits for their kids. Jake "caught wind of this", visited the outdoor pen from time to time, and over the next few months brought the "fur balls" back to Kim, one by one as his dinner gift to the family.

A further memory of the Jones family, was by chance, I finding fairly expensive garden tools, hidden in the bulrushes in the flood plain beyond our property. I returned them to the police, only to find out about a week later that they had been stolen from the Jones' garage. Frank had not communicated this to us. Why they were dumped so close to the house, I do not know. Perhaps Jake was nearby. He probably would have helped them! The police returned the goods, but did not appear to be in a hurry to leave the Jones driveway. Kim was also in the driveway, washing the rear of the van, and washing and washing the rear of the van. I was gardening in the front yard, beside the Jones driveway. The policeman finally got out of his vehicle and I overheard him say "You can stop now Ma'am. I know your vehicle license on the rear plate is out of date. May I suggest that you have this updated tomorrow and we will forget about it". He then left the scene.

The next tenants after the Jones' family left for Saskatoon, were the Martons, Audrey and Les, who had 2 children, and added a third later on. Very nice neighbours, who also had a lovely chocolate lab, aptly named Hershey. It was not difficult to love Hershey, whose tail wagged ceaselessly. One New Years' Eve, the Martons, who knew we would be home at about 1:00, asked that as they were not returning home from a late- night party until 4:00 a.m., if I would be able to let Hershey out, on my return, to do "his thing". I let Hershey out as planned, and threw a ball for him to chase. He returned with the ball, but not on all fours. The hind legs were not supporting him and he came back sliding and whimpering on the snow- covered lawn.

I was mortified. I picked him up, and staggered to their front door. Holding him, while inserting the key, and then opening the door, while stopping their inside cat from escaping, was a challenge. Once inside, what to do? A hand written note on the fridge gave a vet number. I called, and they answered, shortly after 1:00 a.m. I was surprised to say the least. I explained the problem. Bring him over to the clinic on Yonge St., in 30 minutes. I complied, and Hershey was now in the hands of professionals, which he acknowledged by wagging his tail. Back to the house. Left a note for the Martons, and went to bed about 3:00 a.m.

New Years' Day dawned, and I contacted the Martons, to find out that Hershey was "right as rain". It apparently happens now and again to Labs. The rear legs seize, and then release again with time and heat application. She asked Hershey in my presence, if he ever wanted Bob to look after him again, and then jerked his leash back and forth to provide a definitive "no" answer. Rude!

We continued the relationship with the Johnstons, even after leaving Unionville. Larry and I were not close, but we did experience a lot of life together. We jogged (slowly) on sun drenched beaches in Florida. We skied down bunny hills, in Ontario, Quebec and Vermont, completely out of control. We watched sports on tv. We ate good food, and not so good food. We pretended to do "guy things", all under the watchful eyes of our wives.

Larry was not perfect and transformed himself from time to time. In the summer he became a lobster. He hated sun tan lotion; too much trouble putting it on. Put a television remote in his hand, and he became a control freak. Your eyeballs could not keep up with the changing channels. Show him a popcorn stand and he became a vacuum. Quantities consumed in record time.

The fire alarm went off in a movie theatre in Sarasota, Florida, and as the 4 of us made our way rather hurriedly to the closest exit, at the urging of the alarm and loud speaker system, Larry's wife, Shirley, had to yell out "Larry, where are you going?" "I'm going back to my seat to get the empty popcorn bucket". Apparently the second bucket was free, if you produced the first one, empty. Needless to say, Shirley won, and Larry went "popcornless", for the rest of the night.

We were fearless, but not good skiers, and truth to tell, the major challenge for us, was to actually get up the hill without incident. Our uphill report card was so bad, that our wives would not ride anywhere near us. Paying attention was a serious problem. Most chairlift seating only provided room for two skiers on each chair, and you had to be ready and in position to mount the lift at the right time.

In one incident, Larry and I prepared to shuffle with confidence into a position, to mount a two- person chair. We were chatting and perhaps too relaxed, as the chair came around the corner to "pick us up", only to see another skier standing between us, with fear written all over his face. Where did he come from, we both thought, and why is he looking so upset? I think he was having the same thought. Where did these idiots come from? Oops, three bottoms on a space intended for two. A moment of determination on the third party's face as the three of us, wiggled and waggled to squeeze onto the chair. Every bottom for itself! The chair picked up speed and I lost, and went spilling onto the ground. The emergency brake on the chair lift system was applied, and everything stopped. The operator yelled at us, and Larry and I beat a hasty retreat to mount the next chair.

Our actual first downhill ski hill experience together, was on a so called, T bar, on a bunny hill, at an Ontario ski resort. Larry found the T bar challenging, as it did not quite fit the contours of his lower body. I had encouraged him to go well ahead of me, and true to form he slipped off. I then took off, well behind him, but became agitated when Larry waving his arms, signaled that it was his intention to rejoin the T bar, by positioning his non- moving body, on the other side of the bar that was pushing me up.

I waved and yelled that, "this was not a good idea". Mr. Stubborn retorted "It will be o.k." Needless to say the effect of the contact, when we collided with his body, was enough to spin Larry around, and force him to cling onto the pole as if he was climbing up to heaven. Meanwhile the same collision, propelled my body upwards and sideways, and succeeded in having my one ski hook over the horizontal bar, which continued to pull me up the mountain upside down, like a side of beef.

Finally, the mechanism stopped and unknown to us, the operator at the top of the hill had come out of his cabin, doubled up in laughter, while shouting at two female skiers who had just arrived at the summit. "Did you see these two clowns? I have never seen anything like that before." The ladies looked down the hill, looked at each other, and our wives skied away.

Our "uphill' ability improved considerably after visits to the ski hills of Saint Sauveur, Quebec and Killington, Vermont. A day trip to Horseshoe Valley was therefore considered a walk in the park. However, after easily boarding the chairlift, and being halfway up the hill, Larry started banging his pair of skis together to remove some ice and snow. "Not a good idea", I said, as we watched one ski depart from his boot, and plunge downwards to the brush and deep snow below. We both let out a childlike, "Oh. Oh" and pondered the inevitable "what do we do now".

I'll need your help when we get off", he said. "If you lean on me, we are going down", I said. As the chair approached the top of the hill, Larry asked me if the operator would stop the lift. "Probably not", I said. "We're going down", he said. "Probably", I mumbled.

We linked arms, and straightened up, like a pair of ski hill jumpers, as we prepared to dismount. Leaving the safety of the chair we managed to maintain balance for about 1.5 seconds. About then, the 3 remaining skis intertwined, and we started to perform side by side double toe loops, before crashing to the ground in an ungainly heap. Needless to say, the occupants of the next chair crashed into us, and we all eventually managed to hobble to the exit ramp while avoiding the next group, and the spirited comments from the lift operator. We did not let this "one off" incident, deter us from, "soldiering on". It was obviously our mission in life, to terrify our fellow downhill skiers and in this regard, we were very successful.

With the birth of Daric on July 13, 1986, Jamie on July 14, 1987, and Kyle on November 13, 1992 (Michele and Doug's children) and Melissa on November 18, 1988 and Danielle on July 25, 1991 (Susan and Mike's first two children), the family was expanding rapidly and therefore it was the season and the reason for, great grandmother visits from Peterborough and Vancouver. Great aunt Maureen also visited, but hated, and would not permit us, to use the word "great", in her title.

With the joy of births, comes the sadness of deaths. During the following seven- year time frame, we unfortunately lost our super Ancaster neighbour, John Hunter in August, 1986, Eleanor's father, Sid Storey in July, 1988, and my very close friend Tom Jepson, who died at a very young age in November, 1993. The Lord giveth and the Lord taketh away!

Fiona, who always wanted to organize us, had used her voice to become the official answering service operator on our phone, with a lengthy message. Mum Greve, in answering a phone call late, had picked up the receiver, and heard Fiona's recorded message, while thinking that she was receiving a call from her and then reported to us, that she had had this long one- way chat with Fiona, who sounded well. She was confused. I probably snickered, and that did not go down well with her.

During this visit, Mum Greve also encountered a fairly scary situation. El and I were awakened about 3:00 in the morning, Christmas Eve, by Mum's voice indicating that she had a problem. Her bed was on fire. We shot up from a deep sleep, and rushed into her room to indeed find smoke billowing from her bed, and the sight of small flames on the bed covers. She had complained of being cold, and we had located and given her an electric blanket, which had not been used for years. The electric cord must have been frayed, and the unit caught fire. El and I ushered her out of the bedroom, and told her to stay on the landing, while we dashed downstairs to get a bucket or container for water.

Meanwhile on hearing the commotion, Maureen had come out of her room, smelled the smoke, and seeing Mum on the landing yelled at her to get back in her room for safety. We came back upstairs with the water, found Mum in the room, yelled at her to get out and back on the landing, poured water on the fire, and wrestled the mattress downstairs and outside for safety. As usual Mum was obedient to all our demands.

Sleep was not on the menu after that. We opened our presents fairly early that morning, had breakfast, and then called Larry Johnston, to have his company come asap with their special equipment, to remove the smoke smell from the house, together with the mattress and burnt covers.

1988 brought two more traditions to the Coyle household. The first was limited to El and I, and involved royalty. This involved celebrating our November 15th wedding anniversary, by going to the Royal York hotel on the closest Friday to the 15th, followed by an afternoon and evening at the Royal Winter Fair, which is always held at that time of year. Our love of horses always prevailed, and we would stay to the bitter end of jumping competition, which sometimes continued until 11:30 at night.

Referring to weddings, June 11 of that year, was their day, for Jeff Gray and Monique. They were and have remained a favourite couple of ours. Not because Jeff was such a valuable addition to the office sales staff, but because they are such a darned down to earth likeable, sensible pair, who have done so well in life. They also have this magnificent 40 foot- long yacht named "Entre Nous", which I have enjoyed sailing on, El not so much.

A yearly tradition, was taking the girls out for a December evening celebration, including dinner and a theatre show. Because of Michele's location and commitment to the family, she unfortunately missed out on most of these. It is now hard to believe that we did this for 16 years in a row, dining at downtown restaurants such as La Fenice, Far Niente and others, followed by these theatre shows; Suds, The Importance of Being Earnest, the girls favourite Dick Whittington, Les Misérables, Chorus Line, The Phantom, Show Boat, Beauty and the Beast, Ragtime, Rent, Fame, Needfire, The Lion King, Handel's Messiah, Contact and The Colours of Christmas.

Sixteen years in a row. Now that is tradition for you. A decision was made to end it, perhaps due to the sons in law being left out, or the possibility of us now also favouring the grandchildren, who numbered 7. To wrap up this tradition which ran from 1988 to 2003 inclusive, we had dinner in 2004 at Oakland Hall in Aurora, with Susan, Fiona and their husbands. End of an era, but what a ride! By the way, we still hosted Christmas dinner for all immediate family and in- law members, who could attend.

These early years in Aurora were active years. Fiona was with us, just! I joked with my Mum, that if she borrowed our car, not to park on the right side of the driveway, because it was reserved for police cars. There was some substance to my humour. El and I came home from an overnight ski trip, to find the flood plain behind our house crawling with flashing lights. It was similar to the time of year, when we would see male fireflies in the flood plain, flashing on and off to attract females during the mating season. Fiona had arranged a girls' sleepover, which some males had got wind off and wanted to crash. Fiona quite rightly, called the police and they arrived in force, to try and locate the boys, who had fled into the flood plain. People do not understand, that when you call the police with an emergency, they do react in a serious manner, and in numbers. This scene is applicable today, and has been played out on television many times!

On another instance, we came home to find Fiona, holding a number of blood- stained bath towels. Our house was on a bend of Murray Drive, and due to the camber on the road, which in my opinion was incorrect, speeding cars made a habit of crashing on the bend. She was home alone, when one such crash occurred and actually knowing the occupants, provided first aid and bath towels. If emergency services were called, we never saw them, or any evidence of a crash or vehicles. Hmmm!

One Halloween, Fiona dressed as the Pillsbury Doughboy and arrived home well after 1:30 a.m., breaking her curfew. She then proceeded to tell us a "cock and bull" story about helping a man, who had tried to rob the local LCBO store, and in breaking a window, had severely cut himself in the process. She said, that she had stayed with him until the police and emergency services arrived, hence the delay in getting home. The store is about 20 minutes from our house on foot…but hmmm. That was a Sunday night and the next morning while driving to work, I was shocked and surprised to hear the radio announcer give details as to a break in at the Aurora LCBO and the subsequent arrest. I was more than distracted, and confused about the similarity between Fiona's assumed "story telling", and the radio report, that I was pulled over in a police speed trap and charged with speeding. I explained in detail, the details of my daughter's experience, and the radio report, which had caused me to lack focus. The officer nodded and said the story seems very believable, but the fine for speeding still stood, and he then issued me with the applicable ticket. I was being punished for not believing my daughter.

Our Toronto business results began to strengthen during these early years following 1988, and our production numbers were well in excess of our branch targets. I do not know if this gave me permission to take more, or in fact any vacation time, but 1989 was the year that El and I started to aggressively take major vacation trips, which we have managed to continue for the last 30 years. In April of that year, we vacationed for 2 weeks at a "3- star resort" called Jolly Beach in Antigua. We were not prepared to leave Fiona at home, and she came with a girl friend named Lee. They slept during the day and partied at night. El and I did the opposite and we hardly ever saw each other.

The exception however, was at the award ceremonies at night. I suspect that some of the hotel staff had a soft spot for Fiona, because every night she seemed to be onstage, accepting a prize and usually a first prize, for whatever competitive event she had entered. The beach at Jolly Beach was quite beautiful, the hotel and food not so much. But this was the start of many, many vacations, and we had yet to discern the good from the average.

At the resort, we met a delightful Swiss couple, Marianne and Marco Poltera, from New York, who worked for the Swiss bank and were being transferred back to Switzerland within months. Maybe you will visit us, they said. Never suggest possible free international vacation accommodation to a Scot!

We received a letter from Mum Greve, later that year, that based upon a video we had sent her of her now 3 great- grandchildren, that she was coming for a visit. She was now 76, frail, with intestine problems and poor lung capacity, and facing a 5- hour flight from Vancouver, but the thought of seeing and spending time with these kids, was just too strong to resist. Good for you Mum!

October,'89, we accepted an invitation to join the Johnstons in Sarasota, and were introduced to a condominium site called Siesta Dunes. The property is on Crescent Beach, which is the main beach on Siesta Key. The 2.5 mile- long beach is quite beautiful, and sports white flour- like sand, that never gets hot. This was to be the first of multi visits to this Florida location and although in reality we could never afford to buy a unit there, we have rented 24 times and probably spent more money on rent than the buying price would have been. I have run and walked that beach more times than I can remember, but of late I have noticed that the beach itself gets longer and longer with every vacation, and oh those hills!

We finished off the year by spending post- Christmas days with the Johnstons in Saint Sauveur, Quebec in a condo, on the ski hill. Fiona joined us, and the memories of that trip were more than pleasant. I recall the village setting, and the ambience of the village restaurant we would have dinner at on several occasions. Quebec really has a lot to offer. Larry and I, at his urging, tried the moguls, which was stupid. But that was Larry, he would try anything, and I went along with it!

Our strong '89 and '90 branch new business numbers, qualified El and I for a President's Club business trip with Standard Life to the U.K., in May/June 1990. Mary Laudadio, and her husband Vito also qualified. We were entertained royally by the U.K. staff in London, Edinburgh and Gosforth Park, which has a major conference centre, near Newcastle.

Our hotel in London was memorable, because the room allotted, which apparently others smarter than us had refused, was like a rotunda on the top floor. The roof tiles above, were either metal or tin, and home to a flock of pigeons, day and night. We were convinced that they all wore clogs, and were into line dancing.

The commissionaire we met, to escort us and our luggage to the room, was a young lad in a long gray ill- fitting coat, and a hat that also did not fit. The elevator was, as is in many older cities, quite small and could only accommodate him, and the luggage on the first trip. On exiting the elevator, he piled our luggage and perhaps others, on the top floor landing, at the edge of a beautiful winding staircase. We arrived on the elevator to find him struggling with the pile of bags, and to the sound of "thump, thump, thump", on the staircase. I noticed, that for every case he piled up, one would leave, and make its' way out of sight, back down the stairs to the lobby below. I pointed this out, and his not to be forgotten cockney answer was, "Bloody Hell, you're right"! We never saw him again.

An older gentleman, perhaps his father, replaced him the next day. I was promised "a good deal" on dry cleaning my pants and on tickets to the theatre to see the show "Cats". I never saw my pants again, but we did receive some compensation months later, on our return to Canada, from the commissionaire or the hotel itself.

We did so much on that trip, that I have to confess, I fell asleep watching "Cats". We flew to Munich the next day and I found myself sitting beside a "Cats lover". I dared not admit that I had barely seen the show. El and I rented a car and drove to Austria to stay at a time share, gifted to us by

Els' friend Donna Purkey, and her husband Hal. The hotel was nestled in a small community in the Alps, called St. Johann. El had met and befriended Donna in Toronto, at a girls' residence, when El left her parents' home in Peterborough in 1961, to "adventure out and see the world".

Donna had met Hal, while vacationing in Germany. At the time Hal was in the U.S. armed forces, also based in Germany. Donna, was originally a Canadian girl, with a duel passport, who he married. She in turn, helped put him through university, when he returned to the U.S.A. He was a very smart man and went on to own, and run a very successful bond investment company in Connecticut. Donna's claim to fame and quite rightly so, was her curling ability, and the fact that she represented the U.S. national women's curling team on many occasions, helped coach female U.S. Olympic curlers in her later years, and was President of the United States Women's Curling Association in '94 and '95. In the years that El resumed contact with Donna, she lived in Chicago, Illinois, Connecticut, and then eventually retired to a beautiful residence in Phoenix, Arizona.

Donna was warm and friendly. Hal not so much. But they were both given to generosity, and gifted us, most of that time share stay in Austria. The hotel was dwarfed by the Alps, and so remote that our only neighbours, were the milking cows in the adjacent pastures. The air was so clean and crisp. We took a one- hour side trip to Werfen Ice Caves, which sport the largest ice cave in the world. It takes a tortuous car drive, a cable car ride and then a steep hike to get to the cave entrance.

After the door to the cave was opened, you experience a huge rush of wind. You are given an open flame lantern to light the way and proceed on a short path to the first flight of stairs. Stairs are up and down, and total 1400 plus steps. The natural formed ice sculptures are quite beautiful, impressive and breathtaking. No photography is permitted, and therefore you have to just take in what you see. English speaking guides have to be reserved, which we did not know. El spoke up and asked within our group if anyone spoke English. A young Austrian university student volunteered with enthusiasm, to practice her English, by interpreting for us, and she would not accept anything, other than our multiple thanks when the tour was over.

Later that night we met a delightful couple from Florida, the Robertsons, who were in the dining room. Our first meeting was fairly short. El had ordered a pizza. The only one available, had sea- food toppings. I will not forget the looks on the faces of most in the restaurant, as this "specialty" was brought to our table. Everyone got a whiff of the pungent smell coming from the pizza, which was honestly disgusting. Its' arrival was a signal to vacate the restaurant, which most did, even after the pizza was returned, untouched, to the kitchen. Anyone for salad!

I had contacted the Polteras. Remember them from our Antigua vacation last year. I indicated that we would be in Austria, and would love to visit them now that they were back in Switzerland. Arno, call me Marco's, response was, "So soon", but if we would give them a few more days, they could accommodate us. We managed to extend our stay in St. Johann for a very reasonable price, and then set off to drive to their small town near Zurich. The ride took us through a never- ending multiple kilometer tunnel under the Alps, linking Austria and Switzerland. They do some magical things in Europe.

Austria and Germany are dotted with excellent high- speed roads called autobahns up high, with high speed train rails in the valleys below. Switzerland is so different in that their valleys are lakes, and therefore a great amount of travel there, is by boat, and the ferry system linking the lakes is very organized and punctual.

The Polteras' had an under 1- year old son, that Marco would let you speak to, but was reluctant to let you hold. Dad was noticeably possessive, but enthusiastic that we experience some of the best of Switzerland. We set out one day, complete with child backpack harness, to explore the local mountains. This involved "climbing" the local mountain, via the funicular railway, a five- kilometer trail hike across the top of the mountains, lunch and then descent to the lake below, via an enclosed chairlift. We then boarded a ferry to return home, only to find out that it was headed the wrong way. We disembarked at the first stop and waited patiently, with an understandably impatient child, for about ninety minutes, before boarding the correct ferry to return home. A long day but worth it!

We left our Swiss friends to drive to Frankfurt, Germany, in a rental car. While transferring from one autobahn freeway, to another autobahn, on the way to the airport, I ended up in the middle of a police escorted convoy of black SUVs, flashing lights and all. I was chased out quickly.

A wonderful 28- day trip with so many memories. I recall at the time, of the joy of being introduced in Austria, to the warmth and comfort of a duvet for the first time and in Switzerland to a bowl of fresh fruit at breakfast every morning, complete with whipped fresh cream. Yummy!

The year continued, with a last 2 weeks of October vacation, in Sarasota at Siesta Dunes. The weather always seems just perfect in Florida at that time of year. The timing is important because, as Standard's year end is November 15, I would not have gone on vacation, unless the branch had already exceeded its target for the year. Maureen joined us for the first of many vacations together.

She had tried vacationing with other ladies from Vancouver, including Hawaii, but these had not worked out to her satisfaction. As a single person, who had lived alone for many years Maureen was opinionated and particular, but tried to be on her best behavior with us, and I am sure held back some of her thoughts. This was the beginning for her, of an extensive travelling pattern, and certainly not all with us. I know she ended up, visiting in excess of 50 world countries, many with us, but also many through a group sponsored by a Ballantrae neighbor turned travel agent, Betty Shukster, who enhanced our lives with these trips.

We wrapped up the year by booking a ski trip to Killington, Vermont with the Johnston family. The resort was nice, the weather not so much. It was extremely cold, and the green (beginner) and black (expert) hills were both closed due to a lack of snow and extreme icy conditions. The runs down the blue (intermediate) hills were therefore challenging, because you encountered falling beginners, and crazy dangerous expert skiers aplenty. Our children were also stranded on a chairlift for a while due to freezing conditions.

A significant memory was the cozy dining room, good food and a terrible lounge piano player. I think he was booed on occasion, and just a song away from dinner rolls being hurled at him. His favourite phrase was "Thank you, thank you very much", recognizing the one tone deaf guest, who had applauded him.

1990 was noteworthy from a family point of view in that our oldest daughter Susan was hired as a full- time temp in Standard's Toronto group pension office. As I was the manager, she was not permitted a permanent full- time position, while I was in that role. She achieved permanent status when I retired in 1997, and all along was considered an extremely valuable employee, finally focusing her talents on a consulting role in the area of defined benefit pension programs. A noteworthy part of her career, was that she had to be treated by me, as an employee and not a family member for so many years, to the extent that some staff who were hired later, did not even know that we were related. This must have been difficult for Susan, but she distinguished herself by doing her job, being accepted by the staff as one of them, and never being singled out with a complaint.

Our office new business results were really picking up. We introduced two annual perks for the brokers, we hoped to do more business with. The first was a business meeting in a hotel environment, where we introduced them to legislative changes, new ideas and Standard Life concepts to help them look after the retirement needs of their corporate clients. We, (both the branch and Head Office marketing staff), put tremendous effort into writing professional scripts and presentations (huge screen and technical staff), that it came across to the 65 attendees or so, as something they had not witnessed before, and they went away with a more than favourable impression, and solid information for their clients. This was the first of many such education meetings, to achieve our goal, of wanting these brokers, to direct all of their client pension business to us.

The second, was an inaugural annual golf tournament, held initially at Sleepy Hollow in Stouffville, for both brokers and pension consultants from the major pension consulting firms. This was attended by over 100 participants and became an annual feature for many years. A sit- down dinner followed the golf. Purely a marketing feature, to consolidate our relationships with these middle men and women, and to say thank you for their business. We went on to hold several of these, at Angus Glen, before this renowned course achieved its notoriety. I clearly recall the large tent that was used for our sit-down dinner, before the clubhouse, and dining area buildings were completed.

Was this strategy successful? Yes! Our branch target for the year 1991 was $8.5 million production credits. We surpassed this figure by some $2 million credits. Due to the branch business results, and a general feeling of success among the staff in general, I was able to build a more complete family atmosphere starting in '91, by including them in social outings, such as a Blue Jays game, a pool party at our Aurora home and a year-end Christmas dinner. Our branch as a whole was coming together.

We were fortunate to book an island- hopping trip to the Caribbean late April '91, involving 1 week at Jolly Beach in Antigua and 1 week in Barbados (nicer hotel and better food). The week in Antigua was spent on the water, because of an influx of German tourists, who hogged everything, and were quite rude and disruptive. The week in Barbados was much better. The beaches are spectacular and allow you to walk for miles. Barbados is quite British, with a cutlery display on the table, that would be the envy of Downton Abbey fans. Our booking permitted us, to have dinner at a different hotel restaurant each night.

An eventful dinner was the invitation of a cockroach to our table. It fell from the ceiling or purposely jumped and landed on Els' shoulder. She immediately jumped up and let out a blood curdling scream. We managed to bat it onto the open dance floor. It was empty save for the snoozing cat, which let out a yelp and vacated the area "tout de suite". Our dinner arrangements were for the early sitting, and the few occupants settled down to the calm, that followed the debacle.

A shade later we witnessed a foursome, who could not decide which table to sit at, and consequently moved upon 3 different occasions as the evening progressed. A buddy of our uninvited guest, had stationed himself above their location, which they had witnessed, and as they moved, the cockroach followed suit. They were obviously smarter than us, but we did not stay long enough to see who won. I also recall on the walk back to our hotel, how pitch black it was. You dare not walk back via the beach, and even when you used the sidewalk, you were startled at the sight of the white of some ones' eyes, as you suddenly came upon them.

Later that summer El and I qualified for a Standard Stars conference at Chateau Montebello in Quebec. Maureen also qualified, in her role with Standards' brokerage office in Vancouver. As usual, she encountered a problem. This time she was given a key to her room and on opening the door encountered a male having a nap on "her" bed. Another blood curdling yell!

I believe, that from that time on, El and I had to accompany her to her designated room, to find that either the key did not fit, the room was not made up, or there were signs of it still being occupied. The highlight of this conference, was that we could not go outside and enjoy the beautiful setting of Montebello. It rained nonstop for 3 days. However, the food and wine were excellent and true to Standard Life, they did their best to make our stay as comfortable as possible.

One of our younger office staff members, and a favourite of mine, Richard Keeley, was getting married and I was invited to his stag, which I could quickly see was getting out of hand. I was smart enough to leave early, as Richard sporting a "getting married" sign, was tied to a post at the corner of Sheppard and Yonge in Willowdale, to enjoy the honking of passing cars. Although, I think he was probably oblivious to the goings on. He was obviously released unharmed, as he went on in life, to become a very successful insurance broker.

Mum Greve visited us in '91, and Danielle was born July 25, 1991 to Sue and Mike (4th grandchild). A memorable wedding that year was the joining together of the Johnstons' son Brad, to Jacqueline. A significant guest, and participant at the wedding, was the great Canadian tenor Ben Heppner, whose children had been nannied, throughout his tours of North America and Europe by the Johnstons' daughter, Leanne. Very few opera singers, performing an aria at a wedding, would be as down to earth as he was, and "ask you to join in".

Ben, despite his notoriety, had no airs and graces! He later was to experience a vocal crisis, which kept him away from the opera house and concert hall in 2002-03. Unfortunately, his crash and burn happened in Toronto, at The Roy Thomson Hall. El and I were there, in about the fourth row. He just stopped singing after missing some notes, and walked off the stage. As he put it, "I was embarrassed, but I also wanted to save you from any more pain". That was Ben Heppner!

Gerry and Kathy Guilfoyle exhibited a significant part of their nature, generosity, by insisting that we use their tickets, to see The Phantom of The Opera, as due to a conflict they were unable to attend. I will refer to them from time to time in the years ahead. Very good friends and classy people. It was a lovely gesture, to see a wonderful show, from great seats.

We rounded off the year by going to Siesta Key for 2 weeks. The Johnstons, were with us for a week, and then we were fortunate to meet a couple from Glasgow, Scotland, at a local restaurant. David and Bobby Hepburn were very guarded at first, until we discovered, that he was a police superintendent for a large slice of Glasgow, and she was on the police office staff. They relaxed and were fun to be with and we visited each- others condo during the week. They disappeared very quickly, explaining that as a member of the police- force he would have access to the next soccer game, being played at Ibrox Stadium, to watch his home team, Rangers. They had decided to change their flight home, to get back to Glasgow in time for the kick off. The lure of soccer!

Success at Standard Life translated into rewards, and El and I again qualified for a Presidents' Club business award trip to the U.K., in April '92, to be entertained royally in London, Edinburgh and the Gosforth Park Convention Centre. Side trips complete with guides, took us to Westminster Abbey, the Tower of London, Stirling Castle and Bannockburn. These were truly high-lights for a Scot born in the U.K., who had never in person tasted the history, and legacy of such well known sites, brought to light by Mel Gibson's portrayal of William Wallace in Braveheart.

Jeff and Monique Gray and the Lieschs from Vancouver also qualified. El and I chose to stay in England for the rest of our vacation. I wanted to view

Plymouth, from where I believe my father set sail with the Royal Navy in the 2nd World War. We took a train to Bath, to stay in a comfortable bed and breakfast there, and to then view the highlights of this ancient and historic town. We then rented a car, to tour further south in Devon and maybe to Cornwall, if time permitted.

Plymouth was heavily bombed by the German Air Force during the 40s', and appeared to me to have been rebuilt with a "hodge- podge" group of buildings, which did not match each other in height or shape. We took a conducted bus tour, but I was not impressed. At the bed and breakfast in Bath, a young staff member, recommended that we stay at a hotel near Chudleigh, called Sampson Farms Country Hotel. It was a first- class recommendation. A very countryfied 15th century building, complete with a thatched roof, where the locals gathered at the intimate pub inside. The kitchen, was in the area of the renovated cow byre. It was therefore a very long renovated room, but now sparkled with modern aluminum counters, cabinets and appliances. The chef was trained in St. Catharines, Ontario, of all places.

We stopped off on the way to the hotel at Wells, Anglican Cathedral, a beautiful Gothic structure, built over a period ranging from 1176 to 1490 A. D., in the medieval heart of England's smallest city. So old, so historical, but so modern in many ways. After a meal on the grounds, you could wash your hands in a wash area, that was motion sensitive in every way, whether it be the soap, water or drying one's hands. I mean this was 1992 service, in the proximity of a building finally constructed some 500 years ago.

This technology continued at the Sampson Farms hotel, where the water for the shower, would only flow, if you turned on the electric switch on the outer wall, and then turning the taps on. This had us puzzled for a while! To celebrate our last night, we had pre ordered the duck for dinner, which required 24- hour notice. The dining area was small and near the bar. The main course, was served in separate, "his and her" silver tureens, brought from the kitchen, and held high by 2 staff members, accompanied by a chorus from the locals, at the nearby bar, who proudly proclaimed in their Devon dialect, "They be having the duck".

When the lids of the tureens were removed, the sight of these huge, cooked golden brown, meals almost defeated us, until we started to peel away the thick and bloated skin, to reveal portions, that we knew we could handle. The food and service there, could not have been better. The morning we left, they had made up a cold, but appetizing breakfast for us, and set the table beautifully, knowing that the time we were departing for a London flight, was truly early and before anyone else was up.

The hotel was surrounded by fields and greenery, and the area is a hive for artists and artisans. We walked to Chudleigh, to view and talk with the many, who were selling their works. We actually purchased 3 originals from a lady by the name of Jan Lunn, who I have fantasized as becoming very famous. Over 25 years and still hoping! Her work depicts the walls or reaves, as they were originally called, found on Dartmoor, and believed to be built in the Bronze Age. The paintings are as she saw them, and feature three of our seasons. The fall season was missing. We have proudly displayed them in our living room, for many years. In typically, British humour, there is also a small community nearby called Upper Chudleigh, but there is no Lower Chudleigh.

The timing we chose to leave Devon, and specifically Bath, was poor. Professional rugby is a big- time sport in the U.K. and especially Bath, whose team had apparently won the rugby league championship game, just prior to us leaving. A roofless double decker bus was parading around Bath, the day we were leaving, to show off the players and their trophy. I imagine that the social life around that sedate sleepy historical town was going to get a lot more exciting. We passed many honking vehicles travelling to the celebrations in Bath, on our way to London's Heathrow Airport. Bath itself is so historic, but the atmosphere was about to become hysteric.

The Romans commenced construction of a limited bathing facility in 1 A.D., enhanced it over the next 300 years, only to have it destroyed in about the 6th century A.D., after their departure. It is estimated that Rome had about 40,000 troops in Britain at the height of their occupation.

Our twenty- one day trip to the U.K. was so memorable. Once again, we had been blessed by a Company that said, "If you perform for us, we will perform for you". At the time, I was not consciously aware, that I had adopted the same attitude with the staff, whether sales or administration, "You may suffer the odd disappointment", I would say, and then endorse the phrase, "Try harder to perform. You will enjoy it, and the rewards that automatically follow".

September 22 marked the wedding day for our Fiona to Steve Ferstl. The reception and dinner, with over 100 guests, were both held at the Boulevard Club. Tom Jepson was the Master of Ceremonies and on our side, the Coyle, Storey and Smith families were well represented. Bride and groom families are not always familiar with each other, and as I was wearing a tuxedo, I was frequently asked, the way to the washroom, or if I would fill up their wine glass.

I recall Daric, our oldest grandchild, and then only 6, providing some lighter moments by referring to the Japanese chef, who was carving the roast beef, as the Japan guy with the cow! His other great one liner, was his shouted comment from the bathroom closet, with several club members present, to the effect that, the bull his Dad and Mum owned, was being, denutted. "You mean it's being castrated Daric", I said. "No grandpa, its being denutted", was the reply. A chorus of short polite guffaws from the members present, echoed through the washroom.

David Smith was the best man at our wedding, and I was David and Jana's best man at their Victoria B.C. wedding. They were now living just outside Phoenix Arizona, with David continuing to do consulting work for Cemex, the huge cement provider, head officed in Mexico. Because of our love of horses, El and I decided to take a trip to Arizona in October, to view a ranch near Tucson, called Tanque Verde, that Maureen had referred to us. We stopped by and were impressed by it. We also visited the Grand Canyon, Sedona and the Smiths themselves in Tempe.

The Grand Canyon is pretty amazing. For our first visit, we stupidly loaded up with ham sandwiches and luckily water, and set out down the switchback path to Plateau Point, which is halfway to the Canyon floor and the Colorado River. The difference in temperature is remarkable, the further you descend into the Canyon, and hydration is a must. The hike to Plateau Point and back is 12 miles, with 3,000 feet of elevation lost and gained. Summer heat can make this hazardous, but this was October. We spent an hour or so, just looking at the spectacular views. Just enough time for El to tell me that her hips had seized, and walking back would be a problem. What problem! A helicopter ride for $400 per person, is available! Plateau Pont is flat and full of vegetation and deer, and was negotiable by El.

Now we came to the steep winding climb. I suggested that she walk in front of me, and I would put my fist in her belt, and provide her with the force to loosen her hips, and help her walk. We agreed to rest every 10 minutes, knowing that it would take about 2 plus hours to reach the top. My "Andy Cap" hat, made me look older than 52, which prompted a fellow climber to admonish their friend from complaining, by saying "Stop moaning. Look at that woman straining, to pull that old man up the hill"! The old man and El, made it in time to get a South Rim hotel room that night.

The mule ride for a group of Japanese tourists, was led by a mustachioed male wearing a black hat, long black skin coat, chaps and boots. In reply to Els' raised thumb for a ride, his response in perfect English, was, "Mummy told me to never pick up strangers". A delightful comment!

We headed south the next morning, to spend our final 2 days with the Smiths. They in turn, took us on two different sight- seeing trips; the first to see the famous fountain at Fountain Hill which shoots water about 560 feet into the air and comes on every 15 minutes, and the second to experience part of the Salt River Canyon. The latter involved wading in the river, which was mainly not more than knee deep, for a couple of miles, to a beautiful waterfall, where we could swim in the pool below the fall. The attraction of this setting, was the privacy. We did not meet or see anyone, while wading in the river, other than the Smiths' daughter on the way back, who was able to greet us in her car, which unfortunately was stuck in the sandy bottom of the river bed. We rocked the vehicle out. We did meet a young indigenous man, when we initially entered the canyon by car, who asked for a few dollars, as the entrance fee to the canyon. Whether this was legal or not, David did not argue. It was certainly worth it!

We took the Smiths out for dinner, as a thank you for their hospitality and witnessed sports history in the making. The restaurant had a wall mounted television and we were able to see the Toronto Blue Jays win the World Series, in six games over the Atlanta Braves. This was achieved 15 years after they had been awarded a franchise, and of course, was the first time the ultimate baseball trophy had been awarded to a team outside of the U.S.A. A fitting end to a great Arizona trip, and we were determined to come back, again and again. And as you will see, we did.

November 13,1992, our daughter Michele gave birth to Kyle, our fifth grandchild.

Because of the '91 branch results, H.O. marketing increased our new business target for '92 by about 20%, to $10 million production credits. We were on a roll however and ended up the year by producing, $12 million production credits. This success was going to reward El and I, with more Company sponsored and paid for trips over the next 2 years, and on the negative side, increase our new business targets even further.

The backyard pool had for years, entertained so many family members, staff, neighbours and guests, but was beginning to show the flaws of its' initial construction. The wood retaining wall had not been built on a cement foundation, and there were insufficient cross beams near the top of the wall. The result of cold Ontario winters, was the heaving of the pool base, as the wall started inch by inch, to move away from the pool. There was therefore the danger, of the retaining wall giving way, and the pool wall following suit, with a tsunami of water dumping any bathers in the pool at the time, into the flood plain beyond.

Suffice to say we would have to build a more solid retaining wall, and construct a more solid base for the new pool. Our first undertaking of the spring and summer project, was to build a small screened in porch of the family room, with steps leading down to the pool deck. While this was being completed and painted, the painter dropped a full open can of paint into the pool below. Luckily, we had begun to drain the pool in advance of the renovation work.

Options for a new retaining wall were the pumping of cement over the house to build a 10- foot high concrete wall, a gabion wall used in building dykes, which involves the packing of multi stones into a wire cage, or a man- made wooden wall with appropriate cross beams built on a cement foundation. The latter proposal was accepted by us, and built by an Italian team of workers, recommended to us by Larry Johnston. To see these men, work and build the wall without any machinery, was a thing of beauty, and the cost was reasonable.

When the wall was built, Mayfair pools after some reluctance agreed to install the new pool. They reinforced the heavy- duty cement- based pool, with extra rebar, claiming that short of an earthquake "this time, this thing isn't going anywhere". The cost of this replacement seriously damaged any financial gain we had made, between selling in Unionville and buying in Aurora. But based upon the joy and bonding, the backyard pool brought to all the family it was well worth it.

Our '93 Standard trip, was to The Stars conference to be held in Halifax, Nova Scotia. Early June is a bit chilly there, but once again we were entertained royally. Maureen also qualified and after the conference, we rented a car to explore P.E.I. We stayed in Summerside and Charlottetown.

My first impressions of P.E.I. were; well- constructed Canadian taxpayer subsidized roads, farmhouses that had been updated on the outside with siding, with no people or farm machinery in sight, the friendliness of the people, and multi offers to sample their cooked rhubarb. The young people were friendly, but most had never been off the island. The Japanese in particular are fixated with the story of Anne of Green Gables, and flock to the island in droves. As our car license plates were registered elsewhere, the bus groups who stopped near our car, would enthusiastically take photographs of them, for what reason, we know naught.

I had this whacky idea, that on leaving Halifax, we should fly to Toronto, and then connect to Sarasota, to experience some warmer weather. It certainly was warmer, and very humid and very wet. The 3 of us stayed in a building close to, but not on the beach. It was not the same as Siesta Dunes, and I was firmly told by "you know who", not to do this again. Complaints about the excessive rain I thought, were exaggerated, but on at least one night, we did have to take our shoes and socks off, and wade through the parking lot, to a village restaurant. The side trip to Florida was not a good idea!

To celebrate my mothers' 80th birthday that year, El and I went to Vancouver in October. Maureen hosted the day and evening, and it was quite a tribute. Funnily enough, I then considered Mum as old, but as I am writing this, in the vicinity of the same birthday myself, I don't feel the same way about my age. El and I took a side trip to Vancouver Island to visit her Aunt Ollie and husband Jim, who lived in Parksville. Jim was a Scot and very likeable. Ollie has always been my favourite "aunt", but don't tell her that or she might want to kiss me! Jim loved to paint seascapes and was quite good. We purchased one, not because he was kind of family, but because it was a quality piece of work, which we liked.

We came back to face a tragedy, in that as mentioned, our close friend Tom Jepson died, after his heart went way out of rhythm, while playing hockey. Tom was a GP and knew too much. Family members, including his younger brother Jim, who was a federal M.P. for London East, had succumbed to heart disease. Tom knew his life was going to be cut short, and in the few years leading up to his death, he determined to live life to the fullest. This included unfortunately, divorcing his wife Barbara, and probably hurting other family members on the way. Had this been today, Tom, due to the advances in treating heart disease, would probably have survived.

Our 1971 to 1978 years together as Ancaster neighbours, and the many meetings we had, after I left Ontario, were some of the best male friendship times, one could ever wish for. Tom was truly my friend, and the eulogy that I have kept, and included with my memoirs, speaks for itself.

I have tried to maintain contact with his sons, Gordon and Kenneth, who are both lawyers in Toronto, and we have shared suppers on occasion, in down town Toronto. We keep in touch and continually agree to meet, without fixing a date and place. Cathy, his daughter is in Ottawa and Barbara is we believe, still in Ancaster. The Jepson family is one our remaining family links, to our Ontario history, starting almost 50 years ago. Call it nostalgia, but we should maintain the relationship. Time to call!

El and I qualified for the '94 Presidents Club trip to Argentina. A trip of a lifetime, so attractive that we added Brazilian stayovers, to both ends of the business trip. Unable to sit together on both the Miami and Rio flights, El voiced her displeasure with the booking agent in Miami. We were upgraded to first class on the 747 Aerolineas Argentinas flight to Rio. We were told however, that we would not be sitting next to each other. "That's o.k." said El! Way to go El.

First impressions of Rio were mixed; many homeless people begging on the streets, many missing a limb, a volcanic landscape with hotels and nice houses on level land, "barrios" (poor living cramped quarters) rising up steep hills, beautiful scenic beaches, highlighted by the Copacabana and Ipanema beaches with milky white Atlantic waves crashing onto the shores. Rio has many impressive tour sites, such as Corcovado, sporting an iconic 125- foot high statue, known as Christ the Redeemer and Sugarloaf Mountain, rising 1200 feet above the harbour, and only accessible by cableway.

It is said, that if you are born or move to Rio, you will never leave. Over 6 million people are currently supporting that theory. The Samba music and dance is a Brazilian genre, with its roots in Africa. We visited a nightclub in Rio. The show was terrific, but it came to light, and surprised many, that most of the female peacock feather adorned line dancers, were male!

The Guilfoyles, and ourselves took a side trip to the coastal town of Buzios. The former Brazilian fishing village, was made famous by Bridget Bardot, the French sex symbol actress of the 1950s and 1960s, who winterized there. An enjoyable day, despite the many tourists, and the obvious presence of the army, who walked around in groups of four. The tour bus return trip emphasized the problems in Brazil. As we entered a new state (Brazil consists of 26 states and 1 federal district), we were boarded by men in army uniforms, who demanded money from the driver. This apparently is not an unusual happening, and is usually only restricted to the bus company, and not the passengers. The driver merely said you will have to speak to my employer in Rio, and the army types seemed to accept this and left the bus. They did not speak to us.

We returned to Rio, to a message, that the then President of Standard, Claude Garcia was expecting us to join he and his wife for dinner at 6:30. We arrived home at 6:10. Much earlier in the trip, I had suggested to Claude that he and his wife, join the Coyles and Guilfoyles for dinner, at one of the beaches in downtown Rio, to escape the restriction of the hotel. We had all been warned, for safety purposes, not to venture out of the hotel in the evening. A rebel I can be!

I had forgotten, that I had asked him earlier in the week, not really expecting a positive response. We got ready in record time, and joined them for a delightful dinner and evening in an open downtown Rio restaurant. Because they have open access to you, you have to expect a stream, of usually very young children, attempting to sell you their goods, only to be chased away by the waiting staff, from time to time. These kids are poor! Claude and his wife Danielle were good company. She is very likeable and for the six of us it was a lasting memory.

We were staying at the Sheraton Hotel. El and I left for dinner the next night on our own, to get a taxi outside of the hotel gates, and we were shouted at by the hotel staff, as to the danger. I think the danger is overrated. We met a couple with their kids, over dinner, who spoke English, joined us, and drove us back to our hotel. Gerry Guilfoyle and I ran along Ipanema Beach. El purchased goods on the beach, and we were made to feel very welcome in their "paradise". Swimming in the ocean although exciting, was challenging, because of the waves and riptide.

Those of us staying in Rio, all flew to Buenos Aires after our three or four day stay, and as usual, were royally entertained by Standards' social schedule. A memorable night in Argentina, was attending an evening show influenced by, the haunting sound of their native accordion, which is called the Bandoneon, and the Tango couples dancing as one. One young blond lady in the cast, proved she could sing, dance, and play various musical instruments, all through the show, until the final act revealed that our talented actress, was in real life, actual identical twins. It was very clever and totally disguised, until the performers came out at the end of the show, with the twins appearing on stage at opposite ends to thunderous applause.

There are many beautiful statues and fountains in Buenos Aires, which have been desecrated by graffiti. This is done to mark gang territory, and is also obvious on many public buildings. Most statues have been donated by various other countries, and the joke was that, if a foreign country fell out favour with Argentina, the statue would be blown up, and replaced by a similar donation from another country.

The downtown streets are majestic and sometimes as much as 10 lanes wide. Gerry and I had to run really fast over those, before the traffic lights changed. One such run led as to a downtown square, where the Argentinian Government had constructed a commemorative wall, to remember those lost in the undeclared Falkland War of 1982. A battle over two British dependent territories in the South Atlantic. Argentina invaded the islands. The Brits responded by sending a naval task force to recover them. It was a short war, with the Brits claiming victory. 649 Argentinian and 255 British servicemen and women died, together with 3 Falkland Island civilians, during the 74- day conflict. War is war, but in this case, it was a stupid war. Margaret Thatcher enhanced her position and the popularity of her Conservative government by sending a task force, almost 11,000 kilometers. Argentina did not anticipate that the Brits would react. They were sadly wrong!

I recall Barbara Frum being hired by the CBC, to host the forerunner of The National on television, just as the war drums were sounding. The whole show, every night, was dominated by the Falkland happenings. A British nuclear submarine torpedoed an Argentinian light cruiser, called the General Belgrano, causing 323 deaths. The Argentinians replied, by hitting a British destroyer, HMS Sheffield, with an air force fired Exocet missile resulting in 20 deaths. The British were devastated, as the ship was crippled and eventually sank. The Brits lost several more ships to the Argentinian air force, but gradually gained the upper hand. Cooler heads prevailed and a peace, of sorts was finally negotiated.

The Falkland War commemorative wall referred to, was guarded by Argentinian soldiers, who did not look straight ahead, as the British ceremonial soldiers do, but they followed our every movement, in almost a threatening manner. Mind you, being sweaty and in shorts, did not really enhance our looks, or lighten their suspicions. We got out of their eyesight, as quickly as possible.

A more positive tourist option, was to view the spectacular opera house in Buenos Aires, including the below ground, maze of rooms, where the costumes and props for the various operas were kept. We then toured a local arts and crafts fair on a Sunday, which was shaped as a square, with an open area in the middle. Unknown to us, the tradition was to have around 40 or so of the opera company members come to the fair, dressed as locals. They suddenly burst out in song. No instruments, just the refined voices of these professionals. I have seen this done on television, but to experience it first hand, and be right in the middle of these professional singers was amazing.

We purchased a beautiful original painting at the fair, and have proudly displayed this in our homes, for over 25 years. It is simple, but effective, depicting a small courtyard with an outside staircase, leading up to a partial second story Spanish style dwelling.

An interesting out of town trip was to a ranch, to witness a day in the life of an Argentinian gaucho, who is defined as a skilled horseman, reputed to be brave and unruly, who takes care of cattle on the endless grasslands of Argentina. The South American version of our cowboy. Beef cattle is big business there, and they really are accomplished riders, with enormous skill at throwing the bolas and performing various precision drills, while riding bareback at breathtaking speed. The day ended with a barbecued side of beef on a revolving spit. The meat looked terrific, the volume of flies they allowed to alight on the beef, before the spit got going, not so good.

The highlight of the trip had to be the day we were flown to Iguazu Falls. This indigenous word means "big waters", and sums it up perfectly. The site of the falls is in Northern Argentina, bordering, Brazil and Paraguay. These falls are shaped as a staircase of two step, multiple waterfalls, which mainly drop into a narrow chasm, called the Devils Throat. The Iguazu River has a huge dam on it, which reputedly provides 40% of the power required by Argentina and Brazil.

Several of the group, including El, were not well that day, and declined the small boat trip to the edge of the falls. The water level and flow were low, but it did not deter some on the boat from screaming, as we approached the edge of one of the falls, which we observed later on, fell some 100 feet to the water below, and then dropped another 125 feet, to the Devils Throat chasm. The boat operator casually threw an anchor on a small island, several feet from where the water disappeared, and calmly explained the highlights of the falls, in broken English, while most of us on the boat stared, at what seemed "certain death" a few feet away.

The final night party and award presentations were enjoyable, and Standard again organized everything with class and precision. El and I left the next night to return, not home, but to Rio. We had booked an additional 5 days at a resort on the Atlantic, south of Rio, called Porto Gallo. Our flight arrived about midnight, and I think we were the only passengers to disembark, before it went onto Miami. Our luggage was not deposited on the carousel, and we spent 20 minutes worrying that it had not been taken off the plane. Finally, an airport employee found our bags elsewhere.

The cab ride to the downtown hotel, where we were to be picked up, was scary. Cars do not observe red lights in Rio after midnight. Probably because it is dangerous to be stopped in the dark. They slow up, maybe, and speed through the stop light. As we were being picked up at 6:00 a.m., the Scottish in me, elected that we spend the 4 hours or so, on the lobby furniture. The staff said, no problem, and immediately dispatched a number of cleaning staff to vacuum and clean around us forever, it seemed.

The driver assigned to pick us up, asked no questions and left the hotel, on finding out that we were not registered. The front staff did not try to contact us. I wondered why, but the answer came quickly. We were contacted by a young man, who offered to take us in his small car, which pulled a hand made trailer for the luggage. "It's a long way to Porto Gallo. Can I bring someone with me for company on the return trip?", he asked. We agreed and away we went. We soon found out that "the someone" was the love of his Latino life, and I had to remind him from time to time, to concentrate on his driving, and stop pecking her on the cheek. We arrived safely at the hotel and were impressed by its' height location overlooking the Atlantic, and the fact that other than "jungle", there was nothing else around as far as the eye could see. It was gated, with a guard on duty. This was truly Brazil!

Our first impressions were overwhelming. The music was blaring. The hotel was jumping. Drinks were on the house, courtesy of Cutty Sark, the Scottish whisky distributor. With the language difficulty, El and I were not aware, that this was a one night drop off point, in a leg of an around the Cape, ocean going yacht race. The party and excitement went onto late in the night. The next morning, we woke up to silence. Virtually everyone and the yachts were gone, leaving perhaps 30 hotel guests.

On the positive side for me, the social director had organized a soccer game for the remaining few male guests, most of whom were German or Argentinian. At age 54 I held my own, and then asked what we would be doing tomorrow. "Nothing, you are on your own", said the director. "My contract is finished and I am going home. This is now the slow season, with very few guests". It was the middle of March and at this latitude, their weather is equivalent to that in our September, and therefore their quiet season. The exception are Argentinians, who due to lower costs, find Brazil attractive, at all times of the year.

The hotel location was beautiful, but isolated. The beach could only be reached by a North American style chairlift, which ran continuously at slow speed. The beach was very short, with poor swimming capability. The other exit, from the hotel guarded gate, revealed a highway and jungle.

Most guests did not speak English. One lady kept saying "The water is very yellow". She meant warm! We sought space by booking snorkeling trips on the local yacht. Time to leave.

On the return trip to Rio, we were taken via a sister resort, called Porto Bello, to pick up other tourists. A name I am familiar with (Portobello), as it was a wave pool site outside of Edinburgh, attracting thousands including myself, every summer. Sean Connery was once a lifeguard there. Times change however, and the pool site has been closed, and the facility is now utilized for basketball and tennis courts. Although Porto Gallo was quiet, we were fortunate. The resort of Porto Bello, in Brazil, looks out onto an ugly part of the Atlantic, complete with a breakwater, and dockside tanks, for receiving oil, from unsightly rusted, offshore oil tankers.

Our trip home on an Aerolineas Argentinas 747 to Miami was noteworthy, in that there were only 12 passengers on board. We just outnumbered the crew, who were more interested in sleeping the trip away. If you wanted anything to eat or drink, other than hot food, you just helped ourselves. A strange way to end, what was probably the trip of a lifetime.

I returned home, to be assessed a 20% increase to our '94 new business target to $12.25 million credits, which was what we had achieved last year. Once again, the whole staff rallied, and we produced $13 million credits. The branch was firing on all cylinders. We had developed a swagger.

A short 2- day trip to a "Managers Skill Building" seminar in Montreal, allowed me to see other managers, but its' content did not impress me. I decided then, that "the bloom was somewhat off the rose" and that with a possible 40 years of service, I should be considering retiring in 1997. I was reading a John Buchan thriller entitled "39 Steps", and decided to use that title as a guide, and give my verbal notice 39 months, before an anticipated retirement in August of 1997. I communicated this verbally with Head Office officials, but no one believed me.

We managed once again, to go to Sarasota, late in the year. Gerry and Kathy Guilfoyle joined us for a few days, and El and I visited the Robertson couple, whom we had met in Switzerland in 1990. They had a beautiful house on Tampa Bay. The restaurant they took us to, was unique, in that once seated, you had the opportunity to visit a room off the kitchen, and pick out from a tank, the fish or lobster you wanted for dinner. Ordering dessert was from a telephone style cubicle on an upper floor, with the order placed by telephone, directly to the pastry department.

Our '95 Standard Stars trip was to Whistler B.C. We met the Guilfoyles, and drove there from Vancouver. On arrival, Gerry noticed that his wallet was missing. I know that sinking feeling, and after some retracing and phone calls, it still could not be found. We had parked the rental car in a nearby building, and I suggested we walk back, and search the vehicle again. There it was on the floor, tucked under the front seat. Thank you, Lord! We did a short jig together. What a relief! A special evening, was when for "the gala night", we were asked at the last minute to dress up. El did an amazing job of converting me to the Straw Man, and herself to the Wicked Witch, from the Wizard of Oz. Gerry and Kathy dressed as Elvis and Priscilla.

After the conference we met Maureen, and journeyed to Whidbey Island, in Washington to visit Ruth and Reidar for a few days. We took a ferry to Port Angeles, and then a Black Ball ferry to Victoria. The scenery in entering that harbour, and subsequent docking is magnificent. Supper that night, was on a hotel porch, overlooking the water, complete with an entertaining group of seals. The next night was at Painters Lodge, a lovely hotel. We had arranged through a Vancouver friend for a "conducted tour" of the forest the next day, and as we had to bring lunch, Maureen ordered, what turned out to be designer sandwiches, from the hotel.

Life can be full of misunderstandings. First of all, the "conducted tour", consisted of meeting a yellow school bus with about 25 grade 5s, and a teacher on board, to teach us as to what a forest has to offer. The second was Maureen's food order, which was plentiful, in that there was enough food for 6 of us. When we all sat down to lunch beside a lake, we the "adults" tried to isolate ourselves away from the hungry looks of the children, as we wolfed down our designer food. At the days' end, we had to all raise our hands on the bus, to answer the teacher's questions. I continually raised my hand, and was completely ignored. Her loss! Nah, nah, nah, nah, nah!

We continued on the next day, to drive on the only road, to the west side of Vancouver Island, stopping on route at Cathedral Grove in the MacMillan Provincial Park. A 157 hectare stand of ancient Douglas Firs, some of whom date back over 800 years and are 9 meters in circumference. Having reached the west side we walked on Long Beach, stopped at the famous Wickaninnish Inn, toured Tofino, which is noted for its' whale watching trips, and returned to Ucluelet for dinner on a docked ship, the Canadian Princess, complete with a restaurant. Ucluelet was stocked with beautiful art and jewelry. We were introduced on the ship, to Bumbleberry Pie as the dessert, which according to the staff, was first made available at a pastry shop in Victoria. We could not find the said shop, but it certainly is available in many restaurants and shops in Vancouver.

Our fall/winter trip to Siesta Dunes was shared with the Johnstons, and also involved the bother of splitting our time, between buildings 2 and 5. Larry had some business concerns which he would not reveal, and wanted to return early to Toronto. They had driven, and El volunteered her airline ticket, which he used to return with me. He was not questioned. You certainly cannot do that today. El drove home with Shirley, via a visit to the Hoffmans, in North Carolina.

September 2nd, 1995 was memorable, but in a very negative way. And now the story behind the story. The first world passenger commercial jetliner to take to the air, was the de Havilland DH 106 Comet, which was designed and built in Britain. Its maiden flight was July 28th 1949, and it actually only beat the inaugural flight of the Canadian designed and built Avro Canada C102 passenger Jetliner by a mere 13 days. As the British plane, which finally entered commercial service in 1952, the Comet became more popular, before a series of mechanical problems and structural failures, resulted in the loss of three aircraft within 12 months of entering service. Of course, more seriously, there was a loss of almost 100 passengers and crew, from these three incidents. As expected, the plane was grounded, mainly because of voiced public concern. Shades of the 2019 grounding of the Boeing 737 Max 8 planes, which even after U.S. FAA safety approvals, will in my opinion, have difficulty in winning back public confidence.

The structural failure problems were finally identified, by a series of studies in a water tank, using pressurized water to simulate the air pressure, that the jet was encountering at speed and altitude, never before experienced, by propeller driven planes. The study revealed that under these conditions, the plane structure was aging at a phenomenal rate, causing structural failure. One of the major changes recommended for future jet aircraft was the installation of viewing windows with rounded edges, as opposed to square windows, to lessen the effects of pressure on the cabin structure. The decision was finally made to abandon the Comet program as a passenger airliner, and its future was handed over to the Royal Air Force to further develop and reconfigure it, as a submarine hunter, with the revised name, the Hawker Siddeley Nimrod R1, or mighty hunter, which entered service in 1958.

And now, the rest of the story. The RAF agreed to the participation of one of their four engine Nimrods in the 1995 Toronto Airshow, to demonstrate the plane's ability to maneuver at low speed and low altitude, in carrying out its major purpose as a submarine hunter. As social members of the Boulevard Club, whose property sits adjacent to Lake Ontario, El and I had asked our Aurora neighbors, Ron and Fran Hine, to join us for lunch there and watch the show. Following lunch, we walked to the Club's boathouse structure next door, which afforded a better viewing.

I had the binoculars on hand, at the time the Nimrod was coming into view. The others were chatting, as I yelled and uttered these exact words "He's not coming out of that turn", as the plane plunged headlong towards the waters of Lake Ontario. The inquest determined pilot error, as the engines had stalled, due to an overly tight turn at low altitude. There was insufficient time to restart the engines, before the plane hit the water.

Following my alert, the four of us watched, as the plane almost elegantly slipped into the water. What followed, was a moment of disbelief and doubt, that we were actually witnessing a tragedy in real time. The mighty four engine Nimrod had entered the water, in a similar fashion to a high platform diver, with what seemed total grace and slow motion. The reality came seconds later, as the eerie silence was followed by a mighty roar, from the delayed effect of the plane making impact with the water, and the impact sound finally reached us. All seven crew members died. At our distant location, we could only imagine the mass confusion that followed, as we were left speechless, with only our individual thoughts and prayers!

We lost a close Ancaster neighbour, Bill Jopson, in March 1996. Bill was the quiet man in any conversation. A secret smoker, quietly accepting the scolding he would receive every so often from his wife June, for his bad habit. June's bark was really worse than her bite. Bill was simply a nice man. A jack of all trades. Happiest, when building or repairing something. El was out of the country, but I went to the funeral and delivered one of the eulogies, which I have included with these memoirs. Bill was deserved of having nice things said about him.

'96 saw El and I win yet another reward trip to the U.K. After the usual quality entertainment, tours and dining, we flew to Athens to spend the next 3 weeks touring much of Greece. We had arranged a 7- day cruise of the Greek Islands to visit Mykonos, Santorini, Rhodes, Ephesus in Turkey and the Isle of Patmos, where the disciple John was sentenced to isolation, and penned the Book of Revelation. The Greek ruins and artifacts are amazing. The only place in the world that trumps those holdings, is the British Museum in London. The Brits brought back treasure troves of Greek history, all illegally.

The cruise ship was small. Most of the tourists were Japanese, who were always first off, "en masse", ignoring all the instructions as to how to disembark, and continually getting on the wrong bus, of many that were parked dockside, to take groups on various tours. We left via Athens' port of Piraeus, which is now totally owned by the Chinese, who 25 years after we were there, are buying commercial and residential property in Athens at an astounding rate. Earlier, we had met a group of Chinese businessmen in Athens, who said they were in the oil business. I said, that being Canadian, we were also in the oil business (different oil). I probably was misunderstood, because I became an instant friend, complete with multi business cards from all twelve of them, and they wanted to take a photo of their group, with me in the middle. They insisted that El take the photo. Oops! Women were not high on the Chines pedestal in these days. And today?

Ephesus in Turkey is an amazing place to visit. The Greek ruins and history surrounding this former vibrant location are fascinating, especially when this is explained in detail by a guide. If you examine a map and refer to the New Testament in the Bible, and follow the exploits of the Apostle Paul, you will see where Ephesus sits in relation to all the various cities that Paul visited and wrote about, such as Laodicea, Pergamum, Smyrna and Philippi. It is a visit going back 2,000 years in time. Ephesus once, was a port city. You can see the water now, way in the distance!

Part of any tour, is the inevitable required commercial visit to a specialty store. We were bussed back to the Port of Kusadasi, where we bargained for, and purchased a beautiful leather jacket for Eleanor, with an agreed upon major discount in Turkish currency. When it came to the financial transaction, at the cash register location, which was on a different floor, the discount had "mysteriously" disappeared, but was reapplied after a short and crisp debate. A clerical error? Hmmm! You have to be on your toes, purchasing a product abroad, labelled in their currency, and then converted into Canadian dollars. You also have to be able to say, no. There were several tourists on our ship, as we sailed to our next destination, bemoaning the fact that they had been talked into purchasing carpets, which they now felt, they did not want or required.

Our return trip to Athens on the Aegean Sea was not pleasant. The seas were very rough, the evening entertainment was cancelled, and El and I were in bed, very early on. We survived and flew to the Island of Rhodes the next day. Our hotel, The Steppes of Lindos, was at the top of a hill overlooking the Mediterranean. The view was spectacular. A short walk down the hill, a painful walk without shoes on the pebbled beach, and then into warm water with a silky texture. Maybe it had too much sun lotion in it. It still felt good. The lounges complete with umbrellas appeared free, but as per the European custom, a fee was collected late in the afternoon.

A lady had lost her ring in the water, appeared quite upset, and swam up to me for assistance. I had noticed a young boy snorkeling nearby, and said I would ask him to help, but maybe she should find the top of her swimsuit, before he came by. He responded eagerly to my request, maybe because she had remained where she believed the ring was lost, and therefore not taken my dress code advice. I left them to their searching. European bathers like to travel light!

The hotel was fine, apart from the fact that only one other couple spoke, or wanted to speak English. After they left, we were on our own, "so to speak" or "not to speak". A further negative was the lack of air conditioning. Only available, in July and August, and at a higher room rate. We are blessed in North America.

To compensate, we left the front door of our suite open, to get what little breeze there was. The result was either a fat lip or a swollen eye in the morning, from the marauding mosquitos. One morning, we found a cat wandering about the room. You get, what you pay for!

There is an acropolis on Rhodes and some very interesting sites. Rhodes has a powerful history, in that folklore has it, that the total civilization of the island, was washed away by a gigantic tsunami, brought about by an earthquake, near the Island of Santorini, which sheared off a major part of the island, sinking it into the sea. The evidence of the damage and loss of land to Santorini is very visible. We drove to the west side of Rhodes, via the ring road and decided to come back directly, through the middle of the island. The "road" as such, was a dry creek bed, with most of the large rocks removed. A definite challenge for the suspension system of the rental car.

We were away 25 days in the 33rd year of our marriage and being Scottish, I labelled it our slightly delayed, 25th year anniversary celebration. Greece is special, and El and I both agree, that if you are interested in seeing the world, you absolutely have to visit and take in the majestic beauty of the Greek islands, enhanced by the contrasting colours of the clear light blue skies, the deep blue waters of the Aegean Sea, and the white washed island buildings.

Home for 5 months and then off to Arizona. The Guilfoyles joined us, and we stayed with the Smiths in Tempe. Gerry had just run the Toronto marathon, and was visibly showing the signs of every ache and pain throughout his body. We sympathized by driving to the Grand Canyon, spent a couple of hours there, and then drove to Sedona, to enjoy the comfort of a Guilfoyle timeshare. On the way, it started to snow and Kathy who likes to drive, turned the driving over to me, by exiting at a layby, and insisting that I take the wheel in these dangerous whiteout conditions. We no sooner got back on the freeway, than the snow stopped, the sun came out, and it was clear the rest of the way. Sorry Kathy!

We journeyed onto Tucson, and introduced the Guilfoyles, to the Tanque Verde horse ranch. We got sumptuous living quarters, for a very reasonable price. The accommodation consisted of wing suites, joined in the middle, with a living room, kitchen and dining area and a fabulous view of the nearby mountains. Gerry was a trooper, but his legs after his marathon run, did not appreciate being spread over the back of a horse. The after-ride photos, showed his clear discomfort.

We elected to spend New Years' in Vancouver, and were met by an extensive snow storm, which paralyzed the area. Maureen's driveway is not short, and her shovels not worthy. I believe that over a foot of snow fell, and Maureen insisted on climbing onto her roof, to clear the heavy snow from the roofs of the shed and her sunroom. The glass roof of the greenhouse did not survive.

My Mum was not feeling well, and Maureen, El and I, spent New Years' Eve of '96 in a restaurant. Maureen had developed laryngitis courtesy of snow clearing, and lost her voice. The three of us, conversed, by way of notes, passed back and forth. The waiting staff were at times confused, as to whether or not we could actually speak to them, or ask for our food in writing.

My mother's health was deteriorating. She had been diagnosed with a form of lung cancer, and the doctor indicated that give or take, she only had a few months left. El and I agreed that we should send the girls out to Vancouver, to say goodbye. Michele could not go, but using a movie camera, she made a beautiful DVD, featuring her family members in their country location, with a January snowfall adding to the scenery, their just purchased Christmas winter wear and their sleds, including a snowmobile.

Mum was impressed and especially with her 3 great grandchildren. But in true form, after 20 minutes of watching, turned to me and said "It's awfully long"!

Susan and Fiona went out to Vancouver, and regaled us with stories of washing and cutting Mum's hair, and of driving her Chevrolet Chevette all over the City. Mum had been given steroids by her GP, and she responded by barking at the girls, in her usual fashion, if things were not done properly. One such incident occurred in Stanley Park, when her wheelchair complete with oxygen tank, was allowed to roll somewhat down a hill, before being stopped. Fiona chauffeured, and recounted the story of driving into a Richmond full -service gas station and asking the staff to "fill her up". The fuel charge was less than $8. Mum's chevette, was not a gas guzzler. Although their visit was short, the girls and Mum, had shared a long lasting and precious memory.

El also went out to Vancouver, and I arrived shortly before the effects of the steroids subsided and Mum passed away. Her memorial service was held in Richmond, at the historic Chapel in The Park. The social following the service, was catered at Maureen's house. Both were extremely well attended, and went off without a hitch. Although, in the scramble to get back to Maureen's, both El and I were left at the Chapel, without transportation. This was noticed, eventually, and we were rescued after a short delay.

Mum had limited possessions, and the apartment where she and Ralph had lived in Vancouver, was rented. The apportioning of household items to surviving family members, can sometimes be somewhat cold, difficult and divisive. Maureen and I had no problems. Maureen, El and I, did also agree, to try very hard, to keep the family together, despite geography, and where possible, visit and vacation together. The 3 of us did keep this pledge, and in the years following, these words will testify to this fact.

Never physically strong, but mentally determined, Mum lived into her 84th year, despite being a lifetime smoker. She epitomized the 20th century; the hopes, the fears, the struggles brought on by world events, wars and everyday challenges. My short poetic testimony of her life is:

You lived a life, that was never free, of war, of peace, of victory.
You've seen it all, we can agree, the hopes, the fears, they're part of thee.
We salute you Mary, your strength, your brie,
you were, what we would want to be.

Having declared my intention to retire in '97, at the age of 57, the qualification for the Standard Stars conference at Niagara on the Lake, was to be my swansong. I was saddened by Mum's death, but not my decision. Forty years of service, still employed, and still being queried as to my decision to retire. Our branch target for '97 was $18.5 million production points, and although I was not physically the manager at year end November 15, we ended up the year accumulating $23 million production points. I was blessed to have my career end on a high note!

The Niagara hotel was quality, but the food was lacking. The ownership was now in the hands of an Asian lady, who decided, that all guests must now be nourished on Asian food. Where's the beef? It was fun to see the speed with which a plate of pre- dinner chicken appetizers evaporated.

An infamous outing was a boat trip on the Niagara River, to view the whirlpool and run the rapids, which are rated 5 plus, and are therefore too dangerous for white water rafting. The boat held about 50 passengers, mostly Standard staff and spouses, and we were suitably dressed, to allow water to pour in and out of portholes, on the sides of the boat, as it pitched up and down. As the boat descended in the rapid, the operator would "gun" the engine, and we would come shooting back up. As the boat descended on one rapid however, there was a thunderclap right above us, whose noise echoed scarily throughout the river canyon. It was accompanied by a hailstorm which showered down large pebbles of hail, pounding our heads and arms, as we held on to the rails in front of us.

It was June! Where did this freak storm come from? Due to the horrendous thunderclap, and sudden downpour, the boat operator must have frozen for an instant, and instead of riding the rapids up, we appeared to be still descending, as in the mode of a submarine dive. Screams of fear, echoed throughout the boat, and the operator snapped out of his shock, and we shot back up again. It was an amazing ride, which most of us, would not want to duplicate, but which we proudly had to broadcast that evening, to those who had tried other activities, during the day. "Did you hear about….."?

The closing Standard Stars dinner, was memorable for me. As usual, I was prepared to say a "few words", especially as Scott Bell, our now world- wide General Manager (President), was in attendance. Scott and I had come full cycle in those 40 years, from young lads, who had drunk beer together and played soccer for Standard Life in Edinburgh. Mind you, he was then quite young, but a determined mind from Falkirk, who was to qualify as an Actuary, and achieve a notable position, as world- wide General Manager, of a huge financial institution. Scott and I were not close, but I like to think that we respected one another. There appeared to be some hesitation about my speaking, but "somebody" intervened, and I gave what I considered as an entertaining, but poignant speech. At least two people came up to me afterwards and congratulated me. Out of 125 attendees, that's not bad!

We continued our tradition of going to Siesta Key in late October, but this time we took Susan and Mike's daughters, Melissa and Danielle. Fiona and Bruce came along as "sitters". The girls really enjoyed their time there, especially in the pool. They were not beach lovers. The energy they expended, was frightening. At dinner one evening, a couple congratulated us, on having such lovely and well- behaved grandchildren. The truth was, that they could hardly stay awake. They left after a week and the Guilfoyles joined us, for the rest of the vacation.

As of August, '97, I was approved by Standard Life, to assume an in- house pension consulting role, to look after the many Defined Benefit pension corporate clients, serviced by our Toronto office. Our professionals in Montreal, provided the necessary actuarial, administrative and employee statements required by these clients. My role was to present and explain these, and to assist them with their day to day questions., and servicing. All of my services were provided at $120 per hour, with 50% of the fees going to Standard. My billing target was easily makeable and I would average 1000 hours per year for the next 9 years. We expanded our professional services during this time period, headed by a new employee Kurt Dreger, assisted by our daughter Susan Hamelin, who after my retirement, was granted deservedly so, a full- time permanent position.

1998, brought the first full year in 4 decades, that I was not at my desk by 8:00 a.m. I had been given an office, a parking spot, and the availability to have steno assistance when necessary. We of course were now in the computer age, and I really was able to self- manage, with no reporting or assistance necessary. What a treat! I just had to avoid giving advice to any of my former staff. The branch problems were now the responsibility of someone else. Call it luck, reasonably good management, or the Lord looking after me, I was at the helm of the Toronto Pension Office, for 16 years. During the next 9 years, that I was there in a consulting role, we had 4 managers. Still having the management role inside of me, I wondered how much that had cost Standard Life.

For a change, we planned to vacation in Mexico, on the Mayan Riviera, but had to cancel our plans, because of Mum Storey's ill health. After her recovery from a stay in a Peterborough hospital, El felt it would be better, if we moved her, to a location nearer to us. The sale of her house in Peterborough, certainly gave us the funds, to make this move possible.

El found a retirement home in Aurora, not far from our Murray Drive residence. Unlike most seniors, who strongly resist such a move, Mum Storey did not object with much vigor, and the move went off without a hitch. The home was close by, and was also located on Murray Drive.

We moved her on a Friday. I know, because at 9:00 a.m. on Saturday morning, the front door bell rang. I yelled out, "El, it's your mother". Mum Storey said only one thing. "That was a long walk". What I thought next is not important! There never was another "long walk", as her legs said, that this would not happen again. She settled in. It was a quality residence with good staff, and good living and social quarters. She was very happy there for the next 5 years, and with us being so close, made it even better, for more frequent visits, to look after her needs and solve her problems, such as her TV remote, which she managed to discombobulate at least 3 times a week.

On reflection, many of these pages suggest, that most of my life was spent on vacation, with some work thrown in along the way. Possibly true, but when I was at work, the hours were long and I probably did not give as much of my time, as I should have, to help El raise the children. But she did a good job! The proof of this, is the longstanding close relationships we have had, and continue to have with them.

I made a point of being available, during North American vacations, to talk with staff members twice a week, and during emergencies. To compliment them, my words of wisdom were rarely required! I also continued to run 3 km, at least 3 times a week, and therefore was in reasonably good shape in my 50's. I was not yet aware of the health trials ahead of me. My eventual motto was "to get in shape for the next operation". But now, it is time to reflect on the next vacation!

We rebooked Mexico, late October '98, for a 2 week stay in the Mayan Riviera, in a hotel called Playa. Fiona and Bruce joined us. We arrived October 24, and were flown back October 28, because of the danger posed by Hurricane Mitch and its' 300 kph winds. The Mexicans prepared for this in orderly fashion. We were moved from the ground to the second floor of the hotel. All windows were covered with sheets of clean plywood. The palm trees on the beach were roped together, and newly planted palms were dug up, wrapped and laid on the ground. The pool furniture was stacked together and lowered into the deep end of the pool. Had they seen this before? Oh, yes, they were prepared.

With the knowledge that our stay might be short, the German tourists mobbed the bar, and drank all the beer. The Brits received a promise to be flown home, by the British Air Force. The Americans were reassured that the 6th fleet was on its way, and would have their back. The joke was, that each Canadian would receive a postcard from the prime minister, saying "have a nice vacation". In the end, our tour company realized the seriousness of the situation, and dispatched 3 planes to the area. With a warning, not to miss the pre-arranged pick up at our hotel, we were hurriedly loaded onto the planes in Cancun, without seat allocation, and set off for Toronto.

All went smoothly and we were brought home safely. It was interesting to be part of a convoy of 3 planes in the sky, visible at times, to each other. Were El and I, once again being shown a path to safety in our life's journey? I recall being on the beach in Playa, the day before we were evacuated, with the leading edge of the hurricane, still well over 150 miles away, and experiencing even then, the force of the wind gusts.

"Mitch" did not reach Mexico, but it did turn into the second deadliest Atlantic hurricane on record. It did an abrupt turn in the Gulf, and slammed into Honduras, Guatemala and Nicaragua. It had become a category 5 hurricane. In essence the worst of the worst. Over 11,000 persons died as a result of "Mitch", and the flooding that followed, caused by an estimated 75 inches of rainfall. There were so many missing persons in underdeveloped places, that the true death toll will never be known. Wind gusts exceeded 325 kph. It destroyed hundreds of thousands of homes and has been deemed the deadliest hurricane, to hit the Western Hemisphere in more than 200 years. The total damage cost was estimated at over $6 billion. To this day, I do not believe, that we truly understood the danger that we, and the locals were possibly in, and we were selfishly more focused on the inconvenience, of our vacation being cut short.

To close out 1998, with a bang, Susan gave birth to Taylor, our sixth grandchild, on December 06.

1999 dawned, and the rumours and speculation started. At year end, we would be entering a new century. How would the tools of technology react? Would computers shut down on the stroke of 01.01.2000. Would the banking system, as we knew it, become paralyzed? To us today, this fear mongering may sound silly. But, believe me, the concerns then were real, and huge amounts of money were spent, preparing options for damage control, in the event systems crashed.

To show how concerned El and I were, we picked up the cancellation option from the cut short '98 vacation in Mexico, and headed for the Hotel Iberostar, which we had seen and admired on our last shortened visit, this time hopefully for a full 2 week stay. The hotel of these days was different. The Mayan Riviera was in its infancy of being developed, and our accommodation was truly in a jungle setting, with flamboyant spoonbills and flamingos all around, and spider monkeys in the trees, reaching down to your porch, for handouts of food. It was so, "au naturel".

Swimming, sunbathing and eating, were the strenuous exercises of the day. We also took walking and cycling trips to Playa Del Carmen, the local small town, and to Xcaret which is a wonderful entertainment park and zoo, with local birds, sea life and wildlife, offering insight into Mexican historical culture. This was topped, by an evening show, performed by all the people, who served and entertained you, during the day. Peso for peso, it has to be, among some of the best entertainment value, we have ever purchased. Don't miss it, if you visit the Mayan Riviera.

We also wanted to see the historic Mayan ruins at Chichen Itza. The bus trip is too long, and we chose to fly from Playa. The prop plane flew initially, to the Island of Cozumel, perhaps to pick up other passengers, or to refuel. We had to disembark, and were led into the terminal, to a glass partitioned area, which separated us from other flight passengers. I was in conversation with an American tourist, who had volunteered that he was a glass contractor.

Looking out on to the tarmac, we noticed a jet passenger plane start its engines, to taxi away from the terminal. It was noticeable, because the plane was facing out towards the runway, and not in the traditional push back position. The plane started to move, and when the pilot tried to make a 90- degree turn, he revved the engines, and the sudden blast, blew out all the terminal glass windows in its path. Luckily, we were one section over, and missed the flying shards of glass hurtling through the air. The contractor turned to his wife, and simply said, "Wrong glass!" Thank you, Lord! It would have been a disaster, if our group had been directly behind the windows affected. We saw the plane continue to taxi toward the runway, and majestically take off. I wondered aloud, if any lawsuits had already been filed.

We flew on to Chichen Itza, a preserved Mayan township in Mexico, dating back to 1000 A.D., and landed on a sun baked, dried up river bed, with earth walls on either side, just barely offering room for the wings. This was the airport runway. This is Mexico! Most rivers are underground in this part of Mexico, but the landing strip, if not an old riverbed, sure mirrored one, with the odd patch of asphalt, sprinkled around to harden the ground. Chichen Itza is a wonderful site, especially when you are informed by a local guide, as to the symbolic use and nature of the designs, of the various buildings and their intricate carvings. The main attraction there is the Castillo Pyramid, 100 feet high, steep, but at the time climbable, even though it dates back over 1000 years. In its days, Chichen Itza was the powerful regional capital of the Northern and Central Yucatan Peninsula. The site, also has many Cenotes, (deep sink holes with fresh water), which in parts of Mexico have been turned into tourist attractions, for exploration and swimming. Mayan history suggests, that the cenotes here, were used initially, and they stress, only many, many years ago, as locations for sacrifices to the "gods".

The site also contains the Great Ball Court (over 500 feet long and over 200 feet wide). We sat and watched a game called the Mesoamerica ballgame at one of the smaller ball courts, in which the opposing teams try to put a large rubber ball through stone hoops (rings) attached to the side walls of the ball court, using their hips. Yes, their hips! The walls are vertical on each side and the floor then slopes down from each wall, to the flat area of the court. The participants are talented, and their ability to "hip" that ball so close to, or through these rings, is quite amazing and entertaining. Mexico is just not, luxury hotels, sunshine and beaches. We will go back to the Yucatan Peninsula, and in particular the Mayan Riviera, but we will witness a deterioration of the natural, to provide for the lure of the many. We experienced the best of the best in the '90s.

We were then invited by Tom and Eleanor Beckett to join them and other former Unionville neighbours in April, to a vacation in Nerja, a small coastal town in the southeast of Spain. Tom, in his art gallery ownership position, had assisted an Ottawa art dealer, who in turn, offered him a two week no cost vacation at his condo, in Nerja, on the Costa Del Sol. Seven of us were included in the invite.

To further enhance the experience of being in Spain, and therefore to extend the vacation, El and I signed up with Brian and Rosemary Burley, also ex Unionville neighbours, to join a bus touring group labelled The Highlights of Spain, which toured the major cities of Spain to the south, and would immediately follow our stay in Nerja. We were to be away 25 days. A memorable holiday was coming up.

We flew from Toronto to Montreal, to Madrid, to Malaga. A total of 21 hours. Oh, to be young again! I met Claude Garcia, a former Standard Life president, at the Toronto airport, as we were about to leave. When asked where, and how long we would be away, he immediately quipped, on hearing the length of our vacation and destination, "I was obviously paying you too much!"

A van had been rented, and was awaiting our arrival at Malaga airport, with another car and two car rental employees, who had to handle the overflow of luggage for 7 persons, staying 2 weeks. El, Rosemary and myself, had obtained international driving licenses, to handle the necessary driving, while we were there. We however, had not counted on all 7 of us, being "backseat drivers, who all knew best". After multi comments and criticism the ladies said no thanks, and I was appointed by default, to drive. We started out for the one- hour drive to Nerja, to a chorus of, "turn right, no left, no straight ahead". We circled the airport twice to the waves and whoops, from other passengers, standing at the terminal doors, as they awaited their rides. I finally got it right, and we were on our way, as peace and quiet, descended on the vehicle.

The condo was on a hill and due to recent heavy rain, there was some water on the ground floor level and basement, including bedrooms. The Becketts of course got to stay upstairs, and because I was now the designated driver, El and I got the remaining upstairs bedroom. Nerja, is a small tourist loaded community, serviced by multi restaurants. Luckily, we had a list of these, and their locations. As I ran every day, I would select a name and address, check out the local map and run to that location. At night, following my notes, the drive was easy, and the group would wonder at my accuracy, at getting them there. One run proved more difficult, because, as

I turned a blind corner, I found myself smack in the middle of a funeral, complete with mourners, a donkey pulled cart, and of course the coffin. Removing my hat, and ignoring the puzzled glances, from the mourners, I managed to eventually glide off into a nearby lane.

Every second day, we drove to a local tourist highlight, such as the caves at Nerja, Frigiliana (a cobbled hillside village), and Granada, to experience the Alhambra Palace and Fortress, dating back to the year 900 A.D. Alhambra, means "The Red One", after the reddish colours of the earth used to construct the outer walls. It was the royal court of Queen Isabella 1 of Castile, the first Queen of Spain, and Ferdinand 11 of Aragon, who gave their blessing and "money", to fund the Columbus expedition of 1492. This led to the opening of the New World, and probably paid off handsomely for them, as it established Spain as a global power, which dominated Europe and most of the world, for more than a century. The royals are better known, for completing the "Reconquista", which entailed the conversion or exile of their Muslim and Jewish subjects. This was 15th century Catholicism. On a positive note their places of worship were not destroyed.

Our trips to the sea, included the beach at Burriana, and the Balcon de Europa, a viewpoint, giving stunning views across the Mediterranean, where Napoleon is believed to have decided, that all he could see from there, would be part of his empire. On the more practical side, we had a pizza lunch there one day, served on a burning hot metal stand, which kept the pizza hot outside through the whole meal, and is an idea that should be adopted in North America.

Our trip to the gorge at Ronda was memorable, because we chose to have lunch at the Parador de Ronda hotel, part of a state- run hotel chain, perched on the edge of the gorge, very expensive and just a high- class place. The lunch menu, was a fixed 3 course midday meal, and not cheap. Our Ontario fellow tourists totally ignored this, and started to order customized meals.

"Salad only. I'll have the soup. What sandwiches do you have?" Spain is not North America. The beautifully dressed Spanish waitress was to say the least, confused and flustered. She rushed off to seek her manager, while we continued to tear the menu apart, a la North American style. Bless him, without hesitation, the manager authorized our custom meals. Now when Brian Burley, heard our orders, and that the pricing was now somewhat limited, he immediately chipped in with, "This one is on me". I so wanted to change my order.

Nerja, is known for its caves. They were discovered in recent modern times by 5 friends, just poking around. This occurred in 1959, and although they are deemed a national treasure, they have also brought enormous wealth to the Nerja area, due to tourism. They stretch underground for 5 miles, and a walk through is fairly extensive, complete with commercial purchases for this and that. They are so large, that concerts can and are held in one of the chambers, which is formed perfectly into a natural amphitheater.

I was not aware that our host Tom Beckett, was subject to bouts of depression. It happened just before they were due to return to Toronto. We arrived in Malaga, to find that the scheduled flight to Toronto, that the Becketts, and June Jopson were booked on via Madrid, had left. The next flight was due out the next day. I spoke with Iberia Airlines staff, explaining Tom's dilemma, and with only a short delay they transferred the Becketts and June, to a flight bound for Toronto, via London England, without any cost differential.

The Burleys and ourselves left a little later for Madrid, to meet our guide Elinor, for the 10- day bus tour of Spain. We were on our own for dinner that night, and wandered to a restaurant called El Pardo. We arrived about 7:00 p.m., to a locked door, which was finally answered by the owner. "You must be from North America. No Spaniards eat this early." He let us in and served us the special for that day, Wild Boar with prunes. It was delicious. As we were finishing our meal, about 9:00 or so, the locals, with their young children were filing in. A different world!

Our tour took in Zaragoza, Barcelona, Peniscola, Valencia, Granada, Alhambra, Seville, Cordoba and back to Madrid. A truly amazing trip. Some highlights were, the Mosque in Cordoba, the organized tour of the

Alhambra, the flamenco nightclub show in Seville, the tour of the Palace in Madrid and the tour of the Museo del Prado, the famous museum in Madrid. I did not get to see Barcelona or Real Madrid soccer games. It probably was not on the tour! Nor was there time.

We did however purchase a print called "Las Meninas", which depicts the ladies in waiting and the daughter of King Philip 1V of Spain. It was painted by Diego Velazquez in 1656, and shows the child, Margaret Theresa, and parents (reflected in a mirror), and their entourage of maids of honour, and dwarfs, that were purposely hand- picked to be equal in height with, and not dominate the children.

It was a quality trip in every sense, with the bonus of being introduced to the various cultures, that dominate the makeup of Spain. The Spaniards are loyalists to their various geographical locations. The Basques have emphasized this in the past, and recent events in and around Barcelona have brought this to the fore. I recall being in a restaurant, explaining to a waiter, that we were from Canada, to be greeted by him, yelling at the top of his voice that, "He was from Sevillia"! It was scary.

Fiona and Bruce were married on May 15. The wedding ceremony was held in the basement of our Aurora home. Family members, Els' mum and Maureen attended. All went well. The only humerous incident I can attest to, was at the wedding dinner in our favourite Aurora restaurant named Joia, where a family member of Bruce, insisted that he have thousand-island dressing on his salad. But its Caesar salad sir, the waiter said. Funnily enough the waiters' name was Caesar. The guest prevailed and the "mixed" salad was served. Later that month we enjoyed a weekend, at the Guilfoyles cottage.

With our connection and love of the West, still being strong, we organized a trip to Vancouver in August, which on reflection at the time, seemed like a farewell trip to visit friends that we might never see again. Collected at the airport by Maureen, we had dinner with her long- term friend and mentor Kay Liss, and then drove to Whidbey Island in Washington State, to spend 2 days with Ruth and Radar Nordhoy, and their loveable dog,

Rusty. Then we took the ferry from Port Townsend, to Port Angeles, to Vancouver Island, to visit Els' aunt Ollie and her husband Jim, a very good amateur painter, in Parksville. From there, we went by ferry to Salt Spring Island, to visit Bob and Judith Young, our former Calgary neighbours. I climbed the 1200 feet of Mt. Erskine with Bob, to view the many little fairy villages, that he has secretly built on the mountain. Please note the word secret! You can refer to The Fairy Doors of Salt Spring Island on the internet. Just do not share what you have learned here.

From there, we visited Maureen's friends, Maureen and Peter Rowell. Then onto another ferry, from Swartz Bay, back to the mainland terminal at Tsawwassen, to visit Els' close friend Sylvia Loutit, who was celebrating her 60th birthday. The next day, we had dinner with Brian and Rosemary Burley (Spain partners), at their beautiful home perched on a hill overlooking Horseshoe Bay in North Vancouver. The following day, as pre- arranged, I met Bob Young and we climbed the Grouse Grind in North Vancouver, in a time of 53 minutes and 56 seconds. Not a world record, but not bad for an almost 60 year- old. The "Grind" as it is known, is a local and tourist highlight climb, which takes you on an "au naturel" vertical pathway, over tree roots and loose earth "free of charge", to the top of Grouse Mountain. The alternative is to pay for the ski lift. I will take the alternative from now on.

We visited my cousin Kathleen, and her husband Graham, an ex- fire captain and nice man. Due to a major fall and head wound, Kathleen is both physically and mentally challenged. Graham has given most of his life to look after her at home. Today she is in a facility, that can look after her, and Graham can now pursue a more normal life. I played soccer for Peebles Rovers and we were drawn against Hibs of Edinburgh in a Scottish Cup game in 1959 or 1960. We lost 9 goals to 1. Graham said he was at that game and did not remember me, but thought that our team was rubbish. Nice going Graham!

Our next step, was a "free" ride in a balloon in the Fraser Valley, courtesy of a gift Maureen had received. It was only for two and El, who has not forgotten, was not included. The pilot said at the time he was a pilot for

Wardair, and based on the speed of the wind, and the number of power lines, his expertise was welcome. There were 6 of us plus the pilot. It was extremely windy, and the pilot was having trouble finding a suitable landing spot. Every balloon has a chase car, to collect and bring the passengers and equipment back to their base. Therefore, any landing site must allow access to the chase car, that is in frequent radio communication with the pilot.

The pilot found what he thought was a suitable site, and started to descend. Only to be greeted by a man, bursting out of his small house, complete with shotgun, pointed upwards towards us. He yelled "You are not landing that blankety, blankety thing on my property". The pilot applied a short burst of hot air and we soared up and away, in search of another, perhaps less hostile landing spot.

One of our fellow passengers, was an obnoxious realtor, who Maureen and I thought was continually rude to his lady friend. When we finally landed, the basket was dragged onto its side, and we spilled with it. Both Maureen and I made sure, that we landed on top of "nasty", with sharpened elbows at the ready. As we lay there, an old woman came out of a nearby small hut, located on the side of the field, and sauntered over to question, where we had come from. I believe that Pluto or Venus, was on her mind.

There are 2 noticeable things when you are ballooning. Silence from below, which is only challenged by the hot air being released to keep you afloat, and now and again, the sound of dogs barking. They do not like hot air balloons, and in fact are so intimidated, that they go berserk, jumping in circles, until the balloon moves on.

Our return to Vancouver ended with visits with Doug and Joan McArthur, Ron Moir, the Cartmells, the Scharfes, and a final dinner at Jericho, Maureen's tennis club. It seemed that we packed a lifetime of activities and visits into a short 2- week period. We were afraid to say that we might not be back, but on reflection, if we did return, we would not try to duplicate the energy expended on this trip.

Tom Jepson's son, Kenneth, whom he championed as an NHL hockey prospect, married Jane in September. Kenneth was a very talented hockey player, but unfortunately topped out at about 5 foot 7 inches, and a professional career in ice hockey as harboured by his dad, was apparently dashed. El enjoyed a Women's Aglow conference in Orlando in November, and while she was away, I went to the Royal Winter Fair with the Hamelin family. Melissa and Danielle, found the animal side of the fair to be a bit messy, and not in the least fitting with their ladylike thoughts of a suitable outing, and we quickly moved to the rides and the fairgrounds.

Our late fall trip, was to Texas. We stayed in a Houston airport hotel overnight, to await Fiona's arrival on a later flight. We then drove to Fredericksburg, to meet up with Frank and Francine Simpson, whom we had met on our trip through Spain. They had a beautiful ranch style home, with a magnificent open view over a valley. U.S. President Lyndon Johnson and Ladybird Johnson had an original 800 - acre ranch in the area, only about 25 or so miles, from the Simpsons' location. All the roads in and around Fredericksburg were very well paved.

The Simpsons' history was interesting. Francine's first husband was the commander of a U.S Navy submarine, and when he died from cancer in his 50's, Francine, after an appropriate time, married Frank, who was divorced, but well known to her, as he was her first husband's, second in command, on the submarine. Francine is talkative and gregarious. Frank is quiet, but a man who you grow to like and trust.

After his retirement from active service, Frank became very involved in the National Museum of the Pacific War in Fredericksburg, which honours Admiral Nimitz of the U.S. Pacific fleet, and the sailors and staff he commanded, during the 2nd World War Pacific battles against the Japanese. We have stayed in contact and met with the Simpsons, as they travel extensively in the U.S.A. and Canada. Maureen, met and entertained them in Vancouver, as they returned from an Alaska tour.

The three of us left Fredericksburg, for a stay at the Flying L guest ranch, in Bandera Texas. This area is known as Hill Country and is the origination area, of the famous cattle drives from Texas to the U.S. north east, before rail and road transportation. On arrival the social director asked if we were "TLW's". "What does that mean?", I asked. The staff member said he would let us know tomorrow. The next day, he clarified the meaning as, "Texas Lottery Winner". All such winners over the last number of months, had been invited to the ranch, for professional financial counselling, long-term investment advice and prudent care of their recent winnings. Most folks around us were really happy. I wonder why?

We took a side-trip from the ranch, to San Antonio to view the famous Riverwalk, and to watch a movie of the Alamo, provided free for tourists. Both were so interesting, that we vowed that we would go back. Our next day ride, was to be in the state park with a guide. The horses had to be trucked over to the park, which offers miles and miles of free -range riding and rivers to cross. A lady by the name of Rebecca Culbertson, asked if she could join us and the three of us had a wonderful exciting ride, allowing us to say "Yee ha", for the first time on the ranch. To show appreciation Rebecca asked if we would join her and her husband Frank, for a pre-dinner drink the next day.

Frank preferred golf to riding and joined us, after his round. As per normal, I quizzed him as to where he worked and what he did. Houston and the aero industry, were his abbreviated answers. "In the engineering field", I asked. "No, more to do with the flying", he replied. "You are a pilot", I countered. "Do you test planes?", I pressed. "I guess, I do, but the ones that go a bit higher", he stated. I paused, "Frank, are you an astronaut?", I stuttered. "Yes" was the reply. "Have you been to the space station?" "Not yet", he replied, "However I am going to Russia next year, to learn Russian and to meet the Russian cosmonauts, that are going up with me in 2001".

How amazing was that encounter, and how low key can you be? The only memento I have, is the NASA pin he gave me the next day. But I have the memory. Frank Lee Culbertson Jr, was selected as a candidate for the Astronaut program in 1984 at the age of 35, having been a navy pilot for many years. He had logged over 8,900 hours flying time in 55 different types of aircraft and had made 450 carrier landings. He has since spent over 146 days in space and served as Commander of the International Space Station for 129 days in 2001, with his 2 fellow Russian cosmonauts, and in essence, was the only American not on the planet, during the 2001, nine eleven terrorists attacks on the twin towers in New York. He is now retired from what became a later role, as President of the Space Systems Group, at Northrop Grumman Innovation Systems.

We took Fiona, back to Houston airport, as her stay was over, and headed back to the ranch. We however, stayed overnight in San Antonio, and watched the River Walk boat parade. This is held over the Christmas season, which they have determined, starts with the American Thanksgiving Holiday. A never- ending procession of boats, highly decorated with Christmas lights, pass through the downtown tourist core, already decorated with 100,000 lights. It was quite the sight.

I recall we two Canadians, standing among thousands of Mexicans, enjoying the parade. The Latino population of San Antonio is huge. That night, after asking re a suitable spot for dinner, we were directed to The Little Rhino Steakhouse, by bicycle riding police, as "the place to go in town". Because of the river network, police cars in this area, are not practical. It was a pretty posh place, and when I ordered a reasonably priced bottle of red wine, which was probably the lowest cost bottle, and was actually numbered 365, on the hard- covered wine list, the waiter in as loud a snooty voice as possible, said "Oh, we are having the Chilean tonight. Excellent choice". Grrrr.

We returned to the Flying L. ranch for 4 more days. Again, we preferred the additional cost state park rides, to the normal rides, which due to many young novice riders, were slow and involved multiple "potty breaks", where the horse stops to pee. Horses are very fussy about peeing, including coming to an abrupt halt, and the spreading of the legs. They do not stop, when they are pooing, and create no fuss what so ever. You explain the difference! It must all be in keeping the legs dry! We returned home without incident. Although, I did mislay my reading glasses at the ranch, and my hat on the airport bus, returning from the rental car location. Both were recovered, after some anxious moments.

As '99 drew to a close, there was a fair amount of nostalgia about the closing of 20th century memories, and a wondering about the dawning of a new century and what lay ahead. Maureen arrived for a 2- week break, to participate with the family in Christmas celebrations, Coyle traditions and the New Year fellowship that we had planned.

We celebrated a traditional family Christmas dinner at home. Then Maureen joined Susan and Fiona for dinner downtown, on December 29th at La Fenice Ristorante, followed by the show Needfire, a Celtic Celebration of song and dance. For New Years' Eve, the "three amigos" went for dinner downtown at Il Fornello, and from there we attended a Roy Thomson Hall special presentation, to close out the 20th century. This was a New Years' Eve concert featuring multi Canadian Tenor talent. The only talent missing was Ben Hepner. We never found out why, unless he perhaps was still having vocal- chord problems. The night was not over. We then drove to the Cricket Club, having accepted an invitation from Gerry and Kathy Guilfoyle, to celebrate and bring in the New Year with them.

It was a memorable evening, lasting almost 10 hours. And guess what! Computers and systems did not crash, and the sun came up the next morning, right on cue. Happy New Year and welcome to the year 2000, and a brand- new century. Maureen left for Vancouver on January 3rd, fairly exhausted.

What could we do to top our end of the century activities? First of all, I started a brand- new tradition, by attending the first Burns Supper dinner and entertainment evening, to be held at the Old Mill in Toronto. I had met a fellow by the name of Gordon Hepburn through the years, by attending various Burns Supper evenings, throughout the city with Jeff Gray. Gordon, was the Canadian G.M. of Thomas Cook Travel, a well-travelled man, a Burns fanatic, a scotch lover, and a great M. C. at these evenings. He had now settled for the Old Mill, as a preferred place to celebrate January 25th, and Jeff and I obediently followed. It was certainly classier, than prior locations we had been to, and I wanted El and some family members to experience this at subsequent gatherings.

We wanted to make contact again with some U.S. couples that we had met through the years. We called the Robertsons in South Carolina, the Hoffmans in North Carolina, and the Purkeys in Connecticut. We made positive contact with all three couples, and planned the trip accordingly, but starting in Nashville, which we both had wanted to experience. We were going to squeeze a considerable amount of driving, visiting and entertainment, into a short 2- week April/May, 2000 period.

We started, by finding a neat restaurant in Tipp City, Ohio called the Coldwater Café, which we have consistently visited on each subsequent road trip's first night, on the way to a Sarasota vacation. The restaurant was a former bank and you can eat in the vault, if you like thick wall enclosure and heavy doors. Onto Nashville, and a stay at the Opryland Hotel, which is basic, but is only one of many buildings and shops in a completely covered huge block long dome structure. The restaurant we ate at in the dome, was 3 or 4 stories in the air, and looked down on the pedestrian traffic below in a climate- controlled dome setting.

We did the tourist thing with a bus trip, to visit highlights, including the Ryman Auditorium, which was the original theatre used by the Grand Ole Opry. We then had great seats, at the Grand Ole Opry House to watch Little Jimmy Dickens, Vince Gill, Amy Grant and many other talents. It began as a live music radio show dating back in 1925. The producers were initially concerned, that it would not be accepted by the listening audience, because its' time slot, was preceded by serious symphony music. They, therefore used the name Opry as a play on words, in the hope that listeners would initially interpret the content as being operatic, and continue listening.

On to Bluffton, South Carolina, to meet with Luellen and Doug Robertson, who we had met and befriended in Austria. They had recently moved from Tampa, and we were not sure of their exact location. The good Lord, put Luellen right beside us, as she arrived at a service gas station, shortly after we pulled in. We followed her, to their magazine trophy house by the river, leading out to the ocean. The only drawback to their location, was that there were gators lurking in the water, just 10 feet below their elevated walkway, which ran from the house, out to their gazebo.

Doug was now in the land development business, having been "retired" from his Pepsi sales management position in South Florida. I believe, that Luellen's parents had left this South Carolina land to them, and they were intent on developing it, for a new residential sub division. I had specifically asked them, where we should park on their extensive driveway, but Doug with business thoughts distracting him, still managed to hit our car, which was parked well away from their house.

An estimator was called and a sum of $700 U.S. was paid to us, which turned out to be right in line, with the ultimate repair bill at home. Our future relationship was never the same. The car accident, their business development plans, Doug's health, something we said? We will never know. I do know, that before leaving the area, we purchased a gift to thank them for their hospitality, and left it at the house. We will never know, but sadly a last conversation with Luellen, about a year later, was short, and not so sweet. I do not look at myself as being biased, but my experience in life has been, that friendships with Canadians, are more binding, and long lasting, than with Americans. We Canadians, appear to be more trustworthy and not suspicious of motives. Americans tend to be continually on guard and wary of one's intentions!

The next stop was Charlestown, North Carolina, to meet up with our former Unionville neighbours, the Hoffmans. Unfortunately, Rolland, who is a C.G.A., was out of town on an audit. As a member of the local golf club, Quail Hollow, he as an accountant, is appointed to be the "money man", when the U.S. P.G.A., holds their tournaments there. In this role, he moves around the course and clubhouse, and distributes cash when requested by players, sometimes only with the authority of their agents. It seems silly that these high- profile golf professionals are monitored so, but there were "groupies" around, who cannot be trusted, especially if their target is single. His wife Mary, was such a nice lady and did her best to entertain us. Except that Mary, did not make any meals, and I mean any meals. We even went out for breakfast. There just was no food in the house. She was "temping', at a Country Day school, and we went to an open house. It was obvious that the kids really loved her.

We made our way to see the Purkeys, in Greenwich, Connecticut, by driving through New York City, which I found scary. The locals have no patience. Once again Donna was a great hostess. The next day, we left early by train, for Grand Central station in New York, toured the United Nations Building and had lunch at a Deli restaurant near Carnegie Hall, to enjoy a huge corned beef sandwich. If you ask a waiter there for anything, after they have brought your meal, in true New York City style, they completely ignore you. Following lunch, we went to see a Broadway play called "True West", which was pretty good. Almost 20 years later it is back on Broadway.

Donna was going out of her way to entertain us and we loved it! We walked around a bit, and later in the afternoon, we made our way to a Spanish restaurant called Solera, which was located (now closed), in Midtown Manhattan. It was too early to eat, and were chatting, prior to Donna's husband Hal, joining us. El had gone to the ladies' room, and Donna and I were discussing the best route to take on the way home, from their house, to our house in Aurora, Ontario.

I had spread out the map of Ontario over the table, and completely forgot about the lit candle. As we discussed the most favourable route home, Lake Ontario started to disappear. We hurriedly threw what was left of the map, on the floor, and stomped on it. El returned, and so did the maître d', both of whom said, "Do you smell smoke". I admit, that I was a tad late in replying, and before I could speak with Canadian honesty and fess up, the staff member said, "It's those people in the kitchen again. They have burned something", and rushed off. We quickly got rid of the evidence and the ladies disguised the smoke smell with all sorts of "products", that they had in their purses.

Following dinner, we went to the Lincoln Centre to see the show "Contact", which is a musical dance show, with no words spoken. Not every ones' cup of tea, but El and I thought it was terrific. It won the Tony award that year for best musical. Coming out of the theatre, we walked across the esplanade to a waiting, chauffer driven Lincoln limousine, which whisked us back to Greenwich. We saw a sample of Hal's successful bond business, which allowed him to use a, chauffer driven car, on demand. The Purkeys were not only friendly, they were very generous.

The 2000 summer and fall, apart from family get togethers, seemed to be occupied, eating out with couples, such as Ron and Fran from Aurora, the Becketts, the Easts, the Grays, the Guilfoyles, the Johnstons, Aunt Ollie and Jim, and "Old Uncle Tom Cobley and all", as the Brits would say.

Sylvia Loutit visited us in September from Vancouver, and we arranged a downtown dinner and theatre visit, to see "Mama Mia", along with Susan and Fiona. It is such an entertaining show with great audience spontaneous participation, including dancing in the aisles. October, brought the sad news that my former Hamilton boss and mentor, Lloyd East had died. I have included one of the many eulogies, that were delivered at his Ancaster funeral, and my words say it all. His wife, the Lady Ida, survived him for five years.

El flew to Edmonton in October for a week to attend a Women Aglow Canadian conference. She returned, and Maureen flew in from Vancouver. The three of us left in days, for Siesta Key in Florida, for our annual fall vacation. We flew to Tampa. Els' luggage arrived the next day. October weather is very nice in Florida. Swimming, sunbathing, eating out, and some shopping was the order of every day. Very stressful! To experience Halloween in the U.S.A. is different. The kids, for safety reasons, do not parade outside, but in the safe confines of shopping mall corridors, where the various store staff, distribute candies and treats. In addition, parents go above and beyond, and rent dress up costumes, to be alongside, and in many cases, outdo their kids.

We picked up Gerry and Kathy Guilfoyle in Tampa, and they joined us for the second week. I played some tennis and golf with Maureen, and ran the beach with Gerry. Maureen was a good tennis player and beat me handily. I played some tennis in Scotland as a youngster, and thought I was pretty good. My sister called me a "blocker", and would not play again with me. Her loss! We drove to Anna Maria Island, to meet with Jim and Barb Marcolin, ex Standard Lifers from Montreal, who the Guilfoyles, and Maureen knew well. El and I were in the front seat. The three in the back, influenced by the alcohol they had consumed, sang their heads off all the way back to the condo. It was fun, but we could have been arrested for excessive vehicle noise.

November 3rd, while still in Florida, we received the news that Fiona had given birth to Cassandra. El had spoken with Fiona, while in hospital, and Susan was at her side for her birth. Joy was shortcoming, as Cassandra's father was about to disappear, from her life. We now had 7 grandchildren; Susan 3, Michele 3, Fiona 1. Obviously, Fiona was devastated, but on returning home we were there to assist, and they moved in with us, while retaining her house in Keswick.

Our former neighbour in Aurora, Audrey Marton, had invited us to a local church Christmas play, that her family members were participating in. Fiona and a sleeping Cassandra joined us. The play was not very good, but as we were seated at the front, it was difficult for us to leave, before the intermission and second act. I asked Fiona, if I could hold Cassandra. "She's fine Dad. She's sleeping.", was the answer. I insisted with the words, "Give me the baby!" Cuddling Cassandra, I got up and said to our family members, "We are out of here". On the way out, I motioned to some church members, that the baby although quiet now, was about to act up, and therefore we had to leave. They nodded their understanding, at this mild untruth. The words "Give me the baby", have become a family expression, when someone wants to get out of doing something.

New Year celebrations entering 2001, were a bit quieter, than those in the prior year. We had dinner New Years' Eve, with Larry and Shirley Johnston and the Stirlings. Larry had lost his business, and was now working in a different role with General Motors. Shirley, understandably was a bit on edge. Larry with his carefree personality, not so much. Her life style had changed, and we as friends, understood this, but notwithstanding, she was not yet ready to accept this.

We had booked a 10- day vacation with Maureen at the Iberostar Hotel in Playa Del Carmen, Mexico, and flew to Cancun on February 01, 2001.

It was an excellent vacation, with tourist trips, by bicycle into Playa, and by taxi to Xcarets' entertainment park, and Coba near Tulum, to see and climb the pyramid there.

The only negative was Els' reaction, to the local drinking water. After 7 days her system says, that she has had enough of Mexico. At the first sign of trouble, we obtained medical help, in the form of antibiotics, and within 2 days, she was feeling much better. But it was a warning for the future. Most hotels in Mexico have excellent medical services and drugs to help you. At a cost, of course!

Fiona was posted on a temporary basis to a branch office of her company in Ottawa, and we visited her and Cassandra in March, and then saw Chris Temple, whose husband Bob, a former Standard Life manager in Vancouver, had died in 1982 at a fairly young age, from heart complications. Bob and I had a very good relationship, especially in the 3- year period ended 1981, when I was in Vancouver, before being transferred back to Ontario.

I look back with skepticism, on some of these decisions made by Standard Life, in appointing their managers. Bob was in my opinion, a good assistant manager. The elevation of his appointment to manager, was a very heavy burden on him, which I am sure created stress. Even as an assistant manager, I had noted that, he took on and shared the problems of his sales representatives, far too seriously. Add in branch administrative staff problems, and overall new business sales difficulties, and you have a recipe for disaster.

This pattern of automatic elevation from being an assistant, to a managership position, is not unusual, and it certainly does not always work. Sport, is a perfect example of this ladder approach to management. Good top management has to recognize, that not every assistant can handle the pressures of the top job, and if passed over, it is not a crime, or the end of that person's career. An assistant role, tends to allow you to remain as one of the "boys". The appointed management position changes that role, and you not only feel more isolated, you are!

BALLANTRAE

2001 - 2006

El felt that it was time for us, to look for a house with an adequate one floor plan. I had no reason to disagree, and she began investigating. Fiona called her, and said, that while driving north on Highway 48, she had noticed major advertising for a condominium setting of bungalows, just north of Aurora side road in Ballantrae, about 20 kilometers east of our Aurora home.

El followed up on what Fiona had reported on, and excitedly called me, to come and see for myself, what she said, was special. We toured the 6 models available, and both agreed that the model, Schickedanz Homes called Castle Pines, was the house for us. As a bungalow, it offered 1850 square feet on a one floor plan, with about 1000 square feet in the basement, for future development. Without delay, we signed a conditional offer, giving us until May 01, to finalize.

The Ballantrae setting, was a condominium site, similar to those, Schickedanz Bros. had built in Florida, but we believe this new project, was to be the first multi single family separate home site in Ontario, built under condominium legislation. It was a huge site, accommodating 900 homes, a recreation centre and multi ponds, all built around a championship golf course. The plan was impressive. The land was a former potato farm. The developers, a family from Austria, had purchased the land, and received approval to build, based upon the inclusion of a separate sewage plant, to service all homes, and then water the golf course with the treated water.

After finalizing the initial purchase agreement, and making a down payment, we celebrated on May 02, by having dinner with the Scharfes, who were visiting Toronto from Vancouver. We met them at the Prince Hotel at 6:00 for dinner, and left at 11:00. We probably dominated the conversation by talking about the house purchase.

May 07, 2001, we listed our 283 Murray Drive Aurora home, and its 14 years of memories, with Els' cousin Jackie, for a selling price of $409,500. One- week later Jackie, brought in a counter offer of $405,000, with only one condition from the buyer. That we be out by July 03, which was only 7 weeks away. El did not like to leave so early in the summer, but somehow, I managed to convince her, that the financial offer was favourable, and that we were setting out on an adventure of being homeless, until our Ballantrae home was completed, by an anticipated date of August 31. The rest of the family were seriously not pleased, that they were losing access to our pool, so early in the summer.

Our first stop was the Staybridge Hotel in Markham. The Atlanta based parent of the hotel chain, BHMC Ltd., had been a pension client for years. I was fairly friendly with their controller, who arranged a favourable stay for us, until July 21, after which we had "volunteered" to house sit the Grays cats, while they vacationed. You see what I mean, by adventure. We were now down to one car, having returned the Honda CRV at the end of its lease. El had our other car, while I agreed to GO bus it back and forth, to my Standard Life consulting role workplace, at Sheppard and Yonge, in north Toronto.

The Grays house was really large, so much so, that El could roller skate in the basement. We saw the two cats for their morning meals and petting, and then they disappeared within the house, for the rest of the day and night. One of the cats, would bring a stuffed toy mouse to the upstairs floor, where we were sleeping, about 3:00 every morning, and would moan out loud, as celebrating a real- life kill. They were not happy, that we were the residents of their "house", and sorely missed their "Mum and Dad", Monique and Jeff.

To maintain the adventure, we moved to the Guilfoyles' house. They were heading to France, for a biking trip, and agreed to let the "weary wanderers" house sit, for a while. We stayed in their fully furnished basement, which was very comfortable. After hearing some disturbing and confusing news on the radio, we turned on the television, just at the moment that the second plane was flying into the twin towers in New York. We witnessed the explosion, and for a moment I was puzzled, thinking that we were seeing a recording of the first and only suicide plane attack. I recall wondering, how they had filmed this initial attack, until I realized, we were seeing a second plane attack, in real time. The tragedy that unfolded that day was evil, and the long- term effects of the 911 terror attacks, against the U.S.A. are still in effect today, and will last for years to come, both medically and psychologically.

Most Canadians gave back that day, in the form of blood donations, room and board for stranded American travelers (all flights were grounded for days), and comfort by telephone to their American friends and family members in the U.S. The Canadians in Newfoundland certainly gave from the heart, to hundreds of American airline passengers, as their planes were diverted there, and held on the ground for days. Witness the amazing Canadian theatre production of "Come from Away", which tells the story of Maritime hospitality. The father Rocky, of the female co-producer of this production, lives about 100 meters away from us. Rocky is a pretty proud man.

By now, we had passed the fictious August 31 house deadline closing date. We had visited Ballantrae, almost every day, to witness the house construction, from the ground up. We had been chased off the property, for security and liability reasons. We had danced on the floor platform, before the walls went up. We had praised and criticized the work crews as they completed, what we wanted. We had made suggestions and recommendations, re plumbing, electrical and interior construction work, which was totally against the rules, as the Castle Pines house design was as per Schickedanz, and was not a Coyle custom designed house. We won some changes. We lost most.

We were still homeless, and Eleanor's cousin Jackie came to the rescue, and offered temporary accommodation in her Richmond Hill house. A last- minute glitch to moving into our new house, came in the form of tiling in the front hall. The colour of tile El wanted, and the builder had approved, which was identical to that in the model home, was suddenly no longer available. El agreed to a change in colour, but stated that they would therefore now, have to change the colour of the surface finish in and around the kitchen sink, the carpeting in the master bedroom and other areas in the house, for colour matching purposes. Schickedanz's representative went pale, and pleaded with the tiler, to find and upgrade the tile in the front hall, to match the exact colour, El initially wanted, ensuring that the other work could continue without change. They found a much more expensive tile in the colour initially approved, and installed it, without additional cost. Good for you El. You called their bluff and you won!

El, had planned a trip to Houston, in September, for a Women's Aglow International Conference, which was hosting thousands of women from around the world. Due to the 911 disaster, this and countless conferences and meetings had been cancelled. We now concentrated on moving into the house, and setting up appointment times and meetings, for the many diverse projects required to make a new property functional.

This spanned the first week of October, and after a verbal fight with the builders' lawyer we got the keys to the house on October 9th. Our furniture had been stored in climate- controlled pallets over the summer, and these were delivered, and emptied. We also had moving staff, assist in putting small items away, especially in the kitchen. We were busy for days, but we are good organizers, and all was planned for a move to this special house, destined to be our last home.

Every home you live in should be special, but several factors made Ballantrae extra special. First of all, due to all of its supplementary highlights, we truly believed that this location would be the last home that we would occupy. Secondly, we were able to watch its construction almost daily, from the ground up to completion. It was not custom designed by us, but the Castle Pine model was our joint automatic pick, from the range of models available, and some of our ideas had been incorporated. The final positive was that this home was truly ours. We were mortgage free! The net proceeds from the Aurora sale exceeded the Ballantrae purchase, even with upgrades. Admittedly, we now had monthly condo fees.

In order not to gift the Houston hotel and Air Canada, with the down payments, El had made for the cancelled women's conference, we decided to build on those reservations, and spend 12 days or so in Texas and visit a much more basic, non- touristy horse ranch, that I had researched, called the Running R., near Bandera. The ranch only served breakfast and lunch, and we drove the 25 minutes or so every night, into Bandera for supper at Billy Jeans restaurant, which served a variety of quality dinners and cozy service. We had dinner one night at a Gun Show, which was in Bandera that week. The meal was excellent, and more than reasonably priced. The atmosphere however, for we Canadians, was weird and unnerving, and shows another side of Texas.

We know the problems, that Americans have faced through the years, with frequent mass shootings. Attend one of any gun marketing shows, and the answer is in your face. Unashamed selling of warlike weapons, guns and knives, all in the interest of "The right to bear arms". That is in their constitution, but in my opinion, those words are completely out of context today, especially when you compare the likely rationale for them then, and todays' application of them, as promoted by the gun lobby, through gun shops and gun shows. Background checks for example, are still not required at gun shows. The gun lobby makes that difficult to legislate otherwise. El and I felt, we could not eat and run, but were mighty pleased to be finally out of there. Talk about kids in a candy shop. Dangerous candy! Guns are openly displayed in vehicles!

Back to the ranch, which seemed positively peaceful. The riding was extensive and excellent. Horses can get you somewhere in a hurry, or almost lull you to sleep with a slow walk, which is hypnotizing. Texas is the final stop for Monarch butterflies, in their journey south from Canada, through the States, to their final destination in Mexico, to winterize. We have driven the highways in Texas, through clouds of Monarchs, and have ridden horses in similar circumstances. Horses spook easily, but when it comes to butterflies, and I am talking clouds of butterflies at eye level, the horses seem to easily accept their presence and act as if completely oblivious to them.

We drove to Fredericksburg after a week, to visit our friends the Simpsons and stayed 2 nights. Then on to San Marcos, which is a factory outlook tourist trap, but a quality one, and then on to San Antonio to stay at the Marriott Hotel, in a room overlooking the Riverwalk, which at most times is impossible to book. But this was following 911, and we were told, that we virtually could have any room in the hotel. Things were that bad!

My other sad, but poignant memory, had been arriving at Houston airport, to witness a U.S, Marine standing at the foot of the escalator, in full battle dress, sporting an M15 Carbine rifle. We so enjoyed the 3 days in San Antonio, helped by the lack of tourists, and the effort the locals extended to make us feel welcome. We drove to Columbus and then flew home from Houston.

Caution is the word when you travel, and we complied on this trip. In Houston, we asked for a suggestion as to an off- site restaurant. The staff obliged, but said that they would drive us there and pick us up, when we called to say dinner was over. This is U.S. reality. This is Houston at night!

Our "gypsy like" adventure, had lasted over 4 months. It was time to settle down, and enjoy our new house. This was home number 9, spanning 38 years, 3 provinces and 7 communities. We strongly believed, that this would be our last home. We now had a one floor plan with a basement, which when finished, would give us every level of comfort, and the ability to entertain, and offer comfortable sleeping quarters for visitors. With a front porch facing east, and a back patio enhanced with a screen, facing west, we will be able to spend hours outside in relative comfort during reasonable weather, in a park like setting. As members of a gated community with long term neighbours, we can now vacation for weeks on end, with limited concerns about break ins. The condominium set up, gives us trees and shrubs, acres of lawns and a golf course, all which are quite beautiful. A valued word in the condominium vocabulary is "green". The country style setting, has just improved with time and after almost 19 years, we have no desire to live elsewhere and God willing, we will here for many years to come.

The Ballantrae house of 2001 was not quite finished to Els' liking and although I was satisfied, she had plans to upgrade in time. The bank was in standby mode, and I didn't know it. With our first partially customized home, we were eager to share our enthusiasm, either at home, or over a dinner table, with photographs. We enjoyed evenings with family members, the Grays, the Johnstons, the Pollocks, the Hines and the Guilfoyles. My Christmas celebrations, included 2 separate Standard Life staff parties, and the Standard client luncheon. El and I enjoyed the main Standard staff party, Christmas Day and Boxing Day family dinners, and our downtown dinner and theater evening with the girls. I look back in awe at the energy expended in travelling and socializing, in such a short period of time. New Years' Eve was held with the Stirlings and the Johnstons. A reasonably quiet evening with nice people. We welcomed 2002 very peacefully.

To kick off 2002, Maureen joined us from Vancouver, and we flew to Cancun on January 24 on Sky Service, a small start- up airline offering discount fares to vacation spots in Mexico. You must be careful with such, as most go out of business, as this one did. We broke tradition, by leaving town, the day before Robert Burns celebrations. I cannot explain why, other than the timing of the discount fare to Mexico, had something to do with it. I promise to be more faithful next year!

We bussed on arrival, to the Iberostar hotel in Playa Del Carmen for a 2 week stay. To explore we had decided to travel to Xel-Ha park, a tourist attraction for snorkeling and swimming with an abundance of tropical fish, sting rays etc. Our ride was interrupted by an American having a stroke or an anxiety attack, who initially refused medical assistance. I managed to persuade him to leave the bus, and see a doctor in a hotel we had stopped at, to pick up additional passengers. He appeared to hold a dim view of Mexican medical abilities. My practical comments were, that our family experiences with their doctors through the years, were favourable, and "Oh, by the way, you really don't have a choice!"

We got our chance to test my words, as Els' stomach acted up again. The magic drug Cipro, was administered, and successfully worked within 48 hours. Gastro enteritis, is common among North American visitors to Mexico, regardless of how safe they claim their water is, and if anti biotics are not taken quickly, the results can be ugly. The hotel was lovely, but being our third visit here, we noticed how much busier it was. A lot of the natural trees and vegetation had been cut back. There were very few birds flying free, certainly no monkeys swinging in the trees and the beach, much narrower, due to higher ocean water. We agreed that we would not be returning.

We visited the Xcaret park again, for another entertaining day. While walking past the "island", where their two long term jaguars are on show, we noticed that the cats were showing interest in what we thought was us. The jaguars were keeping exact pace with us, and a Mexican male, who was walking beside us, in normal clothing, holding a fairly large package in his hand. The package turned out to be a dead chicken, which he suddenly hurled towards the land area, occupied by the jaguars. The chicken carcass did not make, what we believed was the target, but fell, about 50 feet into a gully below, and landed in the water, into a type of "moat" that surrounded the island. What a poor throw, was our first thought until, our thinking was interrupted, by the mouth and then body of a huge alligator, which exploded out of the water, grabbed the chicken, and then disappeared just as quickly into the murky water, which quickly resumed, its undisturbed tranquil appearance. We gulped and moved on, reminded that nature's violence can be sudden, violent and the outcome resolved in an instance.

February saw Scott Bell, our worldwide President, visit Toronto as part of his farewell tour of Canada, prior to his retirement at age 60. As young men in the 50s', we were teammates on Standard's soccer team, carefree and mischievous friends. After achieving the number one position in Standard Life, our relationship was not the same. I understood, but found that sad. Some people have difficulty in handling this type of change in their company relationships.

El celebrated her 60th birthday in March and we honoured her, with a sit-down dinner at the Joia restaurant in Aurora, with 26 guests, including her favourite aunts, Dorothy and Ollie and her Mum. Open restaurants can be noisy, but it was a lovely evening, and Marco and his staff provided the usual quality food and service. I of course wanted to congratulate El, and read out the contents of a few telegrams we had received from friends across Canada. I used that, as a reference to a very special telegram, I had received at the very last moment, bemoaning the fact that the senders had not seen her for a long time, despite various attempts to contact her. It also wished her well, and hoped that they would see her shortly. I motioned to El, who looked puzzled as to who "they" were, and shook her head. I paused and then said "It was signed by the Shoe Manufacturers Association of Canada". Most of the guests got it, and exploded in laughter, and if you looked into her closet, you would quickly get it too.

The evening was memorable, but alas turned out also to be remembered tragically, for the last time we would see our close friend, Larry Johnston. He was to die 3 weeks later, in an automobile accident, after his car had a head on collision with a van, coming down a hill, on the wrong side of the road. I still cannot understand the reason for his senseless death. The van driver, was apparently blinded by the effects of an "Alberta Clipper", which occurs in Ontario late winter from time to time. It is named after a sudden and blinding snowstorm, which appears out of nowhere, and offers little or no vision to drivers. It then leaves as suddenly, as it had appeared.

El was in B.C., when the accident occurred, visiting friends and Maureen, ahead of my coming out for a visit. Our family was united, in insisting that she had to come back immediately, for the viewing and the funeral. She agreed, and was back in Ontario the next day. The church memorable service in Markham, was attended by a huge number of mourners. There were several eulogies, including one from Ben Hepner, offering solace. I was honoured by the family, despite the sadness, to include as much humour and lightness as I felt appropriate, in my words. There were certainly comedic events in the life and times, I had shared with this lovely human being. A copy of the eulogy will form part of my memoirs. I had been intending to join El in B.C., before the tragedy, which befell the Johnstons.

And therefore, as planned, we later headed out to Vancouver and Maureen's house, a week or so after the funeral, to have dinner with the McArthurs and the Lumbs, at Maureen's Jericho Tennis Club. The next day we headed for Vancouver Island, to visit Els' aunt Ollie, and husband Jim. We purchased one of his waterscapes entitled "High and Dry". Then onto Salt Spring Island, to revisit Bob and Judith Young. Yes, he of the secret little people villages, on Erskine Mountain. Remember please, it is a secret! Then another ferry ride to Departure Bay, on the north shore of Vancouver, to meet with Rosemary and Brian Burley, our former Ancaster neighbours and Spain co- trippers. We have always placed a premium, on re acquainting ourselves from time to time, with old friends, because you never know. We have lost three of these dear male friends, since then.

Returning to Vancouver, we now became party to, and unpaid staff, at one of Maureen's world -famous buffet style dinners, for a group of 40 plus guests, mostly from Jericho Tennis Club, and her golfing groups. Believe you me, we worked very hard, days before, and during this soiree. A service person was hired to prepare some of the food, and assistance in the kitchen. I was the barman, stuck in the laundry room. Dispensing drinks was relatively easy, because most of the guests were Brits, and therefore gin and tonics, were the order of the day. A long day!

We recovered enough, to drive to Whidbey Island in Washington, to visit Maureen's friends Ruth and Reidar Nordhoy, and their beautiful home, overlooking an inlet in Puget Sound. And of course, their lovely golden retriever, Rusty. This dog, had an extraordinary long body, like a freight train with a caboose bringing up the rear. But so playful and loveable. Late afternoon every day, Rusty was brought inside, and more than several deer showed up at the side door, to sample Reidar's distribution of apples. To be so close to nature is wonderful, and then you regret it, because the deer become so familiar, that they eat all the tree and bush vegetation, within earshot of the house. We returned to Vancouver to enjoy an evening with the Scharfes in their beautiful second floor condo, facing the water of False Creek and Granville Island. We count them as true and dear friends, dating back to 1964. Then home to Ballantrae.

Our doctor for many years, has been Dr. Eileen Lougheed, who I based at one time, on my running and believed general fitness, did not see very often. After a routine physical, she requested, that I have an ECG, which I questioned, as it revealed nothing. Maybe in testing, she had detected a heart defect of some kind, which was not confirmed by the procedure. I of course, dismissed thoughts of any current or looming problem, which I now believe she may have foreseen, and actually was to come to pass, within the next 4 years. Mr. Fitness, continued my 5km runs, three times a week.

I worked with Fiona to obtain a formal divorce from Bruce and full custody of her daughter. True to form, Bruce did not show up, and our petitions were approved by the court. I found the whole procedure interesting, especially for the manner in which our lawyers conducted themselves. They were neither efficient or organized, and it took urging from Fiona and myself, to come to the successful conclusion that we did. I recall losing my cool at our first meeting, based upon the questioning of Fiona, by one of her lawyers. My comment, based upon his statements was, "Are you representing us, or the other party, because if your tone continues, we are out of here". Obviously, he thought better of it, and changed his ways.

We continued our socializing with friends, probably because of our excitement about the new house, and the fact that at that time our only close neighbours, were construction sites, as more homes were being built. The Leightons, Shorts, Martons, Frenchs, McVickers and Atkinsons, were our dinner victims. I started to dabble at golf, influenced somewhat by the links course on our doorstep. Neighbours, such as Brian Birkness, John Van Velzen and Mike Pyle became golf partners at various times, on courses such as Ballantrae and Spring Lakes. We were not good, but we were honest, tried hard and had fun. Brian and I played one very windy day, at his home course of Spring Lakes in Stouffville. Brian's mighty tee shot on the first hole, hit a tree head on, and came roaring back to end up, about three feet in front of him. He looked at me, but said nothing. I merely said "Strong wind", and we carried on, in silence.

El and I got into the habit of going for a walk after supper on the golf course, to locate and gather misplaced balls in the woods. A short walk would bring, over 12 balls some nights. Collection of these balls, gave birth to an amateur career in 2001, writing poetry. I intend to attach to these memoirs, some of the poetic words, I have penned over the years, not because they are wonderful, but to give you an insight, as to what interests me, and to how I react to the good, the bad and the curious. I have included below two stanzas from the golf ball poem entitled, "Fore Whom It May Concern". This may give you reason not to read the rest of them.

"We sally forth every night, hunting golf balls out of sight. They're white and dimpled and don't belong, in rough or fescue, alone, forlorn."

"Bring them on, we're up to the test, now neatly stored in our golf ball nest. For winter pickings are poor at best, a time ball- hunters get to rest."

Our fall vacation in Florida, included a visit from Fiona, with a very young Cassandra. Unfortunately, the baby laboured with a heavy cold, and the only comfort she would accept early on, was by watching her Barney videos. The term "Elephant", which is relative to the children's' series, was heard again and again. She did recover somewhat, but only in time to travel home.

Fiona was then flagged for an interview, with Canada Customs, on her return to Toronto. We had earnestly ensured, that because she was travelling as a single parent with Cassandra, the necessary papers to take her to and from the U.S., were complete and in order. I was therefore annoyed. On my return, I contacted a senior official in Canada Customs, to complain about the treatment she had received during the lengthy interview. The ridiculous fact was that, if there were any worries at all, they were not even relevant, because she was bringing the baby back to Canada. The official agreed. I hope someone was reprimanded for their officious stupidity.

Maureen joined us at Siesta Dunes for two further weeks. We all enjoyed the warm weather, sunbathing, swimming, walks, runs, shopping, many dinners out, the latter of which pleased El. mightily. We also went to the Golden Apple Dinner Theater to see Mame, and the Players Theater to see My Fair Lady. For amateur productions both were enjoyable.

Upon return to Canada, we attended the usual run of pre- Christmas dinners with neighbours, staff and friends, the Standard client lunch, family Christmas dinners and our downtown dinner and theater night, with the girls. As usual a fairly active and hectic time. New Years' Eve was as usual, with the Stirlings and the Johnstons. A quiet evening, which suited the six of us just fine!

January 25, 2003, saw us resume our Robert Burns dinner celebrations, at the Old Mill. A great evening! Maureen flew into Toronto, and the 3 of us left for Mexico at the beginning of February for a 2 week stay at the Grand Palladium hotel near Tulum, which is a good 90- minute bus ride from Cancun. A quality hotel, with good food and entertainment. Once again, El experienced stomach cramps, and Maureen joined her this time. Did all the tourist things, including a trip to the local Mayan ruins. The lake nearby is full of Caimans (crocs), which are not considered overly dangerous, but can bite. The locals said that we could stand beside them for photographs, suggesting they are only interested in eating chickens, on land. My response was. "You stand beside them. I'm chicken".

April/May, saw us spend 12 days on the west coast, using Maureen's house as a base. We visited old friends. I played some golf, and we ended up on Whidbey Island, at Ruth and Reidar's. On return home, it became obvious that Els' mother's health, was deteriorating. She welcomed us home, and congratulated us on getting married. When El pointed out the photos of Mum's grandchildren, on the wall, she could not identify them. We took her to Southlake and they admitted her, with a statement that if she remained in hospital, they could prolong her life, but otherwise the end was probably not far away. The system usually prefers and sometimes mandates, that this type of patient, be moved to a nursing and care environment, for their remaining days, to keep costs to a minimum. She was moved to the

Willows Estate Care Centre in Aurora and died peacefully after a week, on June 06, at age 85.

El tried to communicate with her in these last days, without much success, but knew that she had accepted the Lord, much earlier. We held 2 memorial services; the first at our Aurora Cornerstone Church, and later at Little Lake Memorial Park in Peterborough, her home town. Both were well attended, and conducted with class and reverence. A fitting memory, for a very nice lady.

I played a lot of golf over the summer. We were fortunate to meet Betty and Bernie Shukster, who were in among the first group of residents in Ballantrae. Betty was a travel agent, intent initially on winding down, but who on seeing the number of new people in Ballantrae and their profiles; mostly in their 60s, many mortgage free, and most physically able to travel, decided to resurrect her travel skills and organize multi trips, to many parts of the world, over the following years. The fact that she did this, certainly enhanced many of our lives, and I for one, have complimented her on how successful she was in opening our eyes, to the world at large, while reducing our bank accounts. El and I visited over 30 countries and Maureen made it to more than 50. Thank you, Lord, for introducing us to Betty. The bank was happy also!

Our first taste of "Shuksterism", was a trip to Italy, and mainly to what I will, call Rome North. The official Trafalgar Tour guide was Elio, a tall handsome married Italian, from Rome. He should therefore be called Roman, because that is what citizens from the city are called. Every female in our group, average age 65 plus, fell in love with him. He stayed with us the whole trip, and was just excellent. He was purposefully delicate with his English. Every reference to the bathroom or a toilet break, was described by him, as a "Situation", or, the next "Situation" break, will be in 20 minutes, and so on.

For those who care to read these memoirs, including myself, I wish to include some specific detail around our travel, and the many locations that we visited, to make the world a smaller place, that you might be interested in, and give thought to visiting. I am not a travel agent! Despite the violence, that seems to invade our world societies every day, I have to encourage you, to at least sample, what the world has to offer. Saint Augustine, author and Saint, quoted some 1500 plus years ago, that "The world is a book, and those who do not travel read only a page". These words are as relevant today. Just do it.

It is almost inevitable, that North American tourist flights arrive in Europe in the morning. As hotels are not available until mid- afternoon, you stretch your already tired eyes, and head out for your first tour. Our destination in Milan was the La Scala Milan, the famous opera house inaugurated in 1778. We then proceeded to witness Leonardo da Vinci's painting of The Last Supper (circa 1495), which of course is a world treasure. This was painted, on the wall of a former Dominican monastery, Santa Maria delle Grazie. The painting depicts, the consternation that occurred among the Twelve Apostles, when Jesus announced that someone would betray him. It measures 180 inches by 350 inches. It is truly amazing to behold. For safety and preservation purposes, security is tight, and only a maximum of 25 people can be admitted after they are "air sanitized", to the viewing room, every 15 minutes.

We then bussed to the north, to witness the beauty of Lakes Como and Maggiore. These lakes are shore lined by the homes of the rich and famous, such as George Clooney, who has property on Lake Como. Access by car or bus is not easy, for obvious reasons, and therefore our viewing was done by an organized boat trip. We then moved on to Lake Garda, Verona and Venice.

Venice is a city built upon 118 small islands. There are no roads, just canals. Water is the attraction, but also a serious problem. The level of water has risen in the canals, as there is a gradual lowering of Venice's surface, and many of the buildings' basements can no longer be used. It is estimated that the city continues to sink, at a rate of 1-2 mm per annum and this problem, combined with an anticipated rise in sea water levels, will challenge the authorities, well into the future. The main square, Piazza San Marco is frequently flooded, and it would appear that it will only get worse, but life there carries on. The tourists keep coming. Flood gates have been installed, but to-date have not been effective.

To remain dry, we viewed the famous Rialto Bridge, and attended a demonstration of the blowing and making of beautiful Murano glass objects, by true artisans. We then took a ride through the canals, on an infamous gondola boat. The gondolier did not utter a word, other than to accept the gratuities. He looked bored. Sorry all, but it really bordered on boring, and certainly was not as romantic, as they portray in the movies.

A new day started by visiting Bolzano at the foot of the Alps. In comparison to North America, Europe is small, and as Italy borders Austria, it was interesting to see much of the town's signage in German. We took a great side trip from Bolzano, on a funicular railway to Soprabolzano, and then on a train to a 5- star Alpine restaurant at about the 2,000 feet level. To eat and drink outside, in the warm and very dry fresh air, while taking in the incredibly beautiful Tyrolean scenery, was more than therapeutic. Nobody wanted to leave after lunch. We had found our "Shangri-La."

We returned to Bolzano, which was featuring its Armed Services Day, complete with military vehicles, and extravagantly uniformed Italian armed forces members, representing the various branches of the military, based in that area. The most colourful were the Alpine specialists with their huge hats, each featuring a huge feather. It was very interesting, but honestly looked more like a fashion show, and was way short of portraying a protective presence.

We then witnessed in The South Tyrol Museum of Archeology, the resting place of the male body discovered in September 1991, frozen and preserved in the alpine ice. That, of a believed to be, middle aged merchant man, who had lived some 5,300 years ago. The Iceman or Otzi, as he is known, is quite a draw for tourists and Italians alike. His body was tattooed. Items found with the body, include a copper axe, a bladed knife and a quiver of 14 arrows. It was believed that he was murdered. His body represents the oldest preserved human being ever found.

We bussed via Mantua, and Bologna to Florence, where we witnessed Michelangelo's incredible 17- foot marble statue of "David", in the Academia Gallery of Florence. His masterpiece was created between 1501 and 1504. According to legend and our guide, Michelangelo included the word "sinceramente", on all his works, which indicated that each sculpture was original, honest and true work. This was later translated to English as "yours sincerely", which of course, was how most correspondence is finished with, prior to your signature, indicating that, all that was written above, was honest and true. I could not really prove this, but the story has a nice ring to it!

On to Pisa, to view the bell tower, the famous leaning tower of Pisa, built in the 12th century A.D. to showcase the city's prosperity. Recent shoring up of foundations have reduced the lean by 40 centimeters, thus adding multi years to the life of its stability. Our next highlight was Siena, which in the 15th century, was the centre of power for the Medici family, who established their bank there in 1457. "They", would be horrified with the current fiscal position of most Italian banks.

Siena hosts the famous "Il Palio", the Il Palio di Siena horse race, which is a 3- lap race, around the Piazza Del Campo, located in the heart of the city. It is only run twice a year, in honour of the Madonna of Provenzano (July 2nd) and the Assumption of Mary (August 16th). Obviously, it has a strong religious background. It features jockeys in colourful outfits, riding 10 horses bareback, and each race, represents 10 of the City's 17 districts or wards, each known as a contrada. It is not just a race, it's a passion. The square is covered with dirt and sod to form a circular track on the outside of its perimeter. This 2- minute morning horse race attracts about 40,000 spectators, surrounding the track on both sides. The event has been running, virtually without change, since 1649. The winner is the first horse to cross the finishing line, having completed 3 laps, with or without a rider. The loser, is the horse that comes in second, not last! The draw for the participants, gives each of the 17 wards, equal exposure over time, as the track, only permits a maximum of 10 horses and their riders, in the race.

Winning the race does not give the rider, or the owner of the horse, a financial reward. It is all about bragging rights for the residents of the ward, or "contrada", represented by the winning horse. Betting, cheating, jockeys hitting other jockeys, or their horses, with their "whips", before or during the race are all permitted. In essence virtually, anything goes. The closeness of the excited horses and their riders, and the huge crowd, combined with all the noise, makes for a spectacle that can be dangerous to both humans and animals alike. It has been cited by, animal rights groups as cruel, but the tradition continues.

All we could do, the day we were there, was to witness the empty square, and perhaps imagine the excitement and commotion of the event, while eating our lunch. We were ready to rehearse what little Italian we knew, in preparing to order the local cuisine. Only to find out, as we closed in on the outdoor restaurant, that we were required to order by number, based upon options pictured on a wall. I believe, that I chose numero quatre, (number four). Yes, you guessed right. The restaurant in this plaza, with hundreds of years of history, was Pizza Pizza. A bit of a disappointment, plus it served pizza whose taste and consistency, were not quite in line with the Canadian formula, we are accustomed to.

A more leisurely time was spent the next day on the cobbled streets of the province of Siena hillside town, of San Gimignamo. This, out of the way community, was the perfect antidote, for all the hustle and bustle, we had encountered in previous days. There were other tourists present, but there was such an aura of quiet, peace, and dignity, reflecting throughout the town square, and surrounding narrow streets, that the experience, proved to have a calming effect on all present.

We left for Rome, via Assisi. This was to be our initial visit to Italy's major city, where Italians are called Romans. They do have the history to wear the name. We in essence, visited the Colosseum from the outside. Once inside, you are at a lower level and do not get a true view, or a true feeling of what transpired in this majestic building. A lot of bad things happened here, and it was the ruling powers way of entertaining the masses, and focusing their attention on, "those that did not adhere to the power of Rome, or were potential threats to that power, or were not understood (Christians), or were convicted felons." We quickly saw St Peter's Basilica, the Trevi Fountain and the Spanish Steps, where tourists love to sit and watch the world go by. The authorities, annoyed at the lack of space to walk up and down the Steps, have now deemed it illegal to sit on the Steps, or to receive a fine if caught. This is Italy. Over time this ordinance will not fly! We also viewed at length the famous Tivoli Gardens, a 16th century Villa, built on a massive sculpted garden property with 51 fountains and nymphaea and then our final visit for the day was to St Peter's square, facing the Vatican, which was fairly crowded, as the Pope was actually giving those present, his blessing.

The next day was a visit to the Catacombs, which were originally excavated for Christian burials, beginning in the 2nd century A.D., but were later used by all religious groups, due to overcrowding and shortage of land. Over 40 of these have been discovered. To walk underground in these narrow low ceiling corridors, is certainly a walk back in time. To many, including El and I, it was certainly spooky, to see multi 4 to 5 feet long burial chambers carved out of the walls. When the group moves on, led by a guide, you do not hesitate to keep up. There are no signs that say "This way out".

Our next tour was that of Pompeii, on the Bay of Naples, which was totally buried in 79 A.D., by 4 to 6 meters of volcanic ash, with the eruption of Mount Vesuvius. Massive excavation has revealed parts of the city, its road structure, and skeletons intact, in essence mummified. The city population was believed to have reached 12,000, with about 2,000 trapped in Pompeii, when the massive explosion occurred and the mountains of volcanic ash descended on the city and smothered the inhabitants. Mount Vesuvius is currently not active, but volcanic experts believe that a similar eruption could happen again, at any time. Only this time, there are 3 million people living within 20 miles of the crater. House are actually being built on the lower slopes of Mount Vesuvius. Crazy!

Lunch was at a farm restaurant called Azienda Agricola La Sorgente, where we were given demonstrations, as to the making of mozzarella cheese and limoncello liqueur. The demonstrations were interesting, but the samples were even better. We closed the day, by visiting Sorrento and driving parts of the Amalfi coast to Positano, where a picturesque view of the Tyrrhenian Sea, accompanied by more limoncello, was the final highlight. This area of Italy is beyond beautiful!

We then returned to Rome for a final day of sightseeing and of saying goodbye to an Italy, that as a tourist, is not hard to love. We viewed the Vatican museum and the Sistine Chapel, which features amazing artwork and sculpture, including the 16th century Michelangelo's, Ceiling of the Sistine Chapel. When you walk through the corridors of the Vatican museum, all frescos, murals and paintings are facing the opposite way. In essence only those, who live and or work in Vatican City, can walk in the direction that these treasures face. Seating in the Sistine Chapel is limited and the ability to look up is limited, by age and fitness. Silence is golden, but is usually not observed.

Our signature night, including dinner, much vino, entertainment and singing was at La Carvana, a restaurant in a major Rome square. A wonderful evening. A wonderful trip. Arrivederci Italia! We will be back. An early morning flight to Milan the next day and then onto Toronto and home.

Prior to leaving for Italy, Michele had indicated, that Kyle was suffering from extreme back pain, the cause of which, they could not pinpoint. A procedure finally indicated that "something", was putting pressure on the spine and nervous system. Surgery was scheduled at Kingston Hospital, to remove 80% of a tumor that was causing the pain. We spoke with Michele from Italy, to find out, that they labelled the problem as Ependymoma, or cancer of the spine and brain, with a number of very small tumors attached to these areas. It most often occurs in young children. Initially Kyle's tumors were confined to the spine, but are now also in the brain stem. We were aware that he would require significant radiation following the surgery. However, his having to bear the burden, of the effects of radiation at such a young age, would have a significant impact on his physical abilities in later life. His back is not strong, and any physical work today is definitely a challenge.

We arrived home to celebrate our 40th anniversary at the Joia restaurant in Aurora, and Maureen left for Vancouver. A spate of Christmas lunches, and dinners followed. Boy, were we social in these days! In keeping with tradition, we spent New Years' Eve, with the Stirlings, and ushered in what 2004 might have in store for us. We, of course, knew what Kyle was about to go through, but the results of tests and his recovery, following his operation, were promising. The family had all agreed, that we would be on call, from the middle of February, to help and counsel Michele and Doug in any way.

We started the 2004 New Year, with an Old Mill visit, to celebrate Burns in January, and then Maureen joined us for a first and very memorable visit to the Dominican Republic. A 2 week stay at the Iberostar Hotel on Bavaro Beach. A beautiful beach, good food and entertainment at a hotel, which was starting to look tired. To clarify the "memorable" comment, Maureen had multi problems. She mislaid her keys to her luggage, "lost" her binoculars, yelled at the operator giving her an early morning wake-up call, without realizing that it was a computerized system, that had called the room 3 times, because she in requesting the wake up service, had registered 3 requests with the front desk, for such a wake -up call.

In addition, El without our knowledge, had become dehydrated during the first few days, and almost fell off her horse, while riding at a pretty fast pace on the beach. After dismounting, showering and then going for dinner, she passed out temporarily in the restaurant, and we had to call for medical help. She recovered quickly and all was well. A few days later, "Dumbo" here, being somewhat distracted, while looking in some shop windows in the hotel complex, spotted El and Maureen seated at an outside dining table. I took a direct line approach by stepping of the causeway, right into the lobby pool, complete with tropical fish, and then waded fully dressed, in water above my knees, over to their table. The waitress, who happened to be right there, taking their drink orders, looked at me in amazement, and without missing a beat, I climbed up, sat down, and ordered a rum and coke. Check the poetry section of these memoirs for "Dominican Gaffs".

We, as grandparents responding to Kyle's situation, found it difficult to know how to help. El and I tend to be pragmatic about getting going and doing things, and probably tried to coax Michele and Doug to agree, to the medical recommendations without delay. In this case, however the medical staff were unable to determine, what negative effects radiation might have on Kyle, weighed against the results of not doing anything. Following the surgery, Michele and Doug agreed to seek radiation at Sick Children/ Princess Margaret hospitals, commencing the middle of February 2004, and as this involved 5 consecutive weeks of Monday to Friday treatments, Michele and Kyle, stayed with us, and went home for the weekends. He is currently working for his brother in law, Tony, who has been extremely helpful. The physical part of the job is difficult, and he has had to endure frequent MRI procedures, intended to keep an eye on the status of the tumors, but he is alive.

Michele and Kyle arrived at the house on February 16th for the start of his radiation therapy. The actual time in the hospital was short some days, and Michele was so good to him. She took him to see many of the City's highlights, and any meals were customized to his liking. She was a wonderful mother. As mentioned, the radiation lasted every weekday for 5 weeks, and this gave them the opportunity to go home Friday afternoons, for the weekend. March, saw Fiona and Ian sell the small house on Tampa Drive, and buy a larger 2- story home in Keswick.

We left on April 29, to spend 2 weeks on the west coast. First to socialize with Maureen and friends, and then the 3 of us drove to Summerland, in the interior of B.C., to spend 4 days at the Wild Horse Mountain Ranch. Our rides were two hours each day. The horses were frisky, but the terrain was hilly. A nearby ranch had "curlies"; horses that have a gene in their coat, that makes them hypoallergenic. As they are non- allergenic, they are therefore valuable, being available to those individuals, such as our Susan, or groups, who are allergic to normal horse hair. We have seen the effects that such allergies have on the face, and particularly the eyes, if they touch any part of their face, following having touched the horse. It is not pretty, and in fact it is quite scary.

The summer of '04, was the start of my playing much more golf. Inspired somewhat by Maureen, who could now be termed as a "golf fanatic". I played with her and her friends in Vancouver, and Brian Birkness and Mike Pyle in the Ballantrae area. Michele and I had a meeting with the oncologists in Toronto, to discuss their concern about the brain stem, and the possibility of exposing Kyle to further radiation. A decision was reached to not submit him to the ongoing radiation, but to MRI him on a fairly frequent basis. As a youngster, Kyle was so athletic and gifted. He was the young quarterback, the older kids wanted to run their team. Unfortunately, the radiation damaged his pituitary gland and his thyroid gland. His physical energy and capability, was lost and has never been the same.

Summer with the family, saw us journey to Madoc to witness the graduation of Kyle's older brother, Daric, and his selection as the school Valedictorian. Well done Daric! Susan's daughter, Danielle, is also very talented, with her guitar playing and singing among her strong abilities. She was featured doing solos at the Keswick outdoor music street festival. We spent a day at Bon Echo provincial park, at the Cook family, campsite. The lake water is so clear and pure, but a wee bit chilly.

One of our original Ballantrae neighbours, Tom Popovich, died that summer. Tom and his wife Joyce were incredible cheerleaders, for newcomers to the development. Tom was a happy man, an organizer, and unfortunately, the first of many to leave us over the past 19 years. I was honoured, to give a eulogy on behalf of the community at his church service, and have included this in my memoir notes. Sorrow followed by joy, as Fiona and Ian were married in August. The reception was at the Schoolhouse in Markham, a restaurant home to many of Ian's company management team. A family dinner followed. It was a great celebration, with a very young Cassandra in attendance and in the wedding party, but not at the dinner. Bedtime required she be taken home by a sitter!

Following the wedding, Maureen, El and I, spent the weekend at the Guilfoyles cottage, in Muskoka. We were then advised, that Ian had won a golf tournament prize of a weekend at the Taboo Resort in Muskoka. The accommodation was the cottage "owned", by the Canadian golfer

Mike Weir, and El and I were invited to join Fiona and Ian, and spend the weekend there.

I was "babysitting", a 3 year- old Cassandra, who did not want to leave the resort's adjoining lake where she was paddling. Trying not to upset her, but to convince her that I was serious about leaving, I walked about 50 paces away to be greeted by her yelling, "Grandpa, I am doing what you told me to do. I am peeing in the water." A chorus of throat clearing noises, echoed up and down the beach, from the men in deckchairs reading their morning newspapers. I had to interpret this, as criticism of the advice, I had given my granddaughter.

We continued the fall ritual of going to Sarasota. The first week, we were able to host our close Ballantrae neighbours, Jeff and Sheri. The surf was extremely high while they were, which was fine for Jeff, because he is tall. I, on the other hand was swamped continuously, to say the least. Maureen joined us for the 2nd and 3rd weeks. These vacations were Els' favourite, and rightly so. Warm days, warm water, sunbathing, eating out every night! Not cooking at all any night was a real treat!

Our Christmas theatre and dinner night tradition for the girls was finally broken, and we ended up taking Susan and Fiona and husbands, to dinner only, at the Oakland Hall restaurant in Aurora. Why had the tradition ended? Probably, because of the busy lives that the girls now had, and the fact that they had growing families, with activities to attend to. Sixteen years of Christmas theatre shows and downtown dinners, is a pretty good run, and although it was sad to end, we had good evenings, and even better memories. Hosting Christmas Day family dinner, was not over yet, and we were also able to visit Doug and Michele in Madoc next day. We had the usual Standard Life and Ballantrae, Christmas celebrations, but as a change, stayed home for New Years' Eve.

2005 saw another change of tradition, in that we celebrated Burns Supper on January 25th, in the house. El had to be persuaded to go along with this, because Burns suppers are not just about Haggis, but a sumptuous menu of Cock-a-Leekie soup, Haggis with Neeps and Champit tatties,

Aberdeen Angus beef or Lossiemouth salmon, with a closing "piece de resistance", of Tipsy Laird Trifle (Drambuie soaked cake, whipped cream and raspberries). This in essence is a feast, which requires a whole day's attention to the presentation. I helped a bit in the preparation, but all honours go to El.

We invited our closest neighbours, the Van Velzens, the Cannons, and the Pyles, as our initial Ballantrae group. It was our intention over future years, to invite different groups of neighbours each year. This idea would eventually backfire. The evening is not just about eating and drinking, but of Burns education, involving a quiz, a piping in of the haggis, an address to the haggis, and the reading of an abbreviated history of Robert Burns, and some of his famous poetry. This requires a 4 - hour evening. A Coyle rule was also implemented, to compliment the meal. "You no eat the haggis, you dina get the trifle!"

Maureen joined us for the Scottish celebration, and we then flew to Cancun, early February for a 2 week stay at the Grand Palladium White Sands resort near Tulum, Mexico. We had been there before, but now noticed that the influx of mainly American young American tourists, had left its mark on the hotel, and not in a nice way. El also had stomach and headache problems not long after we arrived, which were medically solved. The signs were there, that this might be our last trip to Mexico. We did not keep that promise.

A trip to Xcaret Park, brought the highlight of watching an animal keeper, complete with underwater breathing equipment, feeding a very young Manatee underwater, with a very large baby bottle, full of mothers' milk or formula. The Manatee was obviously very attached to the young man, and it really was a very touching scene. He was the provider of life, and the young marine mammal's eyes, followed him everywhere.

The beach, the ocean, the food at the hotel were all excellent. Everything was good, if you ignored the damage that previous visitors had caused, which had not all been attended to. When you stay at an all-inclusive, there is still a desire, to get off the property and explore, especially if you feel it is safe enough. We have never felt nervous in Mexico, but the number of police road checks, and the display of weapons by armed guards at banks, was certainly increasing. We signed up, for what the hotel advertised as a Mayan Echo Adventure all day trip. It turned out to be a super value trip!

The day trip involved cycling through a "tourist" jungle, to various adventure spots. We started on a zip line, which was pretty tame, because the elevation angle was very slight with little slope. The hardest part was getting up the tree to the platform. The next "adventure", was repelling down a dry cenote, while getting the hang of the equipment, and controlling your speed. The most difficult part of doing this, was the feeling you had, after stepping of the cliff, into thin air, of course while still attached and locked onto the guide wire, and then controlling the speed of your descent. Having managed that, you walked back to the top of the cliff via a path.

Our next challenge was repelling into a wet cenote. All rivers in this part of Mexico are underground, and many cenotes (deep craters), are full of crystal, clear lakes of water. To get there as a group, we were all issued bicycles and told to follow the path, until we were met by the next guide. To stop the bike, we were instructed to pedal backwards. Get this into Maureen's head, not possible! Her legs would only turn one way, forward, and if she went of course while tackling a hill, the legs continued to churn forwards, at an even greater speed. Consequently, instead of stopping or slowing down on a hill or bumpy surface, her legs turned faster in the wrong direction, i.e. forward. This meant that now and again, she would go of course, leave the path and disappear into the jungle growth, to reappear some 50 or so meters, further up the path, wearing some of the green vegetation, legs still pumping furiously forwards. This happened several times, until thankfully we arrived at the next challenge, the wet cenote site.

Access to the cenote and the platform, some 50 feet below was by, a not very large hole with a rickety looking wooden structure, complete with a pulley system, to which you attached your repelling equipment. A Mayan, helped you hook up, and then swung you into the hanging position in the middle of the hole. You then repelled at the speed you desired, out of the sunlight, into what seemed murky darkness. As your eyes, became accustomed to the difference in light, you could see that you would be able to land gently onto a floating platform, surrounded by water. Swimming was optional, but the water was clear and fresh, and not cold.

El had examined the whole procedure; the Mayans, the hole, the repelling equipment, and "the what was down below in the inky darkness", and decided that this challenge was not for her! We discussed her concerns, which include claustrophobia, which is very real. I gently suggested that this was perhaps, her one and only chance to do this, and after getting a solemn promise from the Mayan lad, that she would be brought up and into the sunlight first in the group, she consented to give it a try. By the way the Mayan's nod of agreement, had nothing to do with him understanding what she had asked him to promise.

I had gone just before her and was able to help her out of her gear and onto the floating platform. To keep cool, she went for a swim, but as soon as the whistle went as a signal for us to return, she churned through the water at Olympic speed, and muscled herself to the front of the queue. We were pulled up, one at a time, in a harness, at what seemed record speed. I wanted to congratulate the Mayans, on their effective machinery, until I noticed that the power was being provided by 6 beefy Mayans, who were running up a side path, and providing the necessary power to pull us up, and back into the sunlight, in record time. We ended the day by going to Coba, to reclimb the Pyramid there, and to visit the various Mayan ruins. As a tourist trip, this was certainly full value for the experience. We also were entertained royally by Maureen's cycling antics, which were like something out of a Charlie Chapman movie, and just as amusing.

> After returning home, El left for Vancouver on April 26, and I followed her a few days later. Using Maureen's house as a base, we enjoyed time and meals with our Vancouver friends, and then vacationed with the Nordhoys again on Whidbey Island and with the Scharfes on Bowen Island. We returned home in time to attend Ida East's memorial service in Ancaster. She was truly a lady, whom we both liked and admired.

June saw me turning over many of my Standard Life defined benefit pension clients to daughter Susan, who had been elevated to a Defined

Pension Benefit Specialist position. Maybe Standard thought that I was taking too many vacations, and they were probably right. I was also about to turn 65, and it was their way of saying "Your time is a hup".

Later that summer we turned in our Honda CRV, on the expiry of its lease, and purchased a Toyota Highlander CRV, which I grew to love, but never drove, because El loved it more. Golf was now a major part of my life, and I played a lot that summer with multi Ballantrae neighbours.

July 8th 2005, brought a huge surprise. We were going to dinner with Fiona and Ian at the School Restaurant. They wanted to show me the renovation work just completed in the main dining room. I recall that I really was not that interested, and therefore they literally had to force march me there, to be greeted by a roomful of 60 family members and friends for a surprise 65th birthday. Maureen had flown in from Vancouver. It truly was a total surprise, probably because it was 2 weeks before my actual birthday. A photograph taken at the time, clearly shows my dropped jaw, as I entered the room, and tells it all. El, Fiona and Ian get credit for a wonderful job in organizing this secretive and very special occasion. The company, food, comments were all just excellent, and I was speechless, which I am sure suited most people just fine.

I was invited to two events in late summer. The first, was the Guilfoyle Consulting annual golf tournament at Wooden Sticks, which was of significance, because I was not a client. The second invitation was to Graydon Hulse's retirement dinner, at which I was asked to speak. Graydon was the Secretary Treasurer of Local 153 of the I.A.T.S.E., members union, which represents movie theatre and theatrical employees who work behind the scenes, and make the presentation of the screen film you see, satisfactory. I had "baby sat", the pension plan for many years, and to be invited to a union function, was a recognition of the close relationship, that Graydon and I had cemented over the years. I was able to express those thoughts in my congratulatory speech.

I did not know why, but starting August 15th, 2005, El and I were getting up early and going to the Ballantrae Rec Centre to swim, before breakfast and my going to work. Swimming is not a passion of mine, and I do not like getting up early, so what possessed me to get up at 7:00 a.m. and do this, was beyond me at the time. I was to get more than a clue, early in 2006.

Without divulging right now, what was to transpire in 2006, I want to say a few words about my belief that one's life if you allow it, can be guided by a power much greater than yours. There are so many instances in my life, where decisions were made "outside of my reasoning", but virtually all in my favour. We tend to, without thought, attach the label of "coincidence" to such happenings. I believe there is a God, and He certainly has looked after me many times, and charted my life and future, even when I was stubborn enough to believe at one time, and for a long time, that I was the sole factor in influencing all that went on around me.

The success of Betty Shukster's led trip to Italy in 2003, had echoed throughout the Ballantrae community. This encouraged her to arrange another full trip, also to Italy, but this time to visit the highlights of Rome and southern Italy, including Sicily and the Amalfi coast. Arriving in Milan in October 2005, we flew to Palermo, as our starting point to cover Sicily. During our first two days we toured Palermo, Mondello (vacation resort), Cefalu (town on the water), Monreale (cathedral town), and Erice (walled town with a Norman castle). Interesting, but pretty basic stuff!

Our tour bus took us next to the south of Sicily, to Agrigento overnight, and then to the Valley of the Temples, which is a World Heritage Site. The valley includes remains of 7 Doric style Greek temples, with the mainstay being, the Temple of Concordia, built in the 5th century B.C., but still in a good state of preservation. Having been to Athens and Rhodes and witnessed a fair amount of Greek archeology, I was more than impressed with the size and condition of the Concordia temple. It still had the vast majority of the roof in place and all of the columns. It is spectacular.

Bear in mind that we are in Sicily, which is very much a part of Italy, and we are witnessing all things Greek. One does not realize the dominance and spread of the Greek Empire at its height, and especially its coverage of much of the Mediterranean. As an example, we drove for supper to the town of Selinunte, located by the sea. This was an ancient Greek city on the southwest coast of Sicily, featuring 5 temples, of which only the Temple of Hera, has been re- erected. At its peak before 409 B.C., it is believed that the city may have had a population of 30,000.

These sites, plus our visit to a large and preserved, elaborate Roman Villa called The Villa Romana del Casale, complete with artwork dating back to the 4th century A.D., gave us some meat to satisfy our tourist appetites. It contains some 3500 hundred square meters of flooring and is also designated as a World Heritage Site. Before excavation, and even with parts of the villa showing above ground level, the locals were not at all curious, as to what lay below, and continued to seed and cultivate the land above and around it.

It is now time to give credit to our guide on this second Italian tour. His name is Romano and he was the younger brother of Elio, our guide in 2003. He had big shoes to fill, and boy did he fill them. He was not just technically good, he was hilarious, and entertained us on the odd long bus trip, with stand- up comedy routines. He spoke and we laughed at length, at his monologues about his flying lessons in Florida, and his brilliant portrayal of himself as a young Italian immigrant attempting to integrate into American society, and in particular how to be favoured and admitted to a night club by the bouncer, after being in the line- up for so long. His "stick", re his returning to the clothing store, to exchange his recently purchased shirt for one with "the horse" (polo insignia), and using this to persuade and gain entry to the nightclub, and successfully dance with the girl of his dreams, was truly hilarious. All this was delivered by him, standing in the bus aisle, while we tourists roared our heads off.

We stayed in a beautiful 5- star hotel in Giardini Naxos and then visited the famous tourist trap of Taormina, which is high on a mountain top. Very famous, but very expensive. The only purchase I almost made was a sweater, which turned out to be a ladies' garment. I almost purchased it, because it was so tight, that I could not get it off. Later, our local guide had great difficulty in finding our restaurant, and we wandered the streets of Taormina, like lost sheep.

Taormina is beautifully located, and within reasonable distance of the ferry docks at Messina which links Sicily with the mainland, with a fairly short ferry ride. The Italian government has discussed for many years, the possibility of linking the island of Sicily and the Italian mainland, with a bridge. Based upon cost estimates, they may continue to talk about it, but "it ain't gonna happen".

A trip, partway up Aetna, the active volcano, was more than interesting. At 11,000 feet it continues to be the most active volcano in Europe, with multiple eruptions. The last one being in 2018. The damage to buildings in 2001 and 2002, from active lava flows, points out the threat that this monster poses, to this part of Sicily. We then bussed through Catania to Siracusa, to the Isle of Ortigia, to view more Greek antiquities and a cave in Siracusa. The cave was bored out of solid rock to originally store fresh cool water, but is now used as a tourist attraction, because when one speaks in it, the sound of your voice is echoed multiple times, and in some cases up to 16 times.

We returned to Naxos, for a last night celebration in Sicily. Everything, including the wine was excellent. So much so, that our group of 40 plus dignified Canadians, ended up doing a conga line through the restaurant, much to the pleasure, surprise, and I am sure some annoyance of the other patrons. Take your pick! The conga music was available also on a CD, and when this was played on the bus system, our driver Alphonso got into the act, by using his brakes and steering wheel to move the bus from side to side in a jarring motion. Luckily, we were not far from our hotel, and the avenue we were on was wide, and with little traffic. Otherwise, we and the driver would all have been thrown in the "hoosegow", if the police had stopped the bus.

We travelled the next morning to the Messina crossing referred to earlier, and ferried over the short distance to the mainland. We then stayed at a very garish hotel near Pompeii, but declined the excursion, as we had toured the area in 2003. Betty exhibited a nice touch, by including our guides, Romano's and Alphonso's families, for a night at the hotel, with dinner. We took off the next day for Naples, to then cross by hydrofoil to the Isle of Capri. After a zigzag bus trip up the side of a mountain, we hopped on a chairlift, and were transported to the top of the island, for a magnificent view and lunch at the Bellavista restaurant. The name says it all. You could stay for many days on Capri. You might not be able to afford it, but at least you could, try it for a little while. A small cup of coffee later in the day, cost about $9 Canadian, but the warmth of the day, the breeze, the views, the Isle of Capri setting, made it worth the cost, and taste even better. We returned to the mainland, visited Sorrento, drove a portion of the Amalfi coast, and celebrated at a viewing stop, with samples of limoncello and pastries, courtesy of the Trafalgar tour company. We were off to Rome the next day to again tour such sites as the Trevi Fountain, the Spanish Steps and the Pantheon. The latter is one of the best preserved of all Ancient Roman Buildings. Formerly a temple, dedicated about 126 A.D., it has continued to be used throughout history, and since the 7th century, the Pantheon has been used as a church. The building is magnificent. Such are the wonders of ancient civilization, and they are there for the viewing. You just have to go!

Our gala night was at the Canova Restaurant in the Piazza del Popolo, in the heart of Rome. It is still in business today. We had a really good clean fun night, with lots of singing and dancing. Highlights, included Betty Shukster, attempting to climb on the piano, to render a goodbye song to her group, in a prone "sexy" position. The only problem, was getting her up there. Not so sexy! Two men and a stool, finally did the trick.

David Parsons, who is a very accomplished pianist was itching to play, and when the resident pianist took a break, David was there in a shot, asking permission to take over. The fun part, was when the restaurant manager passed by, heard him play, did a double take, rushed off, and returned with a 50 Euro note, which he deposited in the tip jar. I am sure it was taken out before the night ended. Our official trip ended there, but a few of us, had decided to unwind and stay 3 more nights in Rome, and to make it worthwhile, we had booked a visit, to a relatively unheralded museum, the Villa Borghese.

The museum features Bernini's sculptures of Pauline (Napoleon's sister), David with the sling in the act of slaying Goliath, and Phoebus (Apollo) and Daphne. The latter depicts Daphne, at her request, being transformed by her father, Peneus, into a tree to resist being sexually assaulted by Apollo. You "gotta" see it! In my opinion, the whole exhibition just cannot be topped, and a visit to the Villa Borghese is a must, if you are in Rome. You must book ahead, as admittance is by organized groups at stated times.

We visited the Vatican again, as there is just so much to see. In climbing the narrow staircase, which looks down into St. Peter's Basilica, the Italian Renaissance church in Vatican City, we became separated. El did not want to be a part of a narrow staircase. Maureen viewed the stairs as a physical challenge, and took off like a gazelle. I staggered up with the masses. The result was, that I never saw them again for about 4 hours. We were in the Vatican, however, and viewing makes the time go by! We linked up, at about 3:30, at a flea market outside of the Vatican. The location makes one wonder, as to how much effort was put in by the ladies, to re-locate me!

The next day, we were up at 5:00 a.m., on a plane to Milan, and then on to Toronto, arriving at 8:00 p.m. Italian time, a mere 15 hours of travel. There is a penalty to travel and you have to accept it, or stay home. Once again Betty Shukster's led trip, was well worth the money, not only from what we saw and experienced, but bonused by very comfortable accommodation, quality guiding by the Trafalgar Group representatives, and a busload, of easy going Ballantrae tourists. The memories are treasured, and there is more to come from the same source.

The remaining 2 months of 2005 were uneventful. It would appear that the transfer of my consulting clientele was successful, as my diary work entries were now, few and far between. We enjoyed our usual Christmas functions and hosted 18 family members for Christmas Day dinner, complete with the traditional "string game", for our daughters and grandchildren, to provide fun and an extra gift. New Years' Eve, was celebrated with a Marlene and Paul Egan dinner invitation, along with Shirley, Marilyn and Myrna, ladies who had lost their husbands, all of whom we knew.

For a change of pace, Betty Shukster organized a Caribbean cruise in January, 2006, aboard a Royal Caribbean cruise ship, the Brilliance of the Seas, a 2400 passenger liner. When we arrived to embark in Fort Lauderdale, we were met by television cameras covering the fact that CSI Miami investigators were on board, to follow up on a murder investigation, not a television show. The ship had been repositioned in the Mediterranean for the summer months, during which a recently married American male, on his honeymoon, had gone missing. He was last seen in the ship's gambling casino, and although the body was never recovered, there were blood stains on the balcony rail of his cabin. Hmmm!

The weather had not been good in the Mediterranean, and the cabin we were assigned to was next to a damaged bulkhead of the ship, which continually banged against the hull, making sleep impossible. With reluctance, and after several request, we were met by a crew member, about 3:00 in the morning and moved to a cabin on deck 7.

The 10- day cruise, featured stops in Haiti, Aruba, Curacao, the Panama Canal and Costa Rica. We had a catered lunch, on shore in Haiti, at a port stop called Labadee, which the cruise line has exclusive rights to. To my knowledge the locals that stay in a nearby township, and have access to the land owned by the cruise line, must be born there, or must have a direct birth relationship to the families, who live there. After we left, they rushed in to collect what food had not been eaten. The local merchants are given sole rights to sell their goods to the ship's tourists, and literally overwhelm you, in a frightening and desperate manner, when the park gate is unlocked. I had to yell at them to back off, or El would have been knocked off her feet. Sad, but that is Haiti!

Aruba and Curacao with their Dutch heritage, are very touristy, with colourful attractive buildings. We went snorkeling in Aruba, which created some problems, as the water was quite turbulent, and the reefs are shallow, causing the odd scratch to the body. The other problem was that when you surfaced, everyone and I mean everyone, had the same coloured equipment on, and finding El and Maureen in a hundred ocean bobbing bodies was not easy. Communication was only achieved by yelling out their names repeatedly, and finally getting a response.

Our fellow Ballantrae residents at our dining table were good company, and we were well served by our waiters, Hector and Victor, who always brought the correct customized meals, to the right person. To be devilish, I suggested that while the waiters were in the kitchen, the eleven of us switch seats. The looks on the faces of the waiters, was priceless, as they glanced over again and again, before serving us, trying to figure out what was different. Hector implored, that we never do this again. It was the last night. He was safe, but I was no longer his favourite.

El, had what we believed was motion sickness during the first few days. I would apologize for her absence and then minutes later, she would show up at the dinner table. This happened several nights in a row, and indicated that although something was not quite right, it was not long lasting. We visited the ship's medical staff, and they gave her an injection, which seemed to work. When we returned to Toronto, tests indicated that her thyroid gland readings were not balanced, and after the appropriate medicine, she returned to normal.

To experience the working procedures behind the Panama Canal locks, we entered one at 6:00 a.m., and then disembarked in a lake, before taking a train west to Panama City, and then back by bus, to rejoin the ship. The young Panamanian staff on the train were just delightful. You are aware that their expectation is, that they will be tipped along the way. However, these kids were so genuine and innocent in their joy and group singing, that you wanted to take a couple home.

To understand the Panama Canal, you have to realize that the cruise ships and freighters that travel through, are designed to just fit into the width and length of each lock. To ensure that the ships do not bang into the sides of the lock, they are attached on each side of the ship, by heavy duty cables, which in turn are attached on either side, to small electric train locomotives.

These locomotives naturally run on train tracks. The tensions on the cables are adjusted by computer sensors, to ensure the progress of the ship entering the lock is dead centre, without causing damage to either the ship, or the walls of the lock. The train tracks are not level, as they at times run uphill to compensate for the topography of the land, and therefore the height of each lock. A complete transit takes eight to ten hours.

The Panama Canal is an artificial 82k waterway that connects the Atlantic with the Pacific. The U.S. took over the project in 1904 and opened the canal in 1914. France began the work in 1881, but stopped due to engineering problems and high worker mortality, from mosquito bites. Annual traffic, before the building of parallel locks in 2016, was about 15,000 vessels per year. From east to west, there are 3 locks up and 3 locks down. The locks vary in their number of stages (12 in total). The record toll for a single cruise ship was in 2010, an amount of $375,600. The average toll is under $100,000, and is related to the number of occupied and unoccupied berths on the cruise ship.

Our last stop was Costa Rica and a zipline adventure. We were met, with strong winds and pelting rain, and by guides carrying huge golf umbrellas. Most of us pretended, that nothing was going to stop us. Sanity prevailed, and the outing was cancelled by the manager, shortly after we arrived at the departure area. He explained that the strength of the wind and rain, might prevent us stopping at the transfer point to the next zip line, and that those with glasses, may not be able to see. In essence, as we were zipping between trees, short of death, we would be in trouble.

Exercising on the ship, was mainly walking around the deck, in lanes clearly marked. For some reason, I was not able to keep up with her, and militant Maureen yelled at me frequently. As a matter of course, El and I gave blood and then had medicals in February, as requested by our GP, Dr Lougheed on our return from the cruise, with follow up tests scheduled for me in March at Markham Stouffville Hospital. I then had a further examination on April 13, to investigate my shortness of breath, after repeatedly only being able to swim 2 lengths of the pool at Ballantrae's rec centre.

Being a typical male, I believed that all this testing, was much ado about nothing. Consequently, El and I set out on a 2 - week vacation to Vancouver on April 28, to arrange for and bring back Maureen's Toyota Sienna van, which she had sold to us. It was in terrific shape. We did our usual visiting and made arrangements to send the van by train to Toronto and assist Maureen in purchasing a new car. She settled on a fire engine red Nissan Trailblazer, which she loved. We helped Maureen around the house and garden, and made some new friends at Richmond Pentecostal Church. I played golf with Maureen at Country Meadows and while practicing there, somehow lost my wedding ring, which sadly, no one had the courage or the honesty to turn in. It was a 3- diamond beauty. A sad day.

We returned from Vancouver, in time for me to have an X-ray and scheduled stress test on May 15. I will not soon forget the female medical technician overseeing the stress test, bursting through the door of an adjoining office, and yelling "Stop the test", as my vital signs were moving down and way out of normal range, indicating an extremely low blood pressure reading. A May 18th appointment with a cardiologist, Dr Hacker, was then scheduled for an ECG and an Echocardiogram. The results were discussed with Dr. Lougheed on May 25, and an angiogram was booked for May 31, 2006 at Southlake Hospital.

The angiogram revealed 3 arterial blockages, 90%, 75% and 65%. Conclusion… bypass surgery. A meeting with the surgeon Dr. Moon, was scheduled for June 15th. I thought there was urgency to the situation, but in reality, surgeons have to have time off, and at the time he and Dr. Peniston, were the only heart surgeons at Southlake, having started the program together in 2004. The preop was set for June 28. It was extensive and impressive. But all I heard, was that I was physically in good shape, with good legs to provide the bypass veins, and therefore there was no rush. I was being deemed as elective and not urgent. I was not exactly happy with this news, and pushed Dr. Moon's secretary by phone, to try and get me an earlier time slot for my surgery.

She called back on July 18, to state that they had an opening on July 20, due to a cancellation. Instructions were to arrive at Southlake at 6:00 a.m., stop your blood thinner now, and read the night before instructions, given at the preop. I had my last client appointment for Standard Life, on July 19 at 4:30 p.m., and joined El for dinner at Joia Restaurant that night, to celebrate my 66th birthday. The next a.m., El and I sat in an isolated hospital anti-room. El was very nervous, and she was the one who required a warm blanket, which made her look more like the patient. I received an intra venous line, and was out cold, long before I entered the surgery. The surgery room by the way, is huge, with intricate piping to handle the blood flow, during the bypass surgery.

Surgery, which started at 8:00, revealed a fourth blockage at the 60% level. Bleeding became a problem, and consequently, I was in surgery for about 7 hours, while the staff determined how to solve my problem. Dr. Moon spoke to family members at about 3:15 that afternoon, and indicated that although I was still bleeding, this should stop. It was difficult for the family, to believe this, as the drip, drip, continued in the CVICU intensive care ward. I spent 48 hours in intensive care, most of the time asleep. The family (caregivers), are the ones, who suffer most in these times of waiting, hoping and praying. I was finally transferred to recovery room 5627 on the hospital's 5th floor on the afternoon of July 22nd. This, I now know, was a good "out of danger" sign.

I had been given 3 units of blood during and following the operation. I am Rh positive, which is the most common, blood type available, and there is usually plenty in stock. Pre- op always knows your blood type. My stay in room 5627, was not the most pleasant. Nursing attention was excellent, but due to the length of the surgery, I had a reaction to the anesthetic and drugs, and just felt "punk", for a few days. Even nausea relief Gravol pills, did not help. I did not have pain, because of the length of my stay in ICU, and because Dr. Moon had a very special technique of removing the vein from your leg for the bypass procedure, with 2 small incisions, as opposed to a leg long incision. To qualify you had to have "good legs". My fitness had paid off in this area. Not everyone can accept this technique, but if you qualify, you do not have to be burdened with your leg being opened up from top to bottom to retrieve the vein, have the wound stapled, and then wait further for full recovery, which can take longer than the chest wound to heal.

Moon was more than satisfied with my recovery, and authorized my discharge on July 25, that is 5 days post, surgery, which was the norm in those days. It is 4 days now. El was mortified, "Look at him, he is pathetic", she echoed. "Better out of here than face the danger of infection", he countered, and we left that day. This statement makes you less likely to argue. I have summarized events in a poem, entitled "A Heart Stopping Experience". A copy of that poem, possibly still unread, was still on Southlake's CVICU reception area noticeboard, 14 years after the surgery.

The following, to those without belief, may seem a bit strange, but on the Sunday night of my stay, I was saved. I had prayed to God, that if He brought me through the operation, I was His. I have joked, that due to the length of the operation, He perhaps had hesitated somewhat. That Sunday night, about 3:00 in the morning, the silence in my room was deafening. All noises from beeping medical equipment seemed to have stopped. I was "visited" and my conversion was complete. I have volunteered in that CV Surgery ward since December 2007, and every time I enter room 5627, during my Friday shift, I am comforted and consoled by what God has done.

Post bypass surgery, requires dedicated walking and exercising, to speed up and ensure recovery. I had lost my voice, due to the breathing tube being inserted for such a long period, such that when I was home, my positive, but hoarse response to a consoler, was not truly convincing. In addition, to assist with the irritation around one of the drain holes in my stomach, a staff member at Markham Stouffville Hospital had applied a band aid. The irritation got worse, and when the band aid was removed, there were signs of infection, which is a no, no, after surgery.

We left the house about 11:30, on the Friday night of July 28, just 8 days after the surgery, to seek help at Southlake's emergency. After being discharged with an antibiotic prescription, from a doctor, who I did not think much of, we had it filled at an Aurora Drug store, and set off for home about 2:30 in the morning. Poor El, had encountered multi red lights, after leaving the hospital. The icing on the cake, was being stopped, at a railroad crossing, by the longest freight train ever, crossing Aurora side road, just west of Warden. I was not happy. The memory of these flashing red lights, and that endless line of freight cars swooshing past, will remain with me forever.

The next 6 weeks as for all cardiac patients, was spent recovering, walking and thinking about walking. You are limited in the first week to 5- minute walks, 6 times a day, increasing gradually to 30- minute walks at the end of 6 weeks. Summer surgery is better, as you can walk outside with your red heart pillow, and get lots of sympathy. El, as the care giver was the nervous one, because she had experienced the anxiety, and saw how fragile I was. To avoid the possibility of an air bag injury, the cardiac patient has to sit in the back seat for 6 weeks. As you get better, you become more like a back- seat driver, if you know what I mean. El looked good in the chauffeur's hat!

We enjoyed a weekend at the Guilfoyles' cottage, where I was treated royally with kid gloves. A stress test followed, prior to admittance to Southlake Hospital's Heart Recovery program. They now have quarters at the Magna Centre on Mulloch, complete with 2 and soon to be 3, fully financed heart stress testing units. The program then, required visitation twice a week for 26 weeks. The numbers of patients using the program now, has required lowering the visits to, once per week. I was given an ECG and Echocardiogram by Dr Hacker, followed by a meeting with Dr. Moon in September. Both were pleased, and gave me the green light to travel. I took my recovery seriously, and El joined me for frequent swimming at the Rec Centre.

Recovery was going well, and remember my "working life", was over. We were free to travel and after medical approval, undertook to drive to Sarasota for a 5 week stay on October 27th. El, bless her, did more than her fair share of the driving, and we arrived mid- afternoon of the 4th day on the road. To say, I was nervous, as a backseat driver, was an understatement. We encountered 2 days of inordinate traffic holdups, due to accidents. I had no patience, was agitated and beside myself. Presumably, biproducts of a fairly long operation and recovery! Eleanor was the one to be patient!

The weather, at that time of year in Florida, is usually spectacular, as hurricane season comes to a close, and we were not disappointed. The Leightons joined us for the first week and Fiona, Ian and Cassandra came during our second week. Later on, we visited our Ballantrae neighbours, Charlie and Johanna, and Fritz and Margaret, in separate trips to Northport, and a new local couple Christine and Al Vermeer, whom we had met at The Shining Light church picnic.

I was tired at times, but had to be at my best to leave the condo at 7:00 every morning for a week, to "explore" the beach and parts of Sarasota, with Cassandra. I am sure that her early morning rise in the other bedroom, was greeted by her mother with, "Go and see your Grandpa". Even El feigned sleep, when Cassandra came in, stood by the bed and stared. Not a word was spoken by her, until I got up and got dressed. I did get a kick out of Cassandra introducing herself to fellow morning beach walkers, at almost the age of 6.

Upon leaving Sarasota, we drove to Orlando, to visit former Aurora Cornerstone Church members, Tony and Pat Klinakis, both very talented musicians. Tony on drums, and Pat singing and on guitar, were a treat to listen to. We then set off for Charlottetown, North Carolina, to see Mary and Rolland Hoffman, who had been our neighbours for several years in Unionville. Mary does not cook, as previously mentioned, so we ate all our meals out, before leaving.

To say I was tired, when we got home was accurate, but we just had such a great vacation, with lots of company and memories. Just lovely couples, but time and distance, tend to test and eventually break relationships. You have to keep working at it. However, it is a human failing, not to do so! El and I, have always gone out of our way, to maintain and foster relationships on a long- term basis, as long as the other parties were willing.

Our trip to Florida, although enjoyable, was made in lieu of a Betty Shukster, organized trip to Peru (Machu Picchu), the Galapagos Islands and an Amazon location in Brazil. A very special trip, that we had to turn down. As the doctors advised, "The altitude in Peru, so soon, would be a problem. The lack of heart recovery medical services in and around Machu Picchu, would be more than a problem." Maureen had signed up, and enjoyed the trip of a lifetime, which she enjoyed relating to us, again and again.

Maureen joined us on return from her trip, and we took advantage of her presence, to invite our Caribbean cruise table mates, the Gormans, Crosses and Andersons for an evening of reminiscing about the cruise. John Anderson joined the RAF as a fighter pilot during World War 2, but was shot down on his first mission, flying 603 squadron spitfires out of a British base, which amazingly was my home town Edinburgh airport, called Turnhouse. He was recovered by the Germans from the waters of the English Channel, and became a prisoner of war for many years, until the last of his many pow camps were liberated by the Allies in late 1944. A great story to end the year!

9

BALLANTRAE

2007 -2012

In early January, 2007, Andrea Kreutzer arranged a farewell lunch for me, with Jeff Gray, Robyn and partners. A nice parting touch, which had been delayed, due to my busy 2006. The three musketeers were the members of Sales Unit # 1 in our group pension sales office, who for many years, had put their heads down and worked very hard, to achieve successful sales results

Later that month, Susan and Fiona joined us for a renewal of our family dinner at Oakland Hall, claiming that the husbands could stay home and "kid sit", if necessary. Maureen arrived on January 24, in time for a Burns night celebration at the house, with 3 invited couples. It was too successful, and I could see the storm clouds gathering, if as intended, we disinvited those neighbours next year, and invited a completely different group. We were then, up, up and away, on January 28, by Transat Air to Cancun, for what would be our last planned vacation in Mexico.

We encountered multi small, but nagging problems, at our hotel near Tulum, which I have included in a poem entitled "Grand Palladium White Sands, Playa Kantenha". It seemed obvious, that the hotel expansion had got ahead of itself, and they had opened up too soon, before the various problems we encountered, had been addressed. Management and their service staff could not keep up, with the number of mechanical breakdowns they were encountering in the rooms.

The weather, the beach, the water, the side trips to Tulum and Playa Del Carmen, were all excellent. This however was our 6th trip to Mexico, over 9 years, and was destined to be our final visit. Later on, you will see that I have "white lied", but all for a very good family reason. Good times, good memories, no regrets, but we had to weigh these experiences, with the increasing health problems that we were encountering in Mexico, despite their claims of "totally safe drinking water". Another factor was, that we had pretty well seen everything, that the Mexican Mayan Riviera had to offer.

On return, we were about to attend a 75th birthday celebration for one of our neighbours, when we received an urgent call from Fiona. "Dad I'm in a telephone booth and I can't move. My back's out." "Call 911", I said. "I did and they don't want to come, I am in a building across the street from the hospital". "Call them again and stress that you cannot move. They will come. We are on our way and will meet you in Southlake's emergency". Under Ontario law, a person taken to emergency on a gurney, by para-medicals, must be attended by those same persons, until released into an approved hospital bed, or seen by a doctor. This can mean hours of waiting in the emergency area, until this happens. You can perhaps understand, the reluctance of the para-medics to transport Fiona less than 100 meters.

The cause of the back pain and resulting spasms, was never revealed, but we witnessed the stress she was under, from an excruciating pain trip to the washroom in the hospital, before she was examined, and the exam itself. This was followed by relaxing shots, pain medication and a drive home with Mum. We got her into bed and somewhat relaxed ourselves, after a mere 6 hours.

Happy birthday Fieny Van Velzen! We never got to your celebration, due to Fiona's emergency. We did however attend a marriage anniversary luncheon, for Albert and Marion Stirling at Angus Glen, later that month. A very small, but a very dignified celebration, for such a lovely couple.

March 6th, saw ECG and Echocardiogram testing by Dr. Hacker, my cardiologist, with a good report and "A come back and see me in one year's time". I graduated from the Southlake Hospital Heart Recovery program on March 13, 2007, following the 6- month program. I decided then and there, that I had the time and the desire, to apply for a hospital volunteer position with the same program. I applied March 19, but was to be faced with some unknown obstacles and consequent delays.

The balance of the month is historic for the following. March 21, 2007, we held our first Wednesday night bible study in the house. The first of many through the years. March 22, Gordon Pritchard and I started to meet weekly, if available, following us jointly going through the Southlake Heart Recovery program together and forming a good relationship. This was the start of our two- hour, on and off weekly meetings, that have lasted for 13 years, during which we reshape the world, and solve all of life's problems. March 23, El had an open- ended MRI, to try and determine the cause of the ringing in her ears, later confirmed as Tinnitus. This is caused by stress, and despite years of intervention in the U.S. and Canada by medical procedures and specialists, the ongoing problem has not been alleviated.

To volunteer in a hospital, you must pass a police check and be free of tuberculosis. I was fine with the check, but the medical procedure indicated, that I was testing positive for TB. I had to guess that this was related to my life in the U.K., where TB was rampant, and everyone was inoculated, following the war years.

El and I flew to Vancouver late April, using Maureen's house as a base, and renewing the bonds with our friends. A special time was that during our trip to Whidbey Island in Washington, we took a day side trip to the Boeing Aero manufacturing plant in Everett, and enjoyed a conducted tour, to observe the building of the 777, 767 and the Dreamliner 787, Boeing passenger jets. Well worth the visit. However, the massive building intended to house the newest Boeing plane, the 787 Dreamliner, was empty, as they were well behind with this new project, as many plane parts which were being manufactured in various countries around the world, had not yet arrived. Points of interest were the size of the hangars, the moving assembly lines similar to automobile lines, but much, much slower, and the 747s bringing the 787 parts to Everett. These 747 planes had been modified, to have the bubble upper part of the plane extended all the way to the rear, to accommodate large assembly parts, such as wings. Also, of interest were the huge number of bicycles, that staff use on site, to get around the massive plant. The bicycles are colour coded, to represent each department. You can take any bike, as long as it relates to your department.

I had been a candidate for left hip replacement surgery in 2006, which of course was delayed, due to the heart bypass surgery. I finally met my hip surgeon, Dr Haider, on May 14, for scheduled surgery in July. That same month, El had further investigative procedures to follow up on her ear problem, to try and solve the chronic ringing. I also had my first visit with Dr. Lynde, a skin specialist, to review my sun damaged skin, encountered as a youngster in Scotland, which was now coming home to roost, and will be with me forever. Due to the lack of sun in Scotland, one tended to get burned and not just sun tanned.

May 30, 2007, saw a historic meeting in Ballantrae. John Graham, from Condo 1, had witnessed a program to enhance inter condo relationships in Florida, by the organization of "friendly", competitive sports games, with representatives from all condo groups participating. He presented this to the four Condo Boards and a legend was born. Originally called the Ballantrae Olympic Games, the name was revised to the Ballantrae Fall Games, about which I have written a poem. Commencing the fall of 2007, it originally included 4 condo groups, covering 11 sports. Since then, it has been held every 2 years, and now include 5 condos, and covers many more sports and card games etc. Participation has been faithful, with extensive organization leading the way. The 7th games have just been completed. Sadly, John Graham passed September 2020 in his 91st year.

June 1st saw us set off for Europe, on yet another Betty Shukster inspirational trip, which would take us to 8 countries, on a Trafalgar bus tour over 21 days. I estimate that we covered over 20,000 kilometers by air, bus and foot over that time. The poem "Big Scandinavian, Belarus, Polish, German, and Beeg Russian trip", with 54 stanzas, summarizes it all, and if you are looking for physical tourist locations, please read the poem and take notes.

Memories of that trip are a plenty, but I will only dwell on a few. Denmark and Sweden were playing an international soccer game, when we were in Copenhagen. The city was invaded by thousands of, Swedes, marching through the city, all with their faces painted in their national, blue and yellow colours. We think our Toronto Leaf hockey fans go overboard. You had to see this. By the way, you can reach Copenhagen in Denmark, from Sweden, by crossing a bridge.

Russia brought so many highlights. We stayed at a hotel in Smolensk, after leaving Moscow, but before reaching Belarus. To say it was strange, was unfortunately very true. You could hardly swing a cat, in their one elevator, but if you complained of mice in your room, the staff offered to send up the hotel cat to solve the problem. The single beds we slept on were converted sleds. The bathroom sink, and bathtub, were served by the same tap, not taps, but a single tap, which swung over both units.

On the way to a town in Russia called Zakorsk, we visited a widow's cottage with basic living conditions and walls that you could see through. She was however content with her life, as she was receiving a monthly pension from the State, and was able to grow her own vegetables in her small lot. Prominent in her kitchen was a framed photo of Stalin. After leaving her cottage, we rejoined the main highway across Russia, which is, a one lane each way, road. As you drove through each village, there were always women dressed head to toe in dark clothing by the side of the highway, selling food, and tea from a large water boiling container known as a samovar, to passing lorry and passenger car drivers.

Museums in Russia require that before filming, you purchase a sticker for your camera. Volunteers, predominately women, called Babushkas (older women or grandmothers) circle the rooms, to ensure that you have complied with the rule. If you are caught without a sticker, they will embarrass you by slapping your wrist, before requiring you, to make the purchase. I had the sticker on the movie camera, but covered this with my hand. A babushka started to take interest in me, and as she tried to close in, I continuously circled away from her. When she finally came alongside, after 5 minutes or so, I removed my hand to reveal the purchase. Her eyes widened at the sight. I motioned her to hold out her hand, slapped her wrist, and walked away. I wonder what a Russian jail looks like from the inside.

I believe, that as a person born in Britain, during the 6- year Second World war, I viewed, what I saw in Poland and Germany, with more personal significance, than most of our group. Sites in Germany, included several locations, relating to Hitler and the Nazis. Polish museums and statues in Warsaw, set out with frankness, the horrific treatment of the Jewish community, the bravery and cunning of the underground movement, their activities and the consequences of being caught. The atrocities of the Warsaw ghetto and internment concentration camps like Treblinka, are not forgotten, and should be passed down generation by generation, in order that these tragedies never happen again. Unfortunately, hatred and cruelty, continue to be a part of our society, in our so called sophisticated modern world, and we must be on our guard, to curb and stamp these out, whenever and wherever they surface. In actuality, the passion to do this, often comes, only after you have experienced, first- hand the wrong doings themselves.

Shortly after our return, I attended my pre-op hip surgery class, following a meeting with a Dr. Dancy to discuss my positive TB results. He dismissed those, as related to inoculations I had received in the U.K., to counter any possible contact with TB carriers. He further indicated, that I was just as TB free as anyone else, and would confirm this finding, for Southlake's needs. We enjoyed a weekend at the Guilfoyle cottage, and later in July, started a new Coyle tradition, to have as many family members as possible, attend a dinner in Peterborough, at the Burnham House, to celebrate the many summer birthdays among family members. It was "on the house", and we had 14 family members attend.

I had my left hip surgery on Tuesday, July 24th, and was home by Friday of that week. Home nursing and physio followed. I was a tad disappointed, that the surgeon had not been in touch with me in the hospital, until I received a call from him, on a British Airways flight heading for London. A nice touch! Staples and clamps removed, I headed for the fracture clinic and final clearance from Markham Stouffville hospital medical staff, that the surgery had been successful.

My mind was now on organizing the walking competition for Condo 1, in the upcoming Ballantrae games. I had suggested to the committee, that as a final walking event, we should feature a 10- person, 3km event, on the final day. This would involve 10 walkers from each of the 4 condos, each starting at 15 second intervals. On finishing, depending on their position, cards numbered 1 to 40, would be given to each walker, and the condo with the lowest total points would be the winner. Lots of fuss and muss, to prevent running, and ensure that the finishers were awarded their position number, as they finished. It is difficult to control the pride and will to win, and not penalize the tendency to run. However, we have managed this through the years, and the 10- person relay has survived criticism and arguments, through 12 years and 7 games.

I have to recall the opening moments of the 2007, 10- person event. Using a megaphone, I explained to the 4 condo line ups, how it would work. At the crack of the gun, the first walker on each condo would set off, followed at 15 second intervals by a subsequent walker from each condo etc. Fairly simple, but one of the intelligent condos chose not to listen, and when the second walkers from each condo, were called to go, all of the remaining 9 walkers on that "not listening to you" condo took off. I was still using a walking stick, due to the hip surgery, and I recall hobbling after them, as opposed to chasing after them, and yelling through the megaphone "Come back you stupid…!" We did get everyone back, and the race was restarted, without incident. Of course, my instructions were blamed, for lack of clarity. Yea right!

We attended cousin Jackie's daughter's wedding (Amy French to Donnie Blair). I attended a staff farewell dinner for Jeff Gray, who was leaving Standard to join a pension consulting firm. We had some great moments working together, and we equally gave honest time during our working relationship. Els' thyroid check was positive.

We left October 24 by car for our fall vacation in Sarasota. Our suite in Condo 2 was excellent with clear views of the pool, beach and the Gulf.

Maureen joined us for 2 weeks and Fiona, Ian and Cassandra came for the third week. On return we stopped in Orlando, to visit the Klinakis family.

I began my Southlake volunteer career on December 11, 2007. We hosted 2 social nights for volunteers, and Condo 1 walking participants in the 2007 Games. 50 of them came over the 2 nights. To challenge the groups, we organized teams for quizzes, covering sports, politics and Canadian history. After spending time at the Fiona/ Susan households, we hosted the family Christmas dinner. Geoff Coleman saved the day by using his "know how" to bypass our jammed garburator and save a kitchen disaster re clean- up. The Cook family visited us on Boxing Day.

January 2008, saw meetings with the hip surgeon Dr. Haider, and the heart cardiologist Dr. Hacker. Both gave me clean bills of health and the same closing message "I will see you again, if you need me." This gave El and I clearance to head for Arizona, for a 2- week vacation. Because of recent surgery, we agreed that riding horses, should not be on the menu. Our flight out of Toronto was diverted to San Francisco on the west coast, and a separate flight returned us to Phoenix.

We are fortunate that many of our friends also like to travel, or have settled outside of Canada. We stayed with the Smiths in Tempe, visited the Loutits in Mesa, and then headed south to Tucson and Tombstone. A quick visit to the Tanque Verde horse ranch to savour a location, that we would definitely be coming back to, and then on to a short stay in Tombstone, home of the real "Shoot Out at the O.K. Corral."

Tombstone does a fabulous job of hosting, what some consider to just be a Hollywood western movie, and not real history. The street corners downtown, are populated with unshaven, long leather coat wearing, rough looking gunslingers. The saloons have the honkytonk music, with the female waitresses in sparkling dresses. Boothill cemetery is full of graves, many from the 19th century lawlessness. One such grave's tombstone, was engraved with the words "Here lies Jim. He was shot dead." Now that is descriptive writing at its best!

The reenactment of the "Shoot Out at the O.K. Corral", takes place every afternoon, in an open simulated western main street setting, but with a stiff admission fee. The show lasts about 15 minutes, but the shoot- out lasts less than 30 seconds. Led by Wyatt Earp, who was a Republican from the north, and his three fellow lawmen, (Wyatt's two brothers and Doc Holliday), they represented the local business owners and town residents. They confronted ranchers, named the Clantons, and supposed rustlers, the McLaury brothers, and Billy Clairborne, who were lawless and, resented the growing influence of the town residents, who wanted rules and regulations re local politics and law enforcement. 1881 was obviously a long time ago, and how historic events are remembered, are somewhat convoluted, but in the end, some of the participants were killed and injured, in the shootout. Billy Clanton and both McLaury brothers were killed. Doc Holliday and Virgil and Morgan Earp were injured. The rest survived unscathed.

On leaving Tombstone, we headed for the Kartchner Caverns State Park, and a conducted tour of the 4 kilometer- long, underground passages of the show cave. Discovered in 1974, it was kept a secret until 1988, and finally opened in 1999 with a high-tech system of air locked doors. The caves are closed for 6 months, because it is a nursery roost for cave bats. Eleanor is claustrophobic, and after the second air lock door was closed behind her, and the guide offered a "get out of jail card free", she was gone without delay, via the escape tunnel, rather than joining the 40- minute tour.

Both Tombstone and Kartchner, are just short of 5,000 feet above sea level. A few days, in this area makes you aware of this fact. You actually climb almost 4,000 feet as you head south from Phoenix to these locations. On return to Mesa and the Smiths residence, we attended the Scottsdale Arabian Horse Show. We like horses and the animals on show were magnificent. This is a wealth area of the U.S., and everything about the show, the people and the animals, reflected this. El celebrated, by buying a very nice customized leather jacket. On observing her interest, the booth owner said "Try it on, take your time, walk around the show". He knew how to market.

El had befriended Sue and Doug Black in Ancaster, and we were both saddened by the sudden and unexpected passing of Doug in Barrie, at the age of 65, in 2008. He was not athletic, but always seemed hale and hearty. The cause of death was an enlarged heart, which would appear to indicate that a large portion of the heart had stopped working. El has maintained a close relationship with Sue. We see her often, and she has joined us on many occasions, vacationing in Sarasota. Not long after Doug's funeral, we drove to Ancaster, for a post wedding celebration, for our former neighbour June Jopson, who had found a new partner in Hal, a very nice man.

We spent the first 2 weeks of May out West, mostly in Vancouver, using Maureen's house as a base, while also visiting and staying with the Youngs on Salt Spring Island. Our attachment to Vancouver and the West, has always been solid, and is considered by us as a second home, due to strong bonds with several long- term friends. On May 24, we attended the wedding of Stan and Lynn Leighton's daughter, Rebecca. As guests invited by the bride or groom's parents, weddings can be strange, in that, you may never have met, either the bride or groom before the wedding, and you may never meet them in the future. If you do, you must be prepared to say with confidence, "We were at table 24. Don't you remember us"? Disturbing news from Vancouver was of the death of Doug McArthur on June 08, in North Vancouver. Doug was the individual life office manager for Standard in Vancouver for many years, while I was there. I really liked and admired him We later attended a memorial service for Alma Hunter, our dear friend and neighbour from our years in Ancaster. Alma left a monetary gift for Fiona, whom she loved dearly, and I believe that she and husband John, considered her, as the daughter/granddaughter, they never had.

Shirley Johnston joined us for a road trip to Philadelphia, as guests at the wedding of Jenn Hoffman, the daughter of Mary and Rolland Hoffman our American neighbours in Unionville. We knew their 3 children fairly well as youngsters. The pre wedding activity organization, was excellent for guests, and even included a major league baseball game in Philly. The receptions, wedding and dinner celebration were first class, and I managed to find time to pen a poem entitled "A Celebration of Love". Our hotel room overlooked a Casino parking lot, and I found it fascinating that at 8:00 a.m., it was empty, but by 9:30 a.m., it was jam packed. This was every morning, we were there. I take pride in remaining "Casino free". I am not a fan!

Cassandra was now going to a dance class weekly, and we attended a show night at the Stephen Leacock Theatre in Keswick, and later celebrated Jamie's 21st birthday. Our grandchildren were growing up. July was a packed month, as I volunteered to assist at Aurora Cornerstone Church's first summer sports camp, for about 70 children, featuring basketball, athletics, baseball and soccer games and lessons. The camp was only 5 days long from 9:00 to 4:30, but seemed much, much longer.

We took some family members to a weekday showing of Mama Mia, and followed this with an outing to the CNE, which finalized a pretty busy summer. Oh yes, I also did find time to play golf.

I volunteered as a federal election polling clerk on October 14. The Conservatives won a minority government with 143 seats vs 163 opposing. Maureen arrived two days later, and the Scharfes two days after that, as we gathered for yet another Betty Shukster trip of a lifetime. This time we were heading for a truly amazing tour of Israel, Egypt and Jordan. Most groups would only go to one of these destinations, but not Betty, who wanted us to get our moneys' worth. She also wanted us to experience the magic and contrast, offered by these three middle east countries, that have common borders, but hold differing religious beliefs, leadership structures, customs and history. They tolerate each other, but do not permit unfettered freedom of movement, and are suspicious of each countries' motives. But, oh the history!

I have set out the multi locations and sites that we visited, in the poem entitled "A Ballantrae Caravan to Israel, Egypt and Jordan". If you decide to go there, read the poem. It will help you plan your visit. There is a richness to these countries by way of their history, and regardless of time, it is all right there.

My major impressions of Israel, other than the multi religious sites, included the following:

> Dark hair, muted clothing, multi bridal wear shops in Tel Aviv, active pedestrian traffic.

> Busy road traffic, over- active car horn honking, emergency police flashing lights continuously.

> Multi customers observing life from multi coffee shops, roads subsidized by other countries.

> Subtle security, metal detector machines, waiters with pistols, off duty soldiers carrying rifles.

> Attractive beaches, old buildings, bible referred sites aplenty, bar mitzvah celebrations.

> Passionate Jewish/Muslim/Christian reverence at all religious sites by locals and tourists alike.

Egyptian memories, include the following:

> Poverty, city pollution, garbage aplenty, unfinished building sites, constant tourist harassment, open palms not handshakes, greasy used currency, old cars, used car part shops, Lada taxis, round- abouts not traffic lights, vendors selling food from carts on bumper to bumper roads, multi police and soldiers carrying guns, packed old rolling stock public transportation but always with room for one more body, the frequent sound of call to prayer, a fertile majestic Nile with cloudless skies and crisp fresh air, but with limited expanse of cultivation on either bank, spectacular tourist sites, including Abu Simbel, the Pyramids, The Sphinx, the Cairo Museum.

Despite what some of the above comments might conjure in your mind, Egypt is magical. This is brought to life, by the so many historical sites, some of which go back 2500 hundred years. These are listed in the poem. Although many were located in different parts of the country, you are required to fly from Cairo, and to always return there overnight, for your next excursion. We did spend several nights in the same Cairo hotel, witnessing daily, a post wedding "no holds barred" dinner and celebration.

The "haves" in Israel and Egypt, appear to spend freely in preparing for, and celebrating such events.

To fly to the Abu Simbel site, relocated in 1968 in Upper Egypt, and witness the Great Temple, dedicated to Ramses 11 and the Small Temple, dedicated to his chief wife Queen Nefertari, is so striking. Because of their imposing size, these two massive rock temples defy a satisfactory description. Egyptian power of old, and its influence on the world, is reflected in these and many more historic sites. The Museum of Egyptian Antiquities in Cairo, also features an extensive and stunning collection of Tutankhamun antiquities. Most of the Egyptian characteristics of these bygone years no longer apply. This was a society that fashioned the Pyramids, the Sphinx, and on and on, but now!

We did not spend much time in Jordan, and therefore cannot comment in great detail. I stopped on a street in Amman, and spoke with a lady, while she was shopping in a downtown area. Her head was covered, but she was wearing, what we would consider as regular western clothing. She appeared happy with her life, and did not complain about anything. I did uncover a strong example of Muslim belief, via a young lady dressed head to toe in black, wearing a hijab, who turned away from us uncovered westerners, to face the wall of the elevator, as if we were unclean. A different attitude was shown by some Jordanian males, who obviously lingered by and ogled, some western female tourists, who were wearing shorts.

Travel over the 3 weeks, brought out the reality of travelling in the Middle East. Tight, but very disguised Israeli security when flying. On leaving Tel Aviv to fly to Cairo, we were engaged in conversation and laughter by several young friendly Israeli youths in the line- up. They were not fellow passengers! They were security, checking up on us. There is a scheduled flight each day from Tel Aviv to Cairo with a return flight. These are not shown on any posted listing in the airports, or listed with travel agents. How you book a ticket, I do not know, but the flights exist.

Egypt does not have many major commercial airports. Most flights to distant Egyptian cities, originate from Cairo, with an always return to

Cairo. At the time, we were told that there were only 2 female pilots, flying for Egypt Air, and one of them was actually flying our plane to Abu Simbel. The site is beyond the massive Aswan Dam, which was financed and built by the Russians, in exchange for Egypt buying military weapons, such as the MIG 17 fighter aircraft. The fighter planes signature extended radar nose cones, can be identified by the matching shape of the many individual hangars housing them, as soon as you enter the grounds of Cairo airport.

Nasser Lake, which was formed, after the Aswan Dam was built, borders the Abu Simbel site and at first glance the blue sparkling waters seems inviting, until you witness the fencing. When the lake was formed, the massive crocodiles were removed or moved from the Nile River, and took up residence in the newly formed lake. Their presence has become a large tourist attraction. There may be the odd crocodile still inhabiting the Nile River, which is fairly shallow in some areas. I had no intention of testing the veracity of that possibility.

A bus trip to Alexandria on the Mediterranean was important to me, as it brought back memories of my father, who although he was a sailor on the British cruiser Cleopatra, during the 2nd World War, was injured just outside Alexandria, while ferrying arms to British land troops. Alexander the Great in essence, built the first city, and it was dominated by the Greeks and then the Romans, before Egypt rightly took possession. The city was home to Cleopatra, who was born into royalty as a princess, became a queen, and then anointed a Pharaoh. When the Romans dominated the Egyptians, Anthony and Cleopatra were in Alexandria. There is really no hard evidence, of these historic figures in this area, but there have been discoveries in the Mediterranean, that suggest that her empire was destroyed by an earthquake and tidal waves over 1500 years ago. Based upon the Roman Amphitheater discovered on land there, I have to believe that future excavations and underwater exploration will produce the required evidence.

The most unusual hotel, we have ever stayed at, was the Taybet Zaman hotel and resort in Jordan, just outside of Petra. A 5- star hotel with rooms, seemingly carved out of rock, in a cave like manner, but with total comfort, including electrically heated floors. A one- night stay was not enough! We left the next day for the marvellous Petra site. Home to the Nabataeans, its entry is through a narrow gorge, called the Siq, to reveal homes and buildings carved out of the rock. This safe haven provided shelter, food and water to its inhabitants, and to travelling caravans. The tomb called The Treasury, carved out of the rock is stunning. It was highlighted in the movie, the Last Crusade, featuring Harrison Ford as Indiana Jones, in the series of mythical movies about this character. We also viewed the area outside of Petra which harbours Aarons' tomb, and the Moses Spring at Wadi Musa, where Moses struck the rock and brought forth water. Did Moses and the Israelites he led out of Egyptian bondage, stay in Petra? There is no such compelling evidence.

On return to Canada, I had agreed with our GP doctor to have a colonoscopy, performed by a Dr. Fu. This was carried out on December 2nd and shortly after, I was informed by her, that I had a growth in my large colon, which she did not want to excise, because it was attached to the colon wall. The remedy was immediate surgery, and I was referred to a Dr. Pallister for an operation on January 9th, 2009. She was likeable, and when I confirmed, based on a scar she saw, that I had gall bladder surgery in 1972, she replied "Oh dear, I was on my tricycle then". She was a character.

With more surgery in my future, in fact the third within 30 months, we closed 2008, with the traditional family Christmas dinner, a turkey dinner at the Cooks on Boxing Day, a celebration for the Van Velzens' 50th wedding anniversary at the Recreation center, and a New Years' Eve dinner and dance also at the Recreation Center.

The January operation, called a partial colectomy, removed 12 inches from my large intestine (colon). The growth was at a non-cancerous stage. I was discharged at the end of a miserable 9- day hospital recovery. I say miserable, because this surgery requires that you are pumped full of post-operative antibiotics, to prevent infection, which leaves one feeling nauseous continuously. To add to the problem, my bladder always goes to sleep following surgery anesthesia, which requires that you be catheterized.

Removal after 2 days and I am fine. The nurses, who I argued with, stated that their hospital rule, was removal after a number of hours, to avoid infection. Consequently, as I pleaded after several attempts, that this would not work, and only after my requested intervention of Dr. Pallister, did I get agreement to my time table. Finally, all was well, but it was a long 9 days!

I was cleared by the surgeon at a post- surgery meeting on January 26, as mission accomplished. We had to turn down an invitation, to the wedding of the Hoffmans' son Paul in Georgia, because I was getting back on my feet, and we had already committed to a vacation in Sarasota. I managed to fit in a root canal procedure, and then head for Florida the next day. Our 4 - week stay at Siesta Dunes saw visits from the Leightons and Sue Black, and time with the Bolsbys, Van Velzens, and the Bridges, who were all in the same area. Driving home via the U.S. East Coast, gave us the opportunity to visit the Hoffmans, in North Carolina and to congratulate the newlyweds. We arrived home March 21, and flew to Vancouver 5 weeks later, to see our many B.C. friends and be hosted by Maureen, who was always so helpful in accommodating us, when we were out west. As usual, we spent a weekend on Whidbey Island, at Ruth and Reidar's island house in Washington.

May was very occupied, with preparation for the 2009 Ballantrae Summer Games, including golf pitching and slow pitch practices. At the end of June, we purchased a Toyota Highlander for under $20,000. The vehicle had less than 17,000 km, having been utilized by the manager of the Toyota Markham dealership. El drove this car for many years, and we both agreed, that it was probably the finest looking car we had ever had. It had nice lines and although an SUV, it was a touch shorter to fit in our garage. After extensive personal car repairs by her husband Doug and a body shop, our daughter Michele is still driving the vehicle 10 years later.

Watoto Ministries, sends children's choirs from Uganda, to visit North American churches and to raise money for the Charity. My research had indicated that this ministry does an excellent job on behalf of these kids. El and I agreed to billet 2 of the children and their "uncle", for 2 nights in July. It was heart- warming, as these children were orphaned at an early age, and have been subject to abandonment, hunger and danger in their homeland. As the first of several years, that we would be involved, we felt that we were also blessed.

El and I continued our volunteer act, by helping out at the Aurora Cornerstone Church's 2nd annual sports camp in July. It was held in Aurora's central park, and adjoining high school, to permit 50 or so kids, to participate in various sports, while learning from the Bible. Our grandson Kyle, stayed with us, and I arranged some golfing lessons at the Ballantrae course. He can hit the ball a mile, but hitting it straight, is not his strong point. El and I also volunteered at the Church's vacation bible school, and our granddaughter Cassandra was able to volunteer and stay with us.

We had a wonderful 3- night stay at the Guilfoyles' cottage in Muskoka, where Gerry and I played some early morning golf. I then became knee deep in helping organize the walking events for the Ballantrae 2009 summer games, and also signing up walking participants, to represent our Condo 1. I also finally decided to participate in some walking events, and to also play slow pitch.

Maureen arrived August 25, to witness some of the events in the games, and to get ready for yet another Betty Shukster organized trip. The family got together, and had a kind of farewell meal for us, before El, Maureen and I started packing for a flight to Europe. This time, we were going on a riverboat cruise on the Rhine, from Basel in Switzerland to Amsterdam in Holland, aboard a Uniworld boat, called the River Ambassador. We left on a British Airways flight on September 2nd for Basel, via London, England. Time for the connection at London's Heathrow airport was short, and as usual, Maureen's carry- on luggage came under intense inspection, by security, who really took their time to examine everything and especially the liquids she was carrying. She was always the target at airports! We just made the flight to Basel.

Details of the cruise and the locations we visited are set out in the poem entitled "Castles Along the Rhine". There is no need to duplicate those words, but to summarize this cruise, is to see castles, cathedrals and vineyards. How some of the smaller communities could afford to build these cathedrals is beyond me, but it was probably due to the power and financial strength of the Catholic Church in the Middle Ages. As you head west to the Atlantic, the cathedrals seem to get larger, until you come to the granddaddy of them all, in Cologne. Because it was used as a marker by Allied pilots during the 2nd World War, it was not bombed to any extent, and survived with its twin towers intact.

At one time Cologne was the center of maritime trade in Western Europe, but as larger ships became the norm, Cologne, situated on the less deep waters of the Rhine, lost its status to deep- water ports on the Atlantic. How to continue to attract pilgrims, traders and tourists to this inland city, with this magnificent cathedral. Answer, build a golden tomb, in the largest Gothic cathedral in Europe, and state that this contains the bones of the three Magi; Balthasar, Melchior and Caspar. One cannot dispute, what one does not know, but it worked, and Cologne continues to flourish to this day.

To prepare for the cruise, we bussed from Basel to Lucerne, for a 3- night stay, before returning to Basel, and boarding the ship. Lucerne is a beautiful city, situated on the lake with neat tidy streets, attractive buildings, and it is dominated by the sheer beauty and majesty of the mighty Alps. On our second day, we went on an outing to Mount Pilatus, a 7,000 feet mountain towering over Lake Lucerne. The day involved, a walk, a Lucerne Lake boat ride to the foot of the mountain, a mountain railway ride on the Pilatus Railway, which is the steepest rack (cog) railway in the world, to the top of the mountain, lunch indoors, due to wind and the cold, descent on a large gondola, further descent on a small gondola, a bus trip to central Lucerne and finally a walk to our hotel. Then a nap!

Fiona's husband Ian, lost 2 loves of his life in October. His mother Meryl and his longtime pal, Browning, his chocolate lab, both passed away. We did not really know Meryl well, but attended the funeral in Sudbury. The lady pastor after speaking with Eleanor, asked her to be a part of running the memorial service. My last memory of Browning was, of visiting the house, while Ian and Fiona were working, to see him lying in front of the fireplace, wrapped in a blanket, with the inevitable wagging tail. I cuddled his head in my arms, and we lay in silence for a while. I never saw him again!

Later that month we joined Michele, Doug and Kyle in Norwood for a country fair. Taylor and Cassandra were with us, and this made for a lovely family time together with 3 of the 7 grandchildren. We enjoyed the display of animals and to continue that theme, flew to Houston on October 31, to go riding at a horse ranch near Bandera, Texas which is in an area, known as hill country. First of all, we drove to San Antonio, to meet with Frank and Francine Simpson, the American couple, who we first met on an organized tour of Spain. They now lived in a U.S. forces condo site for retired officers and spouses.

We had signed up for 9 hours of riding over the 4 days, at the Running R Ranch in Bandera. This was a working ranch, with about 20 horses, which catered to a few visitors. The package included breakfast and lunch, but not supper, which was available in Bandera at several restaurants, and a short car ride away. The cook at the ranch was a character. Meals were excellent, and he expected you to tell him so. He rang the meal bell with vigour, and did not take kindly to you being late.

The weather was a constant 75 degrees during the day. The menu was, ride in the morning, swim in the outdoor pool in the afternoon, and visit Bandera late afternoon for shopping and supper. Bandera was a basic small Texas town, with touristy type shops, some folks riding horses on the main street and large trucks with gun racks. They love their guns in Texas! Unfortunately!

The ranch horses were excellent, and were only mildly spooked by deer, that would rise up suddenly out of the long grass. They were disciplined and well trained. As an example, one horse broke away from another ranch ride, about half a mile away, which was going in the opposite direction from us. Apparently, the horse's rider dismounted to adjust his stirrups, and did not secure the reins. His horse galloped away, joined our group, and obediently fell into line about 3 feet behind our last mounted rider, until a ranch employee arrived and took him back. I suspect his girlfriend was in our group.

The ranch staff tried to enhance your riding skills. One such ride, involved climbing a mountain, the locals had named Ice Cream Mountain, which was fairly steep, and then have you come down in a sea of shale and loose stones. The lesson was lean back, and let the horse make the decisions, and do the work. They are much better than you, and more, sure footed. Sounds basic, but you have to experience it, to be able to ride safely. On climbing the hill, you lean forward, to take pressure of your horse's rear. The other lesson, was to not let your guard down, until your horse was safely secured by an employee. They spook easily, and are much bigger and heavier than you.

We left the ranch for a night in San Marcos and 2 days at a Marriott Hotel, overlooking the Riverwalk, in San Antonio. The latter is a very lovely location, which we would encourage you to visit, if in Texas. Site of the Alamo, its history abounds. On return to Toronto, El and I were asked by a neighbour and bible study attendee Irene Surgenor, to make a presentation to her fellow church members in Stouffville, regarding our recent trip to Israel. Neighbour, Don Crump assisted me, by integrating photos and slides into the visual part of the talk, and it was well received.

As usual, December 25, saw us host a Christmas family dinner. Granddaughter Jamie and her husband Tony, visited us on Boxing Day, and we spent some time at Fiona's. December 28, we had a surprise lunch with Tom and Nancy Golberg, from Montreal. Tom was my immediate boss at Standard Life in my latter years. I enjoyed working with him, and we had a very good relationship. As usual now, we chose to see in the New Year celebration quietly, at home.

We had already planned a busy 2010, with 3 trips on the calendar, covering 10 weeks of vacation in Florida, China and Arizona. As a bridge between a busy December '09, and the year ahead, we were able to get together with Michele, Doug and the 3 children in Madoc. Because of Doug's health and inability to travel without serious discomfort, they have not been included, in many family celebrations. El and I have always felt badly about this.

For some reason, I logged the number of volunteer visits, I made to Southlake in 2009. The number totalled 68, or over 200 hours of, on the job volunteering. Once again, we hosted a Burns Supper evening for 6 neighbours in the house, but this time, Fiona and Ian helped with the serving and clean up. We finally realized, that we could not do the preparation and hosting of this elaborate dinner, without help. Quality haggis, is most important at such an event, and I know that you will want to know, that you can get this excellent product, at the But "N" Ben butcher shop in Scarborough.

We left for Florida, by car, on February 12, with the usual 3- night stay on the road, before arriving in Sarasota. The Leightons arrived the next day for a few days and we had day visits, from the Vermeers, the Haefels, and the Van Dams. In the continued search of a cure for Els' tinnitus (constant ringing in the ears), we sought out an ear specialist in Sarasota, who advertised a special hearing device that countered the problem. Unfortunately, during the trial period, El received no relief, and in fact the device amplified the overall noise in a crowded gathering, such as a restaurant. We had to return it for a refund.

Michele and Kyle flew into Tampa, for a 5 day stay with us. Their Jet Blue flight was really late, and our "pass the time" stay, with the Van Dams in Tampa, which was due to end at 9:00 that night, was still going on at midnight. Michele was so happy, to see us greet them at the terminal, after a 3- hour delay, without communication. She was so good to Kyle, during these 5 days. Seventeen -year old boys, are not easy to please, but she went the extra mile, to satisfy him. After they left, Sue Black joined us for a week.

On the way home, we visited the Klinakis family in Orlando, and then had a wonderful day at the Holy Land Experience site, also in Orlando. As Christians, and more than interested in the Bible, we both found the day enlightening and entertaining. The actors, and the content in the presentation for the day, portraying the crucifixion and ascension of Jesus, were so moving and more than worth the entrance fee. We met a young couple from Brazil over lunch, who indicated, that there were in excess of 1,000 members at their church. We from North America, immediately thought of the size of the building. They laughed and said "Oh no. We hold all our services and meetings in the open, on the beach". I recalled that in Mexico, many of the church buildings were round, with no doors between the supporting pillars, allowing many overflow worshippers to stand at the entrance ways and beyond, and still participate in the service.

On the way home, we stayed at a Hampton Inn. We arrived very late, and the expectant hot showers were not available. A staff member acknowledged that to monitor costs, they turned the water temperature down, from say 11:00 p.m. to 5:00 a.m. Be aware of this, and at least get a discount room rate from the hotel, if you arrive late, as we did on this occasion. This is not an isolated hotel practice!

On arrival back home, we went to the Chinese Consulate in Toronto, to obtain a visa. Yes, another Betty Shukster organized trip to Asia, and specifically China this time. The consulate visa waiting area was crowded, with very few non- Asian applicants present. Take a number and stay awake, for a very long time. But be alert, because when your number is called, you must fight your way through a packed room of bodies to get to the appropriate window for your interview, or face the consequences of losing your place, and enduring a further long wait.

The majority of our group were flying from Toronto to Beijing, and then on to our starting point in Shanghai. El and I chose to fly to Vancouver, to have a 2- day break, before flying directly to Shanghai with Maureen, and our long- term Vancouver friends, Nick and Diane Scharfe, Sylvia Loutit and Sylvia's sister in law, who she had persuaded to join us, for what I considered as a trip of a lifetime. We left Vancouver on April 12 on a 12.5- hour flight to Pudong International airport in Shanghai, arriving at supper time the next day. China is 15 hours ahead of Vancouver. China is mainly a north/south country and although large, has only one time zone. The official national standard time is called Beijing Time. After a much needed, night's sleep, we joined up with our fellow travelers.

Once again, for sites and cities to visit in China, from Shanghai in the south, to Beijing in the north, you can refer to the poem East meets West. We were in China for 14 days, sampling their history and current ways of life via 3 plane flights, a riverboat cruise on the Yangzi river and multi coach trips. Organized to perfection, with quality English speaking guides, fine hotels and reasonable food. I say reasonable food, because although the breakfasts were excellent, the lunches and dinners lacked substance, such as meat. I lost 5 pounds on this trip. "Where's the beef?", was uttered now and again. By the way, Chinese fortune cookies, are not Chinese. Their desserts were exclusively fruit.

Noted observations include, the constant use by this huge population of their green spaces. The parks were busy from morning to night, with the Chinese, dancing, exercising or playing different board games. A frightening experience was to see 5 lanes of city traffic (cars, scooters and bicycles) lined up at the red light, and then launched towards you, at speed, as the light changed. Traffic volume is so heavy, that the Chinese population, are consumed with not holding traffic up, and it is written all over their strained faces. To see volunteers at bus stops, not just helping passengers board public transport, but pushing and shoving them, to get every last body on board, is quite amusing.

The Yangzi river is like a super highway with volumes of towed barges, mostly containing coal. It seemed that everyone was building boats in China. All along the river bank there were boats and barges in varying stages of construction. The motorways are more than busy. You can buy a car in Shanghai and have a driver's license, but according to the guide, you must await a successful expensive auction bid, to obtain a car license, enabling you to actually operate the car In Metropolitan Shanghai.(about 9,000 license plates a year are issued). Licenses for new energy vehicles have been issued free since late 2016.

Normally, a favourite seat for tourists travelling by bus, is the seat directly behind the bus driver. In Beijing, no one in our group wanted to sit there, to witness our bus inching its way into merging traffic, and coming within centimeters of hitting car after car. No driver is willing to give any ground on Chinese motorways. If you watch from that seat, you required nerves of steel, and the tendency to either say "Oh No", or "Oh Oh", and sometimes "Watch out!"

Shanghai is a European type city. The waterfront promenade bordering the Huangpu River is called the Bund, with buildings architecturally similar to those in various European capitals. The tower clock on the Bund, is similar to Big Ben in London, and was referred to as Big Qing, (or Big Ching) after the Qing Dynasty (1644 to 1912), which was succeeded by the Republic of China.

Beijing comes across as a stark and sterile communist city, with a strong presence of military and street police, especially close to the Communist Party quarters in the centre of the city, which is adjacent to Tiananmen Square, which in turn is linked to the Forbidden City by a subterranean passageway. The Forbidden City houses the Palace Museum, and was the former Chinese Imperial palace from the Ming dynasty, to the end of the Qing dynasty (the years from 1420 to 1912). It served as the home of emperors and their households, and was the ceremonial and political center of Chinese government for almost 500 years. In essence the ownership of the "power" in China has changed, but the central physical location and type of rule, which is not democratic, has not. The current Chinese government offices are located in a former imperial garden, in that same Imperial City, adjacent to the Forbidden City.

There are many dialects in China, but in Shanghai our guide indicated a move to Mandarin or English, as opposed to the local dialect known as Shanghainese, with nearly 14 million speakers. Wine is now becoming a more popular alcoholic beverage. The wine we received at a restaurant was Chilean, but the French are making inroads, as well as many other European countries, and the U.S.A. The Chinese negotiate with their treasures.

My birth town Edinburgh received panda bears in December 2011, and it was rumoured, that part of the "quid pro quo", in ensuring that the zoo received the bears for an agreed upon period of 10 years was, that a certain volume of Scotch whisky be available for China during this period. The female is called Tian Tian (Sweetie) and the male Yang Guang (Sunshine). Any cubs born during that period, must be returned to China. To date, no panda cubs have been born.

The zoo in Chongqing, features multi panda bears, all chewing away happily on their daily bamboo diet, with a relaxed air of confidence that makes you wonder, if we the humans watching them, are not really the inmates on the inside of the wire cages, and the pandas are the viewing visitors. To achieve satisfactory calorie intake from bamboo, the pandas have to eat for 14 hours per day, and normally from a sitting position. Due to the current pandemic, some foreign zoos are having great difficulty in importing, and affording the needed daily supply of bamboo for their "guests". Bamboo is a required food for panda bears, and as most of it is grown in China many zoos to combat cost, and an inadequate supply chain, are now planning to grow their own.

The Municipality of Chongqing at one time, had a population in excess of 30 million people, which was larger than Canada's population. Accordingly, the outdoor/indoor market in Chongqing has to be seen to be believed. It is huge, and jam packed with shoppers and booths, and the "fresh" food area is teaming with rabbits, ducks, eels and so on. The disturbing issue for we westerners, was the fact that the merchants had no problem, with mixing live and dead animals and birds in the same cage.

The Chinese coolies who bring the fresh supplies, are called "Bang Bangs", recognized by the typical cross-bars of bamboo poles over their shoulders, as they push and struggle through the throng, to bring their goods to the merchants. We visited many Buddhist temples, where Chinese religious practices were on display. Prayer appears to require symbolic offerings, such as lit candles, flowers, food, and even drinks. Offering coins were also deposited, for prayers of good fortune and luck.

The enormous population, requires that China's economy continue to surge. During our visit in 2010, I formed an opinion that their political will and economic requirements, would drift them to a closer relationship with the West. However, since the appointment of Xi Jinping, to the Presidency in March of 2013, the goalposts have changed. All their policies and strategy have turned, to a favoured position of self- determination and isolation from the world powers. Their goal is to become, a major player on the world stage. Any, and all public dissension from within, has been stomped upon and eliminated, or at best closely monitored. They have built up their military capability. They have made inroads in parts of Africa, Asia and even Europe, with statements of huge investments. They punish anyone who crosses them (country or individual) with isolation tactics (trade and/or diplomatic). They have so far managed to juggle all the balls successfully, but there is still a long road ahead to complete their journey, such as keeping the multitude happy and content with their lot. Taiwan and Hong Kong continue to be thorns in their side. Dominate these former parts of China by force, risking response from the West, or gradually "educate" them to accept Chinese authority. These are their choices, and how will the U.S.A. and the European community react. Time, and circumstances will tell, which path China takes. I however, predict stormy days ahead for all parties!

It was smoggy in Shanghai, wet in Beijing, but unbelievably clear on the Great Wall of China, with a magnificent undisturbed view, of a range of snow- covered mountains in the distance. This view is just not normally available. The weather had been cold and damp, and inevitable coughing and sneezing caught up with several on the bus. El became a victim and was not well, missing out on a final night's dinner, with the Scharfes and Maureen, in our hotel's beautiful top floor restaurant, overlooking the city of Beijing. A Chinese twist to serving, was that the wine we had purchased, was brought to the table and poured in our glasses from our bottle, which was then taken away to the kitchen. As North Americans, we found this initially, to be surprising and suspicious. It appears to be their sophisticated way of serving, which we found acceptable, as long as our bottle came back to the table.

We flew from Beijing to Vancouver on April 25, and on to Toronto on April 28. I immediately took El to a walk-in clinic, at our doctor's Markham location. She was prescribed anti biotics, and still took a while to recover.

After being home, I signed up to play in a slow pitch league. El and I had dinner, with most of the Cook family in Madoc.

I resumed, an every three- year meeting with the late Tom Jepson's sons, Gordon and Kenneth, who are both lawyers. They have done well, and in particular Gordon, who manages his own legal firm, specializing in patent law. Our dinner meeting was at the Albany Club in downtown Toronto. Very posh and swishy! I did not feel in the least intimidated, as not long after being admitted, I walked by the bar to be greeted with "And how are you Mr. Coyle". The voice came from the bartender, who at one time, was the maître d at the Boulevard Club, where many of our Standard Life functions were held. He now had a different staff position, but an even more important one, because the bartender at a men's private club, is like a sponge, "He knows all, and to keep his job, reveals nothing!" We rounded out mid- year by enjoying a granddaughter's guitar playing and singing, at the outdoor Keswick Music Festival. Danielle was the performer. She is now a very confident and talented young lady.

July, saw our church have the visiting Watoto children from Uganda, participate in the Canada Day parade and picnic. Good for you Pastor Jeff! Maureen arrived, to celebrate and recognize my 70th birthday. The family was summoned and came, especially as "it was on the house", to a family birthday dinner, at the Burnham House in Peterborough. Grandson Kyle, returned and stayed with us for a couple of days, during which I arranged some golf games for him in Ballantrae. After he left, I was persuaded, to participate in our church yearly Vacation Bible School activities for the children, by having a part in a play each weekday morning at 9:00. Practice makes perfect, and believe you me, to remember a different script each morning at my age, took a lot of rehearsing. Later in August we attended Marlene Clement's daughter's wedding. We had known Allison, since our early days in Unionville dating back to 1981.

November 2^{nd,} we returned to our favourite ranch, Tanque Verde outside of Tucson, Arizona. We spent 7 days there, riding a minimum of 2 hours per day. The resort offers many different activities, with riding being the main attraction. You get the opportunity to meet visitors from different parts of the world, but mainly riders from the U.K. and parts of Europe. You cannot participate in the gallop or canter rides, until you have passed a lope or canter test, to demonstrate full control of the horse. Remember, this is Western and not English riding. A major difference being, that your bottom does not leave the saddle in Western riding. We have seen many female English riders actually cry in desperation, after failing the Western lope test, while their usual non riding yahoo male spouses, passed the test first time.

We left the ranch and stayed at the Smiths' house in Tempe, just outside of Phoenix, and socialized with them. Visited Sylvia and Roy Loutit on vacation from Vancouver, and Eleanor's long- time friend Donna Purkey from Ontario, and her husband Hal. Donna and Hal, formerly lived in Connecticut, New York, where Hal owned a bond investment firm. On retirement, they purchased and moved to a beautiful house, in a condominium site adjacent to Camelback Mountain, near Scottsdale, Arizona.

I played some golf with the men, at different courses. Hal and I were not close, but he was gracious enough to invite me to join him and 2 other men, to play at his private club in Scottsdale, where he was the President. I had never met the other guests before and typical of life's coincidences, I ended up sitting next to one of them on our return flight to Toronto. The fairways on the courses there, are manicured, watered, beautifully green, and very playable, until the ball lands in the rough, and you find yourself trying to hit it back on the fairway, from under a nasty cactus. The weather is quite glorious at that time of the year, averaging 30 degrees Celsius during the day, in a dry climate, but it is cool at night, reflecting the fact, that Phoenix in essence, is desert country.

Back in Ballantrae, and prior to Christmas, we suggested to our lovely neighbour Margaret Gilbert, that she join us for dinner. She insisted, that if we brought the main dish, she would host the evening. Margaret was not young, but quite savvy, and very alert for her senior years. For dessert, she offered us home baked cookies prepared by her daughter, that she said were initially a touch hard, but had been softened, by mixing them with cut up apples, or some other recipe to make them acceptable.

I took a generous bite, and watched as four, count them four, of my upper front teeth, broke off at the gum level, and fell it seemed, in slow motion, one after the other, on to a china plate below, each one making a clanging noise, like the chiming of a grandfather clock. Absolute silence followed. Margaret's mouth was open with astonishment. El thought I was joking, until I smiled. I turned to Margaret and said, "Not soft enough!" We all then laughed, in a bizarre sort of way, to relieve the tension.

To be fair to Margaret, I immediately told her, that due to playing soccer competitively for so many years, I had required extensive dental work, including several root canals. This had weakened my front teeth, to the extent that, what had just happened, would probably have been inevitable in the long term, after biting down on something hard. I had no pain, but immediately called my dentist, Dr. Susan Johnston, who as I had been her patient for so many years, permitted me to call her at home, even on a Sunday night, in the event of an emergency. She immediately said, call the office in the morning and we will fit you in.

My initial thoughts were Christmas, family get togethers, friends, dinners, celebrations! This was Sunday December 21st. Be prepared! Practice! Don't smile! Practice at nodding in agreement. Dr. Susan, really pushed the envelope and came through in record time, with a temporary plate, which helped me through, what would have been a very difficult time. My long-term relationship with Dr. Johnston, had certainly paid off and I expressed my gratitude to her, for solving in record time, what seemed at first light, to be an absolute disaster.

To wrap up the very busy 2010 year, we had our Christmas family dinner, with up to 15 members. The Cook family came from Madoc on Boxing Day and we celebrated at Susan's. Our New Years' Eve celebration, ushering in 2011 was held at the Jobbits, with our Church family and friends.

I managed to persuade El, to co-host two "Burns" dinner nights in January. The first on January 05, was a Scottish night (no haggis), to appease our close neighbours, who were asking, no demanding, to attend another Burns evening. As mentioned before, our initial goal was to promote the

Burns celebration throughout the Condo 1 neighbourhood, with varying guests, but its apparent success was working against this wish. Our solution was probably, only going to last for one year, as the time and effort put into these evenings was extensive,

We did however, host the January 5th Scottish evening for the Birkness, Van Velzen and Cannon neighbours, assisted by our granddaughter Danielle. No haggis, but a successful dinner and evening, with all the trimmings and speeches. On January 28, we held a traditional Burns supper evening, with haggis for new guests, the Shuksters, Guilfoyles and Pyles, assisted by our daughter Fiona. Gerry Guilfoyle had to call off, due to a competing business function, which I think was probably another Burns dinner. That night brought a surprise late snowstorm, and Kathy Guilfoyle, who wanted to get home, described the return drive into Toronto, as the worst she had ever experienced, but thankfully she did arrive home safely.

I was now heavily involved, volunteering with the Heart Recovery program at Southlake Hospital, which was held at the Tannery in Newmarket. This program, encourages those who have had some heart intervention, (bypass surgery, valve replacement, stents, heart attack, arrythmia) to follow a program of hospital supervised recovery for 6 months.

On graduation the results will, with testing, indicate their progress physically, and encourage them to adopt these exercise and lifestyle habits long into the future. I also volunteered every Friday afternoon, on the CV Surgery ward on the 5th floor of Southlake Hospital, to engage with patients and caregivers, answer questions and encourage their recovery, on the basis of "Been there, done that". This was the year 2011, that I met Lloyd Wait at the recovery program and we have walked together for many years, and had coffee weekly, if available, ever since.

Each April, the Community Resource Department and Executive at Southlake, who administer a group of over 800 volunteers at the Hospital, recognize them with a dinner and award evening. It is always eye opening, to see and talk with fellow volunteers at these events, especially those, who have given their time and energy for periods exceeding 25 years. The only sad part, is that most volunteers, work a 2 to 3- hour shift on their own, and consequently do not get an opportunity to meet their fellow volunteers, other than on the odd occasion.

We left for our winter break, and arrived in Sarasota by car on March 1st. We were blessed with many guests for our 5- week vacation, including the Leightons, daughter Fiona with grandchildren Cassandra and Taylor, sister Maureen, and long- time friend Sue Black. On return home, we drove via Orlando, to visit the Klinakis family, who were former members of Aurora Cornerstone Church, but now reside in the U.S. A beautiful family.

We had been visiting Sarasota, and in particular the resort of Siesta Dunes, on and off for over 20 years. As the condo is located, only a 5- minute walk away, from a 2- mile long, white sand beach, we probably do not realize the luxury that we are experiencing. We also know the west side of South Florida well and can visit some of our Ontario friends, who spend winters there. We have been regular attendees for many years, at Shining Light Church in Sarasota, and know the pastor well. Sarasota is 2400 kilometers distant from Ballantrae, but what a treat, as a break during our long Ontario winters.

We had a surprise Ballantrae visit in April, from Frank and Francine Simpson, our U.S friends from Fredericksburg, Texas, who we first met in Spain. They are now living in San Antonio. They were able to attend a David Parson concert with us at our Rec. centre, and were mightily impressed. David is our resident musical genius. Later that month, courtesy of the Guilfoyles, who had won a free night at a charity evening, we spent an overnight at the Oban Inn, in Niagara on the Lake. It was nice, but the allotted room had its challenges, which one by one we overcame. The young waitress who served our dinner was memorable. When asked which cabernet sauvignon wine she might recommend, she went to great lengths, to extoll a specific Niagara Red, complete with endorsements. When asked to bring us a bottle of this wonderful wine, she said "I can't, we are all sold out". That was the type of weekend we had, but the accommodation was free. Thank you Guilfoyles.

Summer golf and the Ballantrae Summer games, were coming up fast. I agreed to once again manage the Condo 1 walking/running team and met with Ed Chillman, who was the overall condo games convener for the walking events. Ed was very organized and a treat to work with them. To add to my summer activities, I signed up for the Condo 1 men's slow pitch team and the Ballantrae men's golf league.

We attended Don Crump's funeral in May. Don had been hospitalized in Southlake, following a heart problem and even after surgery, he could not overcome the heart damage. Don was the Maple Leaf Gardens, VP finance, whom I had first met in 1981, as the company was a pension client of Standards'. Don was fairly quiet and a serious man, but with a good sense of humour, which came in handy, as he had to deal with his boss Harold Ballard for many years, and now and again with the Lady Yolanda.

Later that month, our long- term Vancouver friends Nick and Diane Scharfe, surprised us by visiting Toronto overnight. We met them at 6:00 and had dinner at the Westin Prince Hotel in north Toronto, where they were staying. I had one alcoholic drink early on, and we left for home about 11:00 p.m. We immediately, ran smack dab into a Toronto police Ride Program. Thank you, Lord! Two drinks later in the evening, and I probably would have been nailed. A ride program in May! I also remember the policeman, who interviewed me. He was snarly and if I had had, that extra drink or two, who knows!

The Southlake Heart Recovery program, had adopted a U.S. teaching program entitled "Living a Healthy Life with A Chronic Condition", and I had agreed to become one of the volunteers teaching the course, under the supervision of a qualified medical staff member. The proposal was to offer this course to senior groups at Care Residences and Community Centres, in and around Toronto. To qualify as a teacher, you had to attend a 4- day teaching course and pass the ultimate test. The course was intense, including medical staff we did not know, who would represent themselves at the beginning as hospital patients, and with acting skills, break down in front of you, in a very realistic and persuasive manner. Not being aware of this, our reactions were unpredictable, and varied among the group. I was not the only one taken in by "the so-called hospital patients". They were good.

I was once again invited to the Guilfoyles client golf day, at Cardinal Golf Club. A classy event. A great day, and El was able to come and attend the post golf day reception. The next day we attended our grandson Kyle's graduation. To wrap up mid-year I was again conscripted to participate in a bible skit to be performed each week day at ACC's (our church) Vacation Bible School. To me, this was serious stuff, with lots of lines to memorize, which I am not very good at. Apart from this, we had 8 actual rehearsals, before the July 28 week of performances. This was serious work!

Once again, the Watoto children were in the July 1st Aurora Canada Day parade, and we billeted Ivan, age 11, Marvin, age 12, and their "uncle" David, for 2 days, through the Church. Fiona and Cassie joined us for supper. These orphans are polite, innocent youngsters, who want to be loved. However, you cannot forget, that they are fragile, and react negatively to any sense of violence, even if it comes in the form of a cartoon character. We experienced such a problem during the airing of the DVD, March of the Penguins, and had to shut it down, as the younger boy, Ivan, became truly upset.

Our August break, was at the Guilfoyles' cottage, near Bala for 4 days. We are fortunate and blessed to have friends like them. September was more than busy organizing the walking/running program for Condo 1 participants, while I was personally involved, in walking, cycling and slow pitching. It is a lot of work, organizing, scheduling, pleading, and cajoling friends and neighbours, to participate.

In September, I was finally assigned, among others by Southlake Hospital, to participate as a volunteer teacher in the special health course, they were endorsing, entitled "Living A Healthy Life with A Chronic Condition," for members of the Bernard Betel Community Centre on Steeles Avenue in Toronto. This involved, following the course curriculum, and talking with about 2 dozen attendees, on 6 consecutive Wednesday mornings for 3 hours. The initial response from the community members was frankly one of suspicion at what was its purpose, but by the end of the course, we were more than accepted, and even asked to come back in 6 months and do this again. The course is a process of gaining the trust of the participants, as you gradually peeled back the layers of their personal lives, to discover the hopes and fears of their remaining years, while dealing with their current day to day medical, and perhaps social issues.

At first, I did not appreciate the professionalism of the course, which was produced by Stanford University, but eventually realized, by the end of 6 weeks, that the participants had bonded in gratitude, with us the leaders, to the extent that they were more than serious, that we come back and do this again. Sadly, we never did, but it revealed to me, that the course truly had significant value, and could tear down any walls that participants had built, to hide medical and personal issues that they were keeping to themselves. There were more passionate open discussions about family issues, than any other subject. We were guided by the course content, to give them options and solutions.

Maureen arrived October 8, for a short family visit and get togethers, before she headed out on another Betty Shukster tour, this time no less than to Africa. October 28th, we journeyed to Kitchener/Waterloo to witness our granddaughter, Jamie Cook, graduate with a B.A. degree. This was a moment of pride for us, to see a family member invest her time and energy, to get a university education and degree. Well done Jamie! We are proud of you. I have only seen limited amount of her writing ability over the years, but she has talent. I was also amazed at the number of students, graduating that day. I have to confess, that I quietly said to myself, as I looked upon the lines of graduates on the gymnasium building floor, "How are they all going to get jobs?"

Our November break was once again at The Tanque Verde Guest Ranch, near Tucson. The ranch has upwards of 150 horses, but true to form, you find the one you like, and hopefully stay with him. But horses, like humans are given time off on a regular basis to rest, and therefore are not always available. My pick was Ricochet and El enjoyed Tiny, who was not in the least tiny! We rode morning and afternoon, for the 6 days we were there, always under warm sunny skies. We also participated in the weekly competition of rounding up and penning, 6 to 8 boisterous young steers into a corral. Teams are adjudged competitively on a time basis. The key is not to rush, and to let the horses do most of the work. In this case, they are much smarter than you. Certainly, more than me!

We returned by rental car to Mesa, about 30 minutes from Phoenix, to spend time with the Loutits, our friends from Vancouver, who spend the winter in Arizona. Some sightseeing and golf in the area and time with the Purkeys, before flying home on November 22nd. December socialization was active, with us hosting Christmas Day dinner once again for the family. A quiet New Year's Eve followed to usher in 2012.

We were blessed in 2012 to leave early for Florida and specifically Naples, where we planned to stay from the middle of January to March the first. We had rented a condominium through Pastor Jeff Wilson's in- laws, Bob and Nancy Boshart. As a bonus, Pastor Jeff's parents, Gerry and Anne, met us, and we started a very pleasant relationship, with them chauffeuring us around Naples, to give us a feel for this most southerly city on the west coast of Florida.

Its highlights include, the classy shopping and dining area of 5th Avenue South, and conversely the Naples Zoo, which allows you to get up, really close and personal with the tigers, alligators etc. It is probably the most interactive spectator/animal zoo, I have ever been in. The pier walkway is interesting and historic, because at one time, it was the only way for locals and tourists to get to and from Naples, using a very active ferry system. Freeways and cars have taken over, and the pier is now only used for fishing and viewing. Absolutely top- notch Dixieland and jazz concerts are held weekly at Sugden and Cambier parks. These concerts are attended by thousands, and for a mere $5, you can watch and listen to professional jazz musicians for a couple of hours. These professionals have been assembled from various parts of Florida.

Whether it is shopping at Carlton Place, the Miramar Outlets, the markets of Tin City, the Farmers Market, the Art Show in Cambier Park, or the

Vintage Car show on 5th Avenue, there really is always something to do in Naples. You can travel south to Everglades City, or east to gator watching stops, on Alligator Alley.

Tiger Tail Beach, located on Marco Island, is about 40 minutes from Naples. Long sandy beaches, with warm waters and minimal crowding. After parking, the shortest distance to the beach is through a knee-high lagoon of warm water. The only problem might be on returning, when the tide has come in. You will now be walking in water up to your waist or chest. Travel light, because any baggage or chairs have to be held high in the air!

The churches we attended, were large and vibrant. New Hope Ministry was within walking distance of our condo, and pastored by a Pastor Grant Thigpen. You would have to look long and hard, to find a more charismatic pastor, and just a plain down to earth, nice human being. We were very comfortable going to his church, twice a week, and really enjoyed his sermons, which were delivered with gusto.

We were fortunate enough, to attend a concert at a local Baptist church, featuring the Booth Brothers, U.S. professional gospel singers, who are more than talented. What a show! The Leightons and Sue Black stayed with us for short periods and we visited our Ballantrae neighbours, the Fishers in Fort Myers and the Canattas in Port Charlotte. Gord Pritchard, who I coffee with weekly at home, and his wife Leanne, had rented time in a hotel on Marco Island, and we dined with them on 5th Avenue.

We attended local concerts, drove to and around Sanibel Island which is offshore from Fort Myers, and in my opinion overrated, because the roads are too congested. We spent time with A.C.C. church members, the Bridges, the Van Dams and Glen and Angela Myers, the latter having purchased a very nice condo, only minutes from where we were renting in Naples. Younger than us and a delightful couple.

March 1st, we drove north to lunch with Ballantrae friends, Fritz and Margaret in Northport, and then on to register at Siesta Dunes. Maureen arrived the next day and Fiona, Cassandra and Taylor the day after. Fiona does not like flying, but to keep costs to a minimum, she had booked the flights with Direct Air, a start- up airline flying out of Niagara Falls, New York, to Lakeland Airport, near Orlando, Florida. The day they chose to depart, was a nightmare, weather-wise. Extremely strong winds were forecast for the whole east coast of North America, and Niagara Falls, New York, was hit badly.

The length of the runway in Niagara Falls, would only allow the plane in such windy conditions, to board 50% of the passengers. The rest were bussed to Buffalo, where they met the aircraft and then waited and waited, for a break in the weather. Meanwhile, I had driven the 3 hours from Sarasota to Lakeland, and I also waited and waited for their early afternoon arrival. I and others were getting restless, because there were no announcements, and our weather was also quite windy. Suddenly an announcement!

Which had nothing to do with the status of the Direct Air flight. The message was, that due to the lack of air traffic, the U.S. Airforce, Acrobatic B aerial team was going to put on a show for us. It was quite spectacular, watching 8 or so jets screaming 100- feet above the runway and then soaring into the open skies, to perform their various maneuvers. And then after 30 minutes and all the noise, they were gone, and we were subjected again to the eerie silence of a deserted airport. The crew for the return Direct flight arrived. Did they know something? "Nope, we are contract employees. We are not Direct Air employees. We know nothing."

A cry went up. "I think I see them." In the distance a passenger jet was turning in clear skies to assume a flight path to our airport. It had to be them. Nobody else uses this place! They finally arrived about 5:00 p.m., and we made our weary way home by car to Sarasota, after their lengthy 14- hour trip. The kids survived, not so much Fiona. More to follow about Fiona, but I should relate, that their return trip a week later from Lakeland was on time. I had driven them to a nearby hotel the night before, and they flew out the next morning. Direct Air declared bankruptcy the next day, and has never flown again.

The stress and stormy weather did not agree with Fiona's back and I had to drive her to a chiropractor without delay. He in turn called her Canadian chiropractor, and they chatted quite openly, much to the dismay of Fiona, as her Canadian "fixer", called her a complainer. The treatment she received was not perfect, but certainly relieved a lot of her discomfort. The condo was crowded, but we survived. Fiona slept with El and I was in a rented cot. Fiona was somewhat mortified that at age 40, she was sleeping with her mother, and in the same room as her pajama-less father, in a separate cot. Hey we all survived and enjoyed the weather, swimming, beaching and eating quality meals.

Maureen returned home on the 16th and after saying our goodbyes, we drove to St Petersburg and spent time with Bill and Winnie Van Dam. On leaving Sarasota, we stayed with Pat and Tony Klinakis in Orlando, and went to church with them the next day. They are both talented musicians. Tony on drums and Pat on guitar. She also is a beautiful singer and they both led the church gospel ministry. I have said to her repeatedly, that I would like her to sing at my funeral.

May saw the pulling of a tooth and with deep roots, the nasty consequences. I signed for another season of Ballantrae golf. El hosted a wedding shower, for granddaughter Jamie Cook at our house, as two of her bridesmaids had been university friends and lived in our area. It was small, but successful. I attended another Guilfoyle golf/dinner day at Eagles Nest. Cassandra performed very well at her clubs' dance recital in Keswick. Beautifully done, but a tad too long.

We hosted another visit from the Watoto children, and this time billeted Maria and Sharon, both age 9, and their "Auntie" Suzan. This auntie was a goal getter, determined to take as many North American goodies as possible, back to Uganda. She inquired if we could take her to a garage or street sale on a Sunday no less. No, we said, but how about a visit to the Toronto Zoo. Although from Uganda, these kids had never seen a wild animal. Suzan had been to a zoo on a previous trip to Japan, but had no choice, but to join us.

Our Ballantrae neighbor Terri Herbert was a zoo volunteer, and kindly offered to take us, using her volunteer pass to limit the cost. On arrival, auntie Suzan wanted a big lunch, and we obliged. I loitered too much at the gorilla exhibit, mainly because one of the males came right up to the glass window, pressed his nose against it and stared at me, as if we were long lost pals. It was strange! The rest of our group moved on and despite a lot of searching, we did not make contact again for at least 2 hours. El wanted to report me to the "Lost and Found" office. I had not brought my cell. An older man walking around the zoo on his own, is not exactly a welcome character. I could observe the mums, drawing their children close to them, as I approached. I retrieved my phone from the car, and we arranged to meet. As mentioned before, these children are fragile, and when I finally made contact with them, the young ones ran and hugged me for dear life, as if they had known me forever. It was touching, but indicated the severity of their fragile emotions.

On arriving back home, we had home- made pizza for supper. The kids insisted on rolling their slices up and eating them like a wrap. Ever alert Suzan, asked El and I, if that was wine that we were drinking. She then quickly said yes, when offered some. Suzan was quite the girl! El took us into the mid- year, by volunteering again for the church VBS program. We invited Cassandra to join us, to supervise the very young children and she agreed, and stayed with us for the week. I had been enlisted to play the part of a Roman Centurion, Gaius Maximus in a biblical play. The first group of kids seemed not in the least interested, in fact bored, until I stacked about 6 metal chairs on the stage, and when the part of the play came, where I was to roar, and seemingly lose my temper, I pushed the chairs off the platform. They made an awful noise, as they tumbled from the stage to the floor, and were effective in getting each successive group of kids to actually sit up and pay attention. The noise unfortunately, was more effective than the message!

Maureen visited us for a part of August, and we had a visit from the Cook family and in particular grand-daughter Jamie's first- born Cameron, our first great grandchild. El and I celebrated grand-daughter Danielle's 21st birthday, by having dinner with her at La Fenice, a restaurant we had frequented with her Mum and Aunts when we took them out at Christmas. I recall waiting for Danielle outside the restaurant, and when she arrived, we exchanged hugs and pecks on the cheeks. Two senior ladies were passing by on the sidewalk as we embraced, and tutted audibly at the sight of this old man greeting a young chick, in this manner. Looks can be deceiving ladies! Several days later we were able to have lunch with Danielle and Maureen at a very posh restaurant in the Eaton Centre. Danielle knows Toronto better than most!

We were invited once again to the Guilfoyle cottage in September, for a long weekend. As couples we are compatible, and a few rounds of friendly bridge always adds to the warmth and serenity of their cottage, in this Muskoka setting. A special part of that visit was a visit by boat to Windermere House for lunch. This iconic Victorian landmark, has occupied the shore of Lake Rosseau since 1870, and is known by the locals as "The Lady of the Lake".

Although we were not personally affected, I should note, that on October 29/30, 2012, Toronto and various parts of Ontario, were lashed by Hurricane Sandy, with winds approaching 100 kph, causing significant damage here, and later in Quebec and the Maritimes. For the record, El and I had dodged Hurricane Mitch in Mexico in October 1998, but we were both in Vancouver when the remnants of Typhoon Freda, struck on October 12, 1962. It caused today's equivalent of $600 million in local damage and seven storm related deaths, with winds approaching 145 kph.

One side effect of many, from the B.C storm, was El being stranded in her building elevator, laundry basket and all, when the power went off. At the time, she and I were not married, and she was living with her 2 roommates. She managed to get the emergency door to open, and clambered up to the nearest floor about 2 feet above her. Has this incident, had an effect on her? Oh yes! Where possible take the stairs! Do not let too many try to get on the elevator with her, because all you will hear is "We're full, take the next one", as she blocks the doorway. If the elevator shudders at all, or appears to be slowing, she looks at me, a groan or moan is uttered, and a reassuring cuddle is definitely required.

2012 was not to be Els' year, as the next few paragraphs will detail. We left for Phoenix, with granddaughter Cassandra at the time going on 12, on November 06, rented a car and arrived at our favourite riding ranch, Tanque Verde outside of Tucson, for a 7- day vacation. Cassie passed the lope test, which meant she could participate in any of the canter or gallop rides available. One feature was a cookout at night in the Cotton Grove, with multi bonfires. It was somewhat eerie, to hear the snorting of the wild boars (javelinas), as they made their way through the desert to our location, obviously attracted by the food smells. They are not dangerous, but the staff ensured they were located away from us guests, by providing scraps in a specific location. Some of our fellow guests, including Cassie were however unsettled, and stayed close to the bright fires.

That day, Els' unfortunate events had started. We had 3 separate 1- hour rides and on the last one, at the halfway point, she had requested the young female wrangler leading us to stop, as she was feeling faint. The group came to a halt, as she was helped off her horse, and onto the ground, where she momentarily passed out, due to what we discovered was dehydration.

Our guide radioed the ranch, and the head wrangler replied that he was on his way, with a supply of Gatorade. Take note, by restoring electrolytes, it is more effective than water. "Where are you, he asked? By a wadi (dry channel), she said. Not good enough he said, they are a dime a dozen, in that area of the desert". He eventually found us and after receiving the power drink, cold water and a short rest, El was able to continue. Prior to his arrival, and while El was prone on the ground, there was a touching incident. Her horse Tobasco, seemed concerned with her lying there, and came over to snuffle at her face. The only problem, is that the horses' staple diet at the ranch, is green hay (good quality hay), and therefore their slobber is mostly green. El, one minute out for the count, was the next minute warning Tobasco, not to get that "green stuff on her new blouse." She was recovering fast, and at the sound of her stern warning, the horse backed off!

The next day was the team competition to pen young rebellious cattle, using the shortest time as the determining factor. I was inserted into a team consisting of 2 mums and 2 daughters from Jersey, USA. Trying to be humerous, as a Bob teamed with 4 ladies, I labelled our group the "Boobsters". We went on to win the gold medal. These ladies, one of whom, turned out to be the V.P. Finance of a major U.S. drug company, were to prove very helpful in the days ahead. That day, El and Cassie chose to spend time in the pool. Cassie is like a fish and just cannot and will not get out of the water.

November 9th arrived (Els' Canadian Nine Eleven). I was riding a Belgium draft horse called Goose. El was an equally large horse named Lakota. The ride was over, and some of us had entered the corral to dismount. Goose was second to enter, and I had taken my feet out of the stirrups to dismount by sliding down the left side of Goose, while properly holding the reins. Suddenly a large gust of wind, which although not unusual for Arizona, seemed to come out of nowhere. The gate leading into the pen, where the horses are kept for the day, had in error not been latched. It blew open, and then noisily banged shut with a fury. The horse in front of me reacted, by bucking and snorting in panic and fear. This started a chain reaction, as every horse down the line reacted, in kind.

I found myself hanging onto Gooses' saddle as he started to turn in circles. The speed of his turn left me hanging horizontally in mid- air with my legs and feet straight out like a member of the "Flying Wallendas". Goose probably turned full circle twice, before I decided to abandon him. I landed upright on my feet, while still holding the reins. Goose took off. I continued holding the reins, but due to his size and strength, I had to let go. He turned and bolted through the culprit gate at top speed, to what he imagined was safety. Luckily the gate was still not latched, because he hit it, like a freight train and appeared not to injure himself.

I was somewhat self- congratulating myself at surviving the incident, and turned around to see a body lying on the ground, wearing a top that I recognized. El had not been quite as lucky, and now was lying there in a heap, and groaning in pain. Her horse Lakota, had reacted likewise to the panic of the other horses, and had bucked her off, and onto the hard floor of the corral. A ranch employee called for help, and it seemed that in no time an emergency vehicle from the local fire station came charging in to the corral area. Staffed by young firefighters, who swarmed around to attend her. They cut her top, much to her dismay, as it was new, and inserted an intravenous line into her arm, for pain management purposes. Our group was about 75 feet away, watching from the corral porch and all were ordered by the wrangler to turn around as her bra strap was also being cut.

In the meantime, I had run back to our cabin to get the car keys and "whatever" I thought we might need. A hurried discussion with the 4 lady "boobsters", revealed that I was not to worry about Cassandra. They would look after her. The emergency team loaded El onto a gurney and they tore off, with lights flashing and siren blaring to Tucson General Hospital. I followed close by in our rental car, shadowing their truck to take advantage of going through red lights, which of course was totally illegal. We arrived at the emergency doors of the hospital, and I parked our car. U.S. hospitals are so different! Parking, including valet parking is free, but once you go through the hospital doors, watch out!

We arrived at Tucson General Hospital about 2:30 p.m., about 1 hour after the incident. I had called, our out of country medical number in Montreal, and by the time I was "greeted" by hospital staff, all out of country financial matters had been resolved, and only questions pertaining to Els' health history were asked. We never saw a bill! I was permitted to be with her, as she was wheeled on a gurney by a volunteer for an x ray. The excess pain killer medication administered by the firemen, then caused her to be sick in the corridor, and I recall being the only one concerned. "I need some help here", I yelled. Finally, staff arrived, and we cleaned poor El up.

We were then parked in an emergency room, until El was finally discharged about midnight. There is a computer terminal in each of the emergency rooms, and every item is documented, including glasses of water. Staff communicate with the doctor by e mail. A doctor did finally show up, and confirmed that the x ray indicated a break in the Humerus Bone, the long bone in the upper arm, located between the elbow joint and the shoulder. No casting, but a customized sling was provided and a prescription for pain relievers. We now had to drive around and find a 24- hour pharmacy to obtain the opioids. We were so tired!

We returned to the ranch about 1:30 to find sympathy notes, from the "boobsters" and the ranch executive, together with 2 servings of whatever they had for supper, which based upon the elapsed time, did not appear in the least appetizing, and went into the garbage. The next 3 days for El were discouraging and lonely, as she was in bed, and I had to balance my time with her, and while caregiving, keep Cassandra reasonably occupied and happy.

Cassie was young and sensitive, and I recall 2 incidents following her Grandma's accident; one where she was frightened outside somewhat by the snuffling javelinas, while walking back to our room in the dark from dinner, and then secondly by the darkness of an unused part of the dining room, even though I was sitting at the table with her. She was reacting to her grandmother's incident. Her vacation was over 4 days later, and we all returned to Phoenix, and arranged special service with Air Canada to have her looked after, on the return flight home to Toronto. According to Cassie, the airline staff really fussed over her, and she suggested to her Mum, that she would like to be booked in a similar manner, on all future flights. Good luck with that one, Cassie!

El and I, spent another week in Arizona, while she somewhat recovered. We visited the Smiths, the Loutits and the Purkeys. Each time the message was "the good news is, we are here, the bad news is, El has a broken arm". All were understanding and very, very helpful, apart from the Smiths' dog, who thought that Els' arm sling was colourful and attractive enough, that it should be chewed on by him, if permitted. The out of country insurance staff in Canada, were also helpful and caring, calling to make sure that all was well, and to inform us that they were at our beck and call, if any further medical services were required, while we were in the U.S. A nice touch!

On our return home, it was x ray time, followed by a visit to our GP, and the receipt of more pain killers, and then onto the fracture clinic to meet a Dr. McMahon at Markham Stouffville Hospital. He is a long- time general surgeon and talented doctor, who although somewhat gruff and direct, is extremely knowledgeable about bones, especially broken ones, and immediately reversed the method of supporting Els' arm. The support must only be at the wrist, he said, and not on the entire forearm, in order that the arm can hang down, because the Humerus Bone has been forced up into the shoulder, and must be allowed to fall back down into place. Finally, in good hands!

His second revelation was "no more opioids, only Tylenol". Imagine today, if all physicians and surgeons in 2012, had taken that stance. The North American world of medicine might be a different place, and perhaps, we might not have experienced the same opioid problem, and level of opioid dependency, that we see today. Dr. McMahon is still practicing and performing surgery, in the same practical manner. El and I both recall him lightly squeezing the area of the break on the arm twice, presumably to see what her reaction and tolerance to pain was. She was not happy and cried out "don't do that". I had to smile a little bit, as he went from room to room in the fracture clinic, and the same yell rang out each time from other patients. I presume that he was determining the level of patient recovery, based upon the time that had transpired since their accident. El had follow up appointments at the same fracture clinic with a long- term positive result. The only thing she did not like, was me saying, "you have to get back on a horse".

I had several sessions with Life Spring physios, to treat a pinched muscle in the neck/shoulder area. On Christmas Day, we had the usual gift exchanges, first at Fiona's and then at Susan's, but then we had dinner at Fiona's. A huge break in tradition after 50 years, but no pun intended, a good break this time, for El. We did however have a family lunch celebration on Boxing Day for 17 family members. New Year's Eve was quiet, brought in with the Van Dams and several friends.

Commencing 2013, we had decided to go to Florida for 4 months. The first 6 weeks were to be spent in the Boshart owned condo rental in Naples. In between the socializing with Gerald and Anne Wilson, and Glen and Angela Myers, we did the usual touristy things. Naples, and adjoining communities offer many attractions, while not being crowded. We then moved on to Siesta Key beach, in Sarasota, for the month of March. Maureen joined us for 10 days, and together, we enjoyed the warm weather and proximity of the beach, which gives you such a feeling of freedom, being such a large space. There are many people on the beach, but you can separate yourself very quickly, by walking part or all of the 2 plus mile long beach, or by swimming in the Gulf.

We packed our clothes again, and headed south to enjoy the rest of our vacation, in the Gray rental house that they own in Cape Coral. As agreed, we arrived before they left and enjoyed two days on their boat, to explore the waters off Fort Myers beach and Sanibel Island, which are quite beautiful. Later, the Guilfoyles stayed with us for two days, before Sue Black arrived. The local neighbours are very friendly, and we socialized with Allyson and Floyd, Pauline and Richard and Bev and Dan. The Gray house is more than comfortable, with a huge screened in back yard, complete with swimming pool. Most of Cape Corral is built on canals, and renting a winter home there would be even more attractive, if you had access to and could pilot a boat, to take you out to the attractions on the Gulf. We left by car for Canada on May 3rd, with a traditional dinner at the Paisanos restaurant in Willowdale on arrival, and then on to the house and bed by 10:30.

The Scottish expression, which sums up ones return from vacation is, "back to old clothes and porridge!" This is what transpired over the next 3 months. Bible study night, family visits and meals, volunteering, medical and dental visits, including a satisfactory discharge for El from the fracture clinic, and weekly chats with Lloyd and Gord over Tim Horton coffee. One offs, were attending Cassandra's dance concert, (still too long), volunteering at Cornerstone church's VBS week for children, where Cassandra helped out again, and signing up for the Ballantrae Games, to once again participate and organize Condo 1's walking events, and to supervise the signing and cajoling of warm and mildly enthusiastic bodies, to enter the walking events.

We were now at an age, where the possibility of losing acquaintances and friends, was much more possible. Brian Birkness, a neighbour of

12 years, died in August. Brian was a CA, and the head partner in a smaller accounting firm, before it was taken over by Deloitte. He was an easy- going man and a good talker, and believe it or not, I can be a good listener. We appeared to enjoy each- others company. He had a private golf membership at Spring Lakes Golf Club in Stouffville and we played there every week. Neither of us were very good golfers, but we enjoyed the game. Our relationship was typically male. Not very deep, but with a firm foundation and loyal to each.

Later that year, a fellow church member, Gordon Brown died. I only visited him for a few weeks before he passed on, and regretted that we had not met earlier. Gordon had gone to Bible School in Canada, where he had met Gerald Wilson, the more than friendly pastor, who had introduced us to Naples. Where do all these pastors get the savvy and the risk- taking courage to own these condos in Florida? Gordon however did not go into the ministry, and ended up managing a family owned, mortgage lending business with his sons, which has been very successful. I wish our relationship had occurred earlier in our lives. His wife Gail, attends Aurora Cornerstone Church, and is friendly with El. A lovely lady.

Cassandra, now 12, our youngest grandchild and a lover of horses, had the opportunity to come to Tucson with us, for probably our final trip to the horse ranch. I felt it important that after Els' terrible accident, causing the broken arm, that she ride again, to dispel any future fears. We enjoyed a weekend at the Guilfoyle cottage in Muskoka, before leaving the next night for our Arizona vacation. To make the early morning flight, we stayed at a nearby airport hotel, the choice and timing of which was amazing, as Maureen arrived home, from a Betty Shukster trip to Africa, to stay at the same hotel that same night, before leaving for Vancouver the next day. We met in the hotel lounge saying, "Neither of us really planned this". You have to wonder about these coincidences!

We dined with David and Jana Smith in Tempe (just outside of Phoenix), and then drove to Tucson to hotel overnight, before going to the Tanque Verde Ranch, October 11 for a five day stay. Cassie is easy going. I remember her snuggling up on the floor without any complaints, as we went to bed that night at a Tucson hotel. The only room available was small, as the hotel offered steep discount rates to the military and their families, and with a base nearby, it was really busy.

El rode every day, with her favourite horse being Zodiak, who seemed to be aware that he had to take very special care of his precious cargo. After 7 rides of galloping and loping, Cassandra decided, following her observing fellow riders falling off their horses, that she would stick to cross country bike riding and swimming. She really enjoyed both, but quite honestly, I thought that riding a bike in that terrain, was more dangerous than being on a horse.

Cassie was missing a week of school, and was returning to Canada after one week in Arizona, with flight crew fussing over her the whole trip, based on the extra service, which we had arranged. El and I continued on to Sedona, which is located in red rock country and is quite beautiful. We stayed about 20 minutes outside of Sedona, in a small community called Oak Creek Canyon, just as beautiful, and with accommodation rates at a much more practical level. Using this as a base, we took 4 separate one day trips.

The first, was a Pink Jeep tour, up and down the multi rock canyons. The origin of this company which has hundreds of vehicles in Sedona and Las Vegas, sprang from a married real estate couple, who were based in Sedona, and took potential house buyers by jeep to view various properties of interest. The wife finally insisted, that the so- called buyers were more interested in the bumpy rides, than the properties. Her favourite colour was pink, and now you know the rest of the story. The next day we signed up for a Pink Jeep tour to the Grand Canyon. We were the only passengers who spoke English. It was not inexpensive, but included a great lunch and a driver, who knew how to get the best views. The Grand Canyon is unreal!

Day number 3, was a trip in our car rental to Jerome, a small mountain community, chock full of artisans. I found an amazing custom wall clock, which I loved, but decided to order after we got home. I never did. My loss, but maybe it is still there! In lieu, we purchased 2 pieces of wall art, featuring cactus, shaped into what could only be in the artists' customized mind. Very unusual, but proudly hanging in our dining room. My other memory of Jerome, was eating lunch in an outdoor restaurant up high and overlooking the valley, while enjoying the fresh, warm, dry, pure mountain air of a peaceful Arizona. I really did not want to leave.

Our last adventure was going to a Sunday morning service at the Cowboy Church in Sedona, complete with a wooden railing at the front door to tie up your horse. The males all wore 10- gallon hats, which they took off to pray. The whole service was excellent. The pastor chose to single me out, as a church visitor, for the purposes of his sermon. He did not speak directly to me, but was able to weave my being a visitor, into his sermon. This required him standing right in front of me for a fair bit of his sermon. The congregation was very friendly, and if we chose to vacation there, we would certainly contact the church.

10

BALLANTRAE

2013 - 2020

We drove back to Tempe, to have a farewell dinner with David and Jana Smith. The main purpose of this trip to Arizona, was to get El back on a horse, and diminish the memory of her fall. The possibility, that this was our last trip, to the Tanque Verde ranch, was high. Such memories! Back in Toronto, it was time to plan a celebration, that unfortunately does not occur as often these days. It was for our 50th wedding anniversary, dating back to November 15th, 1963 @7:30p.m., exactly one week before the assassination of President John F. Kennedy, to give you a more historic timeline. We decided to have the special event at the School restaurant. Fiona's husband Ian knew the staff well, and we had met the owner Nick, on several occasions.

We chose Saturday, November 9th, for a sit- down fine dining dinner, and sent out 60 or so invitations, prepared by our neighbour Sheri Donald, to family and those friends who had been a part of our married life. The invitations went far and wide in Canada, from Vancouver to Montreal, and parts of the U.S.A., to celebrate the many parts of Canada, that we had lived in or visited for business or pleasure, and to the U.S.A., where we had several friends. The night we had chosen was in early winter, but nature decided to make things difficult, and we did not see our friends and former neighbours from Ancaster or Peterborough, which was disappointing. At their ages, even celebrations do not encourage travelling long distances in snowy and icy weather.

Sister Maureen had arrived a few days earlier, and helped us decorate the private dining room, we were to use. The School restaurant is very professional. The food, special celebration cake, decorated tables and chairs and service, were all of the highest quality and it was an impressive night. I have always been careful, when hosting an event, not to overdo the alcohol, and had arranged that we would pay for the table wine and the first 2 rounds of drinks. It may sound frugal, but you want everyone to get home safely. According to the restaurant staff, my frugality worked, and they confirmed that they had never seen such a low bar bill, for the size of the group.

Mind you we had 3 pastors and their wives. Pastor Gerald Wilson, his son Jeff who pastored Aurora Cornerstone Church, and a prior assistant pastor at ACC, Glen Myers, who we were friends with. A further definitive reason for the low bar bill, was the fact that, I had asked my close friend Gerry Guilfoyle to say a few words, and Gerry being Gerry, would not touch a drop of alcohol until he had spoken. Unfortunately for him, I chose that he not speak, until near the very end. After he had concluded his very nice words, I know he wanted to add "That's it. And now I am going to have a beer… maybe two!" He departed the mike at top speed. I know how to plan things!

The surprise guests of the night, were our very good friends, Nick and Diane Scharfe from Vancouver. They were heading to the U.S. for a vacation, until their son Brad suggested, they come here first, and then head south. It was lovely to have them. As a reminder El and Diane were in the same pre- natal class, for their and our first born. I met Nick in the process and we have been close friends, despite geography, since 1964. The meetings are few, but the bond is strong.

The evening was very special and it could not have gone any better. We displayed photographs a plenty. Ian had enlarged our wedding day photo to a life size portrait, and we proudly display this in our finished basement. All family members were present, including our first great grandchild Cameron, who mother Jamie kept close, as he was 18 months old. He appeared convinced, that the applause for those who spoke, was directed to him. He in turn stood and clapped, and the guests responded, with laughter and applause. The speakers in turn were delighted, with the presumed response to their words and humour. Everybody was happy! We were happy.

Christmas was celebrated with family members in the traditional way. Visits to Fiona and Susan in the morning followed by a family Christmas dinner at our house for 17. After yet another quiet, New Year's Eve, we got ready to leave for Florida by car, for an extended stay. Our first stop in Florida, was again Naples, where apart from seeing our Canadian friends, we socialized with groups from New Hope Ministry, shopped often at the Farmers Market, sunbathed at Tiger Tail Beach on Marco Island and dined on 5th Avenue. Our only visitors at the condo were the Van Dams, before we moved on to Sarasota, staying the night of Feb. 28th at a hotel. That evening we went to the Van Wezel theatre, to see the Rhythm of the Dance concert presentation.

March 01 saw us in Siesta Dunes. Maureen arrived the next day, for a 12 day stay. While she was with us, we had a visit from the Pritchards, and dinner with our former Standard Life president Joseph Ianicelli and his daughter Caroline at Turtles. We moved from the beach condo to a garden condo 1-206, in time to welcome the O'Hares. We always thought of them as the model family with their 4 lovely children, but unfortunately this was not to be. We really like them, but they have since separated. We attended the Van Wezel to see Vince Gill, entertained the Fishers, lunched with the Florida Vermeers, and welcomed Sue Black, before leaving for Cape Coral.

We attended the Assembly of God church in Fort Myers. Excellent sermons and just nice people. If we ever go back to Israel again, I would choose to go with this group. Spent a great day at Naples Zoo, which has to be the most interactive zoo, I have ever been to. Our Cape Coral neighbours, Bev and Dan, had decided to sell their boat and we were flattered to be their passengers out to the Gulf, on their final boating journey. Sue Black left for home on April 12. We went to dinner with Allie and Floyd, neighbours from across the street. Floyd was a real character, long and lanky, and easy going with a disguised sense of humour. The highlight of the evening, was Floyd tipping backwards in his chair, in the restaurant, which was on an uneven floor, in what seemed slow motion, due to the length of his body. He was not hurt, and when a passing customer suggested in typical American fashion, that he might sue the restaurant, Floyd gave her a puzzled look as if to say, "I do this all the time. What's the problem?" I don't think I have ever met a man who had such a laissez faire attitude to life, while being a real charmer, and a very successful business man.

We left Cape Coral May 1st, had dinner at Joia's in Aurora, May3rd, and then home to bed. May 30, we attended a Jack and Jill evening for granddaughter Melissa, and her husband to be, Marc Fowles. Our first for such an event, which presumably is held to share the couples' good news, and help defray the costs associated with today's weddings, which are meaningful. The banquet building in northwest Toronto, was huge, and is designed to accommodate 5 groups at the one time, in separate rooms in a pie shaped structure. I recall the lighting to be somewhat subdued, and my first and only faux pas of the evening was asking a staff member to uncork the bottle of wine on our table. She gave me a funny look and twisted the cap off, with minimum effort.

The evening was a huge success with lots of good food, wine and company. We got to meet some of Melissa's female friends, who would be her ladies in waiting at the October wedding in Mexico, as they were seated at our table. The evening also featured the ability to purchase raffle tickets, with the possibility of winning very nice prizes. I was not party to the net financial result of this evening of extravaganza, but I suspect their gain was somewhat limited. Never the less, a good time was had by all.

July saw us visit the Wilsons in Zurich, On. Gerry and I really hit it off. Gerry was a happy man, a pastor, a man of God, who in his retirement years continued to run seminars for active pastors. He was also a "sports nut", and had an incredible amount of sports memorabilia in his den and garage. The Zurich home bordered Lake Huron, had a huge backyard and a number of albino white squirrels, that El and I had never seen before. August was visit Guilfoyle cottage time. 3 great days of boating, golf and bridge. After leaving Bala, we stopped for lunch with Els' friend Sue Black.

On returning to town, we met with Magdi Nicholas, the spouse of Hoda, an Aurora Cornerstone church member. Magdi owned the Hyundai and Toyota dealerships in Aurora and we purchased a 2014 turbo charged copper Santa Fe for Eleanor. She very kindly, passed the 8 year- old Toyota Highlander to me, and we serviced and gave Maureen's old Sienna Van, to Doug and Michele, as Doug with his mechanical knowledge, could look after the older vehicle to some extent.

Excitement was growing, with 2 of our granddaughters becoming brides, before year end 2014. September was a busy month with Melissa's shower to be held in the Ballantrae Recreation Centre on the seventh, and Jamie and Tony's wedding in the Kitchener area, on the twenty seventh. El had helped Susan with the arrangements for the shower, and I produced some signs to assist guests find the recreation centre. The theme for the shower was Paris, France. Anything remotely associated with the name and the city, was on display for the 75 plus female guests. El and I, had filed away video of Melissa hamming it up in our basement many years ago, and we had a professional video made of her 10- minute antics. Having delivered it to the Rec Centre, to be shown without Melissa's knowledge as the opener to proceedings, I was quietly asked to leave the room. It was girl party time, and apparently, they all put on quite a show for Melissa. Cleopatra, as I liked to refer to her, was very pleased.

To prepare for Jamie and Tony's wedding, Maureen arrived on the 24th and we booked rooms at a hotel near Cambridge, to stay overnight, after the afternoon wedding, and following the reception and dinner. The wedding ceremony was held in a huge backyard of a home in Petersburg, outside of Kitchener. Tony's biological father owned the property. Most weddings have small glitches, and in this case, a misunderstanding caused a short delay in the bridal car picking Jamie up. It was a lovely day, for a lovely wedding, and a beautiful wedding couple. As grandparents of a bride, who had gone to university, and lived in the Kitchener area for several years, we did not know their many friends and the family members from Tony's side, but we were given the opportunity to say a few words, and these are included with my other memento enclosures.

Maureen, appeared to exhibit some out of character signs at the reception. She spilled wine on her dress, which of course she wished to change. Luckily, I still had our luggage in the car and we finally accommodated her when I returned, but according to some family members, not without a lot of undue fussing. I had driven to the hotel to sort out a booking misunderstanding, and missed her frustration. We did not know then, but this was an early warning sign, of what lay ahead.

We had breakfast the next morning with daughter Michele, and Doug, and then drove home, via Ancaster, allowing us to spend a couple of hours with June and her husband Hal. June and her first husband Bill, now deceased, were among our wonderful neighbours, from 1971 to 1978, during the happy years we spent in Ancaster. We were very fond of them.

Maureen had arranged to spend a few days, with her Toronto friends Margaret and Jackie Fyffe. She returned, for us to be dinner hosted by Betty and Bernie Shukster, who had organized such wonderful world trips for us. Maureen had travelled extensively, perhaps visiting over 50 world countries. We spent the next night at a Toronto airport hotel, leaving in the morning for Cancun, and then onto the Barcelo Hotel, near Tulum, as part of our granddaughter Melissa Hamelin, and Marc Fowles' wedding group, accepting the invitation to be a part of their special day.

The setting for this magnificent hotel is eye popping. Right on the beach, with all the facilities you could desire. The Mayan Riviera is quite beautiful, but a beach wedding at 4:00 in the afternoon, followed by an outside reception, dinner and dancing, still requires the cooperation of good weather. It looked iffy at first, but the good Lord was looking after us, and it cleared up.

Melissa had done some modelling in her young life, and therefore her friends as bridesmaids, all looked like a photoshoot out of Vogue Magazine. The wedding ceremony was lovely, followed by toasts, speeches, an excellent meal and dancing. Once again, an incident with Maureen puzzled me, as she was upset in a flash, at El and I deciding to do something, which did not suit her, but when we met up again shortly thereafter, she reacted as if nothing had ever happened.

As we ate our dinner and listened to speeches, there was minimum lighting (torch flames) and for those "non techies", who had hand written or typed speeches, we were really "in the dark". Marc's brother Nick, as the evening's M.C., and a very good and funny M.C., was really helpful, providing his cellphone light for reading purposes. I was able to establish in my speech that in a very short month, I now had 2 new grandsons in law, with historic names of Marc and Anthony. I further reminded Melissa as to my pet name of Cleopatra for her in recent years, due to her modelling and the make-up that goes with it. I then clarified with husband Marc, that Cleopatra was born a princess, subsequently crowned a queen, and then finally anointed a Pharaoh. The comment "Your problem Marc!", closed the remarks. The Tuesday wedding left us three full days, to enjoy the sun, and all features offered by the hotel, such as swimming with the dolphins.

Melissa and Marc, accepted our offer to financially assist them with their honeymoon, and they headed later to Costa Rica. Jamie and Tony also accepted, and went to Jamaica. Our offer is open to all grandchildren, who get married, so step up to the plate, when you are ready, and I mean really ready, to accept the serious meaning of marriage. The rest of the hotel stay was pleasant, but to "educate" our younger grandchildren, we took Taylor and Cassandra to Xcaret, a theme park about 50 km away, which emphasizes the culture and background of the local Yucatan.

It was a full day of swimming, viewing wild animals such as jaguars, a show featuring bareback riding, mainly by females decked in full Mexican dress, a show featuring the beginnings of Mexico and their then worship of Aztec and Mayan gods, and a concert at night in a covered stadium. This concert, although a bit lengthy, celebrates the different Mexican cultures and their customs, their variety of peoples, and includes the ending of the Mexican/American war in 1848, resulting in their loss by annexation of territory, we now know as Texas. It also covers the sale of California and the rest of its territory north of the Rio Grande, to the United States, for what at the time was a large sum of money, but pales in comparison to the resources and wealth of current day California. A reserved car took us home at the end of a full day, and El and I went to bed tired, but happy, that we had been able to expose and demonstrate to our youngest grandchildren, vivid examples of a culture, that they had never before experienced.

While in the theme park, I had found myself limping somewhat. The injury dated back to the Melissa and Marc wedding celebrations, while dancing on a platform, in the dark, on the beach. Our grandson Taylor who normally does not exert himself, was dancing "like a madman", and although completely out of character for him, he was fascinating to watch. I thought, if my grandson can dance like that, just watch grandpa! Oops, not a good idea. The right hip did not like what I tried to do, and I was to face some discomfort in that area, for some time.

On returning home, Maureen left for Vancouver, and El and I had our usual round of doctor and dentist appointments. El, for work on her eye, and yes me, for x rays of my right hip, followed by a referral to Dr. Haider, the surgeon, who had fitted me for my left hip in- plant. To conclude the year, El and I, celebrated our 51st anniversary at Oakland Hall, a favourite but now closed restaurant of ours, in Aurora. Tom, the owner, had started out with a very small Italian restaurant in St Andrews Village, which was always packed. He achieved his ultimate dream of owning a fine dining establishment called Oakland Hall, located in a historic house on a hill. He owned and managed this for years, and then retired. We miss the quality and ambience of his restaurants.

For years, we had been somewhat concerned about the state of the roof tiles. The house was built in 2001, and the tiles had a dubious 30- year warranty, backed by a U.S. company that had closed its doors. Kelly & Sons, the roofers, stated that they were aware of a class action lawsuit, and could obtain some rebate on the old tiles, if we proceeded with them. Despite winter, they got a window on December 22nd, started the job, cleaned up and were gone by suppertime.

Christmas as usual, was early morning at Fiona's, followed by a visit to Mike and Sue's. As all of their children were there, we really got to celebrate the opening of family gifts, as a family. Once again, we hosted the family Christmas dinner at the house, with at least 17, present. After 50 years of hosting, was El to be gracefully retired from this event? As usual, we exited the New Year quietly. You do well sometimes, not to know what lies ahead. 2015 was to be an unsettling year, involving the whole family, with an experience that we were not prepared for, but that would eventually be perceived as a journey, that would bring us even closer together.

I was referred to my hip surgeon's assessment clinic, and they set a date of July 14, 2015 for the surgery. Although 6 months away, it was comforting to know that it would be fixed. I found that it bothered me most, lying in bed, and I was not looking forward to the nightly nagging discomfort. It was pleasing to know that we would soon be in the warmth and comfort of Florida, and we did indeed arrive safely by car in Naples, on January 19th.

Our 6 weeks in Naples, found us busy with visits to Tiger Tail Beach on Marco Island, the Naples outdoor jazz concerts, the weekly farmers' markets, the Naples pier, the Art Festival and downtown 5th avenue, with its many attractions. We also had visits and dining outs, with our Canadian friends, the Leightons, the Wilsons, the Fishers, the Myers and the Cannatas.

A treat, was a visit to the First Baptist Church, to listen to a talk by Joel Rosenberg, a Christian Jew, a best- selling author, who has written so many thrillers about the Middle East, and predominately about Israel and the plight and pluck of the Israelite nation, surrounded by mostly hostile Arab states. Not everyone will read his material, because of the overtone of religion and his affiliation with Israel, but believe me his books are very well written, and will keep you on the edge of your seat.

We left for Sarasota on February 28, to spend a month at Siesta Dunes. Visits from the Van Dams, the Osbornes (ACC pastor and family), and Shirley Johnston made the month go very quickly. We also dined with Canadian, Florida visitors, Joseph Ianicelli and his daughter, the O'Hares, the Simpsons and the Pritchards, and celebrated Els' 73rd birthday. I managed to dislodge a tooth from my dental plate, but with the co-operation of the condo staff, and a friendly dentist, all was back to normal within a few hours. We left for Cape Coral on March 28 to stay at the Gray rental house. We arrived a day earlier, to take them to the airport. The Van Dams joined us for a few days, being the final leg of our Florida vacation.

The average daily temperature was now 82 degrees, but with the screened in pool and lanai, we were very comfortable. Sue Black arrived for a 2 week stay, and her luggage although initially tagged as "gone missing", arrived the next day. All was well, but this was the calm before the coming storm! I called my sister Maureen on her April 09 birthday, and suspected, based upon some of her strange comments, that something was not quite right. After hanging up, I called her close friend Jane Cartmel in Vancouver, voiced my concerns and the probability, that Maureen may have had a stroke, and urged her to please take Maureen to a doctor as soon as possible. Jane responded, that on reflection, in recent post tennis games get togethers at their Jericho Club, Maureen was fairly quiet and appeared to agree with everything said. Jane then voiced, that she now realized, that this was not a "normal Maureen".

The Cartmels, through the influence of a doctor friend, persuaded her, to go to Vancouver General Hospital, much against her wishes, for a pre- arranged check- up, x rays and blood samples. The blood tests and procedures, revealed a much more serious problem. A growth was putting pressure on the brain, causing stroke like symptoms. Surgery was set for April 17th to be performed by a Dr. Honey, who at the time I did not know was a renowned surgeon in B.C., and also in Canada. My decision, supported by family and Vancouver friends, was to stay put. She was in good hands, and the suspected nature of the growth was not being revealed at this time.

I received a call from Dr. Honey, at about 7:30 p.m., following the surgery. He was extremely forthcoming and informative. The growth was 3cm, by 3cm, by 3cm. Determination of whether the tumor was malignant or not, would have to await the biopsy, but I detected a fairly somber tone to his voice, when questioned. Four days later the hospital staff called, to confirm the growth was cancerous, and that Dr. Honey, had only been able to remove the growth external to the brain. The cancerous growth within the brain, is technically known as glioblastoma, with a remaining lifetime expectation of 12 to 18 months, and a history of seizures during this inoperable period.

Sue Black left the next day, and we left soberly for home by car, the day after. At home we quickly handled our personal affairs, and both agreed, that we should go out to Vancouver, without delay. Maureen had made an amazingly fast and successful recovery from the surgery, and her immediate wish on our arrival on May 1st, was that we should visit her close friends Ruth and Reidar on Whidbey Island in Washington State, and we did. Maureen and Ruth were close friends in High School in Scotland, and their relationship covered some 67 years or more.

We organized Maureen's finances, bills, pills, car repairs and contacts with the B.C. Cancer Society. We socialized with some of Maureen's friends, and I returned home on May 16, while Susan arrived in Vancouver the same day, to join El. Maureen had her first 5 day chemo therapy on May 19. Sue returned home, and Fiona came out to Vancouver, shortly thereafter. On reflection, for someone who was accustomed to her own single company, this coming and going must have been unsettling, but we felt, rightly or wrongly, that multi- layer care giving, was important. Maureen felt obliged to be a tour guide, and while El drove, Maureen showed the girls, the highlights of Vancouver, and the Lower Mainland. Fiona returned home, and I arrived June 2nd.

We made contact with Maureen's oncologist, Dr Thiessen, who proved to be very clinical, but had a charming lady assistant Rosemary Cashman, who Maureen got to know, trust, admire and like. The professionals do not like to bond too closely with their patients, but Maureen and Rosemary, seemed to make an exception to this rule. As in essence, "guests" of Maureen, we were invited to the Cartmels' son's wedding, and later met with cousin John McDonald and his sister Yvonne, who had incurred a brain injury, from a fall, and was now limited physically and mentally. Our days were occupied somewhat, with driving Maureen to appointments and procedures, and ensuring her meds were being taken properly.

Once again, we got out of the house, and spent a delightful weekend, with the Nordhoys, on Whidbey Island. This was therapeutic for all, as Maureen was not accustomed to "permanent guests", at home. As promised, Michele was able to take time off and arrived in Vancouver June 15, and El and I checked into a hotel, to give Maureen some space. We took Maureen to her second chemo therapy session, following which she again became the tourist guide, and proudly showed Michele, Stanley Park, Ambleside, Jericho, Sea to Sky Train and Capilano Suspension Bridge. I drove, and we were tourists for 3 straight days. Michele, returned home on June 20th.

Maureen and I met her surgeon Dr. Honey on June 29th, and I recall his immediate facial reaction, as being stunned, as to how good she looked. It was somewhat justification for our constant caregiving, providing proper meals, supervision of her medication, removal of day to day stressful activities, and an outpouring of love from her remaining family members, to show that we cared. I know it was difficult at times for her as a single person, to have so much company, but the more we organized everything for her, the more she seemed to accept. The exception was her insistence that she maintain her handwritten entries in her bank book, even though all was available to her on the computer, in her TD Bank easy web app.

We had brought her through Phase 1 (3 months) of her limited journey, with the probability of 12 to 15 months remaining. By meeting with many of her friends, we had set the stage for the locals to foster their relationship with her, for the next stage, while we returned home. We flew out of Vancouver on July 5, after being there for almost 10 weeks. Thank you, El. Our flight was somewhat delayed, as Airforce One had landed. The U.S. President was in Vancouver, for the FIFA Women's World Cup Soccer tournament, and accordingly all other flight activity was suspended, until his entourage and their vehicles had left the area. I had my right hip surgery on the 7th, and was released from hospital after 2 days. Friends and the Cancer Society were able to arrange rides, where necessary, for Maureen's appointments and procedures, but her independent persona was returning, and with it a firm desire, to not let anyone other than friends, in the house, or for anyone to supervise her meds etc., and therefore problems were to follow.

Over the next few months, we had house visits from the Golbergs, the Shorts, Michele, Jamie and Cameron, Daric and Nicole, and lunches with Glen and Angela Myers to reminisce old times, and the Bosharts, to renew our condo rental in Naples. We visited the Guilfoyles at their cottage near Bala, and the Wilsons at their house in Zurich. We also had our annual visit to the Royal Winter Fair and the horse show. I had, follow -up visits at the hospital's fracture clinic, and responded well to CCAC house visits, for exercise and monitoring of my hip therapy, and was then successfully discharged from further treatment. Having cleared this hurdle, I had to then see my GP, re a possible hernia problem. I was fast tracked to a surgeon, Dr. Ing at Markville Stouffville Hospital in October, the fracture clinic in November and hernia surgery in December. The repair was to the groin, and the discomfort post- surgery was memorable, even for someone, who had been "under the knife 5 times before".

Late in the year, El and I attended 2 funerals. The first was for Bob Luery, who was an original member of the ACC church assembly, but had left to attend Cedarview Community Church, in Newmarket. El was quite friendly with his wife Elaine. Bob had taken up sailing, and in deciding to sail his boat across Lake Simcoe for the purpose of winterizing it, had left unaccompanied. Bob, as a realtor, was a "take charge" guy, and although someone was probably available to join him, he made the decision to leave on his own. Lake Simcoe, is shallow at the shoreline, but quite deep in the middle, and unpredictable, when it comes to weather. A storm did blow up, and he must have been swept overboard, or the small boat capsized. They found the boat, but have not found his body, and never will. This form of death, causes so much anxiety, stress and grief for surviving family members, and legal delays for final settlement purposes. Elaine's eulogy was so touching, and we still grieve for her.

The second funeral was for Jack Flanagan, the husband of Ruth, who was the founding editor of our Ballantrae Community magazine, Home on the Green, which has been published quarterly for almost 20 years. I had met Jack at Southlake Hospital, while volunteering, following his heart problems. Jack was crusty, but we hit it off, and I was able to house visit him more than several times, before he died.

I was still volunteering at Southlake Hospital's heart recovery program on Wednesdays and their Cardiovascular ward on Fridays. El had taken to playing bridge at our community centre. I participated in an evenings' hospital conference, called The Ultimate Patient Experience, where doctors, nurses and volunteers provide ideas and suggestions, as to how we can make the patient stay in hospital, more satisfying. I was really struck by the friendliness and appreciation shown by the permanent hospital staff to the volunteers that night, and their obvious sincerity.

Maureen's health and welfare, were still very much on our minds. Seizures are such a part of brain cancer and so far, we were not aware, of her encountering any. We had agreed, that she should continue playing golf, but not tennis, as the danger of a fall was real. Her first setback, was early December, when she told us, "that I felt tired, lay down on a grassy knoll, and these nice firemen came by, and picked me up". She was admitted to Vancouver General, but seemed to rebound quite quickly, even to the extent of requesting staff in Emergency, to let her have a shower. I spoke with the oncologist's assistant, Rosemary Cashman, who suggested that we stay put. She confirmed that Maureen had recovered well, but it was extremely likely, that this was a further sign, of the choppy road that lay ahead.

We attended a Christmas Eve sermon, visited Fiona and Susan households on Christmas Day to exchange gifts, and had a wonderful Christmas Dinner at Fiona's. Once again New Years' Eve was uneventful, but El and I without saying anything, knew that the year ahead was going to be challenging. You had heard what the doctors said, but you did not want it to become true!

On the basis of the above thoughts, we decided to leave by car for Florida in early January, after I had been cleared by Dr. Ing to travel, following the hernia surgery. The section of road just north of Ocala, Florida, had come to a standstill, as there had been a fatal roadside shooting on Interstate 75, which delayed our trip somewhat. We had been invited to join the Leightons at their vacation spot, in Fort Pierce on the east coast. Their accommodation, did not really provide comfortable sleeping for 4 adults, but we had fun. The ocean can be, and was very turbulent on the Atlantic side during our visit, and we really prefer the calmer waters of the Gulf.

We arrived in Naples on January 23rd by way of Alligator Alley, which does not live up to its name, unless you take a side trip to one of the tourist farms. We had visits from the Leightons, the Van Dams, and the Bridges, and socialized and dined with the Pritchards, the Wilsons, the Myers, the Fishers, and Angela Myers father Mohinder, and his lady friend Trowdel. Mohinder is a home residential developer and builder in Ontario. We had met him on several of Betty Shukster's world trips, having recommended them to him, through his daughter Angela. We had a change of pace, by joining the Van Dams for a weekend at their place in St. Petersburg.

We moved on to Sarasota on March 05, and welcomed Shirley Johnston the next day. We celebrated Els' 74th birthday at Turtles Restaurant, and went to the Van Wezel theatre to see Gordon Lightfoot. The show in my opinion was a big disappointment. He said, that he was recovering from a cold. I think age was, and is a factor. Entertainers do not like to retire, and some do live on their past reputation. We spent some time with the O'Hares, and then granddaughter Cassandra, and her friend Kelsie arrived. Great teenagers, no problems. Just a delight to have them for a week. It was fun taking them out to supper, and seeing them getting all dressed up, high heels and all. El and I were beaming, as we escorted "our models" through the restaurants.

After Easter service at Shining Light church, we left March 29 to visit the Guilfoyles, at their vacation condo on Fort Myers beach. We had dinner that night in a nearby restaurant, during which Eleanor received a text from a Vancouver based lady, Ann Eynon, a close friend of Maureen. She was at that moment in Hawaii, but as the emergency contact for Maureen, she had been contacted by Vancouver General, to inform her that, Maureen had had a seizure, and was in emergency. We in turn contacted most of Maureen's local friends, and then found out that Ruth Nordhoy and her neighbor Stephanie, from the Island of Whidbey, in Washington State, had undertaken to visit her and taken her out of the hospital, based upon Maureen's usual desire not to be there. She was now at home, much against my wishes, as she was not really facing up to the seriousness of her condition.

We left for Cape Coral on April 02, and Sue Black arrived the next day. All was quiet for a few weeks, until we received an urgent message from Ann Eynon, to the effect that Maureen was in trouble, and I should seriously consider coming out to look after her. I left Fort Myers airport April 21 at 2:00 p.m. and arrived in Vancouver via Toronto at 8:00 p.m., western time that evening. Her hairdresser Jackie Lockmuller and husband Len were there in the house, keeping an eye on her. I was shocked to see the condition Maureen was in.

She circled the room, holding on to each piece of furniture, before greeting me. She was not a good patient, and had not let anyone in the medical field enter the house to offer any service whatsoever. I put my foot down and scolded her, to the effect, that this was not just about her, but that El and I and family members cared, and were involved, and that she had to listen and co-operate. She relented and I had representatives from Vancouver Coastal Health visit, and we restored a proper schedule for her intake of meds and eating habits. Typical Maureen, she bounced back. She was now a year beyond her operation, and looked great and healthy once again. I can still see her standing in the driveway, smiling and waving, as I left to return to Florida.

Sue Black had gone home, and therefore El had been on her own in Cape Coral, for about one week, during my absence. The Grays were aware of our circumstances and indicated that we could stay as long as we wanted, without additional cost. We left Cape Coral May 04, stayed an extra night in a Cambridge hotel, and arrived home the afternoon of May 07, fairly rested. Family and friend get togethers followed, together with supervisory calls re Maureen's meds. The seizures and short hospital stays continued; two in May and two in June. Her early releases from hospital were comforting, but we knew her condition was worsening.

Our former street neighbor Margaret Gilbert, who had been living in Ottawa died, and we attended the memorial service. Margaret had lived a long and full live, much of it in South America, and was ever the lady. Introducing myself to family members, who we had not met before, got the response of "Oh you are the one with or without the teeth", recalling the incident with Margaret's "soft" biscuits. I had an appointment with a plastic surgeon, Dr. Backstein, to remove a basal cancer cell, from my forehead, the first of many in the years to come.

Discussions with medical staff, indicated, that I should return to Vancouver. I flew out Sunday, July 17, to find Maureen at her worst. Her stubborn approach to not accepting outside help had returned, and she was now reaping the negative effects, of not managing her meds properly. I spoke with the pharmacy about the remaining contents of her blister pack, comparing the contents and usage from when it was issued, and we came to the conclusion that she had seriously overmedicated herself.

I therefore took her immediately to Richmond General emergency, whose staff in turn admitted her, ran some tests, questioned and spoke with her, and gave me the indication that their suspicions were, that as I had just arrived in Vancouver, I was using their services, as a convenience, in order not to look after her They would not admit her and a neighbour Jim Ferguson, kindly drove us home about 6:00 p.m., to begin a night, that I would like to forget.

The problem started about 9:00 p.m. The overmedication affected her and without telling me, she struggled to reach the toilet, and when she finally did, she knocked the toilet holder of the wall, and into the toilet bowl, plugging and causing it to overflow when flushed, and flood the bathroom floor. I heard a noise, and when I got to the bathroom door, she would not let me in, as she attempted to clean up using her night dress. I finally persuaded her to let me in, clean her up, dress her and get her into bed. We were both highly stressed with the incident.

Having solved the plugged toilet, and following extensive mopping and rinsing, I got the floor and bathroom, almost back to normal by about 10:30. Bear in mind, that was 1:30 a.m. eastern, my actual time. My thoughts at that moment, about the Richmond General emergency doctors, who would not accept her as being sick and ignored my pleas, were not pleasant. The following days were spent stabilizing her meds and food intake, taking her to Oncologist and Cancer Clinic meetings, returning Richmond General's walker, getting a new walker from the Red Cross, picking up her repaired dental plate, and trying to improve her overall health. I finally admitted to El that it was too much for one person, and would she come out, which she promptly did, arriving July 23.

Together we got Maureen back to a proper regiment of medicine and food intake, took her to her Cancer Clinic appointments, started her radiation treatment, arranged controlled visitations by friends and handled a variety of banking, insurance and house needs. She was no longer permitted to drive. The loss of hair, due to the radiation treatment was looming, and she insisted that her hairdresser, Jackie, be present to supervise the wig to be chosen. I recall being in the shop on Broadway, as Jackie and El decided which one was the most appropriate, while Maureen stayed in the background, and scowled through the whole process. As it turned out, she never even got to wear the wig!

Sunday August 7th, Ann Eynon stepped in to give us a break for a few hours, and El and I drove to church. As we approached the building, I felt dizzy, but kept it to myself. During the service, the pastor asked the congregation to sit, while the tithes and offerings were collected. I then said to El, that we had to leave, as I did not feel well. An awkward moment, as everyone else was sitting down, as we stood up and shuffled along the row. I suggested El drive us to Richmond General Hospital about 15 minutes away. I was admitted, triaged quickly, taken to emergency, and hooked up to all sorts of equipment. With limited knowledge of heart disease, I still think I know everything, and would not stop talking, until El suggested that I be quiet. I do recall one of the staff saying "Look, his heart has stopped beating, and he is still talking".

El did the sensible thing and called the girls. Susan and Fiona dropped everything and arrived the next day. Michele, due to Doug's health, was unable to come out, but contacted El. The overall reaction, epitomized the strength and bond within the family, to give all their time and energy for the needs of other family members, without question. Both the attention and care I received at the hospital were first class. I was concerned that one or more of the heart bypasses had failed, but was reassured that this was not the problem. The electrical signal to the heart chambers, which controls the beat, was not functioning properly, and in fact the top chamber was beating at 300 beats per minute, causing atrial flutter and consequent dizziness. The signal would now have to be controlled by an artificial device, commonly known as a pacemaker, which would restore normalcy to my life.

The surgery was performed under local anesthetic at 8:00 p.m. on Monday night. The area was large, circular, empty, cold and appeared to be in semi darkness, apart from the area, where 3 or 4 staff were attending to me. There was no discomfort, apart from the pressure on the chest, as the staff inserted the device. There is no natural cavity there, and it felt, as if they were hammering it into whatever space was available. I seemed to recover well and was discharged Thursday August 11, first of all to see a cardiologist, Dr. Benny Bar-Shlomo, who was terrific, and then to be driven home by El.

To recap my short visit in Richmond General, there were 4 of us in my post-surgery room and being chatty and having volunteered at Southlake on the cardiovascular ward for many years, I was able to give some comfort to the 3 other patients and their families, probably much to the annoyance of the hospital staff. El brought Maureen in to visit, and I recall her being visibly upset, and wanting to leave the room. I had to suppose, that she somehow considered herself as responsible for my condition and family disruption, and that it was time to take "some action".

The action was triggered the day I got home from the hospital. Something she said to Eleanor, signaled an alarm to El, that she was up to something. El had the girls check Maureen's room and bathroom during the day, and they in turn found multiple pill bottles stashed away, which set out clearly, what her plan of action was. They were removed. That evening, Maureen called it an early night, and left us wondering in the living room. Devastated that her secret had been discovered, she was furious with us, leading to fits of sobbing and screaming. It had become apparent that we could no longer handle things, and that we should call 911. The response by the services, and in particular the RCMP, was disproportionate with the situation. After some discussion, Maureen left the house, with these cold words "And good night to you all". She would not return. The subject of taking one's life, even when there is agreement among all the parties and family members, is a difficult one. You want to consider the feelings of the "patient", who has literally been given a death sentence, but also the feelings of family and caregivers, providing reasonable quality of life, during these difficult times. To end it so, without dignity, seemed to me, to be wrong.

Maureen called the next day, and El told her that we would be in to see her with her personal effects, but that we were returning home as "Bob needed rest and healing". The 4 of us visited the next day. She barely acknowledged Susan and Fiona, as she feverishly went through her personal items, for her purse. She was looking for cash, her credit cards and keys, to escape the hospital. The staff confirmed that she had had two seizures, and would be kept in emergency for a few days, before being moved to a palliative care centre. The staff also confirmed, that we would not be needed in the coming weeks. The girls left the next day, and we flew home shortly thereafter.

I suspect that Rosemary Cashman engineered Maureen's subsequent transfer, to the top floor of the Vancouver General Hospital, which is the palliative cancer ward, before final transfer is approved to a hospice setting. As a patient, you are on the 16th floor for the wrong reason, but the space and ambience of the ward, and the care were second to none. We were home for 8 days attending to numerous calls from the hospital staff and Cancer Centre, before receiving a solid recommendation to come out again, as Maureen was having trouble eating and comprehending.

After moving into Maureen's house, we began a daily routine of visiting her in hospital and organizing visits to the hospital by friends. Even

Ruth and Stephanie from far away Whidbey Island visited. Wednesday, August 31, was a momentous day. El and I arrived early afternoon, to find Maureen almost normal. Alert, happy, and wanting to do something. Steroid medication? The staff said no. It was as if the good Lord was saying "I am giving you a lasting memory of the Maureen, that you knew". The staff suggested a wheelchair, and we took her around the ward, to see the incredible view of Vancouver's outer harbour, complete with anchored merchant vessels, and the snow-capped North Shore mountains in the background. We then went down the elevator, to the coffee shop, where she enjoyed sipping some coffee with part of a cookie, before her strength started to wane. It was just as therapeutic for us, as it appeared to be for Maureen.

The next number of days were difficult. Maureen would not go into her diaper and therefore was probably suffering from bowel and stomach pain, but could not relate this to us. She was being sedated for this, and her negative physical reaction to the staff, if they attempted to help her. We had multiple discussions, about transferring her to a Richmond Hospice to live out her remaining days. El and I visited the hospice, and met with the staff. A tremendous facility, with each room sporting sliding glass doors, looking out on to a tranquil setting of lawn and trees. Her transfer was cancelled, as she was deemed too noisy and disruptive.

The last day, Maureen acknowledged us, was Monday, September 12, by simply saying our names and squeezing our hands. Nobody, really knew the source of Maureen's pain, and to her credit, El spoke with and strongly requested the staff, to increase her pain medication. They complied without argument and she was in a deep sleep after that, and I received a call at 11:30 p.m. on September 15th, to the effect that she was slipping away. Traffic from Richmond into Vancouver was sparse and I arrived at midnight, to be told that she had died at 11:45. It was late, and I was balancing an element of grief with an honest sense of relief, that the battle which she had so bravely fought was over, and that El and I were now free of the daily concerns, which had been with us for 17 months. There is such a finality to hospital death, exhibited by the staff, who request you politely to please remove all personal effects from the room, as this bed will be occupied tomorrow, by another cancer patient with a probable limited life span. Having witnessed the hardship of Maureen's journey, especially in the latter stages, I would certainly support voluntary medical assistance (MAID) in dying, where all parties have legally consented.

Maureen and I had discussed her will openly. I was the executor and the sole beneficiary. My business background had trained me to tackle projects without delay. With Els' help, we began the process of informing friends and family, of making contacts and seeking advice as to suitable realtors, lawyers and funeral directors, of contacting insurance brokers, insurance companies, banks, the B.C. Cancer Society and a location for a memorial service and a pastor who could oversee the service.

Maureen had requested that she be cremated, and that her ashes be spread on the Fraser River, where she had spent many a time around noon, in a lay by parking spot by the river, relaxing in her car, and watching the planes take off and land from the Vancouver International Airport, just across from the river. She knew every airline and most makes of their planes. We also had to consider the extensive contents of Maureen's house, and what action could be taken to bless someone, or some people, with the multitude of quality items, and to arrange for lesser "stuff" to be removed.

We decided, not to transport home much of the house contents, other than a few special items, such as her Edinburgh crystal and show cabinets. El spoke with the elders and pastor of Richmond Pentecostal Church, and we agreed to "gift" the house contents, for the benefit of a Syrian family, they were sponsoring, who they expected to arrive in Canada within the next few months. It was a perfect match, and although their transfer from a Jordan refugee camp to Richmond B.C. took some time, they were able to finally move into an apartment, fully furnished, and lacked nothing in the way of household items. The sole exceptions were a Murphy Bed, which cousin John wanted, and Maureen's wonderful set of golf clubs desired by one of her golf partners.

We had decided to work hard, and achieve all of the above, including of course the memorial service, within a 4 to 5 week- period, before returning home. Maureen was not a believer, and not even a church attender, but we organized a wonderful memorial service at Minoru Chapel in the park, on a warm and sunny September the 29th, which was attended by over 50 of her friends and business associates. The pastor was Allen Burnett, a delightful young man, who ran a fairly neutral service as per Maureen's wishes, but ended the service with these powerful words "Is this all there is?". El had arranged for all to receive a memorial rose, and the Chapel location allowed us to host a well catered social gathering in a building a mere 50 yards away. You want to describe a memorial service as being memorable, paying homage and offering closure. This came close.

Due to our short stay, the urgent tasks, were to finalize a lawyer, to set up the probate filing and application process, and to find a suitable realtor for house listing purposes. Els' cousin Jackie assisted with the latter, and we listed the house with a Michael Cowling of RE/MAX. Due to his efforts, contacts, and the then strong activity of the real estate market, we received an offer very quickly, from a builder, with a final closing date of late December 2016, to allow time, for the probate application to be approved, without which the house could not be sold.

Maureen's lawyer, who had prepared the will, had since retired, but recommended we talk with a Roderick Henderson. Rick, the casual name, I was able to finally address him as, adopted the initial lawyer/client relationship, with a business like, and very professional manner. Over several meetings and phone calls, I was able to determine that a favourite sport of his was soccer. Not only had he attended the University of Calgary, but he had played right back for their soccer team in the Calgary amateur soccer league, during the years 1970 to 1973. During this period, I had played right wing, for a Calgary soccer team called the Calgary Caledonians, and both teams were in the same league. This certainly "broke the ice". We established that more than likely we were on the same soccer field over 45 years ago, but because we were on opposite sides of the field, it is highly likely that we ever came in to contact. It can be a small world sometimes! He was extremely capable as a lawyer, but I reminded him, that I was on a much better soccer team.

Ruth and Reidar invited us to their Whidbey Island home, and we spent a delightful 3 days with them. Back in Richmond, we made final arrangements with the church to collect and transport the house contents to storage, awaiting arrival of their sponsored Syrian refugees. An army of church volunteers arrived, and the house was quickly stripped. We finalized the move of a very few pieces of furniture and the car to Ballantrae, with Atlas Van Lines, the removal of "not wanted stuff" by Maureen's former handyman Angus, and the breakdown and removal of the Murphy bed by cousin John. The house was truly bare, and the church staff even dismantled the glass hot house in the garden. We checked into a local hotel, and flew back home on October 15. I have documented some of the major work, that one can be involved in, following a family member death. The work can last for months. Due to geography and hard work, we achieved all that had to be done, in 4 weeks. Thank you, Eleanor.

Before leaving, we had the scattering of Maureen's ashes to consider. You must have special permission to take one's ashes out of the province, and therefore we decided not to wait, but to act on Maureen's wishes, as mentioned previously, that they be spread on the local waters of the Fraser River. It appeared simple and direct, but reality is that, with this action, you are parting with the last connection of your loved one, apart from the memories.

To achieve this simple but touching task, El and I had driven to a suitable spot by the Fraser river, which gave me reasonable and private access to the waters, on foot. What followed, is not intended to make light of the situation, but to detail, what actually happened. El had suggested, after leaving the car, that I go alone to the river bank, which was dense with bulrushes. I ignored the fact that my running shoes were getting heavy with water, as I pushed through the bulrushes, and prepared to open the jar and scatter the ashes on the flowing river. As I separated the reeds, I found myself looking directly at a University of British Columbia eight rowing crew, sitting in absolute silence, at the ready to take off. They were only a matter of meters it seemed, from where I was standing in the water. At the separation of the reeds, the cox of the crew glanced at me, somewhat surprised at my sudden appearance, but without hesitation gave the order to start rowing. Our (Maureen and mine) private moment, had been interrupted, and after what seemed a lengthy time, the boat disappeared, all was quiet, and I honoured her request, and concluded the scattering.

We went back to normal home life for the next 2 months, including medical appointments and socializing with family and friends. Due to the considerable time spent in Vancouver, we had postponed some work due to upgrade the house, and we now were able to devote our attention to replacing the carpeting in the master bedroom, with a wood floor, matching the living room. We also contracted our handyman Paul, to installing a bathroom in the basement. We had purchased the floor tiling years ago, when the rest of the basement was renovated. He did a superb job, finishing in late December.

As the year wore on, we were getting slightly nervous, as probate approval had not been received, and the house purchase agreement expired on December 30. I was requested to sign final documentation by our Richmond lawyer, but under B.C. law, the lawyer witnessing the documentation was required to have B.C. certification, which our Ontario lawyer did not. Should we send the documentation back to B.C., for witnessing signature by our lawyer. Would this be acceptable practice? As it was late December, we had to also be concerned about delays in mail and courier delivery, and staff vacations.

I decided to nip this in in the bud, called our Richmond lawyer Rick, and confirmed that I was coming out to meet him on the morning of December 27. Rick confirmed that, although his staff was on holiday, he would be in the office. I arrived late on the 26th, and on meeting him the next morning asked wryly, if he knew how to operate the photocopier. He responded that "He thought he could handle that". We signed and witnessed the necessary paperwork, and I caught a cab to the airport, and a flight home arriving at 9:00, that same night. Rick promised that this final documentation would be couriered to the courthouse, with an urgent request to meet the December 30 deadline, and that a courier would be in the courthouse, to deliver the probate approval to his office.

Apparently, probate approval documentation is mostly reviewed and signed by judges, in between court cases, or whenever they have a break. Probate was granted, and received on December 29[th,] and couriered to the purchaser's realtor that day, thereby meeting the terms of the buy/sell agreement, with one day to spare.

Before I had left for Vancouver, Christmas gifts were exchanged as usual on the 25th at Fiona's and Susan's, but this year's Christmas family dinner, was hosted by granddaughter Melissa and her husband Marc, in Keswick. They have a "socially friendly large gathering house", which is perfect to host the family. The year ended on a somewhat sad note, due to the death of David Storey, husband to Edith Storey, who is Eleanor's cousin. Their house was directly across the street from Els' family home, where she grew up, before leaving for Toronto and then Vancouver, where we met. New Year's Eve was spent with the Van Dams. 2016 was now behind us and frankly speaking, not a year that we would wish to be repeated.

The first day of this 2017 new year, saw us attend the wedding, of the son of our church friends from many years ago, Tan and Cheng Yeo. The wedding ceremony and celebrations were held in an Eglinton movie theatre location, which was close to Standard Life's pension office in Toronto, where I was transferred to, from Vancouver to become manager in 1981. El and I had watched movies over the years at this same theatre. A theatre business adapting to a changing world! Everything about this wedding was splendid. The table we were at was occupied by Markham residents of Chinese birth, who also called Hong Kong home. They were a lively group. The groom Thomas, and his bride Susan were picture perfect. As I have said before, weddings bring people together, who have never met or remember most of the other guests. We had met Thomas briefly, some time ago and I asked him, if he remembered meeting Eleanor and I at his parents' house. His answer was short and very North American ......nope!

Before leaving for Florida, we attended to finalizing our wills, with a Newmarket lawyer, Cliff Dresner, including naming our oldest daughter Susan, as the Executrix of the estate. I firmly believe that only one person should be appointed to this position, and wish to make it clear, that this does not give this person any advantage over other beneficiaries, just a lot of extra work. If needed, an executor can appoint the lawyer to handle some or all of the work, over and above filing for probate, with additional costs. To follow up on the condition of the pacemaker inserted in B.C. last September, I met with a techie and later with a cardiologist, Dr. Tsang, at Southlake in the Pace clinic. She was thorough and business like, but our personalities clashed, and if all goes well, we will only meet once a year. She was adamant that I take frequent blood pressure readings, and record those for future appointments. We purchased the necessary equipment.

We then set off for Naples, arriving January 30, with a view to staying in Florida, until the end of April. We are blessed! Our first outing, was a day in Ave Maria, a small community inland and north of Naples, which was created by the Ave Maria Foundation, led by Roman Catholic philanthropist, Tom Monaghan, the founder of Domino's Pizza, as a planned college town. The foundation purchased the land, built a cathedral and the catholic university and schools. The cathedral is a magnificent barn -like structure in the centre of town. The surrounding land area has a population of less than 30,000. During our Naples stay, we had no shortage of visits and visitors including the Tonns. The only disappointment was the appearance of Red Tide at Marco Island beaches. This Gulf borne irritant, if present in the water near the shore, kills the fish population and makes you cough repeatedly, and not want to enter the water. Red Tide has been in the middle of the Gulf waters for hundreds of years, and is only noticeable when it comes close to the shoreline.

We left Naples and spent 2 days with the Guilfoyles, in their condo, on Fort Myers Beach, before moving to our favourite spot on Siesta Key Beach, where we received official confirmation, that our granddaughter Melissa was pregnant with her first child. The Leightons arrived with a problem. The driver bringing them from Tampa, had given their luggage to passengers whom he had already dropped off, before reaching Sarasota. I listened to multi phone calls, accusations and promises. Enough I said, give me the address of those that have the Leightons luggage and we will go and get it. A trip to Palmetto, about 50 minutes away was successful. The dear old ladies, who had the wrong bags said "Oh we thought you would never come". When asked if they had contacted the limousine service, their reply was "Oh no, we knew somebody would find us!"

After the Leightons left, our granddaughter Cassandra, and her girlfriend Kelsey arrived, for a week's stay. We took the girls to see the live theatre show Annie, at the Van Wezel theatre. Very enjoyable. The girls were just great, and oh so easy to please, but we did spoil them somewhat, with dinner outings to Turtles, the Olive Gardens and Carrabba's Italian Grill, and a day of shopping in Ellenton. The O'Hares, all 6 of them, came to town shortly after. Two stayed with us, with the balance at a local motel.

We lunched with our ACC interim pastor Rick and his wife Pat, after attending the Sunday morning church service at First Memorial in Fort Myers. This is a great church, with a charismatic pastor, who leads a group to Israel and Jordan each and every year. Although considered, to-date we have not joined them. Following lunch, we drove to Cape Coral, to meet with Bev and Dan, our neighbours, when we vacationed there in the Gray house. The restaurant they chose was excellent, but Dan probably over ate, when he had this huge piece of chocolate cake. Unknown to us, he had loosened the belt around his waist, and as we left the restaurant and passed other guests, his pants slowly and perhaps even eloquently, slipped past his knees to settle around his ankles, and almost trip him. He hoisted them up, without much fuss, to the accompaniment of some "tut, tuts" from two senior ladies, sitting nearby. Dan, without apology, said to Eleanor, "At least I was wearing boxer shorts".

We got very disturbing news, the next day. Fiona called to say that her estranged husband Ian, had committed suicide. His life and demeanour had changed, following an earlier head on car collision. Although not his fault, the knock-on effects, from such a collision are usually drastic. Their marriage deteriorated. His golfing prowess, which had given him status with the executives he worked for, had really lessened, and in my opinion, he experienced a consequent drop in his worthiness. Ian was a changed man, hid his problems and never recovered. The memorial service was well attended, and the eulogies although difficult were warm. To honour Ian, and comfort Fiona and Cassie somewhat, we had a family dinner after the service with 14 of us there.

May saw us head to Goderich, located on the eastern shore of Lake Huron, to attend the 50th wedding anniversary of Gerald and Anne Wilson. They were the parents of our ACC pastor, Jeff Wilson, and we had become friends with them while vacationing in Naples, where they owned a condominium. We were aware that Gerald had been diagnosed with cancer, which they had chosen to treat with natural products. We suspected that Gerry's condition was much more severe, and he actually had been given a medical opinion as to his remaining life span. The turnout was huge and although facing a harsh reality, Gerry and Anne were sparkling and gracious. I tried to engage Gerald in conversation about health, but it was not the right time.

On the way to Goderich, we stopped in at our granddaughter Jamie's house, to visit and see our second oldest great grandchild, Cara, who was now 8 months old. Over all, this trip saw us experience the joy of new life, and the reality of losing a friend in the short term. In many respects, what we experienced, was a snapshot of life. Later that month, we had lunch with our daughter Michele in Peterborough, and met up with and brought home for a few days, a close B.C. friend, Sylvia Loutit, who had been visiting relatives in Ontario. We have known Sylvia, since 1964, due to my playing soccer for Vancouver Canadians, with her then husband Bill Nicol, who was the nicest guy. El and Sylvia, despite the many miles apart at times, have been close friends for those 50 plus years.

Events over the next few months, were what I would describe as firsts and lasts. I went to a school ground to watch granddaughter Cassandra, participate in an all- girls high school rugby game. I played school rugby at Trinity Academy in Edinburgh, all of 60 plus years ago, but I do not recall the games as being as tough and hostile, as to what I was watching today. I was impressed. These girls were physically fit, enthusiastic and mean. These many years, reflect on average, how much taller and bigger, the high school kids of today are, compared to those in my era. The next first, was having our garage floor, front porch and back patio resurfaced by a company called Fluid Rock, which gave us a pleasing design in a solid rock concrete like finish, and certainly enhanced both the front porch and back patio. Good choice El!

I then had lunch with Jay Waters, our Standard Life, Toronto investment manager, whom I had worked with for so many years, as we jointly counselled Standard's defined benefit pension clients regarding funding and investment issues. Jay had called me, and we had lunch in a Scarborough Town restaurant. This was not only his last appointment of the day, but his last "business" appointment full stop, having just been retired by Standard's successor, Manulife. It meant something that he chose to "celebrate", with me. And we did. On Manulife, I suspect!

My next first would hopefully be my last, as I had been summoned after 55 plus years in Canada, to be a candidate for jury duty. The first day, I was able to sneak into a court, and follow some proceedings, posing as a spectator. The next day, the hundred or so of us in the pool, were isolated in a huge room, while the jury selection continued in private, behind closed doors, with the sole excitement being, when the court clerk announced the name of the next candidate to be considered by the prosecution and defense teams for possible duty, and he or she left the room. The case was regarding an accusation of child molestation, and thankfully I was not picked.

El and I attended Ed Ifurung's funeral, in Oshawa. Ed was the late husband of Carol, who was my staff administration supervisor in Toronto, for so many years. Carol was a lovely lady, who at times was not as authoritative as necessary, but compensated by having a pleasing way with staff and clients alike, and helped create the family atmosphere, that I wanted to achieve in the office. I did not know Ed well, but the large turnout must have pleased, and somewhat comforted Carol.

As the funeral procession of vehicles was about to leave the parking lot for the internment, Carol spotted me, and asked the driver to stop. She then got out of the car, and we hugged, with a warm sincerity. Few words were exchanged, before we mutually mumbled our vague promises to be in touch. Our lives, after so many years, have taken different turns in the road, and it is probable that we will never meet again. That "hug", in my opinion, summed up our long- term relationship, our respect for each other, a thank you for coming and a likely permanent goodbye!

The Walk for Life program, that I volunteer at in Southlake Hospital, has a fund raiser each year to obtain about $70,000 for additional stress testing equipment, which is badly needed and is used for new and graduating clients. The rewards from being a volunteer, mainly surface when you talk with a graduating client, and they disclose the value that you have added to their experience. It is not given that often, but receipt of such words, is always heart- warming.

El and I were invited to the Guilfoyles cottage in July for a lovely weekend, and we followed with a family dinner at the Keg to celebrate my 77th birthday. El and I volunteered at the Ballantrae Summer Games, initially as traffic wardens, but graduating to assist with the walking programs for Condo 1. Stouffville had a weekend summer celebration, and we were asked by a member of the library board to do some book reading in front of their library, microphone and all. We rehearsed diligently, did our twenty- minute stints, to an audience of one, and I suspect he was napping.

Melissa had her baby shower late August, and our third great grandchild Logan, was born to Mum and father Marc on September 21, weighing 7 lbs. 6ozs. Earlier that month we had attended our second born great grandchild, Cara's 1st birthday. A good turnout with our grandson Daric, and Doug Cook, Cara's grandfather, looking after Cameron, Cara's brother, who is now age 5 and is pretty active. I can still see Cara's chocolate covered face, as she planted her head into a huge cake, that her Mum, Jamie, had baked. Later that month, as forecast, we attended a memorial service for Pastor Gerald Wilson, in Goderich. We shared a similar lighthearted view of life, and it was unfortunate that our relationship on earth was so short. I will miss him.

Even with the recent birth of their first child, Marc and Melissa, hosted a family thanksgiving dinner. El had a follow up meeting with a Dr. Lorraine, re her tinnitus ear problem, to be told, that there still was no magic cure. One of these days, she will be able to put this cruel condition behind her! El started playing bridge at the local recreation centre, and I think that this socializing with community members will be good for her. We had tickets for a Diana Krall concert, downtown Toronto, but when daughter Michele found this out, I was forced to surrender my ticket. They enjoyed the show, but El found the walk to the upper level in the theatre, to be a bit difficult.

We attended the funeral service of Valmon Howell, the husband of Arlene Howell a very close church friend of Els'. The service, was held at our ACC church in Aurora, but due to today's technological advancements, the Howells' children, living in both South Africa and Australia were able to participate in the service for their father.

Our December socializing and dinners included time with the Grays in Toronto, the O'Hares and of course a family Christmas dinner hosted by Melissa and Marc. All were excellent with an additional star for the family dinner. As usual, we had visited Fiona's and Susan's earlier in the day and exchanged gifts. Christmas is quite a day for us. 2017 proved to be a collage of joy and sadness, of firsts and lasts, of family newborn and family deaths. A life formula for the future?

Our 2018 socializing began with dinner at the O'Hares, followed by a surprising lunch with Els' cousin Edith Storey and her daughter Brenda, from Peterborough. January, 07, we left for a 2 week stay in Antigua, at the St. James's Club resort, to vacation with Gerry and Kathy Guilfoyle, who had encouraged us to return to Antigua after a 29- year absence. We were more than pleased with everything, the company, the weather, the food, the staff and the resort.

On return, I stepped out of character and purchased a brand- new Toyota RAV 4, for delivery in April. We were able to use our relationship with Magdi Nicholas, the owner of the Stouffville dealership to get a reasonable deal. When I say "reasonable", I mean for both the buyer and the seller. While showing me the technical capabilities of a model outdoors, the staff member asked me if he could be of further help. "Yes" I said, "I would like that one", pointing to a fire red sports model that was sitting in the lot. The deal was done.

El and I had our annual physicals, and I was checked at the Pace Clinic in Southlake Hospital as to the satisfactory operation of my pacemaker.

We were cleared for winter travel. Before leaving, we shared in Susan and Mike's delight at their purchasing a larger and more modern home in Keswick. In my opinion, this will, in time, be an excellent investment, before they step down to a smaller retirement home.

We flew to Sarasota on February 18, rented a car, and moved into condo 5-303 at our favourite condo site Siesta Dunes, on Siesta Key beach. Initially El was not feeling well, and we went to a walk-in clinic for relief of her sore jaw, sore throat and what was perceived as sinusitis. The prescribed medication thankfully improved her condition. We celebrated her 76th birthday, visited the Myers, the O'Connors, the Fishers and the Van Dams. Cassandra and her friend Olivia arrived on March 12, and once again we entertained them shopping and food wise, with outings to the Ellenton Mall, and restaurant visits to Carrabba's, Panera, the Broken Egg, Valentino Pizzeria, The Olive Gardens and Turtles. It was a treat for them, but equally a joy for us and they were a delight to have as our guests for the week.

Sue Black arrived on March 20, on the same flight the girls departed on. We saw the Cuban Symphony Orchestra perform at the Van Wezel theatre, and visited a ranch east of Sarasota, where they have several of the world-famous Lipizzaner high stepping horses. Both shows were worthwhile. The latter was well attended, with the stands packed with winter vacationers. Home was a flight on April 06, after almost seven weeks in Florida. Perfect!

I picked up my new Toyota on April 10, registering 11 kilometers, filed my 2017 tax return summary for the auditors, attended a Southlake appreciation dinner for volunteers, and had an echocardiogram to confirm the bypasses and pacemaker were working well. April 28, we drove to Ancaster, to pick up the clothes El had left at the Florida condo, which had been brought home by the Tekkers, at our request. Peter and Kathryn Tekker also vacation at Siesta Dunes, and this may be the start of a new friendship. On the way home, we stopped to see Hal and June, old Ancaster friends. Hal was doing well, but June appeared quite fragile, with what seemed to be the beginnings of dementia.

A visit to the Lynde Clinic confirmed a squamous cell carcinoma on my forehead. Successfully removed, but with a recommendation of 25 days follow up radiation. Referred to a Dr. Woody Wells, to be my oncologist at Southlake and then a Dr Taremi. I was fitted with a custom, baseball catcher-like mask, and the daily radiation treatment began July 3rd. The procedure required a pace maker check- up, once a week, and the only side effect I encountered, was mild tiredness. Very impressed with the Southlake cancer clinic staff's genuine care and attention.

During the summer we attended an 80th birthday celebration for Ballantrae neighbour, Fritz Haefle, and a smaller celebration for my 78th birthday at Sue and Mikes. We later attended Cassandra's high school graduation, which was quite an affair. It was held at the Hilton Suites hotel in Markham, with all the pomp and grandeur, the organizers could muster. Due to the number graduating, the ceremony was more than lengthy. We had attended several of these before, but this was by far the longest. Sorry Cassandra, but as soon as you received your certificate, we were out of there. This was the last of our seven grandchildren to graduate high school, spanning a period of 15 years, from 2003 to 2018.

We saw Cassandra again, as she and her friend Olivia, took El and I out to lunch, to thank us for their vacation time spent with us in Florida. We were then off to spend time with the Guilfoyles at their cottage, where Gerry complained about a pain in one of his legs, and was not his usual mobile self. A lovely dinner evening with Trish and Rob Wright, our young ACC church friends followed. A special, well attended, 1st birthday party for our great grandson Logan Fowles, was next on the calendar.

October saw us spend part of a day, with Michele and Doug and their animals, at their property north of Madoc. It is always relaxing and entertaining to be there, with of course most of the time spent out of doors. We then journeyed on to visit Jeff and Monique Gray, at their beautifully renovated home in Prince Edward County. The house overlooks an inlet, on Lake Ontario, where their yacht is moored. The property seems isolated, but many of their fellow boaters visit them in the summer, and both after finally retiring, have an interest and talent in the arts, and especially in painting and pottery. They of course spend the winter at their property in Cape Coral, Florida

We made another visit to the Royal Winter Fair in November. After so many visits, our enthusiasm is dampening, mainly because of the similarity of the displays, and the fact that it is becoming more commercial, more expensive, and more difficult and time consuming to get to by car, or transit. Age has that effect on you! Late November, we attended a memorial service and a Jewish Shiva for Bernie Shukster. He had not been well for some time. Bernie had been a part of our Ballantrae lives, featured by the many trips we had taken together, under the leadership of his wife Betty, our travel guide. Bernie's role was to video the trip, and produce a DVD after we returned home, sometimes allowing me to insert my poetic words describing the location, and what we saw, as tourists. To achieve this, I spent several hours with Bernie, after each trip in his photography "suite". Bernie plain and simple, was a nice easygoing man, and we will miss him.

I was persuaded by a smooth- talking young church lady, who will remain nameless, but answers to the words, Pastor Trish, to play the part of the Grinch in ACC's upcoming 2018 Christmas Church play, featuring the young children. The script was extensive, and I spent hours trying to memorize the words, which does not come easy with age. Only to be told, that the green intimidating Grinch look alike costume, complete with head mask, which I was required to wear, was not permitting my words to be easily heard. The solution was for me to read my words, appearance by appearance, record them before the date, and then play them at the appropriate time during the play, while I pretended to speak. In essence I was lip syncing on the stage, while coordinating the recorded words, with my actions. All went well. The kids were the main feature, and spoke and sang well. I did not let the side down. I would do this again? No! Do you hear me Pastor Trish? No!

Christmas Day was busy again with the morning at Fiona's, part of the afternoon at Susan's and Christmas dinner, hosted by Fiona. To complete the year, we booked a 2 week stay for early January at the St James's Club resort in Antigua, with the Guilfoyles joining us partway through the 2 weeks, due to a booked medical procedure for Gerry.

2019 started off on the right foot, with the 2 enjoyable weeks in Antigua, with Gerry and Kathy Guilfoyle. We sometimes take these times together with friends for granted. Whereas you should, in reality, celebrate them as precious moments in your lives. You never know what the future holds, and how often you might be able to repeat these times together. On return from our vacation, I continued my coffee time meetings with Lloyd and Gord, and resumed my Wednesday and Friday volunteer sessions at the Southlake Hospital cardiac and heart recovery units.

Fiona and her boyfriend Mike treated us to a dinner at the Joia restaurant in Aurora. It was a greet and meet opportunity re Mike, and he came across as a friendly nice person, who Fiona obviously cares for. I am old school in many ways, but have always felt that the girls must trust their judgement, in deciding who they will partner with. Right or wrong, I will not change. I had a meeting with my electrical cardiologist, Dr. Tsang and received a "see you in 18 months", clean bill of health. Good news for both of us, as we seem to grate on each other. Paul Ellis, at Lady Eleanor's request, started work on a new kitchen backsplash and toilet replacement project.

We flew to Sarasota, on February 24, to begin a 6 week stay at Siesta Dunes. Arriving late, required breakfast off premises the next morning, followed by grocery shopping. After a few minutes in Publix grocery store, I panicked somewhat, as I could not locate my pouch, complete with cash, credit cards and passports. I indicated to El, that I would check the rental car, and after looking feverishly inside, I decided to go back to the McDonald's, where we had breakfast earlier. I drove there like a madman, a few blocks away and despite my desperate pleas to look everywhere, the staff had no success in finding the missing pouch, and I returned to Publix, contemplating the calls I would have to make to cancel and replace the credit cards and the passports…. Oh, the passports! The missing American currency, was also not a small matter.

El could tell that we were in trouble. I muttered, really without any confidence, that I would check with the Publix counter, that handles product returns and general inquiries, to see if they could be on the lookout for the missing pouch. I mumbled to the serving female staff member. "If anyone happens to turn in a missing black pouch in the next little while, I would appreciate being informed"? "And your full name sir", was the reply. I gave it. She reached under the counter, and the pouch appeared before my dancing eyes and boyish grin. I profusely thanked her, and enthusiastically, asked her if I could give her a kiss. "No sir, our satisfaction policy does not extend quite that far". I queried "Was it found in the store?" "No sir, it apparently fell off the roof of a car, that was exiting our parking lot at high speed". I sheepishly slunk away, to share my joy with El, and to explain without much success, why I had apparently placed it on the roof of the car.

Here is my limp excuse. Arriving late the night before at Siesta Dunes, we found that our building elevator was not working. The security guard, was of no help, and we therefore decided to leave almost all our luggage in the backseat of the car, driving to McDonald's and Publix, with the same luggage in the same position. Therefore, when we arrived at Publix and opened the rear door of the car to get "somethings", out of our luggage, I had to place the pouch on the roof, due to the lack of space in the backseat. That is my pathetic story, and I am sticking to it.

We enjoyed our usual visits to our various restaurants such as, Turtles, the Olive Gardens, Valentinos and those at St. Armands Circle. We stayed overnight at the Grays residence in Cape Coral, lunched with the Fishers in Fort Myers, played bridge with the Tekkers from Ancaster, and attended weekly church services at Shining Light church in Sarasota. Late March we saw the Lion King theatre show, at the Van Wezel Auditorium. We had seen this many years ago in Toronto, but with todays' advances in technology, this came across as a superior production.

Sue Black arrived on March 24, and 2 days later we attended a get together with other Canadians, who were members of the Canada Eh travel group, that we were joining for a bus tour in September, in Portugal. Ron Exelby was the host, at his place in Bradenton. He is such a nice man. More bridge with the Tekkers, sunbathing and swimming, and we were fully rested and on our way home on April 05.

I attended a Southlake Hospital dinner for volunteers on April 10, and El and I had dinner with the Guilfoyles 2 nights later, to reminisce about our Antigua vacation. It was obvious at that time, that Gerry was having a medical problem. Els' Aunt Dorothy died on May 2^{nd,} and we attended her memorial service in Mississauga on May 11, with her sister Aunt Ollie. Dorothy was a charming lady with an easy manner and a warm smile. She was well into her 90s, was accepting about dying due to her faith, and it was her time.

We booked our 2- week September/October trip to Portugal with the Canada Eh group, that our church friends the Van Dams, were somewhat familiar with. Some house- hold problems had to be attended to, including a repair to our garage door and contact with a pest removal company, to get rid of a red squirrel, who had decided to take up lodging in the attic. A June visit to the Guilfoyles' cottage followed. Very enjoyable and relaxing. We then had our first medicals with Dr. Martha Carruthers, our new GP, who insisted that I have a colonoscopy, and El have a mammogram, together with bone density procedures. Our new doctor is young and persuasive, and very thorough and a bit pushy, which is what we need, to keep our health up to par.

July 01, saw the family celebrate our first born, Susan's, 55th birthday. On July 11, Gord and I were enjoying our weekly get together in Tim Hortons, when a fairly young girl walked in and in a loud voice, asked who was driving a red Toyota Rav4. I put up my hand and in a matter of fact voice, she said "Well I just hit your car". The damage was not prolific, at a cost of probably under $1,000, and the car was still able to be driven. But it was my, only 1- year old car! The occupants of the vehicle that did the damage, were 3 young university girls, summer working for an Aurora landscaping company, who should not have tried to squeeze their truck beside my car. But they were honest and cooperative, and after exchanging insurance documentation, were on their way.

I had received a call from a lady by the name of Gail Fraser, inquiring if I was related to a Maureen Coyle, whose obituary she had discovered, while researching her family background. She was quite excited to have found a living relative in the family tree, and promised to send material, while expressing a desire to meet me in the future. We did meet and exchanged information. Gail is an Associate Professor at York University with a background in marine and freshwater avian ecology. As a teacher, her goal is to provide intellectually challenging and stimulating courses, while providing the skills to think critically on environmental issues. Currently she is writing a book, and contact with her following our only meeting has been sparse.

Detailed charts setting out the genealogy of the family on my side, courtesy of Ms. Fraser, have been set aside in a separate binder, with my other physical memories. My summary on my side of the family, commences with my great, great grandfather Francis Patrick Coyle born in Ireland circa 1810, and currently ends with four of my great grandchildren, Cameron, Cara, Logan and one conceived, but yet unborn male child; eight generations spanning over 200 years.

Late July, we received word from Michele, that Doug had been taken to a local hospital and then on to Kingston Hospital, due to his body being racked with frequent seizures. After several days of tests, they went home, but the seizures although less frequent, I believe still continue today. I have to wonder, if the pain that he has endured over a period of 30 years or more from nerve damage, and the medication taken to try and alleviate it, has not created a situation, where the body, through the brain has responded in this manner. Doug and Michele are both strong, and have chosen to self- manage the problem. Hopefully, when the ability to meet and greet returns, we hope that we will be able to assist in some meaningful way.

As previously mentioned, with the retirement of our GP doctor Eileen Lougheed, we were assigned a young, energetic GP, by the name of Dr. Martha Carruthers, who impressed us, with her methodical approach to medical service for seniors. At her insistence, El had a mammogram on August 9th, and so began a journey that would last the rest of the year and beyond, requiring us to cancel our September/October 2019 trip to Portugal.

We met with a Markham Stouffville surgeon Dr. Ing, on August 22 and 29, to discuss removal of a 2cm lump from Eleanor's left breast, revealed in the mammogram procedure. A partial day of surgery assessment was held on September 06, and the day of actual surgery, including preparation and discharge was held on September 10th. The follow up meeting with Dr. Ing was on October 03, to discuss the care, that would be required to stop the possible spread of any cancer cells from the breast and lymph nodes under the left arm. El was not pleased with his assessment of the degree of cancer that they had found, and found his comments contradictory and confusing. In addition, his assistant had quickly removed the tape covering the stitched incision and disturbed the wound, causing the healing period to be extended.

Our next meeting with Dr. Ing will be June/July 2020, following a further mammogram. We chose to have the required follow up radiation/chemo and oncologist services at Southlake Hospital. We met Dr. Conrad (radiation) and Dr. Simos (medical), on October 8 and 9. A CT scan was performed on October 11 and after a good report from a Dr. Li on Els' incision, the radiation program began (25 days from November 5th through December 9th). This was not a pleasant experience, and although the Southlake staff were kind, helpful and supportive, it took all of Els' will to finish the program, suffering pain, itch and general discomfort for those final weeks.

Following the radiation, the plan was, to take on a daily basis for a period of 30 months, the drug Tamoxifen, a hormone therapy drug, which when taken orally, is intended to reduce the levels of estrogen in the breast tissue, thereby reducing the feeding and reproduction of cancer cells. As we were heading to Antigua on January 3, 2020, we received permission to delay commencement of the drug until our return, to avoid any possible side effects, while we were out of the country.

It was important to tell Els' journey in 2019, in its entirety, but of course other family events happened at the same time, and affected 2 of them medically. Fiona had a diagnosis of fibroids and required a female operation. Susan's, Michael, began experiencing vision problems, later diagnosed as a symptom of diabetes. Susan had to drive him to and from work for many weeks, until the required medication took effect. His vision has been restored, but the medical requirements of living with diabetes will continue. September saw 2 of our great grandchildren celebrate birthdays; Cara Gies now 3, and Logan Fowles now 2. Our third great grandchild Cameron Gies is 7 years old.

I had a further Basal cell cancer removed from my arm by Dr. Backstein on September 05. This unfortunately is turning into an annual event. The next day, saw us attend a memorial service for Els' Aunt Ollie, who we both had got to know, and love over the years. She, in my opinion, was Els' favourite aunt. We had visited her in Southlake Hospital, as she struggled in her last days. In a manner similar to her sister Dorothy, she was at an age, where she wanted to go, and she died peacefully and with dignity. Her daughter Jackie, together with Salvation Army staff organized a lovely memorial service, with family members and friends in attendance.

September 30, we received approval from First Service, who manage the overall Ballantrae condo site, to place cages over our roof outlets and finally get rid of that pesky red squirrel, who had taken up residence in our attic. According to wildlife services, red squirrels are the most difficult wildlife animals to deal with. What territory is theirs, is theirs, including yours! I finally picked up my repaired Toyota Rav4, on October 17. There was a suggestion that Toyota's parts system had been hacked, and the supply chain interrupted, hence the delay.

I met with Dr. Fu regarding my upcoming colonoscopy, which she would not let me cancel. Reminding me, that the last one performed 7 years ago, revealed a growth in my large intestine. This was surgically removed, together with 12 inches of my large intestine because of cancer implications, by a Dr. Crystal Pallister, at Markham Stouffville Hospital.

Although El was only partway through her breast cancer journey, we both agreed that we should book, a 2 week visit to Antigua in January, to join the Guilfoyles. November 11, Dr. Lynde surgically removed a further basal cell, from my forehead, and took a sample of another growth on my back, which Dr. Backstein removed 2 weeks later, based on the biopsy. I had the shingle and flu shots, and then attended the Markham hospital for my colonoscopy on December 16.

Of course, I had to drink the disgusting fluids you are required to ingest, prior to this procedure, to empty your bowels. Yuk! I was at the hospital on time, changed for the procedure, and awaited Dr. Fu's call. She indicated that this time, I would not be sedated during the procedure, but would only receive a local anesthetic, which as she so delicately put, "Would negate any discomfort, but if not considered enough, to please let her know." Yea right, but at what point!

I was not nervous, as I lay on the operating table, until I heard her slowly say to her staff, "That as soon as Mr. Coyle removes his undershorts, we will begin." Somewhat embarrassed, I struggled in the horizontal position to remove my "very nice" shorts. Not everyone can be perfect! And I restate that I was not nervous. Apart from some small growths, which were benign, she later indicated that all was well, and that she would see me again in due course. I am almost 80. What is "in due course!"

Our Christmas Day was as usual, very busy and delightful. We spent the morning at Fiona's and were spoiled by her endless gifts, as usual. Then on to Sue and Mike's for a pleasant part of the afternoon, and then home for a short rest. Marc and Melissa, once again, hosted a wonderful family Christmas Dinner, with 21 family members present. Their house design lends itself to large gatherings, with everyone giving a helping hand. My hand is very small! It, was a very special day.

We wrapped up the year, by confirming our 2020 March/April vacation booking, at Siesta Dunes in Florida, for our 24th visit to Siesta Key Beach, dating back to our first visit in October 1989, with Shirley and Larry Johnston, who introduced us to this part of paradise. New Year's Eve was as usual quiet. We were not aware then, that, "This was to be the calm, before a very fateful storm".

I have always enjoyed numbers, and especially the coincidences that numbers can reveal or create. 1919 was the year that the Spanish influenza pandemic finally relented after a world death toll of upwards of 50 million. Would the year 2020 in any way shake the world again? We were about to witness another tragedy, but in early 2020 days, life appeared to go on as normal.

However, at the time, and unknown to the rest of the world, a storm was brewing in China, which at the least, was downplayed by those in the know, and at the worst, suppressed by Chinese authorities, who were not prepared to ring the alarm bell.

El and I left early January, for a 2 week stay at the St. James's Club in Antigua, and we may as well have been on another planet, for the lack of any disturbing information relating to, what was about to happen. Gerry and Kathy Guilfoyle were also there, and they more than added to our enjoyment. During the day we mostly did our own things, but always enjoyed their company at breakfast and dinner. The meals and service were excellent, and especially at the Piccolo Mondo private restaurant. El and I knew, that Gerry was not well, was partway through a medical journey, and that this would be the last time we would vacation together, as a foursome. He was so determined to exercise despite his condition, and we did walk together each day. The Guilfoyles have added to each vacation we have taken together. Wonderful memories, that we would love to repeat, without end. But sadly, there will be an end, and 2020 will most likely bring this to pass. Sadness and anger tend to proceed grief. I am certainly feeling both right now.

Returning to Toronto, we were greeted by lots and lots of snow, which after Antigua, is apparently what it does wintertime in Ontario. El started the consumption of the drug tamoxifen and at the moment is free of any major side effects. The drug is intended to reduce the amount of estrogen in a woman's body. Estrogen stimulates the growth of cancer cells. Normal life until the end of February, meant weekly visits with Lloyd and Gord, car servicing, and a new Rogers, box for the huge television, El had purchased for me. We were advised that Fiona's second husband Bruce Thompson had died. He was a bit of a con artist, and a good one, but he was also Cassandra's biological father, and for that we thank him, because we love this granddaughter dearly.

After 11 years of volunteering at Southlake Hospital, and specifically on the CV Surgery ward on the 5th floor, I was advised that the hospital elevator doors were featuring a photograph of myself, talking with a patient. It is me, but I do not recognize or recall talking with this patient, who I thought looked healthier than me. Fake photography! Anything is possible today! Lunch with Michele in Peterborough, and a visit to the Pace Clinic to check my pacemaker followed, before we readied for our winter break in Florida.

We flew out of Toronto for Sarasota on February 29th, 2020, somewhat oblivious to the fact that a smoking gun was about to wreak havoc, on the health and economies, of not just the citizens of Wuhan, China, the deemed initial epi- center, but on the rest of the worlds' 213 countries and territories. The terms "social distancing", "lockdown" and others would become commonplace as the effects of a deadly virus, now known as COVID- 19, or Coronavirus, took hold and threatened the stability of the world, as we know it. Looking back, we were, perhaps naïve to vacation, but the alarm bells had not gone off and the World Health Organization had refused to call the spread, a pandemic. Suggestions that they were "encouraged", not to refer to it as such, have surfaced, and we may never know their true reasons, but they were slow in declaring it's seriousness, and that is a fact!

We enjoyed our first 2 weeks in Sarasota, with dinner visits to Turtles, to celebrate Els' birthday, the Olive Gardens and Carrabba's, and a small group meeting in Bradenton with the Canada Eh travel group, who had travelled without us to Portugal last year. All was well. Restaurants and shops were active and busy, and then from March 15 onwards, "the walls started to close in". More and more visitors were leaving to return home, restaurants and businesses were closing, and the news was dominated by COVID- 19 facts, rumours, concerns, and projections as to what lay in store for us.

To be honest, we felt our Florida and beach location in a cabana, to be safe. The air was warm, the water was warm, and the public were banned from coming on Siesta Key beach. We had a 2- mile beach to walk on, a warm ocean to swim in, and with little or no people. The number of occupied suites in our condo site was down to less than 50, out of a possible 160. What was there to panic about? We deferred our kids' strong suggestions to come home, with this argument.

In the meantime, I had been checking the availability of Air Canada flights out of Sarasota. They had always listed that day's suppertime flight, and those for the following 3 days. A rude awakening after several days of checking, was that the 3rd day out flight, was now missing and nothing was listed as active, beyond March 25. Time for action! The added problem now, was that any calls to Air Canada were listed not as busy, but as "failed". We could not get through to change our April 04, booking.

A basic tenet of business and perhaps life in general is that, "It is not what you know, but who you know". El called Michelle, our daughter Susan's, sister in law, in Ontario, to explain our dilemma. Michelle works for Air Canada, and posted a comment on the company intranet that some family members were having problems returning from Florida, and within 20 minutes we received a call on our cell, from an Air Canada employee in Vancouver, who took down our details, and especially our code for our booked April 04 return flight. She in turn, called her Montreal office with our information, and a further female Air Canada employee called us from there with a number of questions. Within 20 minutes or so, she indicated that our March 25 return air tickets had been e-mailed to us. "Had we received them", she asked. As we were sitting in a cabana on an empty beach, I had no choice but to fudge the truth. "We were just returning to our condo, and would view and print them shortly". We pulled rank, but we were so impressed with the speed and efficiency of these ladies, to serve us in this manner. Thank you so much ladies, especially Michelle. You really "saved our bacon", as the expression goes.

Plan B, had been to stay at Jeff and Monique Grays' house in Cape Coral, and eventually drive our Alamo rental car, with South Carolina plates, to Michigan, switch cars to one with Ontario plates, and then cross the border at Windsor. This had been arranged with Alamo, as a backup plan. It was a sound but not preferred option, and with the mounting pandemic concerns, a choice that we thankfully did not have to make.

The flight home was unusual, as Air Canada staff adjusted to the coronavirus concerns. Most passengers were quite senior, wore masks, and kept putting their faces close to ours, to tell us that they normally did not return to

Canada, until May. Many were in wheel chairs. No food was available, and the single bottle of water distributed to passengers "on the house", contained 5 oz of water! We were blessed as Fiona, Mike and Cassandra, met us at the airport. Fiona had picked up my car, and for safety reasons, El and I were able to drive this home, while our family members took our luggage separately in Mike's truck. It had been a trying day, but we were home safe and sound, and of course bound to the fact that we would be self- quarantined for 14 days.

This coronavirus, referred to as COVID-19, is listed as a pandemic. I prefer calling it a plague, and have penned a sixteen- stanza poem, as to its believed origin, spread and world- wide effect. What the future holds, based upon 9 months of catastrophic experience to-date is anyone's guess, but as at third quarter 2020, the road ahead looks bleak. Our current hope, is the development of a successful vaccine, but the timeline as to its development and extensive delivery, is still out of reach. Initially, some countries, including Canada, lowered the spread. A second wave has brought to our attention the bad habits we developed. We know what to do. We just have to do it!

As some countries know, the negative effects of not taking COVID-19 seriously, can and have been disastrous. By not adhering to health authority guidelines, or by taking matters into one's hands, the offenders have accelerated its spread, and significantly increased the number of infections within their country's population. We also know that patience and staying the course, are not habits that we 2020 humans find as popular, and that after 9 months or so of restrictions, we, at the slightest bit of encouragement, or relaxation of laws, will stray. For some countries, the quandary or challenge will be, if they are prepared to go back to the beginning, and put into effect the same tough lockdown regulations and protocols all over again, or to suffer the ever increasing infections and resulting deaths, with the unproven hope that many more will recover from their infections, and be in effect immune, from further infection.

Canadians as a whole, are an obedient, calm and disciplined people. Our qualities will be severely tested in the months ahead, but we do have the advantage, of viewing the terrible consequences of not adhering to suggested protocols. In North America, we tend to live in a society controlled and influenced by, "not the when", but by, "the here and now". We have to be obedient and patient.

The culling of seniors in Canada, especially in long term care homes, revealed the gaps in our so called highly developed social system, that we believed for those beyond retirement, was secure and protective. The percentage of overall Canadian deaths in long term care and senior retirement homes, will be a statistic, and an embarrassment, that we will have to live with, and hear about, long beyond the end of this nightmare. There will be lawsuits a plenty!

The long- term effects that the prolonged shutdown will have on the economy are unknown. Our governments have tried to ease the pain in the short term, but the printing of bailout money, will have to be accounted for, and will result in higher taxes for us and for future generations. It will be a challenge for future governments!

This "Hollywood scary movie", is real. Post pandemics, as far back as 2500 years ago, had to run their course without scientific and/or medical intervention, and any known vaccine. We have the hope and reality, that our present worldwide scientific resources will, within a reasonable time, solve this medical problem, and we will be able to look back on this, as a "bad dream". But will we be able to learn from the experience and document effective counter actions, for future generations to learn from. Because, as history has shown, this type of plague will happen again!

History lists various plagues and pandemics, from as far back as The Plague of Athens (430 B.C.), the bubonic plagues in various European countries during the middle ages, the Great Plague of London in 1665, and the Spanish Flu (1918/19), with an unaccounted death rate varying from 17 to 50 million lives lost around the world. The examples are not given to scare, but to educate and to lay bare the fact that, that if we do not recognize the deadly capacity of this Coronavirus, we could be victims of a greater disaster than that, which we have experienced so far, in a few short months of 2020.

Since our early return on March 25 from Florida, I have kept busy, writing and assembling family photographs, as far back as the 1930's, to add to my life memoir moments. El has been playing bridge online four- times a week, and when we are both free, we have enjoyed sitting out, on our very comfortable back patio. To be quarantined has certainly not been a hardship for us. Susan and Mike have done our grocery shopping. Fiona and Mike, likewise for the wine. Cassie and her friend Olivia, helped us with weeding and planting. We have kept in touch with other family members by phone.

Although it feels as though the world and our lives have come to a crashing halt, life does go on. For many in density locations and with young children, isolation has been a major challenge. Our Ballantrae location does not present any challenge whatsoever. Single family dwellings in an open space location, has made our lives so much easier than most.

Even in the face of a pandemic, life does go on. Our granddaughter Melissa, and husband Marc, announced her pregnancy, with their second child to be born, late December. Michele and Doug have sold their cows and now have 5 horses. They now have a lake site to park their mobile trailer, close to home. Michele is back working in Bellville. What's next? Even they do not know. Fiona and Mike have purchased a fixed trailer on a site on Shadow Lake, which is north of Fenelon Falls. The boat purchase followed quickly. Fiona has continued to work uninterrupted at Shoppers. Cassandra is working at the post office in Shoppers for the interim, with the hope to get a position in the physiotherapy medical field, at a retirement or seniors' home, when life returns to some normality. Sue's Mike is back at work. Fiona's Mike is working from home, as is granddaughter Danielle, and granddaughter Melissa. Taylor is working stocking grocery shelves at night. Grandson Kyle is back working with sister Jamie's husband Tony, in the siding part of residential construction. In fact, all family members who had a job, are back working again.

I had a further squamous cancer cell removed from my forehead by Dr. Backstein, who is also working again at the Lynde Clinic in Markham. The only difference being, that instead of 50 plus patients in the waiting room, the number was restricted to 2 or 3 at a time. The post procedure analysis indicated no need for radiation treatment, which was more than welcome news. Our neighbour John Van Velzen, died on April 14, from cancer complications. We were not really close, but in the last few years, we spent time, reliving our business pasts. John, in my opinion received treatments at his request in his final months, which materially affected his remaining quality of life. It is not unusual for the medical system, with the approval of the patient and caregivers, to extend radiation and chemotherapy treatment, on the basis I presume, that a miracle cure or extension of life, can be achieved in these later stages. I understand that hope springs eternal, but I for one, am not a supporter of going above and beyond, with these treatments.

Due to the horrific killing in June, of a black man by a white policeman in Minneapolis, the U.S.A. has erupted in forms of unrest, unlawful assemblies, looting and property damage. The division between black and white America has never seemed greater, and the cry of "Black Lives Matter", has started a movement for radical change in the way policing is carried out, and the actual funding of this service. Canada is not immune from this action, and the police here recently obliged by giving the movement first class examples of poor and violent police action, which caused a similar outcry in Canada for "change".

Thousands of Americans have demonstrated their concerns in over 140 cities and support of a similar nature has occurred not only in Canada, but in Australia and the U.K. and many European cities. This crisis has virtually hijacked the media coverage and public concerns over COVID-19, while at the same time adding to the pandemic problem, by the gathering of huge crowds, ignoring the rules of social distancing and the wearing of masks.

The racial divide, compounded by a huge surge in the numbers of COVID-19 infections, has left the U.S., very vulnerable. Regardless of your political affiliation, this once very strong country is being humbled, by not only a lack of leadership from the top, but by the mixed messaging coming from individual states, and the various levels of government within each county, region and city. This problem has been further compounded, by an American "trait" of individual belief, that each person has rights under the constitution above the law, and they can totally ignore their state and regional government instructions, regarding masks, distancing and crowding in bars and beaches. The results are disastrous. This "push pull" confusion is not working, and as of late September, no one has been able to "steady the ship", with a massive increase in infections and hospitalizations.

On a more positive note, El was scheduled for a follow up mammogram on July 07, to determine the outcome of the left breast cancer surgery she had last fall. The procedure was done in the a.m., and I by chance received a call from our G.P., Dr. Carruthers, in the afternoon to remind me of an upcoming appointment. While talking, I mentioned Els' morning procedure, and she remarked that the results were just coming through. "They are excellent", she said. "Absolutely cancer free". Having advised her that the surgeon, Dr. Ing, was yet to call, she asked El, to act surprised. The surgeon did call later, and El had a pleasant conversation with him, while acting surprised, as coached by her doctor. Surgeons, sometimes have difficulty in expressing themselves with patients, in empathetic and non- medical technical terms. This time he was much more relaxed, and they had a pleasant and fruitful conversation. El was more than happy!

Death is a part of life, and for almost 2 years, Eleanor and I have had intimate knowledge, that our close friend Gerry Guilfoyle, was suffering from a terminal cancer diagnosis. We had been Gerry and Kathy's guests at their cottage in the fall of 2018, where Gerry was complaining about serious pain in his leg, which he openly discussed with us. The diagnosis in September of that year, was Stage 4 small cell cancer of unknown primary origin.

Gerry was such a compassionate and caring person, who was interested in you, and with absolute sincerity, wanted to know all about you. But in turn, he was a very private person, who although extremely successful business wise, shied away from talking about himself. When we met after the diagnosis, it was his absolute wish, that only the family members, and Eleanor and I alone know of his condition. Consequently, we were sworn to absolute secrecy, which we have carried for these many months. This we know, was a great burden on Kathy and her inability to share her concerns and worries, with her many friends. We kept in contact with Gerry and Kathy, by phone, every week for almost 2 years, throughout his journey of multiple procedures, hospital visits and diagnoses, which although helpful, was probably only a small conciliation for her.

To compensate somewhat, they spent time at their Muskoka cottage, and Kathy arranged multiple trips throughout the winter months to Florida, Mexico and Antigua. We were blessed to have three wonderful vacations with them in Antigua, and weekends with them at their cottage, during these 2 years. They trusted us and the memories of these times, will not be forgotten.

Our relationship spans some 40 years plus, with multiple experiences and vacations together in such places as, Rio Brazil, Buenos Aires Argentina, London, Edinburgh and Newcastle in the U.K., Antigua, Florida, and parts of Canada, including Vancouver and Whistler B.C., Minaki Lodge in Northwestern Ontario, Queens Landing Niagara, Halifax Nova Scotia and their wonderful cottage setting near Bala, Muskoka. These moments in time were precious, and will never be forgotten. We ran together, we swam together, we drank together, we even danced together, but not very well. I know the latter event happened, after we drank too much together. He was my friend, and he is my friend. His memory will be with me forever. We last were face to face, on June 16, 2020 and Gerry left us on July 13, 2020. Gerry did not want me to see him in his latter days, and although disappointed, I understood. Eleanor and I will miss him. I have now lost the last of my 4 lifetime close friends; Charlie Rennie, George Bennett, Tom Jepson and Gerry Guilfoyle.

My 80th birthday celebration, was postponed. Unfortunately, the weather forecast for July 19 was not favourable, and we decided to postpone the family birthday gathering, until August 23, to allow some to have a vacation break in early August, and probably to test the results of Ontario relaxing some of their regulations, such as reopening indoor public spaces, including restaurants etc. The results of this type of relaxation in the U.S., have been disastrous, and even in some of our Western provinces they have not been favourable. I am not concerned, but I am being quietly cautious.

August 23 dawned and the forecast for the day was identical to July 19, i.e. hot, humid and a strong possibility of thunderstorms. Never the less, the family gathering proceeded as planned, and the fourteen of us had a wonderful time. I was spoiled, but took it in stride! A very special day, and I really was spoiled. For me, the main delight, was to see how family members got on with each other, and to notice the increased maturity in the younger adults, who I do not get to see on a day to day basis. It was heart- warming, and made me realize how fortunate I am.

Having reached the 9- month anniversary of the first diagnosed coronavirus patient in North America, the world as we know it, is in various forms of turmoil. Some countries have mishandled the pandemic, others have had early successes, but we in Canada, are now experiencing set- backs, due to a relaxation of regulations. Many health and economic uncertainties, will have to be dealt with in the months ahead. Currently infection and death statistics, the hope of a successful vaccine, and the continuation of world-wide negativism due to the pandemic, dominate day to day activities.

Eleanor and I can now look back, on almost 57 years of blessed marriage, and realize that through thick and thin, we seized each moment, when the opportunity arose, even though the road ahead was uncertain. We shouldered each risk one encounters, when you move away from your safety net. The girls also experienced their ups and downs with each move, and we salute them for handling these. The five of us have continued to this day, to maintain the strong parent/children bonding, that has seen us through these many years.

What will the future bring and when? The world is experiencing a first for today's generation, and "a what if, a when, and a how", series of questions. Eleanor and I, and our family members, are not immune from today's events, but compared to most families, we are currently blessed to have reasonable health, and in the main, financial security. I would like to continue writing, but see this as an ideal time to pause. I am now age 80, feel in reasonable health, and I am not prepared to describe this story as ending, but rather as:

The End of a Very Long and Fruitful Beginning.

POETRY

POEMS WRITTEN BY BOB COYLE

A 50 YEAR CELEBRATION 319
A BALLANTRAE CARAVAN ISRAEL, EGYPT & JORDAN 320
A BALLANTRAE MEMORY 329
A CELEBRATION OF LOVE 330
A DOMINICAN MEMORY 332
A HEART STOPPING EXPERIENCE 334
THE VOLUNTEER 336
A LETTER TO THE LAND OF TRUMP VILLE 337
A LONG WEEKEND IN MUSKOKA 340
A LOVE THAT ENDURES 342
A MUSKOKA MEMORY 344
A NEIGHBOUR FRIEND 346
A PARTING PRAYER 347
A REPORT CARD FROM THE HIGHEST AUTHORITY 348
A ROYAL TOUR 350
A SOCCER MEMORY 353
A WALK DOWN MEMORY LANE 354
A WESTCOAST MEMORY 355
ALL I WANT IS A 356
BALLANTRAE FALL GAMES 358

BIG SCANDINAVIAN, BELARUS, POLISH, GERMAN AND BEEG RUSSIAN TRIP	360
CASTLES ALONG THE RHINE	368
CEL<u>L</u>EBRATION	373
CHANGE	375
COME FLY WITH ME	378
CONGRATULATIONS! GO AWAY!	380
COVID-19: A 2020 PLAGUE	382
DOMINICAN GAFFS	385
DON'T LET IT SNOW, LET IT SNOW, LET IT SNOW	387
DOUG MCARTHUR A TESTIMONY	389
EAST MEETS WEST	390
FALL	396
FORE WHOM IT MAY CONCERN	397
PASTORS GERRY AND ELAINE TONN	398
GO FLY A KITE	399
GRAND PALLADIUM WHITE SANDS, PLAYA KANTENAH	401
HAPPY BALLANTRAE 2020	403
HI NEIGHBOUR	404
HOME SWEET HOME	405
IN MEMORIAM	406
ISRAEL TODAY	408
IT WAS A SMALL WORLD AFTER ALL	411
IT'S NEVER TOO LATE TO COMMUNICATE	412
LIFE'S JOURNEY, WHILE ON EARTH	414
ODE TO A WAITER	416
OUR BALLANTRAE	418
OUR CANADA	420
PASTOR GERRY	421
PASTOR PAUL HILSDEN	422

RETURN TO ME	423
ROBIN ME OF SLEEP	425
RUSSIAN OBSERVATIONS	426
RUSSIAN REFLECTIONS	431
SCHARFE MANIA	434
SICILY WITH EPIFANI	436
SIESTA KEY BEACH	439
SPRING	440
SUMMER	441
SUPER CALORIFIC	442
THE END OF ANOTHER "CENTURY"	444
THE FAMILY TOAST	445
THREE DAUGHTERS THE FINAL WEDDING	446
THE TRUE MEANING OF CHRISTMAS	447
TWO HOV OR NOT TWO HOV	448
TO MARY WITH LOVE	449
UPON REACHING SIXTY- FIVE	451
WE ALL WANT TO BE FREE	452
WE SHOULD. WE CAN. WE WILL. OR, WILL WE?	454
WHAT WOULD WE DO WITHOUT THEM	456
WINTER	458
YOUSED AND ABUSED	459

A 50 YEAR CELEBRATION

One nine five six, was the year
That friends and family, did declare
The beginning of, a lifetime journey
Starring Betty, the Brit, and a Canuck named Bernie.

Fifty years of active, ebb and flow
Where oh where, did father time go
The memories, too many to relate
Some ups, some downs, but mostly great.

The years at Ballantrae, among the best
A buffet of activity, pursued with zest
We've travelled much more, than we did before
It's been, just one revolving door.

With many, we met along the way
We want to share, our special day
To toast, when all is said and done
Your friendship earned, is number one.

A BALLANTRAE CARAVAN
ISRAEL, EGYPT & JORDAN

A Shukster trip came out of the blue
To Israel, Egypt and Jordan too
A lifelong fantasy, a dream come true
Monumental history, in a magic venue.

Lufthansa's service, was right on cue
A movie, good food, a drink or two
We've done it before, nothing new
Crossing the Atlantic, déjà vu.

Touchdown in Frankfurt, change of crew
Overbooked to Tel Aviv, by quite a few
747 volume, a veritable zoo
Lost Eleanor's luggage, double boohoo.

Crowne Plaza location, gave us a Tel Aviv view
Of a Mediterranean playground, for many a Jew
Roger, our guide, about Israel did spew
As he led us to Jerusalem, the excitement grew.

Jerusalem Ramada, was the hotel next due
To host our group, for 4 days through
A chat with the locals, at the King David venue
Helped understand Israelis, and their point of view.

The Yad Vashem exhibit was a memorial to
The horrors, millions of Jews suffered, and were put through
Followed by the Dead Sea Scrolls, at a museum milieu
And lunch at a Kibbutz, soup, bun and a brew.

King David's Tomb, the Last Supper Room
Gave insight into, Christ's impending doom
A half mile away, was Gethsemane
Where Judas betrayed, and gave Jesus away.

To an untested show, eight said we'll go
Re Israel's Covenant with God, from long ago
The performance was brilliant, lesser said, not so
Inspiration for Israelis, to watch their national pride grow.

Jerusalem's Old City layout, was in plain view
From a Mount of Olives lookout, and a sky of blue
The Jewish, Muslim and Christian quarters we walked through
And followed the Stations of the Cross, to one two plus two.

We found the Western Wall, more or less,
A reflection of intense reverence, and emotional stress
As witnessed by scenes of brokenness
And passion for prayer, by most of the rest.

Masada is a strategic and imposing sight
Where zealots engaged Romans, in a deadly fight
Onto Qumran, discovery site of the scrolls
Into the Dead Sea, for black goo and tummy rolls.

Jerusalem's final night, we answered the call
To eat at Ticho's restaurant, come one, come all
An early a.m. departure for the Temple Mount
The Dome of the Rock is Muslim, of this there is no doubt.

A side trip to Bethlehem was accepted by us all
To see the Church of the Nativity, and Jesus manger stall
Back over the border, from this Arab occupied town
And onto the Lavi Kibbutz Hotel, to park our bodies down.

Monday morning early, we were up and gone
To visit the plain of Megiddo, Revelations Armageddon
King Solomon's chariot city, with a secret fresh water well
Echoed the sounds of history, where 20 civilizations fell.

Nazareth is where it all began
With Mary's immaculate conception
A church is planted, with worldwide willing
Atop Mary and Joseph's modest dwelling.

Kinneret or Galilee, it's up to thee
To determine the name of this historic sea
Where Jesus preached, in 1 century A.D.
Capernaum would have been the place to be.

The Golan Heights say it best
Of the conflict, area nations, can't put to rest
Israel constantly put to the test
By surrounding Arab nations, a viper's nest.

Our final day on Israeli highway
Included Tzfat, Haifa and Caesarea
A tour of Acre gave us insight
As to what Crusaders did, between each fight.

Kibbutzniks purchased Tzfat's artists' ware
With credit cards in hand, they went on a tear
Haifa's Bahai Gardens, were a photo- op
Caesarea gave us Roman history, full stop.

Two days of leisure allowed us to be
Tourists in Tel Aviv, from guiding free
We walked and we shopped and we gawked at will
To learn the ways, of Israelis Israel.

Cairo beckoned via strangely, El Al
We said goodbye to Roger, our guide, our new pal
Through his eyes and words, we had felt just at home
Goodbye to Israel. L'chaim. Shalom.

Israeli characteristics… dark hair, muted clothing, excellent roads, busy traffic, greenery, attractive beaches, old buildings, coffee shops and cafes, pedestrians and active shoppers, car horns honking, police car emergency lights on continuously.
Our vision of Israeli security, is just not right.
Veiled in subtlety, not black, nor white
Not openly apparent, unless you pry
But reassuringly available, in the blink of an eye.

The head covering, worn by many a man
Does not deem him part, of a sect, tribe or clan
But rather acknowledges, there is a higher plan
Namely Yahweh, "I Am, that I Am, that I Am".

Off- duty military, are joined at the hip
With a gun, fatigues and a bullet clip
In the west, car horn noise may end in court
Blaring a horn in Israel, is just another sport. Meep, Meep!

An impromptu trip to Cairo's Mena House Oberoi
Gave emphasis to the expression Oh Boy! Oh Boy!
The hotel elegance and opulence made our interest grow
So, we signed up for dinner, and the belly dancing show.

Le Meridien Pyramids was located just right
For the Sound and Light Show, at Giza that night
Then off to dinner, and the entertainment show
To watch a whirling dervish, crank up his mojo.

A visit to the Citadel of Salah-ad-Din
And the mosque of Muhammad Ali, contained within
Onto the Coptic Museum, and an area of Cairo
To witness the poverty line, many live below.

The great pyramids of Giza one, two, three
Flanked by the Sphinx, on guard for thee
A camel ride accepted bravely by five
The Egyptian Museum made Tutankhamen come alive.

Riding a camel, while drinking tea
Although highly possible, is not for me
Perched several stories up, with only a desert view
Answering the question, one <u>h</u>ump or two.

An Aswan flight, as early as four
Caused great chagrin, and a minor uproar
But clean fresh air, and Betty's rapport
Lifted our sagging spirits, up from the floor.

A review of the Dam and a trip to the Isle
Of Philae, was done in motor boat style
To reclaim Isis' Temple, was an amazing feat
Enhanced by water taxi parking, a smash and grab treat.

A felucca sail, finished the day
On the River Nile, with the sun in play
A gentle breeze, enough to please
Time to savor our stay, in this mystic land, far away.

A couple renowned in history
Are Ramses 11 and Nefertari
The Abu Simbel Temples, are their legacy
A reminder of the wonders of 1300 B.C.

The Temple of Kom Ombo, is a fusion of two
Dedicated to the god, and Horus the Elder too
We returned to our Nile boat, and on request from the crew
We dressed as locals, to be part of their milieu.

The Temple of Edfu, consecrated to Horus
The Divine Son, the god who gave all people solace
Defended by a falcon, in rock of black granite
And a wall with perfume formulae, written upon it.

The Temple of Luxor, for the god Amon-Ra
Has statues and obelisks and columns extra
Of a size and a height that leave you in awe
And devoid of any speech, from your dropped jaw.

The Valley of the Kings, is solid history
A buffet of pharaoh tombs on display
Seti1, Ramses, Thutmose, to name but a few
Tutankhamen, KV5, the discoveries continue.

Queen Hatshepsut temple, was dedicated to
Hathor, Anubis and Amon-Ra too
Following a fight, with her lofty nephew
Thutmose111 destroyed, most of her statue.

The Colossi of Memnon, are in need of repair
But 1400 hundred B.C. statues, still want you to stare
A likeness of Amenhotep, and 60 feet high
They guarded a temple, in an era gone bye.

29 dynasties created the site
Of Karnak, trying to get it just right
A massive combination of temples and statues
Sphinxes and pillars, obelisks and avenues.

A walk, through Luxor market, no hassle, yeah right
Tarek puffed on a Shisha, with eyes sparkling bright
A late flight to Cairo, made without fuss
To Alexandria next a.m., by motor coach bus.

A stop at a monastery in Wadi El Natrun
Where Cedrack, the priest, a joy, full of fun
Explained the workings of a Coptic monastery
A Christian enclave, in Muslim Egypt today.

Alexander the Great in 332 B.C.
Planned to build Alexandria, on the Mediterranean Sea
Greece, Rome and Egypt, shared the occupancy
But of them all, Cleopatra was <u>the</u> Queen bee.

The fortress Citadel of Qaitbay, has been partially rebuilt
With Great Lighthouse blocks, found in harbour silt
The Roman Amphitheatre uncovered, in nineteen sixty
Gave credence to the Roman presence, and city history.

The Mosque of Abu El Abbas
The Lighthouse site on Isle Pharos
The Amphitheatre, Catacombs, Pompey's Pillar
Are some of Alexandria's highlights stellar.

The magic of Egypt's history
Is its carbon footprint, from early B.C.
The overwhelming talents, of this ancient society
Seem frozen in time, at least to me.

Egyptian characteristics…poverty, city pollution, garbage, unfinished buildings, constant tourist harassment, open palms not handshakes, many old cars driving at high speed, lada taxis, multi police and army with guns, old rolling stock, the frequent sound of prayer, a fertile Nile with cloudless skies and crisp fresh air, but limited cultivation on both banks.

Traffic lights in Cairo, are not to be seen
As locals interpret every colour, as go ahead green
Traffic roundabouts, help to reverse the flow
So that you end up, where you wanted to go.

A pedestrian's lifespan, is somewhat short
As crossing the road, is still a big sport
Tourist police will get you over, safe and sound
As long as you give them, an Egyptian pound.

Cairo to Amman, in the early hour
On to Madaba, meaning sweet not sour
The Church of St. George, and then Mount Nebo
Where God showed Moses, the land of his people.

One should not brag, about a night in a cave
But the hotel Taybet Zaman, was a unique 5- star rave
Stone arched units, with old wooden doors
But spacious interiors, with heated rock floors.

Converted from a village, to a tourist abode
Its cave like appearance, gives it a highlight mode
In a village outside Petra, with a spectacular view
And a high- quality restaurant, with a very fine menu.

Petra is a wonder, a vault to unlock
Named after Peter, Peter the Rock
With a narrow winding entrance, they call the Siq
A canyon of rock red- rose, and walls very steep.

Emerging out of the shadow and into the sun
Before you lies the secret of Petra, the special one
A tomb called the Treasury, carved out of the rock
Leaving most mouths wide open, and absent of talk.

Petra's history, indicates caves occupied
By Nabataeans living there, and willing to provide
An exchange of shelter, water, food and more
To the rich caravans, who were found wanting for.

Our last formal night, our night on the town
Was in El Halaby restaurant, on top of the Crowne
A day in Amann followed, to view and relax
To regenerate our batteries, from empty to max.

Jordan's economy, appears vibrant and strong
Reflected by the currency and active construction
Majestic office towers, mansions and late model cars
Where the East meets the West, under Jordanian stars.

For countless years these lands have seen
Struggles among Muslims, Jews and Christian
We pray for a formula, a simple plan
To achieve peace on earth, goodwill to man.

Travelling as a group of sometimes twenty- one
We traversed the land of Israel, Egypt and Jordan
Responding to the calls of Emad, Roger and Tarek
We salute ourselves for being so energetic.

Three countries, ten flights, countless coach trips and more
A riverboat, a felucca, a motor boat tour
Hotel rooms, terminals, museums, temples and tombs
Troopers to the last day, when age caught up,
and lowered the boom. Goodnight!

A BALLANTRAE MEMORY

Mike and Diane are on their way
To St. Catharines, by the winery
We know neighbours, come and go
But we'll miss their way of saying, hello.

Good friends are precious, especially
Those, a mere stone's throw away
House sitting for us, on many a day
While we vacationed, to escape winter's grey.

We broke some bread, and fine dined too
The list of restaurants, grew and grew
But the meal, to which Mike's heart stayed true
Involved haggis, trifle and whiskey brew.

Mike and I tried, to hit the ball
Mostly right, and not well at all
Tearing up each course, mostly rough
Received countless bills, to replace the turf.

We shared the odd beer, watched Mike Weir
Laughed hearty enough, to bring a tear
I'll miss these times, at the Maples nine
Playing two extra holes, without paying a dime.

I suspect greater pedigree, than what they say
Expecting Her Majesty, to call any day
To announce, a recall of Mister and Mum
And address you, as Lord and Lady Pelham.

A CELEBRATION OF LOVE

The parents are happy
It's plain to see
To surrender Roland and Jen
The groom and bride to be.

Orchestrated by mothers
And planned diligently
Their July '08 wedding
Takes place in Philly.

The rehearsal dinner
Honoring the couple to be
At the Glen Foerd mansion
A special night, we all agree.

The celebration continued
With an invitation to see
The Mets play the Phillies
A July Fourth jubilee.

A win for the home team
Most Canadians, did not see
Preferring the indoor warmth
Of room 604 hospitality.

St. Christopher's Church graced
The couple, and their ceremony
Where an attitude of giving
Was the Father's earnest plea.

Strengthened by love
For their life journey
They united themselves
At two twenty- three.

We retired to the Marriot
For a post wedding spree
To catch up on friendship
And talked endlessly.

The Country Club reception
Summed up to a tee
The quality of the families
And their generosity.

Jennifer and Roland
It is obvious to see
The love and support
Family ingrained in thee.

Your friends, your supporters
Wish you sincerely
Happiness forever
And may God go with thee.

The Hafeles, the Hoffmans
Are richer verily
By seeding a forest
And not each planting a tree.

A DOMINICAN MEMORY

Hispaniola hosts
A common coast
Shared land, at most
In part, they call Dominican.

God, with his hand
Graced sea and sand
He carved this land
Dominican.

Lush flowers, palm trees
Warm tropic breeze
The norm, are these
For the host, they call Dominican.

The ebb and flow
Of tourists, sew
The seeds, that grow
This land, they call Dominican.

White caps, green sea
Blue skies, all free
But poor, is the economy
For those, who dwell Dominican.

They laugh, they smile
But, all the while
Some hold back rile
The natives of, Dominican.

Let's say a prayer
That the West, might share
It's wealth, it's fare
With those, who are Dominican.

A HEART STOPPING EXPERIENCE

Swimming at the rec pool, my lungs seemed to say
We don't know about you, but we're on holiday
A shortness of breath, fitness gone astray
I swallowed my pride and saw my m.d.

Reaction was swift, with a battery
Of tests, respiratory, cardio, a mixed array
For several weeks in the month of May
I was stressed and x-rayed, hot and heavy.

The results sifted by, professionals many
With symptoms pointing to a blocked artery
An angiogram ordered, to find a way
Of confirming my problem, I hope and pray.

May 31 dawned, the skies seemed gray
As I entered Southlake, to join the fray
Dye and x-ray proved, as I did lay
Not blockage uno, not due, but, mama mia tre.

Back in recovery, I had time to pay
Attention to the care, in this cardiac sick bay
The doctors, the nurses, put fears to allay
Giving trust and faith in my future big day.

The surgeon confirmed, a slight delay
For a pre-surgery clinic, deemed necessary
Allowing all specialists, to prepare the way
For my cameo appearance, on the big big day.

A Thursday in July, will indelibly be
Etched in the memories, of my family
Quadruple bypass, labeled routine in every way
Concluded with challenges, after an overtime stay.

To my surgeon, I pledge my triple A
Award of thanks and gratitude, for his skill set array
For his supporting staff, I have no memory
But equally acknowledge and applaud, their ability.

Post- operative care, is the road to recovery
Where they straighten you out, and set you on your way
To those who gave selflessly
I will remember for the rest of my days.

THE VOLUNTEER

Most patients say, what have we here
I do declare, a volunteer
To chat, to listen, to bring you cheer
To welcome, to support, your visit here.

Sporting blue, to identify a person who
Wears a smile honest, just for you
Giving time and energy, tried and true
To every department, in this medical milieu.

Now numbered in the hundreds, as this hospital grew
Supporting its' quality service, through and through
Partnered with professionals, to bring what you are due
A promise, a commitment, Southlake cares for You.

A LETTER TO THE LAND OF TRUMP VILLE

An Alternate Reality

U.S. change, has endorsed a leap
A populous inspired jump
From a passive Obama
To a "Make America Greater", President Trump.

Mr. President, you are one of a kind
With your day to day rants
As you twitter and tweet
Your "Trump Truth" slants.

Continuing the setback, of your early days
We earnestly hope, and really pray
Your administration, will eventually function
And not just falter, and be led astray.

We know the Comey dismissal
Although deemed, one of a kind
Was simply an outlet
To let your frustrations, unwind.

To remove him, from the Russian file
Was not on your mind
We know there is, "nothing of value"
The Bureau can find.

The next appointed Director
Knows, he has a free hand
To go about his business
On a playing field, of sand.

Less we forget, let's make it clear
Despite the claims of success, that appear
What you really have accomplished
By the end of your "final" year.

Continuing the verbal disruption
Spread on the campaign trail
Your achievements on the inside
Have gone, from bad to pale.

Executive orders and appointments
Have come flying, out of the gate
To be challenged, and delayed
Before meeting, an inevitable fate.

Barring immigrants, appointing Flynn
Opposed by legislators, even Republican
Deferred campaign promises mean
Support from die hearts, is perhaps growing thin.

A second health plan, submitted for review
To the Senate, which has promised, not to renew
Negative news is labelled fake, not true
An Administration dysfunctional, and run by few.

Promises to handle trade, infrastructure
Syria, North Korea, to name but a few
The ship has to be steadied, by the leader of
The Red, White and Blue.

To many you are, a breath of fresh air
Breaking untold tradition, as you dash and dare
To others, who hold fast to the known, you do not compare
As President, you're a bad dream, a reality scare.

A man of means, accustomed to win
Celebrating each victory, to his opponents, chagrin
Now faces a system, tested true through time
The challenge, a mountain, I hope you never climb.

A LONG WEEKEND IN MUSKOKA

Those with golf, were on a roll
Parring each course, hole by hole
The youth commissioned, a boat with oar
To challenge the neighbours, in a cox's four.

To paddle a canoe, was our weekend goal
Around the lake, food for the soul
With backs straight, legs upon the floor
We wobbled and bobbled, from the boathouse door.

Our stroke pattern, on the whole
Was sapping our strength, and taking its toll
I yelled, she yelled, we yelled some more
Stop, start, left, right, oh just ignore.

We righted the boat, determined each role
Recognizing success, came from you all
Confirmed from the water, you can explore
The mystique of, vast Muskoka's lore.

Finally paddling, as solid as a rock
We glided smoothly, right to the dock
The line was cast, and tightened too
The lady stepped out, right on cue.

Those watching said, oh no, please no
It's far too early, for you to go
You have to move, right up the boat
Or else, you'll find yourself afloat.

But stubborn, grabbed for solid ground
His fingers stretching, never found
The canoe turned over, on a roll
And he entered the water, like a lump of coal.

The judges on shore, let out a roar
And scored the dive, a four point four.

A LOVE THAT ENDURES

In 1955, Frank Sinatra sang, "Love and Marriage. Love and Marriage. It's an Institute you can't disparage". What keeps the flame of love, alive and well, 50, 60 years into the future? This is our perspective. You must do it your way, and you will!

First of all, we should examine parts of the marriage vows. "to have and to hold; for better for worse; for richer for poorer; to love and to cherish; till death do us part". When we step up to the altar, do these words resonate with us in total understanding and belief, or are we thinking nervously in the moment, of just saying, "I do". Time will test us, to put these basic tenets of marriage into practice.

A 50- year plus marriage is a journey, that has to be undertaken, side by side as partners, through the ups and downs, the joys and disappointments, the sorrow of defeat and the beauty of victory, the warmth of summerlike situations and the cold of winterlike events.

You are a team, that must really care for each other, in a manner that adjusts from those initial years when "Eros", or romantic love, makes you a couple, and takes over your lives, and then melds in to "Agape", or unconditional "God love". You must want for your spouse, what you want for yourself. You must be sensitive to the needs of your spouse, as you would to your own desires. You can and will question, but you must support.

As the "two", become a family of three or more, the joy of these additions should strengthen and consolidate your relationship. Your bond of marriage, has now been given an even greater purpose. To jointly raise and love your children, in a manner, which reflects the inherent love between the two of you, their parents.

Couples are not the same. "Opposites attract", is a famous saying, which is correct to a degree in the beginning, but long term success comes from agreement, common goals, the ability to say "I was wrong or You were right", respect, Agape love, sharing your feelings, honesty with one another, trust, kindness, tolerance, friendship, and caring for one another, all enabling the flame that burned so brightly, so many years ago, to remain alive and well.

Marriage has been termed, "as a work in progress". If, in our opinion, you put into practice, the features shown above, you will both be rewarded with an inner feeling of peace, joy and contentment and experience a life, jointly well lived.

Bob, wedded young in the West, to Eleanor the best. Parented daughters so fine, three ladies divine. Births in three provinces, brought an Eleanor decree. Future transfers, will require a procedure for thee.

Proud grandparents of children, numbering seven. God's gift to our earth walk, before entering heaven. The title "great", added to three children more. We pray for their safety, and what life has in store.

Amen

A MUSKOKA MEMORY

Port Carling, sounded lots of fun.
Travelling by boat, soaking in the sun
The weatherman said, you're insane,
I'm sending you, ugly clouds and rain.

The fabulous five, looked at the sky
We best find something, to keep us dry
From store to store, they did nag
For anything resembling, a garbage bag.

The checkout girls, went to the wall
Cutting holes for heads, and arms for all
They started back, in orange and green
Like inmates, from a jailhouse scene.

In the lock, before Muskoka Lake
A guest suggested, a station break
Moving at speed, into the mist
She spotted the loo, and raised her fist.

When deed was done, she addressed the door
Turn left, turn right, it worked no more
The panic rose, within her chest
Trapped by these walls, an unwanted guest.

Over the door, it was too high
Space below, she did espy
A limbo pose, slow not fast
Under the door, free at last.

She joined the crew, and told her tale
The locals listened, faces pale
A future guest, who wails and begs
Will stay in the boat, and cross their legs.

On wings of water, we were on our way
Home at last, a special day.

A NEIGHBOUR FRIEND

In the 70's down Ancaster way
We had the luxury of visiting, day by day
But transfers to Barrie and then B.C.
Could have turned our relations, from blue to gray.

The test of friendship, is the bond
Maintained while living far apart, beyond
Any thought of dropping in to say
We missed you Doug, how did things go today?

We passed the test, and man alive
The years have flown, you're sixty- five
We wish you well, our hearts remain true
To the birthday boy, and your lovely Sue.

A PARTING PRAYER

Lord:

Our precious is ready, to leave the nest
To seek an identity, she knows best
The years have flown, we should have guessed
Her time has come, to take the test.

Surround her, with your love and grace
Trim her, with your softest lace
Protect her, with your warm embrace
Guide her, with your shining face.

Give light, when clouds are all around
Let your wisdom, be her only sound
Let your glory continue, the tie that bound
Her to You, the One she's found.

Amen.

A REPORT CARD FROM THE HIGHEST AUTHORITY

I am totally aware that, you were created first
Born sentient, to a galaxy of planets, moons and dust
Where, I Am, Your Creator, is not for you to know
Waiting and watching patiently, for you and yours to grow.

To grow beyond the wars, that inhabit planet earth
Sponsored by a desire, of control and worth
Inherited from tribal difference; colour, language, creed
Slowing your maturity, limiting your speed.

Each passing generation, has chosen a similar way
To confront one another, in a violent hostile melee
Through disagreements, wars, death and destruction
Using personal beliefs, to justify your every action.

Your stubbornness and stupidity, are beyond the pale
The absence of humanity, is open and very real
Pray to your Higher Authority, to show you the way
And avoid these selfish actions, for which you will ultimately pay.

A haughty attitude of, yea right, we know what is best
Will never pass, my basic intergalactic test
Framed upon love, respect, and equal rights for all
Regardless of appearance, and individual human role.

Yes, I Am that I Am, you cannot see
Light years ahead of the world, you profess to be free
Waiting patiently, for the planet, you call Earth
To earn you a place, and finally recognize your birth.

A ROYAL TOUR

As seen through the eyes of at least one member
Of the Ballantrae Golf & Country Club Travel Group

Betty decreed the trip begin
With an overnight stay, at the Hampton Inn
Those sailing, came from near and far
From B.C. to Ballantrae, by plane and car.

Day one, saw us all check in
A ship run by, Royal Caribbean
Brilliance of the Seas, a maritime star
Against which, cruise lines set the bar.

An electronic fish, a dorsal fin
Cleaving the waters, of the Caribbean
200 feet from keel, to way up there
A floating hotel, for every jack tar.

Day two, we relaxed within
The choice of eating hearty, or staying thin
A formal night, a black- tie affair
Elegant gowns, and jewelry, and coiffured hair.

Day three Labadee, a different spin
We tendered ashore, every thirty min'
To hear the struggles, of Haitian lore
Born as early as, eighteen zero four.

An English chap, with an enormous grin
Entertained those assembled, with a violin
Gary Lovini's magic, made strings dance
Leaving the audience, in a trance.

Day four, Aruba was in our sights
The temperature continued, at maximum heights
The food sumptuous, the entertainment great
Every moment spent, is worth the freight.

Day five, De Palm, beckoned us to swim
With a jacket, a snorkel, a mask and a fin
Colour laden with fish, like a garden floral
We sucked in our tums, as we scraped the coral.

The Shuksters said, come on in,
Day six, we'll host this cocktail thing.
Curacao shopping, has been on your mind,
This break, will help you to unwind.

Sunday at sea, was named day seven
A day to rest, no longer driven
To seek the activities, that abound
Just sea and sun, on paradise found.

Thirty ought six, was our cabin
Accommodation disturbed, by constant banging
A faulty gangway, a mobile floor
Disturbed our sleep and then some more.

We tried so hard, but could not ignore
The thumping coming, from next door
We called, and pleaded for another bed
So, they stuck us, under the bow instead.

A Panamanian day eight, a canal haven
We viewed the locks, from one to seven
An Atlantic train, to Pacific shore
Back by bus, for views galore.

To our surprise, the ship heard our plea
And voila a stateroom, with a balcony
We climbed the ranks, to the seventh floor
Our complaints silenced, forever more.

Day nine, we docked at Puerto Limon
The rain forest beckoned, but all went wrong
The skies opened up, and the rain did fall
Replacing monkeys and sloths, with a shopping mall.

Day ten, saw us free
From rain- soaked land, now meet turquoise sea
An ocean of white caps, creamy
Made cruising seem what it should be.

Day eleven, our group was somewhat weepy
As we rounded third, bound for Miami
Three five double zero, miles at sea
Forever stamped, on our memory.

A SOCCER MEMORY

A pick- up game, that's all we knew
We played every night, we were addicted to
Kicking that ball, scoring a goal
Nothing else mattered, nothing at all.

Come on Mum, it's a quarter to
I have to eat and run, no time to argue
I've done my work, I don't IOU
To be late, overlooked, it just won't do.

A ragtag group of twelve or more
Friendship forgotten, this was war
Two captains picking, who would they select
The last player chosen, noticeably upset.

A bitter east wind, normal for the day
Mix in rain, and skies of grey
We were in our element, young lads at play
No cares in the world, mud, blood, a real melee.

Our fun cut short by voices, mothers led
Game over, wash up, it's time for bed
Summoned so unmanly, embarrassing too
Heads down we trod slowly, to our waterloo.

With legs aching, and bruises black and blue
I was discouraged from playing, for a day or two
But pride and love, of the beautiful game
Confirmed, it was déjà vu, all over again.

A WALK DOWN MEMORY LANE

It isn't a crime
To step back, in time
To remember, those days
And your parenting ways.

A face so sublime
Gave life to, she's mine
And a promise, to praise
To protect, and embrace.

Those years, up to nine
Filled with laughter, some whine
We co-authored, the grace
To meet her life's, second phase.

The next years, were prime
Watching her grow up, on time
Those chats, face to face
Helped her finish, that race.

The twenty's, by design
Place one's values, on line
Was she up to life's, chase
Would she falter, on base.

A confirmation, a sign
She slipped her arm, into mine
Assumed her role, in my place.
To journey, her life's highways.

A WESTCOAST MEMORY

Vancouver B.C. in April, May
Is, where spring lovers yearn to stay
Blossoms burst, from bush and tree
Colours second to none, we all agree.

For luscious growth, you have to pay
With frequent skies, of dark and gray
A price, some sceptics deem obscene
The locals most accept, for green.

Alaskan cruise ships, are on display
In the Narrows First, then English Bay
Recognizing that, there's much to see
The deck lined tourists, point with glee.

Every day jets, soar up, up and away
To feed a growing, Orient gateway
Far from downtown, and in between
The City, the Fraser, a tranquil scene.

In twenty ten, they hope and pray
That cold and snow, will stick and stay
A special year, an Olympic dream
To welcome the world, the sporting cream.

Ranked number one, on a given day
A world class city, in every way
Overlooked by mountains, nestled by the sea
Its scenic beauty is offered, free.

ALL I WANT IS A

I trembled with fear, as the counter drew near
Going over each word, I should say
But before I could speak, a voice havoc did wreak
By asking, what can we get you today.

I had lost my note, the words stuck in my throat
I froze, like the pre-historic ice-man
The silence you could hear, disturbed those to my rear
So, I turned on my heel and I ran.

I pulled up short, determined as not
To be classified, as a runaway
Re-examined the board, I surveyed the hoard
Of coffee lovers at work, that day.

Those responsible for, each specialty store
With a terminology unto itself
Customized here, for the elegant ear
Not packaged, and pulled from a shelf.

A latte double cream, to some sounds obscene
At a cost, they would not want to pay
But to those with the gene, it enhances the bean
Without a thought, to count the calories.

A coffee lover's dream, to sip a mocha cream
Or enjoy a java chip, or cappuccino
A marketing theme, it surely would seem
To return us, to their java joe casino.

To be in, you must go, with the language, the lingo
And know how and when, to roll up the rim
If it's double, double to go, you are in the know
But a small, brings you nothing from Tim.

I rehearsed at the door, as my feet hit the floor
I strode to the server, with ease
It was my turn to show, that I was in the know
A small black coffee, no sugar please.

BALLANTRAE FALL GAMES

2007

The brainchild of a dreamer
From an overactive mind
To exhort those in our community
Their athletic genes unwind.

Assembled willing hands
To plot and plan a way
To design eleven sporting games
And get them underway.

From suits to coordinators
Captains, techies, volunteers
Condo reps met in boardroom style
To get all things into gear.

The community pulled together
Individuals worked as one
To put Ballantrae on the map
As the best games ever run.

The numbers were impressive
To join walking, bocce, golf
Slo-Pitch, tennis, cycling
Horseshoes, bowling, brought resolve.

The condo shirts gave reality
To the presence of the games
With initial heats a plenty
The finals, their goal and aim.

Volunteers led the way
By giving from the heart
Donating time unselfishly
And really playing their part.

The competition intensified
As they began the final week
Participants gave it all and more
As condo points, they did seek.

Talent, teamwork, effort
Brought condos 1 and 2, the cup
The real winners were all residents
Who got involved, by signing- up.

BIG SCANDINAVIAN, BELARUS, POLISH, GERMAN AND BEEG RUSSIAN TRIP

We boarded Betty's yellow wagon
To travel via Paris, to Copenhagen
Anticipation kept our spirits from sagging
On Air France's version, of a magic dragon.

Anne, our guide, was soon at our side
Norfolk bred, but prefers Spain instead
Gave us a quick one, two, three
Of our trip ahead, soon to be.

Strolling Copenhagen's famous outdoor mall
We found flag waving Danes and Swedish meatball
We later noted that transport for a Viking
Is not by galley but by two - wheel biking.

Denmark and Sweden border each other
But soccer wise, they are not brother to brother
A Swedish invasion of yellow and blue
Brought havoc to downtown and the soccer pitch too.

Tivoli Gardens, the Little Mermaid
Copenhagen attractions, considered first grade
A quaint local restaurant played out a charade
Serving Danish Christmas in June, enough said.

Christiansborg Palace was on the tour
Influenced by Queen Margaret and her "haute couture"
Fredericksborg Castle, a seventeenth century lure
Showcased by Gudrun and her monarch "L'amour".

Monday started early with a trip on a ferry
Then with Casey at the wheel, we did scurry
Destination Stockholm, no time to tarry
Six hundred kilometers, of Swedish motorway.
Our evening menu, started up the tower
With a view of Stockholm, to devour
On to the Ice Bar, for a drink or two
Served in a meat locker, at minus 22.

Continuous bird chirping, is a definitive clue
That summer darkened hours in Sweden, are few
You close your eyes, till the next sunrise
About two minutes go by, and then, surprise!

Rune's tour of Stockholm, from 8 o'clock to 3
Covered Skansen Park, City Hall and a ship lost at sea
Home to the Nobel awards, Swedes' cherish earnestly
He talked, we walked, and we listened attentively…honestly!

We were "Serenaded" overnight, by the Silja Line
To a Baltic crossing, on waters sublime
The evening meal delicious, with lots of wine
Contributed by the Shuksters, a couple most fine.

Two squares and a Rock Church, it wasn't very much
We circled Helsinki, with Ralph in charge
Sibelius was there, with sculpted pipes in air
Make of this art, what you can, if you really dare.

We visited a museum, called the Saarinen home
Where Finnish architect ideas, were born and came from
Back to the Radisson, a lovely five- star dorm
A classic hotel calm, before the Russian storm.

Crossing into Russia, was a bit of a zoo
With kilometers of trucks, and customs officers few
A fellow Trafalgar guide, created a somewhat hullabaloo
By throwing a hissy fit, and trying to jump the queue.

Justice prevailed, and our group got through
Ahead of her rabble, "tough luck, boo- hoo"
Lunch in Vyborg, gave us a clue
Of the quality of food, on a Russian menu.

You must be mad, if you think Petrograd
Can be seen in less than a day
Natasha, our guide took us out far and wide
To view, two hundred years of history.

Later on, from a boat, we did nothing but dote
On the palaces, cathedrals, museums
From Catherine and Romanov to Peter and Stroganov
The buildings mesmerize, as you see them.

A church by name, a museum by fame
The Church on the Spilt Blood, is one and the same
St. Isaac's Cathedral was rebuilt again
To honour the people, and its historical claim.

The Hermitage of world renown
Is really _the_ jewel, in the Russian crown
Wrapped in the Winter Palace opulent gown
Its exhibits, make it the talk of the town.

To add to the culture of the day
We attended a performance of the Swan Lake ballet
Tchaikovsky's classic, what more can you say
Performed with beauty, at the Alexandrinsky.

A visit to where Rasputin died
And on to where Nicholas was canonized
From Peter and Paul Cathedral to Peterhof Park
A recreation of Versailles, it really makes its mark.

A Russian evening, of dance and song
Encouraged us to bring our cameras along
To record Cossack dancing, as on fire
Accompanied by the voices, of the Russian Army choir.

The Babushka stare can give you a scare
Enough to make you toe the line
But if you dare to stray from the straight away
They'll slap you on the wrist, as a warning sign.
The Summer Palace of Catherine the Great
Is located at Pushkin, on a picturesque estate
Destroyed by the Germans, in World War Two
Restored with all the beauty, Russian artisans can do.

Natasha 3 wanted us to see, Novgorod, that's suffered terribly
From Ivan the Terrible, and German artillery
But today, June 10th, we are pleased to see
The locals celebrate happily, on this, their special holiday.

Anne has a history, of hiring guides of quality
This pattern has not changed, we all agree
But to keep Russian paperwork nice and easy
She only hires Natashas, so far three!

Novgorod's hotel had a downtown view
Of a fireworks display, in red, white and blue
Their locals celebrate, exactly as we do
Cultures apart, we are from the same world milieu.

On to Moscow, a long way to go
The ladies sang high, the men like bozo
Anne tested our mettle, with a Russian alpha show
As we bounced to Tver, to recover our mojo.

The subway in Moscow, is not serene
In fact, day and night, it is a turbulent scene
With millions of passengers, transporting to and fro
Through the underground "palaces" of the Moscow Metro.

Tania our guide, conducted us at speed
To various stations, through a public stampede
To witness frescos, mosaic and glass
Chandeliers and statues, all rated first class.

On the way to Zagorsk, we altered our course
To view village life, through Katia's years of strife
A tour of a monastery, named after St. Sergeyev
Viewed Russian Orthodox history, on this, their Independence Day.
Back to the Hotel Sovietsky, for a spit and a polish
On City tour again, our eyes getting owlish
Off the bus, dinner rush, walk to the Circus
An incredible balance of Soviet talent, trust us.

Russian history is a major mystery
Of war and peace, that never seems to cease
The Borodino Memorial is quite tutorial
Using 360 degrees of paintings, to please.

Memorial Park, was on our way
To the Novodevichy Cemetery, where Russian notables lay
The park's symbolic structure, of the Holocaust sculpture
Paid war tribute, to Russia's Jewish culture.

Red Square, the Kremlin, the Armoury Museum
Gave credence to the, "If it's big, it's Russian" theorem
While in Moscow it's okay, for you to pay homage to
A City renewed, where ancient history meets new.

Anne's linguistic quiz, gave us Russian on cue
But our ordering of drinks, would have gone askew
Our words for vodka and champagne, in lieu
Would have produced, Volga water and ladies' shampoo.

The Smolensk hotel was Soviet style
With a décor of this and that
We did not object to the compact toilet
As long as the room had a cat!

The Cathedral in Smolensk, was magnificence
With icons galore, gold leaf and an iron floor
Before the tour could resume, we happened on, we assume
A street festival heirloom, featuring independent state costume.

Smolensk's ambience, invited us to say, giddy up and get on your way
Casey circled the town twice and seemed intent to stay
Finally, over the border to Belarus, the new White Russia today
A former Soviet liege, now a proud and independent country.
Svetlana's tour, of the town squares of Minsk
Revealed a city with a historical jinx
Frequently razed, it has come back from the brink
By rebuilding beautiful duplicates, of the missing links.

At our leader's behest, we set off early for Brest
But a blown tire test, forced Casey to invest
His mechanical zest, with two of the guests
Allowing us tourists to rest, and then continue our quest.

Our goal seemed so simple, once again underway
To cross from Belarus to Poland, in one single day
The documentation extensive, hours of grueling delay
Bureaucracy has been maintained, the old Soviet way.

Our frustration and chagrin, turned to a grin
At the thought of two nights, in the Warsaw Westin
We were not disappointed, with the décor within
Even the food was five - star cuisine.

Jacek painfully explained and took us through
The Warsaw atrocities, of World War Two
Where the systematic elimination, of every Jew
Was ordered at the Ghetto and Treblinka too.

For a change of pace, we donned Armani and lace
For a face to face, in a classy palace
A Chopin recital, played "con gusto" by a
Master pianist named Iwona Klimaszewska.

On to a club for Polish folklore
To sample local food and drinks galore
Our group came alive, with polka and jive
A Warsaw night to remember. Man alive!

Early morning departure, was the request
As we left for Poznan, heading west
Over the border, cleared the passport test
Arrived in Berlin, for a good night's rest.
The <u>itinerary</u> of the City of Berlin
Provided a litany, of history German
Rebuilt on a foundation, of water and sand
The recreated buildings, proudly stand.

Checkpoint Charlie, the Brandenburg Gate
The Reichstag, where Nazis generated hate
Cathedrals, palaces, the Berlin Wall
A city of greenery, we couldn't see it all.

A trip to Potsdam, to witness the fall
Of the German 3rd Reich, Hitler and all
Where a Russian, an American and a portly Brit.
Carved up conquered Berlin, bit by bit.

After 19 days of travel haze
We earned the right, for our gala night
Sporting a PhD, in European history
We ended our tour, with a dancing spree.

Anne Sivi our director, was a perfect fit
With a professional manner, and an easy English wit
She regaled us with her knowledge, at each stop and visit
With perfect diction and grammar, as her education befit.

Our motley crew of forty- two
Took Scandinavia on, and Russia new
Crossed Belarus, Poland into Germany too
On a trip, with a quarter million- dollar value.

For the record, it's worthwhile to say
That Betty's travel group, from Ballantrae
Covered 20,000 km in twenty days
Enriching their lives, in every way.

CASTLES ALONG THE RHINE

With Ballantrae flair, we're flying British Air
To join our cruise, along the Rhine
A luxury fare, with castles to spare
The odd walk, good food and fine wine.

A Heathrow stop, brought major hassle
To make the flight, en route to Basel
Emilio coached us, to listen and learn
As he drove our tired bodies, on to Lucerne.

The Astoria beckoned, for the briefest nap
Followed by Mark's presentation, of Swiss tours on tap
A visit to Movenpick, by a fussy group
Brought kudos for most meals, including the soup.

An early rise for some, but not all
A briefing for those, who answered the call
Lucerne is a masterpiece, best seen by a walk
Enhanced from the lake, after leaving the dock.

Swiss folklore, we did earnestly seek
To view Alp Horns, cowbells and yodeling unique
A night at the Stadtkeller, introduced us to
Local customs and usages, all the year through.

A cog railway, brought us to the top
Of nearby Mount Pilatus, a 7000- foot drop
Windy and cool, with a snowflake or two
Forced us inside, with a limited view.

Descended by cable car, not one but two
Out of the clouds, magnificent view
Of Lake Lucerne, and the valley below
An aerial snapshot of Switzerland, how apropos.

Swiss are precise, and always on time
Lucerne streets are tidy, and buildings sublime
Bed duvets and swans, are the whitest of white
Service is structured, with everything just right.

Sunday dawned, just a beautiful day
River walk Lucerne, was bathed in sunray
Bussed to the Rhine, to view luxury and more
And savor life, on the River Ambassador.

From the Swiss Alps, to the distant North Sea
Father Rhine flows, through European history
Fourteen hundred kilometers, of rich waterway
Enhancing six country economies, day by day.

A week on the boat, easy to unpack
We sailed overnight, from Basel to Breisach
An excursion through Alsace, was a dream come true
Scenic roads, quaint villages and a vineyard or two.

Historic Colmar, a middle age site
Brought a mixture of culture, and photogenic delight
Bartholdi, Unterlinden, museums of note
Enhanced by Gilese, our guide from the boat.

On to Riquewihr in France, to taste local fare
Quiche Lorraine, pinot noir, and cold frothy beer
A stop in Obernai, to break up the trip
A final leg to Strasbourg, to rejoin the ship.

Alsace village scenes, are brought to the fore
Enhanced by the beauty, of geraniums galore
Introduced from North Africa, some centuries before
Lifting the spirits, of all who adore.

The wine road offered, life without care
Hectares of vineyards, fruit loaded, some bare
Red roof villages, popping up through the green
Adding to the beauty, of this masterpiece scene.

Strasbourg offered us a cruise, and a walk
Crossroads of Europe, lots of Parliament talk
Dominated by, the Cathedral of Old Notre Dame
And home to a French style palace, Le Palais Rohan.

After lunch on board, we set sail for Speyer
Cloudless skies, a breeze, warm sun, perfect weather
Black Forest Germany east, French Vosges to the west
The Rhine River, creating the boundary test.

A millennium cathedral, is Speyer's lofty claim
A middle age structure, of Unesco world fame
Heidelberg boasts, a castle from medieval time
A university, plus Tun, an infamous barrel of wine.

Traffic on the Rhine, is an endless line
Of tourist boats, barges and steamers
Moving people and freight, at an outstanding rate
Nature's reward, to transportation dreamers.

By tourist design, you can see Rudesheim am Rhein
From the seated comfort of a cable car
Known for quality wine, it has a reputation in time
As the Rhine centre, for raising the bar.

Castle Vollrads, sits amid a wine estate
Making a half million bottles of Riesling, just first rate
Family history ties questioned, as we toured and drank
But we found to our dismay, it was owned by the bank.

With German precision, trains run on a ribbon
Of track, on both sides of the Rhine
Passenger, freight, they're on time, never late
As many as, grapes on the vine.

Koblenz stands, where the Moselle and Rhine meet
The Middle Rhine cultural, and business center seat
Rebuilt after the damage, of World War Two
To simulate the ambience, of the old- world milieu.

Marksburg Castle, was a realistic tour
Of medieval times, for knights du jour
Presented by a guide, in a rather stoic way
We viewed centuries of castle life, instantly.

The Cologne guide, flooded us with facts
About river levels rising, above the max
The water problems ahead, are quite alarming
As they prepare, for the consequences of global warming.

A Roman town, with a heritage of trade
For three hundred years, Cologne exceeded the grade
In 1880, its former fame passed it by
Then enhanced by the Cathedral, and bones of the Magi.

The Rhine Gorge showcases castles, left and right
A reproduction of Europe's history, always in sight
Stately mansions, protecting local frontiers
Reflecting the culture, of much earlier years.

Disembarkation meant, the end of our trip
Others chose a three- day extension, to come to grip
With the sights and sounds, of Amsterdam
A simulated on-land storm, after the river calm.

Any vacation doubts we had, to win or lose
Were put to rest, by this river cruise
A first-class package, from beginning to end
Castles along the Rhine, we recommend.

Cruising the River Ambassador, La Belle Madame
From Switzerland's Basel, to Holland's Amsterdam
Chaperoned by Christine, and a dedicated crew
We loved the experience, Uniworld we thank you.

CELLEBRATION

We are subject to
Its beck and call
Prisoners of technology
Come one, come all.

Dedicated to daily
With, all our heart and soul
Held high in esteem
As a life-saving tool

A modern, must
Without which, we'd fall
It's being used, and abused
It's taking its toll.

Around the clock
Users have the gall
To call, or text you
From even, down the hall.

Wherever you are
In a theatre, or mall
The ringing's incessant
It's off the wall.

On a beach, in a car
Or in a stall
The wireless- free, yacking
Can only make you growl.

Affixed to the ear
Up and down, they stroll
Oblivious to the stares
Partnered with, a scowl.

A lack of manners
Exhibited, by almost all
With the decibels
Set, at big and tall.

A worldwide issue
Deemed by some, as small
Society should heed
This wireless, free for all.

CHANGE

The Arab Spring has brought, will bring
A history of anguish, spine tingling
A loss of humanity, to which all should cling
Resulting in early failure, in almost everything.

For societal change, it is prime
That such can only occur, over time
A staircase of lessons, one must climb
Before you can cross, that finishing line.

Syria, Iraq, to name the quotable few
Afghanistan, Egypt, Libya, too
Expecting instant change, a lofty view
A goal, time will not let them, soon pursue.

Encouraged by the West, with do-gooder intention
Supporting revolt, with active intervention
Strongman, dictator, became our personal foe
Decision made, we know best, out of here, he has to go.
We made room for a plague called ISIS, oh no.

We have lost face, why not, we created the space
For a so- called ideology, to walk in and lay waste
To the very lands, we just set free, with haste
A decision made wrong, and not with grace.
A memory we'll regret, and not soon erase.

The knock- on effect has stunned, and staggered us all
Millions forced to resettle, as peace and order fall
Or is it a combination of this, and that, with war and conflict
A never- ending pact, but added to the mix is a
Migrant tact, to seek a better life, an economic fact.

From Gambia, Eritrea, Ghana, Niger and more
Africans are fleeing, oblivious to what lies in store
Risking dangerous passage, to reach Europe's back door
Testing and straining resources, to handle this downpour.

An Age of change, is upon us now
You can close your eyes, or furrow your brow
But human displacement, will not go away
Without pain and consequences, for many a day.

Globalization, technology, emigration, rank high
In determining the sharing, of earth's questionable pie
To avoid the pitfalls, of current emigration's, do or die
We must show respect and tolerance, from both the you and I.

The tone of change in the U. S. of A
Was echoed loudly in each state, election day
Cries of replace the known, bring in the new
Shock and awe, is much better than you.

Leaving the E.U., it cannot be true
The Brits have closed ranks, better is few
Sending a message to others, who
Will consider exit, right on cue.

Change is the new norm, all in favour say aye
The momentum is building, come on give it a try
Oh, say can you see, is proudly sung, but
Some may not like what they see, from the bottom rung.

The world we have known, is going awry
Anger and contempt, leading people to try
And waive the status quo, good riddance, goodbye
Only time and history, will answer why, why.

And let's pray, for peace and harmony, to be the new global cry.

COME FLY WITH ME

It's modern to fly, you don't want to miss
Come one, come all, vacation or biz
The end justifies the means, they like to say
Let's examine realities of today's up, up and away.

The check in counter beckons, your destiny, fate
To watch your bags, register pounds overweight
A counter voice tries to soften the blow
Will that be cash or credit, before you go.

Approaching security, boarding pass in hand
A step closer to your destination, sea and sand
Body, shoes, and your belt wanded, dignity harangued
Your land rights surrendered, to their air demand.

Re-assembled, calm, you prepare to strut
Wait, your carry-on's been held, did not make the cut
Some personals displayed, for all to see
Do they want me to fly, do they really want me?

It's time to board, the late flight announced
The delay's made you restless, the airline denounced
You've been held incommunicado, for three hours or more
Enthusiasm drained, chin on the floor.

Refreshed at the sound of a computerized voice
Telling all to look lively, to board their Rolls Royce
You jostle like cattle to form single file
And sharpen your elbows, for the walk down the aisle.

Boarding a plane requires a sudden leap of faith
Onto a bullet train, destined to leave the earth
Shoe horned into your seat, without further delay, you are
Instructed how to handle, a catastrophic emergency.

It's all inclusive, served on a silver tray
An echo from the past, a bye gone day
Economy class, now requires you pay
For every item used, on the flight pathway.

To counter, your bag under the seat
Holds pillows and blankets and your favorite treat
Sandwiches, snacks and a bottle of spree
Your first- class response, to life's new economy.

CONGRATULATIONS! GO AWAY!

For years our ears were subject to
Telemarketing pleas, daily on cue
To sign up, to buy, a mulligan stew
An every day offer, only for you.

The initial response, an experience new
Acceptance, tolerance, was the lofty view
Resistance futile, the exposure grew
Never ending prospects, a telephone queue.
A marketing opportunity, they just blew
By stalking daily, tried and true
A never- ending barrage of nothing new
Brought consumer angst, to a record hue.

Defense mechanisms were assembled to
Thwart invasion from this pushy crew
Call display gave most a clue
To place each ring under review.

The government said, what can we do
The public are creating a hullabaloo
Let's pass a bill, in a month or two
The U.S. did it, we can too.

The Registry should buy silence anew
From the majority of calls, oh how we thank you
Post September 30th, if they continue
Government effectively has the right to sue.

Common sense, at last to the rescue
Although exemptions apply, that's nothing new
A finish to the seemingly endless spew
Of rhetoric, invading our peaceful milieu.

Technology offers to those of you
Who become lonely, not accustomed to,
A silent phone, with calls now few
Just text 1-800 what to do.

COVID-19: A 2020 PLAGUE

Most of us call it a pandemic
Others, a world- wide plague
Its geographic origin known
But the cause is, still somewhat vague.

Human to human transmission
Known to a few, early on
Kept under wraps, by Chinese authorities
Within the city limits, of Wuhan.

Chinese government policy, for everything
Is to control the public voice
By doing so, they exercise authority
Silencing critics, and all unwanted noise.

Wuhan was placed on lockdown
Months of isolation lay ahead
Authorities thought they'd confined it
But the virus was on its way, instead.

The curtain of silence, they had woven
Had been pierced, and torn apart
The disease would spread like wildfire
And this, was only the start.

We are a global society, practicing
Frequent travel, in every aspect
We considered human transmission
But ruled it out, as a valid suspect.

Meanwhile, the predator was closing in
On us, it's prey travelling to and fro
Across world seas and borders, oh Lord
Infected numbers were about to grow.

Its initial target, was to land upon
A place, where travel is frequent and common
Behold, Europe fits this mold, with a
Mobile population, and many seniors very old.

Italy and Spain, the first to suffer pain
As the year grew, infected clusters joined the queue
The U. S. of A. also sadly had to pay, with an
Initial attitude of, "it ain't coming our way."

As of September twenty- five
The virus is still, very much alive
Infecting 35 million people, or so
In 214 countries, and continuing to grow.

This presents, a world problem
The last 100 years have never seen
A global risk of poverty, hunger, unrest
Before release, of that magic vaccine.

Meanwhile those in health, have been the glue
Many risking their lives, to pull us through
Front line workers, bringing medicine and food
Have served us as well, as anyone could.

Social distancing, has enabled us to stall
The spread of COVID- 19, to one and all
But economic pressures, and a wish to stand tall
Risk a return of the virus, and a second down fall.

When infections, deaths, are brought to a halt
Each country will be looking at, an empty vault
Return to normality, will take many a day
Pain and suffering, oh how we will pay.

Will the world heed, this wake-up call
We have the means, the wherewithal
To fight the pandemic, and watch it fall
To eliminate this virus, once and for all.

Or, will we just press the reset button
Throw out recent events, as simply forgotten'
And sadly, change nothing at all
It's our chance. No, it's _your_ call.

DOMINICAN GAFFS

She said, oh woe is me
My locks are sealed, look one, two, three
It took a man, with skill and brie
To fix the bag, and her bp.

She said, it's happened again
My binocs' are gone, it's those customs men
We replied, you did not lose
They're on the table, right under your nose.

It's 5 o'clock you say, I'm on my way
To Santo Domingo, for the day
It's 5:01, your efficient son
Don't call again, I'm on the run.

It's 5:02, I'm on the loo
You've had your fun, enough of you.
You ring me again, I'll give you heck
And what is more, I'll ring your neck.

El read a Herriot book, they said
Her knowledge to enhance
But laughter grew to such a hue
She nearly wet her pants.

Horse riding on the beach, by moon
The saddle sores, were present soon
To ease the pain, Eleanor did swoon
Between a fork, a knife, and a silver spoon.

Fully clothed, Bob did wade
Through the lobby pool, the legend said
Although nonchalant, an egg he laid
But he ordered, a rum and coke instead.

DON'T LET IT SNOW, LET IT SNOW, LET IT SNOW

The media warned us often enough
To expect extreme weather, with nasty stuff
A Texas storm heading our way
Bringing blowing snow, and skies of grey.

An early forecast, of 30 centimeters or more
Starting Friday p.m., and lasting 48 hour
Ample time to plan and plot, how they
Will service their customers, the Melfer way.

Alas the plan, died on the table
Effective snow removal, an Aesop fable
The community listened, waited and watched
But nothing happened, had the company botched.

Wait, after twenty- four hours, a truck with blade
Patrolling the streets, we've been saved
No, just creating a solid wall of snow
At the end of each driveway, fully denying any, to-and-fro.

Cooped up, like dwellers in a cave
Held hostage, residents became desperate, brave
Brandishing shovels, we attacked the layers
Ignoring cardiac warnings, and spousal prayers.

Relief for some, as they dug to the street
Others not so lucky, accepted defeat
Finally ploughs appeared, like j.i.t. freight
On Sunday p.m., too little, too late.

Understanding, is a human trait
Extended to those, who are not always great
But the treatment we seniors unfairly faced
Will remain a memory, bitter laced.

DOUG MCARTHUR A TESTIMONY

A seasoned man, a reasoned man
A man, who stamped his mettle
On all, whose shadow crossed his path
He gave, and asked for little.

A loving man, a family man
A man, whose star attraction
Was to win you over, gain your trust
And guarantee satisfaction.

A business man, with acumen
Devoted to his profession
He stood so tall, by giving all
His family, the sole concession.

A nice man, a gentle man
A man, who won his share
Of admirers, friends and comrades
Through his life, now witness bear.

EAST MEETS WEST

We flew from the West, with the best of the best
Family and friends fast, from five decades past
Anticipation of the reality, soon coming to pass
Of witnessing the treasures, of China's land mass.

Joined Betty's group, now numbering fifty- nine
A number Chinese think, is mathematically fine
Sampled the known cities, of Shanghai and Beijing
Also, Guilin, Xi'an and the most populous Chongqing.

A European landmark, in Chinese history
Shanghai city meaning is, "Land above the sea"
A contradiction in terms, we have to all agree
As it now boasts its very own, sea of humanity.

Leon drove Shanghai streets, long, wide and far
To the Longhua Temple and the Yu Gardens Town Bazaar
Huxinting Teahouse memories, will last for years hence
As will Chinese history, in Sun Yat-sen's residence.

The Jade Buddha Temple, prepared many on the tour
For a Silk shopping frenzy, attracting most to its lure
The Oriental Pearl Tower, gave us an aerial view
Of Pudong building activity, each project right on cue.

Following a Mongolian lunch, we did not travel far
To visit the Yu Yuan Gardens, and walk the Town bazaar
Every Chinese garden, is not designed by chance
Containing, rock, water, structure, and many natural plants.

Between Ten Thousand Happiness, and the Smiling Swan
We ate lazy Susan food, just like the average Han
Became immersed in Chinese wonders, a veritable cuisine
Of ancient mystery and customs, the land of Mandarin.

An evening show followed, a fairly ordinary meal
To witness young talent, perform with much skill and zeal
An acrobatic show, demonstrating their ability in this field
And why Olympic medals, become easy for them to yield.

A bus trip to Suzhou, to witness what's at hand
Parts of a historic City, on 2500-year old land
Master of Nets garden, and boating on the canal
The Pan Men scenic, bridge, water gate and well.

Our last hours in Shanghai, gave all of us a view
Of stunning architectural styles, impressive both old and new
On both banks of the Huangpu, the river running through
As seen from the historical Bund, our lasting impressions grew.

Our guides Scottie and Matt, were active lads that
Laid out Shanghai ways, on a warm and welcome mat
Explaining local dialects, were slowly giving way
To most speaking Mandarin and English, almost every day.

Shanghai is buoyant, and reflects the China who
Wants world recognition, as being at the front of the queue
Managing growth and desire, for a triple "A" review
The challenges ahead, will be multiple, and certainly not few.

A host of photo-ops, very hard to pass by
Without clicking your camera, before saying goodbye
The Chinese handle density with skill, aplomb and flair
Adding order, peace, tranquility, to enhance what's partly there.

Equatorial Hotel praises, for several days we sang
Then said goodbye to Shanghai, by flying to Yichang
Viewed finds from past dynasties, especially that of Ming
Then had dinner locally, before boarding the East King.

Xiling Gorge is a highlight, from the Yangzi first we've seen
A mixture of cliffs, channels, and deepest water green
A side trip to witness, the massive Three Gorges Dam
A gigantic human achievement, to make the waters calm.

The Three Gorges Dam project, was a controversy which,
Balanced that of the poor, with the interest of the rich
To eliminate downstream flooding, and subsequent tragic death
It displaced one million people, from their daily life on earth.

Used the Shennong stream, to join the Pea- pod boating tour
Overwhelmed with the topography, and the Three Lesser Gorge allure
Transferred to a wooden boat, rowed by six athletic men
We laughed and yelled and sang upstream,
till they brought us back again.

The Wu, and Qutang Gorges, were the icing on the cake
Cliffs, peaks and valleys, no human hand could make
The river boat shows, highlighted many of the crew
Their costumes, singing, music, authentic, through and through.

Ming Shan had multi temples, as many as drops of rain
And grotesque waxworks, statues, all expressing human pain
A city of ghostly chilling hue, but with an amazing Yangzi river view
Located near displaced people who, will have to start their lives anew.

The Yangzi river scenery, is a multi- tasting feast
The good, the bad, the awful, the Beauty and the Beast
Combining nature's magic hand, to produce a vision, oh so grand
But with industry in on every brand, there are
negative consequences for the land.

A Chongqing visit, to the City zoo
Gave us pandas breakfasting happily, in open tourist view
Viewed savoured Chinese art, and the City market heart
Before flying to Guilin, for yet another new town start.

Guilin to Yangshuo, we followed the river flow
Of the Li Jiang waterway, on a tour boat we did go
To witness limestone mountains, each with their own custom peak
Spectacular majestic scenery, that for itself does plainly speak.

Low bamboo rafts, were everywhere
Poled to tourist boats, to sell their food and ware
Trained cormorants are many, and typical here
Collared to catch fish, nature's on- line fishing gear.

We bussed Guilin, mainly in the rain
The drivers, the pedestrians, they are all totally insane
Don't look, don't yield, your fate seems sealed
But they're all near misses, your death sentence just repealed.

Albert took us through Xi'an
City wall, the Jade store, part of the plan
A p.m. visit to Qin Shi Huangdi's tomb
To see Terracotta warriors, in a 2000 year buried room.

A dumpling meal, gave us a feel
Of local food, tasting really quite good
The Tang dynasty show, depicting long, long ago
Was a costume flow, of colours rainbow.

Our partial day of touring, the old capital Xi'an
Was with Albert and Emily, to show us as what they can
Chinese religious practices, were brought up to the fore,by
The Great Goose Pagoda and The Great Mosque ancient lore.

Chinese thought, we are the one, there is no other
We are the universe, you don't have to look further
When foreigners arrived, from head to toes
They deemed them look-alikes, and all with a big nose.

Beijing's rain showed us no pity
As we toured Tiananmen Square and the Forbidden City
In a sea of umbrellas, we were led by Chou and Matt
We later ate Dim Sum chicken feet, and maybe this and that.

The Square of the Gate of Heavenly Peace
And the Emperors' palace, are China's Chinese
Combining a symbol of power, from centuries gone bye
With a modern statement, don't challenge us, don't try.

A shopping trip planned, mainly for the girls
Introduced many to the beauty of, fresh water pearls
A tourist requirement, by government decree
Includes such stops for tourists, to assist the local economy.

The Temple of Heaven, dominates a park
Green space locals use, from morning to dark
Singing, dancing, playing cards and Tai Chi
They socialize in harmony, as multi leaves in green tea.

The Peking Opera performance, gave us all a taste
Of male actors in disguise, using make-up and paste
Visually stunning, different, with a distinctive music style
We saw a Monkey and a Dam, who fooled us for a while.

The Great Wall of China, is amazing to behold
A wondrous man- made structure, long, strong and very bold
Dating from the Qin dynasty, around 200 hundred- year B.C.
Now considered a world wonder, every traveler, must see.

We trolled the tombs, at historic Chang Ling
The resting place, of 13 emperors Ming
Slowly back on a bus, in rush hour Beijing
To enjoy our final dinner, roasted Duck Peking.

A tribute to Betty, in the hotel lobby bar
Sincere thanks to a gal, who has vacationed many afar
With organizational skills that, always get us home
No matter the highlights, or how far we must roam.

The grounds of the Summer Palace, gave all of us insight
To Empress Dowager Cixi and others', spending might
The building, the lake, the money spent for luxury sake
The Qin Dynasty leaders, did not give the poor, one single break.

The Bird's Nest stadium is empty, but ready and intact
Cost half a billion dollars, and that's a sobering fact
A visual Olympic legacy, supported by tourist yuan
Top down, déjà vu spending, all over again.

The China we saw, left us breathless, and somewhat in awe
The cities, the people, the history, we viewed with dropped jaw
Differences apart, they work hard, and are very, very smart
While offering their friendship, apparently straight from a warm heart.

My initial thoughts of China were confused, and distorted somewhat
I found them sincere, friendly, yet philosophically and socially caught
In choosing between East and West, which path they considered best
I know the Chinese will decide which option, best feathers their nest.

FALL

Remember When

It was in your face.
A vibrant orange ball,
Hanging low in space.

Signals the opening
Of the season of grace
When we all give thanks
When we all give praise.

We cling to the pause
That wants to stay
Before giving way
To winter's day.

FORE WHOM IT MAY CONCERN

Golf club rules, are pretty clear
To trespass, brings up to a year
We talked, debated, cleared the air
We'll take the risk, because they're there.

We sally forth every night
Hunting golf balls, hidden out of sight.
They're white and dimpled, and don't belong
In rough or fescue, alone, forlorn.

Our mission, is to rescue them
Those round white pearls, a hunter's gem
With bug spray, sleeves and long pants too
We scour the course, each day on cue.

Callaway, Pinnacle, to name a few
The more they lose, there's work to do
The hunting season, lasts through the fall
The balls keep coming, enough for all.

Bring them on, we're up to the test
To increase those stored, in our golf ball nest
For winter pickings, are poor at best
A time, ball hunters get to rest.

PASTORS GERRY AND ELAINE TONN

At such times, we struggle as to what to say
Our hearts full of love, words, words just get in the way
Cornerstone, don't hesitate to show, display
Your feelings for them, on their special day.

A day when warmth and care, come into play
A day of affection, in every way
We wish them God speed, on their journey
Our prayers for them, will not go astray.

Pastors Gerry, Elaine, it won't be the same
We'll miss your mantle, your sharing our joy, our pain
Your love, your purpose, in our hands will remain
Your memory, our minds, our hearts, will retain.

Elaine, a pastor, a lady, with gifts galore
Supporting her husband, to help open each door
A spouse, a mother, a partner of four
A complete, who gives her all and more.

Gerry, a man of God, who has followed the Word
Planted a church, with his special touch
Moves on to challenges unknown
With God by your side, your seeds will be sown.

Amen.

GO FLY A KITE

Dad surveyed the kite rack
With a twinkle in his eye
Should he buy the tiger moth
Or the monarch butterfly.

He appeared before the family
With a package, in his hand
We'll fly this beauty tomorrow
Above the golden sand.

The north wind started blowing
The temperature's gone astray
Best time to fly a kite, Dad said
Is any time, night or day.

They strode down the beach
Determined to show their best
The kite ascended quickly
They puffed out, their collective chest.

Mere seconds into the flight
Disaster struck the test
It wobbled, bobbled, and dive bombed
It's not difficult, to guess the rest.

Determined to be noticed
By those who stood around
It scattered them like cattle
As its maiden flight unwound.

Cassandra knelt, and hugged it
To sooth its wounded pride
The next time that we fly you.
I know, you'll soar and glide.

GRAND PALLADIUM WHITE SANDS, PLAYA KANTENAH

Villa 52, is where they had us go
Quite beautiful, sitting westward ho
But far from the beach, too much to and fro
Our initial enthusiasm, went from high to low.

Trips to the desk, met with a maybe, and a no
For a transfer to the beach, far below
After five days, they finally gave us the go
We trudged to villa fifty- nine, with luggage in tow.

For years, the complex has continued to grow
Increasing the distance, between points A and O
The trolley brings relief, to the ebb and flow
Of guests who locate it, or are in the know.

This land train travels, fast not slow
With little warning, when it's time to go
The schedule documented, but dependable no
Palladium take heed, as the objections grow.

Prior trips to Kantenah, gave us a glow
To return to this resort, where the trade winds blow
But this experience, with its troubles and woe
Have turned us from yes, to we really don't know.

Room fan repaired and then replaced. (continuous noise).
Door lock repaired and then replaced. (could access room now and then).
Infestation of ants. Room sprayed. (ground floor rooms have this problem).
Lukewarm water. Following complaint and argument hot water was available.
Television repaired (cable connection had been removed and not replaced).

HAPPY BALLANTRAE 2020

Christmas lights sparkling, on snow laden trees
Frame Ballantrae gripped, in our first winter freeze
The crunching of boot steps, repeat passing bye
Supporting an image, bowed down, low to the sky.

A fierce north wind pushing, snowflakes at pace
Each one competing, in their own wintry race
Snow banks towering, with significant growth
Dwarfing vehicles few, that dare venture forth.

A January night followed, all crisp, calm and clear
The icy silence pleasing, to each attuned ear
Ushering a new decade, of wishful good health and cheer
To all Ballantrae residents, we wish you, A Very Happy New Year.

HI NEIGHBOUR

What's in a word
A phrase not absurd
Make a positive choice
Those in need, hear your voice.

The pace of one's life
Never far from some strife
But it's so simple to say
How are <u>you</u> doing today.

The interest you show
When someone is low
At a price, free of cost
Total gain, nothing lost.

The Samaritan within
Needs awakening now and then
To do what is right
To share your joy and light.

The rewards are in line
With a feeling divine
You have given from yearn
Requiring nothing in return.

HOME SWEET HOME

What is the allure
Of being mature
Of having the time
To do what is mine.

As a Ballantrae guest
We have the best, of the best
We can club by design
Or walk our own line.

If it's cards that you wish
Or to swim like a fish
A club menu so fine
Will let you fine dine.

Or you can walk, jog or hike
Or take to a bike
You can golf 18 or 9
Till the planets align.

If a trip's in the air
To a spot over there
Betty S. can assign
A vacation, divine.

This location unique
Of highly we speak
We savour with thyme
Each day from the vine.

IN MEMORIAM

To critique the war
Is considered taboo
But what oh what
Are they going to do.

Stay the course, leave Iraq
Comply or argue
A contradiction in terms
It's a catch twenty- two.

The Administration adopts
A big picture, view
To counter terrorism
We must fight, to renew.

The public finds solace
At the back of the queue
The protestors, the objectors
Their cries are now few.

The military obedient
Are bewildered too
At the lack of support
From the American, you.

The ribbons, the slogans
Have lost their hue
Expressions of hope
Bound without glue.

Opposing forces, civilians
Prove nothing is new
The head count continues
The body bags accrue.

History will judge all those
And the rhetoric, they spew
But our hearts will remember
The pain, of this tragic milieu.

ISRAEL TODAY

Crowne Plaza location gave us a Tel Aviv view
Of a Mediterranean playground for many a Jew
As, Roger our guide, Israeli through and through
Led us to Jerusalem, our excitement grew.

The Yad Vashem exhibit was a memorial to
The horrors, millions of Jews suffered, and were put through
Followed by the Dead Sea Scrolls at a museum milieu
And lunch at a Kibbutz, soup, bun and a stew.

King David's Tomb, the Last Supper Room
Gave insight into Christ's impending doom
A half mile away was Gethsemane
Where Judas betrayed and gave Jesus away.

Jerusalem's Old City layout was in plain view
From a Mount of Olives lookout, under a sky of blue
The Jewish, Muslim and Christian quarters we walked through
And followed the Stations of the Cross to one two, plus two.

We found the Western Wall, more or less,
A reflection of intense reverence and emotional stress
As witnessed by scenes of brokenness
And passion for prayer, by most of the rest.

Masada is a strategic and imposing sight
Where zealots engaged Romans, in a deadly fight
Onto Qumran, discovery site of the scrolls
Into the Dead Sea, for black goo and tummy rolls.

Jerusalem's final night, we answered the call
To eat Israeli fare, come one, come all
An early a.m. departure for the Temple Mount
The Dome of the Rock is Muslim, of this there is no doubt.

A side trip to Bethlehem was accepted by all
To see the Church of the Nativity and Jesus's manger stall
Back over the border, from this West Bank town
To the Lavi Kibbutz Hotel, to lay our bodies down.

Monday morning early, we were up and gone
To visit the plain of Megiddo, Revelations Armageddon
King Solomon's chariot city, with a secret fresh water well
Echoed the sounds of history, where 20 civilizations fell.

Nazareth is where it all began
With Mary's immaculate conception
A church is planted with worldwide willing
Atop, Mary and Joseph's modest dwelling.

Kinneret or Galilee, it's up to thee
To determine the name of this historic sea
Where Jesus preached in 1 century A.D.
Capernaum would have been the place to be.

The Golan Heights say it best
Of the conflict, area nations, can't put to rest
Israel constantly put to the test
By surrounding Arab nations, a viper's nest.

A tour of Acre gave us insight
As to what Crusaders did between each fight
Haifa's Bahai Gardens were a photo- op
Caesarea gave us Roman history, full stop.

Two days of leisure allowed us to be
Tourists in Tel Aviv, from guiding free
We walked and we shopped and we gawked at will
To learn the ways, of Israelis' Israel.

Cairo beckoned via strangely, El Al
We said goodbye to Roger, our guide, our new pal
Through his eyes and his words, we felt close, felt at home
Goodbye to Israel. L'chaim and Shalom.

Israeli characteristics… dark hair, muted clothing, excellent roads, busy traffic, greenery, attractive beaches, old buildings, coffee shops and cafes, pedestrians, active shoppers, car horns honking, police car emergency lights on all the time.

Our vision of Israeli security is just not right.
Veiled in subtlety, not black, nor white
Not openly apparent, unless you pry
But reassuringly available, in the blink of an eye.

The head covering worn, by many a man
Does not deem him part of a sect, tribe or clan
But rather acknowledges, there is a higher plan
Namely, Yahweh. "I Am that I Am that I Am".

IT WAS A SMALL WORLD AFTER ALL

Saturday mornings, we would often say
It's nice outside, let's main street today
Car in garage, we strode effortlessly
To explore our town, the old- fashioned way.

We entered each store, with anticipation and zeal
Looking for that maybe deal
The reception was constant, warm and real
The small independent had that special feel.

Satisfaction for each, when a sale was made
A product purchased, sold, specific lives repaid
A sense of community, a foundation laid
Mutual respect, of the highest grade.

But square footage growth was in the air
Inspired in part, by boardroom chair
And public acceptance, of it's all right there
Forcing small business, in general, to despair.

Today's box stores tend to dominate
To satisfy consumers' need to satiate
Change inevitable, it is our ultimate fate
With super centers, to have a definitive date.

Alas a trap, unless we rally
Left at the gate, if we dilly dally
We Canadians, through plain and valley
Serviced by Walmart Stores, and the odd bowling alley.

IT'S NEVER TOO LATE TO COMMUNICATE

Following, the pre-bedtime scrubbing, complete with girlish screams of joy, at the warmth and comfort of their bathwater, the young ladies turned their attention, to the only one, who if skillfully manipulated, could prolong their waking hours.

"Papa" they implored. "Papa, please tell us about Beau Beau and Jump Jump, pllease".

By this time, they had been creamed and powdered, by their Mum. The aroma of the sweet smells, combined with their angelic looks, and earnest pleading, squashed any thoughts I had of deferring the inevitable.

I began my story, centered around the antics of the fictional characters, we jointly had named as Beau Beau and Jump Jump. I was not reading from a book. I was just telling a made-up story, while my granddaughters spent their listening time, jumping back and forth, from their two feet apart, side by side, single beds, screaming all the while as the story unfolded.

Beau Beau and Jump Jump, were the figments of a grandfather's imagination, but to these young ladies, they were as real as their school chums. These fictional characters, though perhaps questioned at first by the family adults, gave the children and myself valid passports to visit parts of the world, real and imagined, that we normally only dream about.

We ate porridge with the three bears, fought the fiercest of dragons, descended to the lost city of Atlantis, and whirled around space with aliens.

Beau Beau and Jump Jump, were a non techie's equivalent of R2-D2 and C-3PO, enabling us to enter the realm of make belief, without viewing a DVD, or making a trip to the local theatre.

At the time, I was not aware of the impact that story telling had on these young ladies. Age differential and perhaps shyness can deter any attempt to communicate at a level where you are deemed "one of them", and can enter their world.

We all live fast- paced lives, where time is precious, and where we can be guilty of not devoting sufficient time to "our precious". Using one's natural ability to share or read a story with your grandchildren, will foster and enhance their development. Try it. You and your grandchildren will like it.

LIFE'S JOURNEY, WHILE ON EARTH

The journey, the quest, I was merely a guest
On life's backbone of time, from zero to prime
To confirm I was blessed, I will tell you the rest
Of my fruits on the vine, of a life by design.

Born a Scot, in nineteen forty naught
While World War Two, was being fought
Parents Ronald and Mary, had set the table
By, adding a girl and a boy, to the Coyle stable.

Twenty years, of Scottish youthful fun
The formation years, most battles won
A father lost, so early in his years
A new beginning, to wipe away the tears.

A family reunited, in Canada's West
Sister Maureen, helped Mum and I, build a new nest
A fresh start, we worked diligently, day by day
To become Canadian, the Canadian way.

Wedded young in the West, to Eleanor the best
Fathered daughters so fine, three ladies divine
Births in three provinces, brought an Eleanor decree
Future transfers will require, a procedure for thee.

A single employer, Standard Life, I did test
Both sides of the Atlantic, my whole life invest
Two score and nine, of years toeing the line
Now enjoying the rewards, of a pension just fine.

Proud grandfather of children, numbering seven
God's gift to my earth walk, before entering heaven
The title great, added to three children more
I pray for their safety, and what life has in store.

Have run many a race, to look for that place
That combines home coming, friendship, dignity, grace
The gates of Ballantrae, have brought such a face
Then ultimately, Heaven's shelter, trimmed with fine lace.

Family and friends, church, travel, sport
Each one receives, a more than favourable report
Lest anyone critique, I can proudly retort
The road that was mine, one just cannot outshine.

ODE TO A WAITER

After eleven days of dining
With Hector, our friend
We faced the conclusion
All good things come, to an end.

You served us well
Our Chilean mate
Bringing all sorts of goodies
On plate, after plate.

With arrival of the service
You tended to peek
So, we hid under the menus
To let you play, hide and seek.

You endorsed, all our food choices
But after we pointed to this and those
You showed your true colours
By often, scrunching up your nose.

The only night you flinched
And faced your worst fear
Your motley crew, had ordered
Then changed seats, far and near.

You kept your composure
Responded like a pro'
Never missed a beat
As you made us all, eat "crow".

Your Cancun team-mate, Victor
Worked hard, around the clock
Providing all sorts of service
As solid as a rock.

Every moment in time
Fades year after year
But we will never forget
your signature move…

"The wiggling of your derriere".

On board dining experience, was truly great
We salute the class and fun, of the other eight
With Hector and Victor, adding the spice
Our table 520 evenings, were twice as nice.

OUR BALLANTRAE

It is a shame, that behind each name
There's a story, we tend to ignore
We live, work and play, in Ballantrae
With history, worth to explore.

The Ballantrae, we feel is next to Heaven
Was settled some say, in one eight four seven
Credit for the name, is a mystery sought
Research points to the Irish, and also a Scot.

A service centre, for Vivian's lumber trade
Ballantrae inns and hotels, supplied workers their bed
McMillan, McCordock, Galloway, DeGeer
Pioneered commerce for all, in those early years.

Hamlet growth, activity higher
Opportunity knocked for Macey and Prior
Gray and Reynolds, also joined the fray
Recognizing business could only go, one way.

Add a carpenter, a smithy, a justice of peace
A railway ensured, that growth would not cease
Messrs Hill, Miller, Wright, Davies and Hood
Added structure to the little hamlet that could.

A Gaelic word meaning, place by the beach
Ballantrae's historic namesake, is not out of reach
A former fishing village, in Scotland's south west
Offering scenic beauty and golf access, the best of the best.

A harbor location, fished for lobster and crab
At the mouth of a river, tranquil not drab
Turnberry and Troon, a short distance away
Paradise on earth, some golfers might say.

Our beloved offspring, is up, up and away
Not next to an ocean, a great lake, or a bay
We salute those past, who engineered the way
For us to more than savor, our Ballantrae.

OUR CANADA

Tell us, that you love this land
Show us that you care
Bind your future, raise your hand
Take the oath, and swear.

Everyone, has the right to be
A part of our democracy
Everyone, has the right to be
Here, everyone is free.

The envy, of many global peers
Beset by struggles, wars and fears
A focus of the world community
Attracted to our humanity.

To protect the level, we have set the bar
We must maintain our chosen way
A path that leads us, where we are
Identifying us from the fray.

We welcome those, who come and stay
Bringing their heritage, their customs, a multi array
Embracing this land, and the dues they must pay
To become Canadian, the Canadian way.

Forever, sunshine in the valley
Forever, snowflakes on the hill
Preserving this land, for those to come
Our Canada unchanged, with God's will.

PASTOR GERRY

25 years of……

Opening eyes, opening ears
Giving hope, stemming fears
Sharing joy, sharing tears.

25 years of……

Deed after deed
Helping feed, paying heed
Sewing seed, filling need.

25 years of……

Spreading the Word
Being heard
A servant of God
A voice of The Lord.

PASTOR PAUL HILSDEN

Though, technically not small
Paul's, just not very tall
Some reason, it's due to his diet
We suspect that, by age ten
Mum, Dad said amen
Growth's not in your genes
So, don't try it.

To walk down the aisle
Takes, such a long while
He's taken to adopt the front pew
To open in prayer
He climbs up the stair
The assembly sits up
They have too!

To see him stand tall
Dispensing to all
His sermon, with passion and gusto
But his posture goes flat
Beside Gerry and Matt
In the shade of an oak and a willow.

Blessed our family, in prayer
Celebrated Mum's life, with flair
Married our girls yes, a pair
He's the best of the best
Who's passed every test
God speed Pastor Paul and God Bless.

RETURN TO ME

I left You why, where and when
Life's journey to begin
A pathway, through the wilderness
A walk, through fire and sin.

I want to be, in Your arms again
I want to be free, of doubt and pain
I surrender all, I have and can
Lord and Master, Son of Man.

Your hand nearby, I sensed It's touch
To turn back to the light
My focus clouded, human, frail
I denied You, and chose the night.

I want to be, in Your arms again
I want to be free, of doubt and pain
I surrender all, I have and can
Lord and Master, Son of Man.

A crossroad reached, decision time
Broken, ready for the fall
You never left, dependable, true
I submitted, to Your call.

I want to be, in Your arms again
I want to be free, of doubt and pain
I surrender all, I have and can
Lord and Master, Son of Man.

Peace, inner warmth, and comfort, joy
Rain lifted from my heart
A promise made, to honor my King
And love You, for all Thou art.

ROBIN ME OF SLEEP

I sensed my fingers, around his throat
Itching to stifle, each piercing note
Ashamed am I, but what can I do
My pleas unnoticed, from his lofty view.

The joy inherent, in his pulsating song
Should make me want, to hum along
But every a.m., I suffer sleep deprive
Check the clock, it's only three twenty- five.

His heaving breast, the color of my eyes
Announces boldly, it's time to arise
A new day awaits, he wants me to know
It's the middle of the night, you so and so.

He's out of his time zone, I have to guess
His clock unadjusted, a biological mess
Or perhaps an insomniac, who in lieu of sleep
Has to open his mouth, and flap his beak.

Disturbed, my thoughts should give a clue
Gunpowder, dynamite, to name a few
But love of nature, will carry the day
Close the windows, plug my ears, warble away.

RUSSIAN OBSERVATIONS

Eleanor and I were blessed to take a land trip in June to Denmark, Sweden, Finland, Russia, Belarus, Poland and Germany. To imagine how we travelled, see yourself as playing baseball and standing on 3rd base (Copenhagen) and then walk back to 2nd base, then 1st base, and eventually home plate (Berlin). That's the clockwise direction in which we travelled. However, it took us 18 days and we traveled over 5000 kilometers, mainly by bus.

In the time allotted, we cannot do justice to all these countries and have chosen to focus on Russia, in the main, because we were there for 9 of the 18 days and because we Westerners are somewhat puzzled and confused about this land. This is a country of size, both geographically (17 million square kilometers, almost twice the size of Canada) and in population (over 150 million people). It is a land of controversy, both to outsiders and to the Russians themselves.

The name Russia appears to come from the word "RUS", which means bright, shining and refers to the people who originally settled this land; Vikings from Sweden in the 9th century. This means over 1200 years of significant and turbulent history, with constant war with Mongols, the Tatars, the Swedes, the Poles, the French, the Germans and so on. Their history, unlike Canada, is one of constant violence, and somewhat explains their suspicious nature and isolation from the world stage.

It does not however excuse their behavior through history, especially with their own people. Whether ruled through the centuries by their Czars, or by the 20th century communist dictatorships of Lenin, Stalin and their successors, the average Soviet was treated shamefully, as cannon fodder during their wars, as convicts in their gulags or prisons, if they dared question their leaders' directives, or if they openly displayed their religious beliefs.

Modern Russia in their large cities of St. Petersburg and Moscow is amazing. Both cities were destroyed by siege during the German offensive of the Second World War in the 1940's. All buildings of significance, have been restored, with their original 18th century facades. It is like stepping back in time, yet with all the conveniences of a modern city.

The main streets of both cities are very wide. Buildings are beeg, not big, but beeg.

The highlights in St. Petersburg, are the many palaces and museums of Czars past, such as those built by Ivan the Terrible, Peter the Great and Catherine the Great. Note how everything in Russia has a name which infers it is bigger or better, than anything else.

However, the Hermitage Museum, the Winter Palace, and the Summer Palace of Catherine the Great, are truly spectacular and contain room, after room, after room, of precious artifacts and masterpiece paintings. The Russians of today, perhaps forget that this outlandish richness, was a major reason for the October revolution of 1917, when the then Czar, was forced to abdicate, and was eventually murdered with the rest of his family. The public now flock in great numbers to see the treasures.

Moscow is dominated by the Kremlin. This name means citadel, and many Russian cities have kremlins. Of course, the one in Moscow is symbolic of Communism and the cruel dictators that ruled within its' walls, which by the way are at least 30 feet high and 5 feet thick. The infamous Red Square where the May Day military parades, tanks and all, used to take place, lies within the Kremlin, and is surrounded by enormous towers, beautiful cathedrals, and in particular St. Basil's, which is truly magical from the outside, Lenin's tomb and an impressive 4 story commercial building, which houses very expensive and modern retail shops, which appear to be out of place in such a historical location.

A feature of museums in Russia, is that in each room there is a volunteer, a Babuska, a pet name given to an older lady or grandmother. They watch you with an eagle eye and if you commit an indiscretion, that is if you touch something of value, or lean over a rope or sit on a radiator, they gently take your hand, turn it over, give you a stern look and slap you on the wrist.

Enormous apartment blocks dominate the suburbs. Built by the Soviet government to provide affordable accommodation; some are attractive to look at, others a disgrace.

The State determines if the outside of the building is to be improved. Some have balconies, which do not line up with any windows. "Finish the building, even if the construction is incorrect", was the Soviet way. Others have balconies, which line up with windows, which only move up and down. It's therefore tricky to get out onto your balcony, but they did not change to sliding windows.

The subway in Moscow (The Metro) as it is called, has to be seen to be believed. It was built by convict labor in the 30's and has to be at least 5 times deeper Toronto's. The stations are full of art, mosaic tile and paintings, statues and chandeliers. They are decorated like museums, but still transport 8 million passengers every day, <u>8 million</u>.

Rush hour traffic in a city such as Moscow (population 10 million) makes Toronto look like a village. Cars, big, black, and fast, are plentiful. Advertising is in your face, North American and over the top. Russian women, mostly with blond hair, have a love affair with high heel shoes (minimum 5 inches). Significantly white birch trees are everywhere, and dominate the landscape.

The main religion in Russia is Russian Orthodox. The 20th century purge on religious activity has seriously affected church attendance. The cathedrals and churches are more like museums, than churches as we know them. Their interiors are full off frescos, icons, paintings, mosaics, gold leaf, stained glass and statues. They are rich beyond belief, with the above- mentioned items, but not with people. The cathedrals in smaller and more impoverished areas, boast the same riches, but appear to have a better attendance record.

In Zagorsk, the Russian Orthodox equivalent of the Vatican and the centre of Russian orthodox faith, religious art and architecture, we were told that there was now no shortage of young male applicants for the priesthood. This was the only monastery in Russia approved by the state, to practice their religious faith during the years of "atheism".

There is a huge amount of faith catching up to be done, and we suspect that this will come mainly from the rural and impoverished areas as opposed to the big cities, where "freedom", has turned Russian heads to solely concentrating on individual economic gain.

A Russian parable, as taken from a fictional book about Russia, and recited by a Russian orthodox priest, might assist in understanding the Russian mindset, bearing in mind that the bear has been the symbol of Russia for many years.

"The church elder Basil, dwelt for a long time in his hermitage praying and giving spiritual guidance. It was said that he had a gift with animals, and particularly bears. It was also remarked that a large bear would often appear, and he would talk to it as a father to a child, and people therefore decided that he had a gift.

Not so. The elder was very much afraid when the bear first appeared and he cowered in his hut for two nights. On the third night the elder Basil understood what he must do. He said the Jesus prayer, "Lord, Jesus Christ, Son of God, have mercy upon me, a sinner", not because he asked that his body be saved, but rather that he had considered "What can this bear do to me, who by God's grace, has eternal life"

And thus, his fear of the bear disappeared. We know, what has passed in former times in this our beloved Russia, but in rebuilding the church, we also know, that we must not fear the bear. We must love him. For perfect love, casteth out fear."

Russia is a complex land, with a desperate need to be part of the world stage. We earnestly hope that their history of death and despair is behind them, and that with much prayer and common sense, they can achieve a peaceful and spiritual future.

Thank you for listening, or as they say in Russian……… Spasiba!

RUSSIAN REFLECTIONS

The Hermitage of world renown
Is really the jewel, in the Russian crown
Wrapped in the Winter Palace opulent gown
Its exhibits in Petrograd, make it the talk of the town.

A visit to where Rasputin died
And on to where Nicholas was canonized
From Peter and Paul Cathedral, to Peterhof Park
A re-creation of Versailles, it really makes its mark.

The summer palace of Catherine the Great
Is located at Pushkin, on a picturesque estate
Destroyed by the Germans, in World War Two
Restored with all the beauty, Russian artisans can do.

The Babushka stare, can give you a scare
Enough, to make you toe the line
But if you dare to stray, from the straight away
They'll slap you on the wrist, as a warning sign.

Novgorod's hotel had a downtown view
Of a fire -works display in red, white and blue
Their locals celebrate, exactly as we do
Seemingly cultures apart, we are from the same, world milieu.

The subway in Moscow, is not serene
In fact, day and night, it's a turbulent scene
With millions of passengers, travelling to and fro
Through the underground "palaces", of the Moscow Metro.

To view these "palaces", you must proceed at speed
To various stations, through a people stampede
And witness frescos, mosaic and glass
Chandeliers and statues, all rated first class.

Russian history, is a major mystery
Of war and peace, that never wants to cease
The Borodino Panorama, is quite tutorial
360 degrees of paintings, a master showpiece.

Memorial Park, is on the way
To the Novodevichy Cemetery, where Russian notables lay
The park's symbolic structure, of the Holocaust sculpture
Pays war tribute, to Russia's Jewish culture.

Red Square, the Kremlin, the Armoury Museum
Give credence to the, "If it's big, it's Russian", theorem
While in Moscow it's okay for you, to pay homage to
A City renewed, where ancient history meets new.

The Cathedral in Smolensk, is magnificence
With icons galore, gold leaf, and an iron floor
The economy of the town, seemed less up than down
Suggesting limited opportunity lies in store.

A Russian potpourri of what you see: -

Wide avenues, monuments celebrating victory
Museums, palaces, cathedrals, endlessly
"Beeg" buildings, fast cars, rural poverty
Straight roads, that run for eternity.

Blond hair, high heels, many a birch tree
A police presence, we are not accustomed to see
In your face ads, that cry out to thee
The power, of the Russian economy.

The Rivers Volga and Neva, will always be
Symbols of Russia, flowing through history
A complex land, adjusting to the word free
We pray, they maintain their world role, peacefully.

SCHARFE MANIA

Following a condo tour, we were on our way
For a casual lunch, just "blocks away"
But, after walking, for a mile or more
We could still see the diner, on the other shore.

To swim False Creek, in the month of May
Was out of the question, we would have to stay
And wait for a ferry, by now a hungry four
Hoping to be dropped at the restaurant door.

If returning by boat, we would have to pay
We decided to walk, it was a gorgeous day
We headed east, with a calory charged roar
Soon to be silenced, as our feet became sore.

We finally arrived at Scharfe manor, by the bay
To be greeted by bells a ringing, a real melee
The lobby was as busy, as a Walmart store
With firefighters heading for the seventeenth floor.

The condo residents, mingled with a "hi" and a "hey"
The all clear was sounded, we went on our way
Looking forward to snacks, and drinks to pour
But our peace was to be shattered, yet once more.

The pork chops were a cooking perfectly
On an out- door Ball BQ, coloured silver grey
The aroma drifted and seeped, through the porch door
The smoke alarm reacted, with an angry roar.

Our initial thought was to run away
Recalling the building alarm, earlier that day
But a secret weapon, our hosts had in store
Turn on their fountain and flood the floor.

Like geese, our arms, we did flap and flay
In hope, the screeching would go away
The concierge arrived, and said no more
I'll disarm the circuit, on this floor.

The Scharfes insisted, it's never this way
We always serve quiet, on a silver tray
You can hear a pin drop, never a snore
We believe you, yea right, as we closed the door.

SICILY WITH EPIFANI

Betty's party grew and grew
A European vacation, to pursue
Tickets in hand, and euros too
They left for Italy, right on cue.

The flight overnight, was nothing new
Babies on planes, don't bill and coo
Milano spirits, bordered on blue
A sleepless night, will do it for you.

On to Palermo, in morning dew
The isle of Sicily, was overdue
They held up well, those thirty- two
Ten days ahead, and lots to do.

A Trafalgar relation, pleased to renew
With Romano their guide, the father of two
As Alfonso bussed each avenue
Pino toured Monreale and Cefalu.

The second day, brought a mixed hue
Of Mondello sun and rain in lieu
A gastronomic lunch, a fish milieu
Followed by an Erice view.

Claudio met and took us through
The Valley of the Temples, historic venue
Selinunte beckoned, for us to view
It's ruined temples, one plus two.

Romano's humour, was served like stew
Full of comic flavour, and meaty too
Pure laughter contagious, upon us grew
From the flyer of Cessna, one seven two.

Taormina, a playground of the rich and few
Reached by elevated highway, we named mon dieu
The cobblestones on the street, we did tattoo
Looking for our restaurant, can't find it, can you.

Mount Etna's past, is deadly true
Lava, gas and ash, it did spew
Our climb with Wendy, we did rue
Hoping to avoid, our Waterloo.

Siracusa's skies, were brilliant blue
With a Sirocco temperature, of eighty- two
Theatres and caves, gave us a clue
Of bye gone days, around B.C. 2.

A Naxos meal, we savoured through
An elegant dinner, with a mixed menu
With Allen's approval, the Mafia guru.
Stephanie birthed, a conga queue.

We created, such a hullabaloo
With Alfonso dancing, a quickstep too
The musicians played, the whole night through
Enjoying the crazy, Canadese crew.

Return to the mainland, made us think things through
Of sun- drenched fruit trees, where good things grew
A Sicily remembered, for its coastline too
A Sicily captured, within each of you.

The hotel near Pompeii was, how you say ooh
Like a colourful edition, of an Ed Mirvish revue
The theme established, by urn and statue
With artifacts as plenty, as flies in a zoo.

The families of our tour staff, were invited to
Join us for dinner, what a nice thing to do
We were later awakened, at eleven forty- two
By explosions and fireworks, a Vesuvian preview.

We crisscrossed Capri, on a transport menu
Enzo our guide, said "What a matter you"
And related, how Tiberius punished argue
By dropping the guilty, into the below blue.

Up, down on a chairlift, to savour the view
Lunch at the Bellavista, was simply "merveilleux"
Sorrento, Amalfi, to name but a few
Ending with pastry, limoncello, from the Trafalgar crew.

To seal the trip, Rome was the glue
Viewed obelisks and fountains, and piazzas too
Gala dined at Canova, serenaded by two
Sang "Arrivederci Roma, Saluto to you".

SIESTA KEY BEACH

A beach, offering miles of walking free
Enhanced by the lure, of blue green, sea
Sun drenched bodies relax instantly
As they absorb the beauty of the topography.

For the most part, clean and commercial free
Which is what a five- star beach, ought to be
Providing inspiration, to renew one's energy
To handle life's challenges, and the daily melee.

Each day, a moving sea of humanity
Patrol the beach, watching intently
Those who pass, to view and decree
If, what they see, would be appropriate "for me".

A stroll down the beach, with the setting sun
Reveals fewer bathers, walkers, kids having fun
Most have retired to view their tan
And compare the difference, from where they began.

This white sand beach, has the right to be
Defined as a place of quality
An entrée, full of shore, sand and sea
Carved by the Lord's hand, you have to agree.

SPRING

Remember When

And then give praise
For winter's past
It's no disgrace.

To yearn for growth
Brought by, sun rays
To ponder the joy
Of longer days.

To sense the warmth
Of Spring's embrace.

SUMMER

Remember When

All seemed right
Gardens, lush and green
Not brown, not white.

Water sparkling
In extended light
High skies, warm winds
From morn' 'till night.

Nature's joy for life
Was at its height
To this season, we offer
An open invite.

SUPER CALORIFIC

The buffet table was laden
Hot and cold, in piles amassed
The doors were thrown open
At exactly, twenty- past.

The maitre d's smile faded
As he turned, and looked aghast
At the sight of Stan Leighton
As he slowly sauntered past.

The alarm bells sounded
Phones rang of the hook
The kitchen staff alerted
There's more for you to cook.

The sous chef snorted
We cooked for ninety- four
We know the reservations
They can't eat anymore.

His jaw dropped slowly
As the owner, let out a roar
The group includes Stan Leighton
We've all been through this, before.

As one, the staff acknowledged
The challenge that lay ahead
To prepare reserves aplenty
To ensure the man was fed.

In the meantime, Stan was sampling
All the best parts of the spread
Using his doppler radar eyes
No need to move his head.

The initial plate was modest
What surprise might lie in store
To those who really knew him
It was the first of, twenty- four.

Savoring each bite, with such delight
As he started, to tuck it away
As the evening wore on, the profit was gone
To the owner's, woe and dismay.

After an hour or two, the entrée was through
And focus was turned on the pie
With now not many there, sharing would be rare
Observed Stan, with a gleam in his eye.

Chocolate pie is just right, bite after bite
It's delicious in every way
Smacking his lips, he ensured first dibs
Using a soup spoon, to put it away.

Stuffed to the core, he exited the door
Stomach full, there was nary a crack
With a yawn and well fed, he was ready for bed
But wait, maybe there's time for a snack.

THE END OF ANOTHER "CENTURY"

A penny for your thoughts
Is out, it's no longer so
It'll cost you a nickel
The Feds' have decreed, it has to go.

The original copper penny
Struck in one nine naught eight
Saw out the 20th century
Just in time, for its Watergate.

An abundance of sayings
Spoken through the years
Will cease to be relevant
As this currency disappears.

Penny wise and pound foolish
In for a penny, in for a pound
Pennies from heaven, ten a penny
Classic expressions all out, and outward bound.

Is this the beginning, of the forecast end
Of coins and bills, cashiers and tills
To be replaced by the card, or maybe a chip
Implanted in the wrist, your chest or your hip.

THE FAMILY TOAST

To those of us, who went before.

To those, who've seen it all and more.

To those whose future, lies in store.

To those yet to join, the family lore.

We give you. The Family.

The Family

THREE DAUGHTERS THE FINAL WEDDING

The fourteenth dawned, all mist and dew
Wake up, get up, there's lots to do
We've done this before, it's nothing new
Don't argue, do something, find my shoe.

The car is washed, and loaded too
I'll shower and dress, if that's okay with you
The flowers, the presents, the house is a zoo
There's more to be done, in my view.

I think I'll go, hit a ball or two
Are you mad, your speech, my hair, to name a few
There's hardly time, to visit the loo
I need you here, to be just you.

Head up, tum' in, a smile that's true.
Nod to the in-laws, second pew
Walk slowly down the aisle, on cue
To the pastor, proudly reply, we do.

My feet are sore, how are you
I'm really tired, it's a quarter past two
I don't think, I want to start anew
Hon' it's over, the girls, they're all gone… phew!

THE TRUE MEANING OF CHRISTMAS

On Christmas morn', are your thoughts torn
Between the activities ahead, and the child within born
The gifts displayed, on the outside worn
Our inner self freed, as our sins He's borne.

The lights on the tree, the mistletoe
The family visits, to- and- fro
It's all about us, or is it, no
It's that tiny perfect child, 2000 years ago.

Hours in the day, to stop and say
Why do we celebrate, in this special way
The name Christmas itself, is a give away
To bow our heads, and openly pray.

The faces of children, their cries of joy
Our hopes nurtured, by that that new born boy
A stable, a manger, the basics, no toy
His life surrendered, ours to enjoy.

Does the peace of Christmas, really stem
From the giving that passes, between those and them
No, it's the day of days, a jewel, a gem
For all, who believe in Bethlehem.

TWO HOV OR NOT TWO HOV

HOV, is not going to be
A way of travel, for you or me
It was announced by, a special decree
It must be used, by us or we.

Initial stats, are coming in
They give the trial, a positive spin
Of passing drivers, sitting in
Clogged lanes, of misery and chagrin.

With noses high, and in the air
They say aloud, you can't come here
We're saving, twenty minutes a day
Don't think about it, just stay, out of our way.

In days gone past, when passengers asked
They received a smile but, paid by the mile
Now the driver must say to the rider, I'll pay
If you give me your word, you're on board each way.

The saving of time, has become obsessive
Turning driver nature from passive, to aggressive
The need for speed, like bee to honey
Has forced some to inflate, a front seat dummy.

Progress has required us, to be inventive
To benefit from this, so- called incentive
To clean the air, and shorten the trip
You must share the space, and double the dip.

TO MARY WITH LOVE

The Hoffman clan, are not an also ran
They are tried and true, and very much
American, through and through
And strong supporters of red, white and blue.

A family of equals
With independence of view
Assisted in their bonding
With Mary's emotional glue.

The 80's brought them settling verily
To a northern land, also strong and free
Where Mary's snow shoveling, a daily spree
Became compulsive obsessive, we all agree.

This was our Mary, a sign of things to come
Focused, friendly, giving, and oh so strong
The lady next door, who could do no wrong
A neighbour, a wife, the perfect mom.

The Canadian end came, as it had begun
With hugs and handshakes, they were moving on
Memories, good times, friendships won
A half turn, a wave, and they were gone.

Mary's spirit, kept us feeling close
Enabling us to visit, the Charlotte house
The relationship continued, as the years went by
With the family maturing, under her matriarchal eye.

A Philadelphia wedding brought contact anew
To witness Mary, organize with effect, and on cue
A further celebration, is Athens, Georgia due
But in the meantime, Mary, Happy Birthday to You.

Bob & Eleanor

UPON REACHING SIXTY- FIVE

The journey, the quest
I was merely a guest
On the backbone of time
From zero to prime.

Without your behest
I will tell you the rest
Of my fruits on the vine
Of my life by design.

Wedded young in the west
To the best of the best
Fathered daughters so fine
Three ladies, divine.

Tackled work full of zest
One employer I did test
Finished two score and nine
Years of toeing the line.

Travelled much to invest
To search for that nest
Found a Ballantrae sign
Offering fine wine and dine.

I pinch myself lest
I be taken in jest
But the road which is mine
One, just cannot outshine.

WE ALL WANT TO BE FREE

An echo from the 18th century
A warning shot, from recent history
Les Miserables, spoke to you and me
All peoples are entitled, to be free.

The ingredients, of the human recipe
Self-worth, and the basics of humanity
Giving notice to those, whose sole decree
Requires the rule of force, and a bended knee.

Absolute power, just does not see
One's quality of life, is an essential to be
That one's spirit, yearns for liberty
And to walk, a path of dignity.

Accusers will shout that, this is not so
And propose dictatorship, as apropos
Leading so many, to go astray,
Muddying their future, losing their way.

However, the message is clear, with each sea
Of dissenters, looking for victory
Over regimes that have ruled, for an eternity
With dominance, strife, and it's all about me.

You can't underestimate, the gravity
Of current world events, the destiny
Of human revolt, against totality
To achieve better rights, and equality.

We should support and believe, in every way
That this hunger for change, is not a far-off day
As others join the search, for what should be
Not just their dream, but their reality.

WE SHOULD. WE CAN. WE WILL. OR, WILL WE?

Green, is not a figure of speech
Once thought to be, out of reach
Through education, we can teach
A new way of life, we do beseech.

Nature's response, to our promiscuous ways
Has brought savage storms, and skies of greys
Scorching heat and drought, with endless rays
A pattern of weather, not seen for many- a- days.

To those who sigh, we've seen this before
Accustom yourselves, there's much more in store
As global warming, opens a troublesome door
A pandora's box, of weather galore.

Scientists call, for radical change
To protect the environment, we must rearrange
Our priorities, which we find difficult, strange
And for many the objective, is out of range.

Governments, play a defensive game
Supporting limited change, to achieve the same
But action short term, cannot be by name, but
Put into practice, to avoid our shame.

The shame of what, we gift to those
The next generation, our non-tackled woes
Finance, technology, allow us to suppose
That change and procedures, we can impose.

Problems, solutions, do not develop over night
But to ignore them blindly, is just not right
Planet earth is worth our resolve, our fight
We owe it to all, to make the future bright.

WHAT WOULD WE DO WITHOUT THEM

We rely on them to make a point
To save our bacon, we duly anoint
The use of sayings, that help us teach
So, we can honestly practice, what we preach.

Remember, as far as the eye can see
The best things in life, are always free
Never look a gift horse, in the mouth
But focus, when markets are going south.

Note, all that glitters is not gold
Can apply to, we will not be undersold
Caveat emptor, protects your piece of the pie
But instead its shop till you drop, do or die.

Slow as molasses, quick as a bunny
If you back the wrong horse, you're out of the money
To run the race, is more than half the fun
Even if you don't win, everything under the sun.

You know, pride comes before a fall
So, keep your eye on the bouncing ball
Its better to walk, before you run
Or you will end up somehow, under the gun.

Prepare ready, to watch your p's and q's
Because, if you dare to snooze, you really lose
Don't fall asleep at the wheel
But stay, on a steady even keel.

You could be as good as gold
But revenge is a dish, best served cold
Food for thought, you so and so
Don't make a meal of it, you reap what you sow.

Take off your hat, they're not standing pat
They're going to bat, a second kick at the cat
Delivering tit for tat, take that and that
Two men having a chat, chewing the fat.

We are rounding third and coming home
You have read this far, when in Rome
Another stanza, are you insane.
It would be déjà vu, all over again.

WINTER

Remember When

The chill of day
Gave birth to blow
And skies of gray.

Our spirits sank
As snow did lay
On trees of fir
And fields of hay.

But for those of us
Who've walked this way
We know it, as part
Of our DNA.

YOUSED AND ABUSED

It's sad to say, that everyday
We hear the term, "youse guys"
It's not obscene, but what does it mean
Where and when, did it ever arise.

When lunch is through, we're bid fond adieu
And, have a nice day, "youse guys"
Words though sincere, I don't want to hear
They spoil my shake, and my french fries.

English it's not, I'm becoming distraught
It's time to hear, from "weese guys"
We can stop the rot, if we correct on the spot
And tell them, to open their eyes.

Collective we're not, individual by thought
Sex distinct, to family the wise
We have earned the right, to take up the fight
It's time to listen, to our cries.

We are not blind, to the modern mind
Except for these words, we despise
In dictionaries around, this phrase cannot be found
It's time to see, that it dies.